The Shah's Imperial Celebrations of 1971

The Shah's Imperial Celebrations of 1971

Nationalism, Culture and Politics in Late Pahlavi Iran

Robert Steele

I.B. TAURIS
LONDON • NEW YORK • OXFORD • NEW DELHI • SYDNEY

I.B. TAURIS
Bloomsbury Publishing Plc
50 Bedford Square, London, WC1B 3DP, UK
1385 Broadway, New York, NY 10018, USA
29 Earlsfort Terrace, Dublin 2, Ireland

BLOOMSBURY, I.B. TAURIS and the I.B. Tauris logo are
trademarks of Bloomsbury Publishing Plc

First published in Great Britain 2021
Paperback edition published 2022

Copyright © Robert Steele, 2022

Robert Steele has asserted his right under the Copyright,
Designs and Patents Act, 1988, to be identified as Author of this work.

For legal purposes the Acknowledgements on p. vii constitute
an extension of this copyright page.

Cover design: Adriana Brioso
Cover image © Georges Galmiche/INA/Getty Images

All rights reserved. No part of this publication may be reproduced or
transmitted in any form or by any means, electronic or mechanical,
including photocopying, recording, or any information storage or retrieval
system, without prior permission in writing from the publishers.

Bloomsbury Publishing Plc does not have any control over, or responsibility for,
any third-party websites referred to or in this book. All internet addresses given
in this book were correct at the time of going to press. The author and publisher
regret any inconvenience caused if addresses have changed or sites have
ceased to exist, but can accept no responsibility for any such changes.

A catalogue record for this book is available from the British Library.

A catalog record for this book is available from the Library of Congress.

ISBN: PB: 978-0-7556-3956-4
ePDF: 978-1-8386-0419-6
eBook: 978-1-8386-0418-9

Typeset by Newgen KnowledgeWorks Pvt. Ltd., Chennai, India

To find out more about our authors and books visit
www.bloomsbury.com and sign up for our newsletters.

Dedicated to
Michael Axworthy (1962–2019)

Contents

List of illustrations	viii
Note on transliteration	x
Acknowledgements	xi
Introduction	1
1　Ideology and historical background	13
2　'The World's Centre of Happiness'	29
3　International diplomacy at Persepolis	55
4　The Celebrations and cultural policy	73
5　International cultural activity	93
6　Criticizing the Celebrations	109
7　The cost of the Celebrations	125
Conclusion	139
Notes	147
Bibliography	193
Index	213

Illustrations

1. Shojāʿ al-Din Shafā (picture taken 1971), the Shah's cultural counsellor at the Imperial Court, who first proposed a celebration commemorating Cyrus the Great in 1958. Courtesy of Claudine Shafa.
2. A headline from *Keyhān* (19 Mehr 1350/ 11 October 1971) that reads 'The Immortality of Imperial Iran'. From the British Library's collection.
3. Shojāʿ al-Din Shafā beside a map marking the international committees established for the Imperial Celebrations. Courtesy of Claudine Shafa.
4. Advertisement from Iran Air (Homā), in the newspaper *Keyhān*. From the British Library's collection.
5. Set of stamps from Tunisia commemorating the 2500th Anniversary Celebrations. Author's collection.
6. Set of stamps from Fujairah commemorating the 2500th Anniversary Celebrations. Author's collection.
7. Three stamps from Iran. On the top left corner of each is the original logo of the Celebrations, depicting an image of an eagle found at Persepolis. Author's collection.
8. Stamp from Belgium depicting the tomb at Buzpar, discovered by Belgian archaeologist Louis Vanden Berghe during his sixth Fars expedition (18 November 1960–17 January 1961). Author's collection.
9. Stamp from Oman depicting Iranian footballer Parviz Ghelichkhani, issued as part of a set of six stamps commemorating the 2500th Anniversary Celebrations. Author's collection.
10. Illustration published on the front page of *Iran Free Press*, October 1971. From the collection of the International Institute of Social History, Amsterdam.
11. The Shahyād Tower, shortly before its inauguration in 1971 (Photo by Bettmann via Getty Images).
12. Inauguration of the Āryāmehr Stadium (Photo by Rolls Press/Popperfoto via Getty Images).

13. Soldiers marching during the parade at Persepolis (Photo by Georges Galmiche/INA via Getty Images).
14. View of the tent city from Persepolis (Photo by Georges Galmiche/INA via Getty Images).
15. Frontal view of one of the tent structures (Photo by the author, 2017).
16. The grand banquet in the dining hall of the tent city (Photo by Georges Galmiche/INA via Getty Images).

Note on transliteration

The transliteration follows the system employed by the journal *Iranian Studies*, which adopts the long a (ā), ayn (') and hamza ('). Names which are in common use in English, for example, Mohammad Reza Pahlavi and Ruhollah Khomeini, have not been converted into this style, so as not to confuse non-specialists. Translations from Persian are my own, unless otherwise stated.

Acknowledgements

This book is the culmination of a project that I started in 2013 as an MPhil student at the University of Manchester. Having previously studied politics and ancient history, I was interested in the ways in which historical narratives can be refashioned to support national ideologies, and at Manchester I looked at the role of British academics in facilitating this process in Iran in the early 1970s. I am indebted to my supervisor at Manchester, Oliver Bast, for sparking my interest in the Shah's Imperial Celebrations of 1971 and for teaching me the importance of challenging established narratives.

At Exeter University, I would like to thank my Persian teacher Ali Mossadegh and my secondary supervisor Leonard Lewisohn, who, although we met only a few times, spoke to me at length while I was in Tehran, offering me practical advice and insights into a country it was clear he loved deeply. This book is dedicated to my supervisor at Exeter, Michael Axworthy, to whom I will be forever grateful, for agreeing to be my PhD supervisor in the first place, for supporting my work early on and for continuing to do so even during his illness. Not only was he a great scholar, but he was also everything a great scholarly mentor should be: encouraging, inspiring and dependable. This work would not have been possible without his guidance.

Many people have been extremely forthcoming in offering information and advice over the years, including David Morgan, Roger Savory, John Hinnells, Ehsan Yarshater and Kambiz Atabai. To all of them I offer many thanks. I am especially grateful to Claudine Shafa, who introduced me to her husband's archives and has been helpful in many other ways, not least by allowing me to use pictures from her private collection in this book. I am thankful to Abdolreza Ansari, who met me in a cafe in Paris to share his experiences of the Imperial Celebrations, and to David Stronach, with whom I spent a wonderfully informative afternoon in Berkeley. I thank my PhD examiners, Ali Ansari and Sajjad Rizvi, who made me think about ways in which I could better articulate the central points of my thesis and who supported me in turning it into a book. I hope they will be pleased with the finished product.

Chapter 3 of this book appeared, in altered form, in a collection edited by Roham Alvandi titled *The Age of Aryamehr: Late Pahlavi Iran and Its Global Entanglements*.[1] The book was the product of a workshop hosted by the Middle East Centre at the London School of Economics and Political Science in May 2016 titled 'Pahlavi Iran, 1941–1978: A Global History Workshop'. Dr Alvandi's thorough feedback, at the time of the workshop and throughout the review process, was invaluable and not only improved the published paper, but, ultimately, this book, too.

I wish to thank the Department of Near Eastern Languages and Cultures at UCLA for awarding me with the Jahangir and Eleanor Amuzegar Fellowship in Modern Iranian History. I am particularly grateful to Rahim Shayegan for his encouragement and belief in my work. I feel humbled to have been given the opportunity to complete this project in such a stimulating scholarly environment.

I am indebted to my dear friend Safa Mahmoudian for her help with Persian translations and transliterations, and to David Hiles for his help with French translations. I also thank Cyrus Kadivar, with whom I have spent many hours discussing Pahlavi Iran, and whose insights and passion inspire me to continue studying this fascinating period of history.

My wife Maria has been a constant source of support; accompanying me on field trips, helping to translate documents from Dutch, French, Italian and German, proofreading countless drafts and always giving me love and reassurance. Finally, I am extremely fortunate to have been able to rely on the support of my parents, Sandra and Harry, throughout my education. I am more grateful to them than I could even begin to put into words.

Introduction

In October 1971, heads of state, political and cultural figures, business leaders and journalists from around the world came to Persepolis at the invitation of Shah Mohammad Reza Pahlavi of Iran to celebrate the 2500th Anniversary of the Founding of the Persian Empire by Cyrus the Great. The event was designed as an elaborate and magnificent piece of political theatre and at centre stage was the Shah himself. He was presented to Iran and the world as a great king, at once traditional and modern; the heir and defender of a 2,500-year-old monarchical tradition and a modernizing revolutionary. Kings and emperors, presidents and prime ministers came to the ancient city of Persepolis to pay tribute to the Shah and his vision for Iran. For a domestic audience, the event bolstered the ideological underpinning of the Pahlavi regime by promoting the idea that the successes of the country had been, and always would be, dependent on the throne. To an international audience, the event signalled the beginning of a new period of prosperity and global influence for Iran. No longer was Iran to be the plaything of imperial powers; Iran was now a significant player on the international stage.

Throughout the festivities, the monarchy was presented as the harbinger of Iranian glory, and the Shah as its guarantor. The central figure in the official ceremonies was Cyrus the Great, who was lauded as a benevolent ruler, a father to his people, and one who brought peace to mankind. The Shah, meanwhile, was presented as his spiritual successor. Texts of the points of the Shah's White Revolution reforms were engraved in stone slabs erected in towns across Iran, alongside the text of the Cyrus Cylinder, which was formally recognized by the Pahlavi regime as the first bill of human rights. To emphasize this internationally, plaster casts of the Cylinder were made and displayed at the UN headquarters in New York and Geneva. Conferences and exhibitions were held around the world on Iranian culture and civilization, and in subsequent years, according to one historian, as a direct result of the interest the Celebrations generated, the literature on Ancient Iran 'almost doubled'.[1] The French scholar Jean Perrot further observed that the Celebrations initiated a resurgence in interest in the Achaemenid period internationally.[2] By reminding his people and the world of Iran's historic regional hegemony and global cultural influence, and by vowing to follow the precedent set by his forebears, the Shah promised a future for Iran as glorious as its past.

The programme of events of the Celebrations in Iran included a ceremony at the tomb of Cyrus at Pasargadae, an international congress of Iranology, a parade and *son et lumière* at Persepolis, the inauguration of the Shahyād Tower and Āryāmehr Stadium in Tehran, and a wreath-laying ceremony at the tomb of Reza Pahlavi. The most controversial event, however, which provoked the disgust of the Pahlavi regime's political opponents, was the gala dinner, held for guests at the banquet hall of the specially constructed tent city complex by the ancient ruins of Persepolis. In response to widespread criticism of the dinner, the Shah's regime would later play down its opulence, but at the time, regime-supporting newspapers called it *porshokuhtarin meyhmāni-ye tārikh* – the most magnificent party in history.³ In large part because of the extravagant indulgence of this banquet and the real, or imagined, luxury of the tent city, the Celebrations have been characterized as overelaborate, inappropriate and unnecessary – some even point to the furore the event caused as the beginning of the widespread popular discontent with the Shah's rule that culminated in the revolution of 1978–9. The Celebrations have come to be remembered as a costly mistake, the grandiosity of which, as Marvin Zonis noted, would 'characterize the remainder of the Shah's rule'.⁴ Other historical accounts comment on the event's 'squanderous indulgence'⁵ and the Shah's 'increasing megalomania'.⁶

At the time, while the media in Iran trumpeted the VIP luxury as indicative of its success, some Western newspapers criticized these aspects of the event, contrasting the vast expenditure with the poverty experienced by large parts of Iran's population. A typical article appearing in the *Daily Telegraph* noted, for example, that 'in a country where average income per head does not exceed £200 a year … the peasants, who form the vast majority of the population and who can neither read nor write, know little of what is going on'.⁷ A report from the *Washington Daily News* called the Celebrations a 'vain, pompous, vulgar show of wealth' and mocked the imperial couple: 'To be fair, Empress Farah hasn't said of starving Iranian peasants, "Let them eat caviar." But she is looking a bit peaked and round-shouldered from carting around all those diamonds, and the tone of the party is very Marie Antoinette.'⁸ *Newsweek* wrote that the event was 'a mixture of pomp and pomposity, of regal splendor and petty carping'.⁹ In addition to the purported high costs associated with the events at Persepolis, there were concerns from some states that international participation would be construed as condonement of the Shah's human rights record.

There was a political motivation to such reporting and some reporters clearly sympathized with protest movements against the Shah's regime, which intensified during this period. Jonathan Randal, the reporter for *The Washington Post*, for example, claimed that his derogatory reporting on the occasion was his way of 'pissing on the Shah's party'.¹⁰ According to Andrew Scott Cooper, Randal's reports 'presented a devastating portrait of conditions inside Iran and helped define the Shah as a corrupt, cruel dictator'.¹¹ The Dutch ambassador at the time, Hendrik Jonker, angrily commented on this aspect of the reporting: 'The western press has reported extensively before and after these festivities, with just a few exceptions, in a way which seemed to me at the very least juvenile and definitely not hindered by any truthful or extensive knowledge of the country, its people, customs and development, profound objective analysis or even any thought whatsoever.'¹² The ambassador argued that the journalists who attended the festivities were expecting something to go wrong and described them as 'waiting for blood, for an attack or an accident. In anything else they are not interested'.[13]

Jonker missed part of the picture, though, since not all reports on the Celebrations were negative. Many were quite favourable and focused on Iran's recent economic development. An article appeared in *Le Monde*, for instance, arguing that 'the spending on Persepolis has given the Iranian nation prestige, which will only continue to grow',[14] while the reports of *The Guardian*'s Walter Schwarz were noted in an American article as a response to the accusations of repression and misery in Iran. According to the article, if *The Guardian*, 'a liberal-slanted English newspaper' which 'is not given to apologizing for dictators nor covering up their shortcomings', could commend Iran on its achievements, then this 'is saying a lot'.[15] The response to the Celebrations from the press was generally neither overwhelmingly negative nor positive, but a number of journalists were openly hostile to the event, and their accounts are those most vividly remembered. Furthermore, the presence of so many heads of state in an exotic location and the resulting heightened media attention gave rise to sensationalism as journalists speculated wildly, particularly about the cost. They felt emboldened to suggest any figure, however unrealistic.

There was a degree of condescension in the way in which the Shah was perceived by some diplomats and commentators, and one can sense some contemptuous resentment at the splendour of the Pahlavi court. The former American diplomat George Ball, for example, wrote, first of the coronation, then the Celebrations:

> What an absurd, bathetic spectacle! The son of a colonel in a Persian Cossack regiment play-acting as the emperor of a country with an average per capita income of $250 per year, proclaiming his achievements in modernizing his nation while accoutred in the raiment and symbols of ancient despotism. No wonder we talked among ourselves about the fragility of an anachronistic structure that compounded the doubtful expectancy of an absolute monarch with wasteful display. It was, I thought, a deliberate insult to the wretchedly poor with whom the country abounded. Still, though the prodigality of Versailles had nothing on the Golestan Palace, the greatest affront was not to come until four years later. Then the Shah and his queen spent $120 million on an opulent pageant at Persepolis that enriched not Omar the Tentmaker, but Pierre the Tentmaker and the other luxury merchants of Paris who handled the arrangements. A few minor heads of state showed up to keep company with Spiro Agnew, but the world was either too polite or too humourless to laugh.[16]

As Shojāʿ al-Din Shafā, one of the Celebrations' architects, pointed out in a posthumously published interview, the $120 million figure has no real basis and by the time of the Celebrations, per capita income had actually increased significantly from $250.[17] Shafā attributed disdainful analyses such as Ball's as a reaction to Iran's emergence as an economic power and their 'dissatisfaction that a third world country [such as Iran] had surpassed its limits'.[18] While Ball attacked the Shah for being the son of a lowly Cossack, Shafā argues that the elite families of the United States itself are descendants of prisoners sent to America by Elizabeth I under the control of Sir Walter Raleigh.[19]

Why then, Shafā continues, 'in another country, with many thousands of years of history, may a son born of a Cossack (*qazāq zādeh*) not celebrate 25 centuries of his country's civilization and culture?'[20] Shafā's questionable analysis of American history notwithstanding, he does have a point, and although Iran was a fast-growing economy during this period, one gets the impression that some Western commentators felt that the Shah was getting a little above his station.

Despite the evident allure of the Celebrations to the press, the body of scholarly literature on the event is relatively small, with most accounts appearing in general histories of Pahlavi Iran or political memoirs. At the time, many of the reports of the Celebrations stressed the drama and historical importance of the occasion, which was encouraged by the Pahlavi regime, and influenced how historians later approached the subject. The Shah's speech at Cyrus's tomb on 12 October inspired creative reports, such as this from *The Guardian*: 'A whirlwind raced across the sand towards the Shah. He looked up as he spoke and it turned away, keeping a respectful distance. The appearance of three witches, prophesying fresh glories, would not have seemed wildly inappropriate.'[21] The use of pathetic fallacy here is striking; even the wind is respectful of the Shah, while the Shakespearean reference adds to the mysticism of the event. William Shawcross, in his 1988 publication, *The Shah's Last Ride*, also evokes this image, putting the scene in the context of the Shah's inevitable downfall, which was to occur less than eight years later. The prophetic wind, Shawcross writes, 'was widely thought to be a good omen. It was not'.[22] Instead, the scene was set for a tragedy. The Shah, like Macbeth, would be unable to resist the temptations of power and the Celebrations would come to represent not the Shah's rise, but his downfall. Shawcross continues, 'It was supposed to mark the 2500th Anniversary of the original empire founded by Cyrus the Great in the sixth century B.C. In retrospect it can be seen to mark the beginning of the end of the Pahlavi dynasty, which the Shah's father had founded just fifty years before.'[23]

The perception of the Celebrations as having contributed to the revolution, even constituting the beginning of widespread discontent, or as having revealed fatal flaws in the Shah's character, has become a convenient part of the narrative of the Shah's downfall. Shawcross, whose chapter on the Celebrations is incidentally titled 'The Party', writes that 'For the Shah himself it would bring a complete divorce from reality. He became more and more obsessed with his own kingship and the importance of his direct succession from Cyrus.'[24] Marvin Zonis, in his *Majestic Failure*, also focuses on the 'party' and gives further credence to the idea that the Celebrations represented a turning point in the Shah's reign.[25]

The Celebrations were considered a failure in part because of the negative attention they received, which was stimulated by the idea that they were an irresponsible and expensive endeavour undertaken by a megalomaniac Shah. The excesses and extravagance of the Celebrations are, therefore, generally stressed in the literature. Nikki Keddie, for example, refers to them as 'vastly wasteful',[26] while James Buchan observed that 'Persepolis introduced an element of the fantastical into the Pahlavi style, as if some toy principality had gained a half-million-man army'.[27] Roy Mottahedeh, in his *The Mantle of the Prophet*, wrote that the 'party at Persepolis was more or less a success', but that 'many more Iranians were unimpressed. The whole thing had cost about three hundred million dollars'.²⁸ Fakhreddin Azimi also refers to the Shah's 'steadily nurtured illusion of power' and his 'perilous arrogance' which the Celebrations reflected.²⁹ Such accounts conform to the generally accepted idea of the event as a 'party', organized to entertain international VIPs and massage the Shah's already inflated ego.

A BBC documentary, first broadcast in 2016, titled *Decadence and Downfall: The Shah of Iran's Ultimate Party* repeats the same narrative, focusing almost entirely on the VIP guests at Persepolis and the vast expenditure, while a chorus of aged waiters and chefs reminisce and gossip. Much of the gossip is disprovable, yet the stubborn pervasiveness of the narrative of decadence, and indeed downfall, apparently does not allow space for proper scrutiny of sources. One claim repeated, first made in an article in *Tages-Anzeiger*, was that 50,000 European songbirds were imported to Persepolis for the occasion, most of which died within days as they were unaccustomed to the 'desert climate'.³⁰ While several newspaper journalists and authors have accepted this claim at face value and repeated it verbatim, upon closer inspection one realizes how illogical it is. There are many birds indigenous to the region that the organizers could have used to beautify the site, so why import from Europe? How would the organizers even source and import 50,000 birds? Moreover, historical climate data for Persepolis shows that in October, temperatures tend to vary from a minimum of 10 °C at night to 27 °C during the day; not extreme temperatures by Iranian or even European standards. Aside from these logical problems, there is simply no documentation to verify the claim.

The title of the documentary would not be out of place in a headline of one of the newspapers of 1971, which suggests that our understanding of the occasion is still hampered by sensationalism and a general obsession with the supposed flamboyance of an oriental despot. Indeed, the documentary opens with a quote from a Swiss member of the catering staff, who states that the two-day event at Persepolis had cost the equivalent of the entire national budget of Switzerland for two years; an absurd claim. In response to the programme and illustrating the effect of such programmes, a report appeared in the British tabloid newspaper *The Daily Mail*, titled 'Princess Anne and the £1 billion party that lit the fuse of Islamic terror 45 years ago', which argued that 'the great irony is that the Shah's feast was supposed to reinforce the throne it ultimately toppled'.³¹

Writing shortly after returning from the Celebrations, which he attended as part of the British scholarly delegation, Edinburgh University scholar Laurence Elwell-Sutton argued that 'In view of the discourteous tone of the bulk of the reports sent home by some foreign journalists – rivalled only by their discourteous behaviour on the spot – it may perhaps be worth while to attempt an objective assessment of this imposing and undoubtedly expensive operation.'³² Even during the immediate period following the Celebrations, long before hindsight would lead them to be linked to later events, Elwell-Sutton recognized the need for an objective analysis of their purpose and outcomes. This need has become increasingly urgent in the intervening fifty years. Many historians and commentators have claimed that the Celebrations were one of the root causes of the revolution, and that they helped to cement the image of the Shah as a delusional, out-of-touch third-world autocrat. Still, no thorough scholarly study of the Celebrations has hitherto been undertaken. This work aims to fill this gap.

Aims of the book

The premise of this book is that in order to understand the rationale for the Celebrations and to analyse their success or failure in their own historical context, rather than employing the narrative of the 'doomed' shah, one should look at their origins, and explore the cultural aspects of the event, which were critical to its success and reveal more of the true nature of the undertaking. It proposes a calmer and more balanced assessment of the Celebrations that considers their intended economic, political and cultural impact. The purpose is not to exonerate the Shah but to provide the type of 'objective assessment' that Elwell-Sutton called for. One of the main contributions of the book, therefore, is the challenging of a teleological view of the Celebrations, which supposes that they achieved little and merely set Iran on an unstoppable march towards revolution. The book aims to remove the Celebrations from the revolution, putting them in the context of the Shah's rise, rather than his fall. It will question what the regime aimed to achieve by holding the event, in terms of ideological dissemination, by promoting the Pahlavi historical narrative, as well as in terms of material gains, by encouraging foreign investment and tourism. The success of the Celebrations will, in this book, be judged by the extent to which they achieved the objectives set out when they were conceived in 1958.

The scale of the global cultural operation initiated during the Celebrations was extraordinary and unprecedented; hundreds of books were published, conferences organized, and exhibitions held. This aspect is, however, ignored in most analyses. Two authors have shone some light on this cultural operation in recent years. In his *Life and Times of the Shah*, Gholam Reza Afkhami provides the most detailed assessment yet of the Celebrations, and although he concludes that they were 'too foreign dominated', and thus were 'ill conceived', his account is noteworthy for the attention paid to the cultural initiatives. He states that the Congress of Iranology, held at the Pahlavi University, was one of the 'major events' of the Celebrations, and makes reference to some of the main cultural initiatives, including the publication of hundreds of books and the establishment of the Pahlavi Library.[33] Abbas Milani's biography *The Shah* also makes reference to the cultural aspects of the event, though he concludes that these 'were overshadowed by the rumour and reality of corruption and the embarrassment of nouveau riche extravaganza'.[34]

Given the glamour of the tent city, it is understandable that events such as the Congress of Iranology, in which nearly three hundred scholars from around the world participated, received little international media attention and have largely been written out of the narrative of the Celebrations not just by journalists but also historians. The Congress was, however, a significant event in the programme and stimulated much genuine scholarly activity. In addition to the hundreds of academics who attended the conference in October 1971, many more contributed with publications and by organizing conferences, lectures and exhibitions in their own countries, dedicated to various aspects of Iranian culture and civilization. In terms of expenditure and publicity, these aspects of the event were outshone by the extravagance of the tent city, but in sheer volume and depth of international engagement they reveal more of the essential character of this monumental undertaking.

This book aims to show how cultural politics, in other words, the shaping of politics through the use of culture, helped to promote the Pahlavi national ideology. Because the construction of nationalism and national identity is a process that requires a degree of creative imagination, a degree of artistry too is involved in the articulation of the resulting narrative to the population. Murray Edelman observes of regimes and proponents of political causes, that they 'know that it takes much coercion, propaganda, and the portrayal of issues in terms that entertain, distort, and shock to extract a public response of any kind'.[35] The purpose is not merely to project a narrative, but project it in a way that stirs emotions and incites enthusiasm. Political spectacles, including national celebrations, are a powerful way in which to do this and cultural activity often forms the basis of such events. As Frank Manning observed, 'Celebration is both culture and politics, or, better perhaps, cultural politics.' There are two contrary processes involved in the term 'cultural politics', he continues. The first is the politicization of culture, 'the translation of cultural symbols, beliefs, and values into political discourse and strategy'. And the second is 'the rendering of politics ... in cultural terms'.[36]

In the late Pahlavi period, cultural policies were employed for the Pahlavi articulation of state ideology. The main cultural government and non-government bodies were involved in the planning of the Celebrations, for instance, along with the more overtly political organs of the state. Cultural symbols and historical artefacts, such as the Cyrus Cylinder, were reshaped to serve political ideology and structures such as the tomb of Cyrus the Great served as sites at which national heroes could be remembered. Cultural events, including national celebrations, helped to draw attention to these sites and firmly establish the legendary figures they represented as ones of national significance. As Manning further observes, 'celebration is a kind of "power play," a dramatic arena in which cultural politics assumes style, shape, and significance.'[37] The Imperial Celebrations of 1971 provide an excellent case study of this 'dramatic arena'.

Culture can play an important soft power role in international relations, too, and the Celebrations presented many opportunities for countries to express their friendship with Iran through cultural activities. Special committees were established in countries around the world to direct programmes of activities and according to published figures there were as many as 131 books on various aspects of Iranian civilization and culture published, and 143 exhibitions, 326 congresses, seminars and other academic proceedings and 37 artistic events held, including poetry readings and ballet, theatre and classical music performances.[38] Some of these publications and events were supported financially or logistically by the Iranian state, but many more were initiated independently of Iranian state influence.

These cultural events carried a strong ideological message and served to stimulate greater awareness of Iranian culture and civilization around the world. Through them political figures and the general public were urged to identify Iran not with the Middle East and Islam, but with Europe and accounts of Persian kings recorded in Hellenic and biblical texts, which precipitated an increase in tourism figures in the years following 1971. This reflected the regime's tourism promotion strategy and was not merely a convenient by-product. Responding to criticism of the building projects carried out for the Celebrations in Fars province, Empress Farah said to a reporter in Europe, 'We would have had to do that at some point anyway, and now we've had to do it a bit quicker. In time the tourists will bring us back the money.'³⁹ At the first meetings of the organizing committee of the Celebrations, much attention was paid to infrastructural development, and an article published in the run-up to the Celebrations stated that the organizers expected them 'to bring a flood of tourists to Iran'.⁴⁰ It was not just the tourism industry that benefitted Iran, as the event stimulated much foreign investment.

The type of national celebration observed in Iran under the Shah was not without international precedent and parallels can be drawn between the Imperial Celebrations of 1971 and Tsar Nicholas II's tercentenary celebration of Romanov rule in 1913. Through this celebration, Tsar Nicholas II sought to 'reinvent the past, to recount the epic of the "popular Tsar", so as to invest the monarchy with a mythical historical legitimacy and an image of enduring permeance'.⁴¹ Facing challenges to the throne from modernizing forces, the celebration served as a reminder to the Russian people of the successes of the Romanovs and sought to 'unite the nation around the throne'.⁴² Although the jubilant crowds that lined the streets convinced the Tsar and his queen of the love of their people, the celebration merely, as Wortman has written, 'raised the question of the meaning of the word nation and its relationship to monarch and state … Rather than provide an occasion for consensus, the celebration became a focus of contention between diverse understandings of nation – liberal, statist, monarchical and clerical'.⁴³ The Shah's Imperial Celebrations, too, were a clear articulation of what the Pahlavi state believed it meant to be Iranian, and though some were undoubtedly convinced, many were not, and the event broadened and intensified discussions about the nation and monarchical rule.

Pahlavi history in general has experienced a surge in scholarly interest in recent years, as a new generation of historians has emerged with access to newly released documents and a fresh view on the era unimpeded by experiences of the *ancien régime*. This fresh approach to Pahlavi history is not without its critics. Reviewing Michael Axworthy's *Revolutionary Iran*, published in 2013, the renowned historian of modern Iran Ervand Abrahamian wrote that Axworthy's work tended to 'exaggerate the independence of the Shah' and that 'such a depiction runs counter to the facts'.⁴⁴ Abrahamian disagrees with the perception that the Shah was a 'partner', preferring the typical presentation of him as a 'military monarch dependent on the West'. Such long-held beliefs have, however, been further challenged in more recent works, notably Roham Alvandi's *Nixon, Kissinger and the Shah*, which, through extensive use of documents from archives in the United States, shows that the Shah was an important player in the politics of the Cold War.⁴⁵ In Alvandi's account, the relationship between Iran and the United States was very much a partnership which benefitted both parties.

In his *The Fall of Heaven*, Andrew Scott Cooper explains the problems inherent in researching the revolutionary period in Iran: 'Historians often talk about the "uses and abuses" of history, and researching the Iranian revolution can be compared to entering a dark tunnel without a flashlight. The tunnel is filled with caverns, dead ends, and missed turns and lit only by the occasional flare of rumor, conspiracy theory, and outright lie.'⁴⁶ As time passes and prejudices subside, a clearer picture of the Pahlavi period is emerging. The Islamic Republic's narrative of a decadent, megalomaniac, corrupt and tyrannical Mohammad Reza Pahlavi is becoming more difficult to sustain as new information about the Pahlavi regime comes to light. The Imperial Celebrations of 1971 have been demonized by the leadership of the Islamic Republic, which refers to them as *bazm-e ahriman*, the devil's feast, and they have been subjected over the years to the same flares of 'rumor, conspiracy theory, and outright lie'. This book aims, therefore, to provide a contribution not only to the literature on the Celebrations but also to our general understanding of this important period of the Shah's rule, when he was reaching the zenith of his political authority and when his international standing was firmly on the rise.

Note on sources

As already touched upon, one of the problems with many accounts of the Celebrations is that there is very little analysis of documents and often historians make assumptions based on conjecture, or by using newspaper articles or accounts from opposition figures, which tend to exaggerate and are often misleading. In an example of such misleading accounts, in his *Crowned Cannibals*, the poet and political activist Reza Baraheni wrote an account of the Celebrations which is replete with factual inaccuracies. During the Shah's speech at Pasargadae, for instance, according to Baraheni, the world leaders were present.[47] He even comments on the mannerisms of Spiro Agnew and King Frederick IX of Denmark at this ceremony, despite the fact that world leaders were not present at Pasargadae and did not actually arrive in Shiraz until after the ceremony had finished. In his book *Autocracy, Modernization, and Revolution in Russia and Iran*, Tim McDaniel calls Baraheni's description a 'superb passage, with its pointed contrasts between the shah's grandiose pretensions and his diminished presence, and between the pseudonationalist rhetoric and the foreign audience and provenance of the event, underscores the emptiness of traditional monarchical symbolism in the Iran of oil and SAVAK'.[48] It may, indeed, be a superb passage, but it is factually inaccurate. Baraheni's work was intended to provoke an emotional response, rather than to provide a historical account and serves as a reminder of some of the problems inherent in handling sources from this period.

Similar problems can be found in standard texts, such the abridged English translation of the diaries of the Shah's Court Minister Asadollāh 'Alam, which authors often quote from without checking the original Persian for accuracy. For example, several authors, even in recent works, have quoted Empress Farah on one occasion as saying to 'Alam, 'For goodness sake, leave me alone … I want our names to be utterly disassociated from those ghastly celebrations.'[49] The original Persian, however, reads simply '*Velam kon, digar nemikhāham dar in kār-e jashnhā esmi az mā bordeh shavad*' – 'Leave me alone, I do not want our names to be associated with the work of the celebrations anymore.'[50] Two words are missing here, 'ghastly' and 'utterly', while 'leave me alone' (*velam kon*), is not preceded by 'for goodness sake'. It is difficult to understand why the translators have inserted words that are not there, or how they could have inferred that they should be there from the context of the passage. Granted, these are only small additions, but they are powerful ones, and change the overall tone of the sentence. This emphasizes the need, particularly when studying the Celebrations, for a careful and measured analysis of primary source material.

This book draws on a wide range of primary source materials, including academic publications, official documents, newspapers and oral histories, primarily in Persian and English, but also Dutch, French, Italian and German. Although it is difficult to access sources from the period in Iran, there is a wealth of documentary evidence available at archives and libraries outside of Iran. Among archives and libraries consulted during the research for this book were the British National Archives and the British Museum in London, the Institute of Social History in Amsterdam, the National Archives of the Netherlands in The Hague, the Austrian Staatsarchiv in Vienna, and the Bibliothèque universitaire des langues et civilisations in Paris, which holds the archive of Shojāʿ al-Din Shafā.

Documents published by the Islamic Republic's Ministry of Information were extensively studied. The four-volume *Bazm-e Ahriman* is a particularly valuable source for any study of the Imperial Celebrations, though one should consider that the documents contained within have been selected from a wider range of documentation and do not form a complete account. Kamran Scot Aghaie has noted that collections such as these published by the Islamic Republic 'constitute a strategy to use primary documents to put forth an ideologically motivated view of specific incidents in history'.[51] In the case of *Bazm-e Ahriman*, the purpose was to select the documents for publication that would 'demonstrate the moral depravity of the Pahlavis by showing the affluence, squandering of scarce natural resources, and moral decadence (according to Islam) of those in attendance'.[52] Indeed, many documents detail foreign involvement, the participation of religious minorities, such as the Jewish and Baha'i communities, and spending.

Some of the documents detail rumours of excessive spending overheard by SAVAK spies, without including hard evidence to either prove or disprove these rumours. There are references, for example, to the cost of horses flown into Iran from Hungary, for use during the parade at Persepolis. One source speculates that seven hundred horses were transported for 1.5 million rials each, meaning the total cost would have been around $14 million.[53] Another source claims that 2,500 horses were bought from Hungary and the cost of stables would be 8,000 rials each, which equalled in total approximately $270,000.[54] Although there are footnotes throughout the four volumes offering additional information, in this instance the editors make no effort to find documents that confirm whether these figures were accurate or not. Such documents are interesting because they illustrate the prevalence of such rumours, but the lack of clarification reveals the disingenuity of the volume's compilers. Notwithstanding these issues, there are nearly two thousand pages of documentation contained within the four volumes, printed, aside from a short introduction to each volume, without analysis.[55] They are, therefore, one of the most important sources for research on the 2500th Anniversary Celebrations.

Chapter overview

The Celebrations were the ultimate expression of the Pahlavi state ideology, which gained political traction from the 1960s. This nationalist ideology, based among other things on the glory of pre-Islamic Iran and Iran's immutable and historical right to regional supremacy, was strongly influenced by, and in many ways was a product of, the romantic nationalist discourse that developed in Iran from the middle of the 19th century. The purpose of Chapter 1 is to explore the currents of Iranian nationalism from this period onwards. It will examine the politicization of the legend of Cyrus the Great, which essentially began in antiquity and became an important part of the Pahlavi nationalist discourse in the 20th century. The chapter ultimately seeks to explain the motives of the Shah's cultural advisor at the Imperial Court, Shojāʿ al-Din Shafā, in proposing in 1958 a celebration to honour the legacy of Cyrus the Great.

Immediately after Shafā's idea was approved by the Shah, a special organizing committee was established, headed by Court Minister Hoseyn ʿAlā, and made up of the heads of key government ministries and other non-governmental organizations. In the following ten years, the Celebrations were repeatedly postponed, until 1968, when a firm date was finally set. Chapter 2 charts the development of the Celebrations, from initial conception through to the planning and the main events that took place in Fars province and Tehran in 1971. The chapter aims to lead to an understanding as to what motivated the organizers to hold the Celebrations in the way they did, and how the event helped to articulate the Pahlavi national ideology. It will show that the Celebrations were conceived as a relatively modest cultural commemoration, the highlight of which would be a Congress of Iranology, yet as the Shah's political standing and Iran's economy grew, the event took on a greater significance, internationally and domestically. Despite this, the chapter shows that the Celebrations retained their *raison d'être* of raising awareness of Iranian cultural heritage in Iran and around the world.

One aspect of the Pahlavi state ideology contended that Iran had a right to regional hegemony. The purpose of honouring the founder of the Achaemenid Empire, one of the largest empires the ancient world had known, was to validate the historicity of such claims. It is often said that because Queen Elizabeth and President Nixon in particular turned down their invitations to attend, the Celebrations were a failure. Conversely, Chapter 3 argues that the Celebrations had huge international appeal, as leaders from around the world came to take part in the festivities. Even those who did not were careful to let the Shah down gently, writing personal notes and devising seemingly valid excuses. This chapter puts the Celebrations in the context of this important period of the Shah's reign when his political capital was on the rise and shows that as the Shah emerged as a serious player on the international stage, states from around the world were ever more eager to pay tribute to him, securing lucrative contracts and regional influence in the process. Iran presented itself as a land of opportunity to investors and many states were keen to take advantage of the Shah's regional position. Furthermore, Iran's global cultural policy was not only intended to convey Pahlavi nationalism to a global audience, but it also formed a valuable part of Iran's foreign policy agenda and became a tool through which other states communicated with Iran on a political level.

From the time Shafā became the head of cultural affairs at the Imperial Court, he was a key figure in the formation of cultural policy and devised a number of initiatives to contribute to this. Chapter 4 shows that the Celebrations of 1971, though their scale and ideological message surprised many, fit perfectly into this broader cultural policy agenda. One goal of this agenda was to make Iran the main centre of Persian studies in the world, and to this end the regime established libraries and organized conferences.

One of these conferences was the Second International Congress of Iranology, held in October 1971 during the Imperial Celebrations, which was claimed to be the largest Iranian studies conference ever held. Another aspect of the cultural policy agenda was to promote the Pahlavi historical narrative to the domestic population. This was achieved through the publication of books and in the years prior to and during the Celebrations hundreds of works were published, intended to glorify the monarchy and Ancient Iran, and trumpet Iran's recent achievements.

Chapter 5 explores such cultural activity in an international context. The main way in which other countries contributed to the Celebrations was by arranging cultural events such as exhibitions and conferences, and through the publication of books. Cyrus the Great Committees were set up in countries around the world, and included among their members political figures, scholars and heads of business, in order to direct the cultural operation. The purpose of Chapter 5 is to investigate the types of events these committees organized, in order to understand better the increasingly important role that culture played in international diplomacy towards the Shah's regime. There was a clear political subtext to some of the historical works published, in the sense that they pandered to the ideology propagated by the regime, but many more sought to stimulate genuine scholarly inquiry. Many also showed that it was possible to do both simultaneously, and the Celebrations are deemed to have had a positive impact on Iranian studies as a scholarly discipline.

Despite the regime's attempts to use the Celebrations to promote a positive impression of Iran internationally and to stimulate broad support domestically, many were turned off by what they perceived as unnecessary expenditure and the delusion of an oriental despot. Chapter 6 contextualizes the opposition to the Celebrations, exploring why and how they were opposed by Khomeini and his supporters, student opposition groups in Iran and abroad, Islamic intellectuals and Marxist/Islamic militant groups. It will show that the Celebrations became an important rallying point for disparate opposition groups voicing long-standing grievances against the Shah's regime. Notwithstanding the cultural, political and economic benefits the event stimulated, there was no sophisticated public relations mechanism in place to counter the negative perception of the Celebrations.

The overriding narrative of the Celebrations, one promoted most recently in the BBC film *Decadence and Downfall*, is that over the course of a week in October 1971, the world's elite came to Iran to feast on the spoils of the country's oil wealth. The lavishness of the 'party' is generally stressed in the historical literature, often accompanied by unsubstantiated estimates as to its cost. Chapter 7 will show that much of the spending associated with the Celebrations contributed to the development of industry and infrastructure. The purpose of the chapter is to separate spending associated with the main festivities and spending associated with industrial development as set out in the Fourth Plan (1968–73), and by studying the accounts of the central organizing committee, to give an impression of how much was spent, and on what.

1

Ideology and historical background

Pierre Nora has argued that in the context of nationalism, there is no such thing as spontaneous memory; and that, therefore, once a historical narrative has been devised and described, a country's leaders are faced with the need to stimulate continuously awareness of this constructed past among the population. Leaders do this by such means as creating archives, marking anniversaries, eulogizing, authenticating documents and organizing celebrations.[1] The Shah was certainly not the first to use large-scale national celebrations for this purpose, as demonstrated by the 1913 tercentenary of the Romanov dynasty in Russia, the 1937–8 bimillennial celebration of the birth of Augustus in Italy and the 1940 celebration of the 2600th anniversary of the Japanese empire.[2] Such celebrations help to create or enforce national identity, legitimize one's rule or defend the established order, and to trumpet the leader's power and authority.[3] The purpose is not merely to commemorate past events but to present the current political status quo as the inevitable result of historical forces. As David Kertzer has written, 'In rendering their political system sacred through the use of ritual, people end up legitimizing the power held by political leaders.'[4]

The use of ritual and performance to elicit public support for a ruler or regime has been an important strategy for creating legitimacy in Iranian history. The royal patronage and embellishment of the Ashura rituals in the Safavid period from the rule of Shāh 'Abbās, and the *taʿziyeh* during the Qajar period, allowed the ruler to insert himself into pre-existing religious ceremonies, and in the process establish the state as the guarantor of religion.[5] The Pahlavis also used ceremonies as a means to legitimize the authority of the state, though these were often secular rather than religious. One key strategy employed by the Pahlavi regime was the creation of *lieux de mémoire*, to borrow Pierre Nora's phrase for physical sites designed or repurposed for the collective remembrance of a shared national history. This essentially became the government policy with the founding of the Society for the National Heritage of Iran (*Anjoman-e Āsār-e Melli-ye Irān*) in 1922. Events such as the celebration of the 1000th anniversary of the birth of Ferdowsi and the comparatively low-key inauguration of Nāder Shāh's tomb in 1959, both of which were supported by the Society for the National Heritage, illustrate the Pahlavi regime's strategy of both creating national heroes and establishing sites at which they could be honoured. Although steps had already been taken to glorify the image of Cyrus, the removal of Islamic-era additions to the site in the build up to the Celebrations, the sombre ceremony held at the tomb and the Shah's moving dedication, bolstered the Cyrus narrative and firmly established the tomb as a place at which Cyrus could be honoured as an Iranian hero.

Works such as Reza Zia-Ebrahimi's *The Emergence of Iranian Nationalism* have explained how intellectuals from the middle of the 19th century onwards recast the pre-Islamic period as a golden age in Iranian history, and equated the advent of Islam with the demise of Iranian grandeur.[6] The purpose of this chapter is not to provide an overview of Iranian nationalism but to show how romantic perceptions of Ancient Persia informed the thinking of nationalist authors, and how this romantic nationalist discourse developed into state nationalism with the emergence of Reza Shah, forming a key component of the Pahlavi state ideology of the 1960s and 1970s. The chapter seeks to understand how Cyrus the Great became such an important figure to Mohammad Reza Pahlavi, why he derived legitimacy from such an ancient ruler, and why his regime ultimately held the Imperial Celebrations in 1971 to honour the Achaemenid king.

Nationalism and Ancient Persia

The nation is commonly understood as a distinctly modern form of political society, bound together by a collective consciousness.[7] Although nationalism as a scholarly discipline is relatively modern, for centuries political theorists have been discussing the idea of nation and nationalism. Jean-Jacques Rousseau observed in his *Constitutional Project for Corsica* in 1765, for example, that 'The first rule to be followed is the principle of national character; for each people has, or ought to have, a national character; if it did not, we should have to start by giving it one.'[8] In his understanding, endowing the population with a binding identity is imperative for citizens to be able to understand their place in the community to which they belong. When Rousseau talks of 'giving' a national character, this suggests that national identities as we know them today did not appear entirely organically. Shared language, culture and territory can provide a foundation for a shared identity, but 'for that consciousness to become *nationalist* in any true sense', as Eley and Suny note, 'something else normally has to happen in the form of political intervention'.[9] The idea of a homeland, or a nation, therefore, is not natural per se, but is something chosen, constructed and ultimately politically motivated.

The term *vatan* had been used in Persian to denote a habitual place, or ordinary home, but its meaning was changed to denote a national homeland by intellectuals from the middle of the 19th century onwards.[10] During this period, education was controlled by the Shiite clergy through the *maktab* system, which stifled any open political discussion of modernization.[11] The translation and proliferation of the works of modern Western political philosophers and the increased interaction between Westerners and Iranians helped to change this situation. A number of prominent intellectuals, including Mirzā Fath'Ali Ākhundzādeh, Mirzā Āqā Khān Kermāni and Mirzā Malkam Khān, criticized the role of Islam in public life and utilized the works of thinkers such as Voltaire, Renan and Montesquieu to attempt to construct a modern, secular identity for the Iranian homeland.¹² Renan's work in particular spoke about the usefulness of history in conceptualizing the nation. In a lecture in 1882, he said:

> The nation, like the individual, is the outcome of a long past of efforts, sacrifices, and devotions. Of all cults, that of the ancestors is the most legitimate: our ancestors have made us what we are. A heroic past with great men and glory (I mean true glory) is the social capital upon which the national idea rests. These are the essential conditions of being a people: having common glories in the past and a will to continue them in the present; having made great things together and wishing to make them again.¹³

The rich catalogue of Persian history and literature, in the words of Tavakoli-Targhi, 'provided the pedagogical resources for the making of nationalist subjectivity and identity'.¹⁴

The intellectuals emphasized Ancient Persia for three reasons.¹⁵ First, by focusing on the ancient past, the movement naturally attained a level of authenticity. David Lowenthal noted this phenomenon in our understanding of history when he observed, 'Being ancient makes things precious by their proximity to the dawn of time, to their earlier beginnings ... the more ancient a lineage the more highly venerated it is.'¹⁶ Second, the lack of Persian material on the ancient period allowed for innovation and creativity, and the period served as a convenient template onto which the ideals and ideas of the modern world could be transplanted. As noted above, discussions of modernization had been suppressed by the conservative teaching of the *maktab*, but through exploration of history this dialogue could take place. And third, this innovation and creativity, in a sense the rearticulation of ancient history, allowed for effective comparison with the present. The high point of ancient Persian pre-eminence provided a sharp contrast to the dilapidated current state of affairs. It served, as Marashi observed, as a 'political call to arms'.¹⁷

This contrast between the glorious past and the present reality inevitably led some to question who, or what, was to blame for the decline. One of the first intellectuals to tackle this question was Jalāl al-Din Mirzā (1827–1872), who was the forty-eighth son of Fath 'Ali Shāh. He spoke French and was educated at the Dār al-Fonun, where he was exposed to a number of important Western historical and philosophical texts, including John Malcolm's *History of Persia*, George Rawlinson's *History of the Sassanian Kings of Persia* and a number of works of Voltaire.¹⁸ His *Nāmeh-ye Khosrovān* (Book of Kings), which was written in simple Persian prose and intended as an elementary textbook for the Dār al-Fonun, marked a break from the Persian historiography of the Qajar period, in the sense that it stressed cultural and political continuity from the pre-Islamic to Islamic periods.¹⁹ Jalāl al-Din Mirzā presented a romanticized image of the pre-Islamic period and showed that the Arab invasions were, as Amanat writes, 'a political catastrophe that pummelled the superior Iranian civilization under its hoof'.²⁰

Mirzā Fath'Ali Ākhundzādeh (1812–1878) was another important nationalist intellectual during this period. His romantic interpretation of Iranian history was 'the closest a nineteenth-century Iranian expatriate could come to the Deist ideas of the French Enlightenment'.²¹ Like Jalāl al-Din Mirzā, with whom he was in contact,

Ākhundzādeh contrasted the glory of Ancient Persia with the Islamic period, tracing Iran's deprivation to the barbarous Arab invaders: 'It has been 1,280 years now that the naked and starving Arabs have descended upon you and made your life miserable. Your land is in ruins, your people ignorant and innocent of civilization, deprived of prosperity and freedom, and your King is a despot.'[22] For Ākhundzādeh, Ancient Persia represented modernity and authenticity, whereas the Islamic period was one of backwardness.[23] While the Islamic period provided an example of deprivation, the West was held up as a model to which Persia should aspire. As Mohamad Tavakoli-Targhi has written, 'Identification with heterotopic Europe served as an oppositional strategy for the disarticulation of the dominant Islamicate discourse and for the construction of a new pattern of self-identity grounded on pre-Islamic history and culture.'[24] This shift towards the West and enlightenment ideas and away from Islam and the Islamite tradition was representative of a growing intellectual schism that developed during this period between the modernist intellectuals and the *ulema*.

An important aspect of Iranian nationalism that developed at this time was the Aryan myth, which championed the idea of Iranian exceptionalism, and which later came to have a significant influence on the Pahlavi state ideology under Mohammad Reza Pahlavi, expressed most explicitly through his adoption of the term *Āryāmehr*, Sun of the Aryans. Western scholars such as Friedrich Max Müller and Arthur de Gobineau popularized the idea of a superior Aryan race and at the beginning of the 20th century, the word *Aryan* was used in many scholarly circles to denote a higher race.[25] While some scholars in Iran were certainly influenced by this racist doctrine, and the idea of a superior Iranian race perhaps had some allure, the Aryan myth in Iran reflected specific trends in Iranian nationalism and historiography. While the Aryan myth had distinctive anti-Jewish overtones in Europe – indeed, it was used by some to denote one who is an anti-Semite – in Iran, the ideology had its roots deep in Persian history and reflected, if anything, anti-Arab sentiment.

Ali Ansari has argued that although the Aryan discourse may have been attractive for some, it was by no means popular and some of the key nationalists of the period, including Mohammad 'Ali Foroughi and Sayyed Hasan Taqizādeh, not only did not support the racist doctrine but also argued against it.[26] Moreover, authors such as Ākhundzādeh did not use ideas related to race to make abstract scientific pronouncements but to legitimate their claims and to assert Iran, as Marashi writes, 'as an equal and authentic member of a trans-European modernity'.[27] Like Ākhundzādeh, Mirzā Āqā Khān Kermāni (1854–1896) sought to re-evaluate the ancient Iranian civilization as distinct from the period after the Arab conquests. The idea of an ancient Aryan heritage again helped to emphasize this distinction.

The modern Iranian nationalism that developed from the middle of the 19th century onwards and that was eventually embraced by the Pahlavi regime was stimulated by three factors: an increased awareness of European political philosophy and ideas of nationalism; an 'intellectual awakening', as Homa Katouzian terms it, to ancient Iranian history, in part influenced by Europeans; and the 'psychology of the downtrodden', in which modern Iranian nationalist intellectuals lamented their country's demise, which they associated, as some Westerners did, with the Arab invasion.[28] They harked back to the glories of the Achaemenid and Sasanian periods in their search for the real Persia, a Persia uncontaminated by foreign culture and customs, and a Persia that commanded respect from the world. These ideas were, however, restricted to intellectuals and unknown to the general public, and at the beginning of the 20th century, there was still no real sense of Iranian nationalism. Most Iranians had no concept of *vatan* and considered their local community or town as their homeland.[29] These new ideas found a political voice at the beginning of the 20th century, with the Constitutional Revolution of 1905–11, the publication of journals such as *Kāveh* and *Irānshahr*, and into the Pahlavi period with the educational policies of the Pahlavi state.[30]

As a scholar as well as a statesman, Mohammad 'Ali Forughi (1877–1942) had a profound influence on the politics and national ideology of Iran in the early to mid-20th century. Like his predecessors discussed above, Forughi sought to restore to Iran a degree of dignity and pride in its culture and civilization. He contributed to the literature on Ancient Iran with a general history, published in 1902, as well as a history of the Sasanian period, published in 1898.[31] He dismissed the idea of race as a defining factor in national identity, concluding that history provides a stronger binding force.[32] To Forughi, as Ansari has written, 'Iran represented civilization, one that may have lost its way but a civilization nonetheless, that with a period of "enlightenment" could once again contribute constructively to the progress of mankind.'[33] He helped to found the Society for the National Heritage of Iran in 1922, which attempted to stimulate public participation in the nationalizing efforts of the state, so that Iranians would value their culture and heritage more highly.[34]

Persian nationalism sought not only to transform history but also language. In order to recover the true Iran that existed before the Arab invasions, it was argued that the Persian language must be purged of foreign, particularly Arab, words.[35] A number of organizations took part in a campaign to purify the Persian language during the first decade of Reza Shah's rule. The most important of these organizations was the *Farhangestān* (Academy). Its purpose, as Forughi stated, was to investigate strategies through which the Persian language could be altered in order to contribute to the 'Iranization' of culture and educational infrastructure and to stress the distinctiveness of Iranian civilization.[36]

In the nationalist newspaper *Kāveh*, which was published in Germany and ran from 1916 until 1921, Sayyed Hasan Taqizādeh (1878–1970) spoke of the importance of the 'revitalization of ancient Iranian national customs'.[37] The romantic nationalist intellectuals of the mid- to late 19th century were important in rearticulating Persian history, but *Kāveh* sought to promulgate these ideas to a wider audience in order to instigate a societal shift, as Pejman Abdolmohammadi writes, 'from theory to action'.[38] As well as engaging with orientalist literature and reformulating the history, myths and culture of Iran to the contemporary national form, Taqizādeh also called for fundamental reforms of Iran's education system and women's emancipation.[39] The journal *Irānshahr*, which was launched after Taqizādeh and most of the *Kāveh* staff returned to Iran and which ran from 1922 until 1927, also rooted Iran's national spirit in the pre-Islamic past and presented a utopian idea of Ancient Iran.[40] It also called for a 'spiritual revolution', achieved through educational modernization and by infusing national culture through teaching.[41]

During the late Qajar period, the Iranian elite developed a growing interest in their ancient history. According to Lord Curzon, by the end of the 19th century, the Iranians were so enthused by their ancient capital of Persepolis that the first modern warship of the Iranian navy, a 600-ton steamship purchased from Germany, was named *Persepolis*, while a small river steamer bought at the same time was named *Susa*.[42] In the same period, the Qajars began to show a willingness to engage with European archaeologists in the study of pre-Islamic history. For example, Prince Farhād Mirzā Mo'tamed al-Dowleh, son of 'Abbās Mirzā, led the third major excavations at Persepolis from 14 March to 16 April 1877. Persian interest in European investigations is further evidenced by the fact that Henry Rawlinson personally presented the first Persian language translation of the Bisotun inscriptions to Mohammad Shāh, receiving a medal of the Lion and the Sun for his efforts.[43] The Qajars had previously emphasized their Turkish origins, but during this period began to stress their Iranian roots.[44]

In October 1877, Farhād Mirzā gave permission to a German team to excavate at Persepolis, on the proviso that any artefacts they uncovered must remain in Persia.[45] The Germans refused to accept the condition, but the mere fact that it was set is indicative of a desire among the elite to safeguard Persia's cultural heritage. Artefacts were no longer commodities but were part of Persian identity. Perhaps inspired by his travels to Europe, Nāser al-Din Shāh created the Royal Museum in his Golestān Palace in Tehran in 1876, which further reflects the growing interest in heritage among the Qajar elite during this period. The opening of the Bāstān Museum in Tehran is often attributed to Reza Shah; however, a precursor to the Bāstān Museum, the National Museum, was established earlier in 1917 in the building of the Ministry of Education north of the Dār al-Fonun.[46] As we will see shortly, it was during the early Pahlavi period that the romantic nationalist discourse became part of the official state ideology, however, this narrative had already become engrained in the political consciousness of the elite in late Qajar period.

Ancient Persia and the West

The nationalist intellectual movement that appeared in Iran in the 19th and early 20th centuries reflected, to a certain degree, trends in European orientalist historiography. In the ancient world, the Persians were respected to some extent by their Roman and Greek enemies, even though they were essentially considered barbarians, and Persians were the subjects of plays, poetry, philosophy and historical inquiry. However, this respect disappeared following the Arab invasion when, in the words of Richard Frye, 'a kind of curtain was drawn between the Persians and the West, and this lasted for many centuries'.[47] The classical and biblical sources remained the primary sources for Westerners on the history of Iran and, as Ansari writes, they 'left a narrative legacy that would permeate the medieval mind and be reinforced by the advent of the Renaissance, which, along with the growth in travel, literacy and publishing, ensured an increasing and fertile audience'.[48]

As interaction between Westerners and Persians increased in the early modern period, interest in Persian history developed once again in the West. This interaction began in earnest in the 16th century during the Safavid period. Shāh Tahmāsp (r. 1524–1576) permitted foreigners to access Iranian markets, and the development of travel infrastructure under Shāh ʿAbbās (r. 1588–1629) made it easier for foreign merchants to travel through Persia.[49] Meanwhile, the exploits of the famous English adventurer Robert Sherley, who led Persian embassies to Europe during the reign of Shāh ʿAbbās, further fed the English public's fascination with the romance of the East.[50] Partly inspired by these interactions, ancient Persian kings became popular subjects in theatre between the 16th and 18th centuries and plays were performed with titles such as *Xerxes: A Tragedy* and *The Tragedy of Darius*.[51] At least four plays were written about Cyrus the Great specifically, including the anonymously published *The Wars of Cyrus King of Persia, against Antiochus King of Assyria, with the Tragical End of Panthaea* (1594) and John Banks's *Cyrus the Great: or, The Tragedy of Love* (1696).[52]

In the following two centuries, as Europeans, particularly the British, travelled to Iran, usually on diplomatic missions, interest in Ancient Persia grew further. It was during the early decades of the 19th century that the first attempts were made to excavate the site of Persepolis by British passers-by, such as Sir Gore Ouseley on his mission in 1811, with work continued by his attaché Robert Gordon and later by Lieutenant-Colonel Ephraim Gerrish Stannus in 1825 and Colonel John Macdonald in 1826.[53] The activity that can be observed at Persepolis indicates the enthusiasm that these early travellers felt at visiting the monuments of Ancient Persia. According to one report at the time, 'English who wish to proceed overland from the East Indies, come by sea into the Persian Gulf … land at Bendarabas … proceed to Shiraz … and take pleasure in visiting the ruins of Persepolis.'[54] It was around this time that the first comprehensive history of Persia was published by Sir John Malcolm. Malcolm, who had travelled to Iran in 1800, was fascinated by the country and its history, and declared, 'I employ every leisure hour in researches into the history of this extraordinary country, with which we are but little acquainted.'[55] In his *History of Persia*, first published in 1815, he wrote that 'the English reader should be made acquainted with the history and condition of a people, who have in most ages acted a conspicuous part on the theatre of the world.'[56] Not all visitors were so enthralled. One British serviceman wrote bitterly that Persepolis 'has been crammed down my throat, upon every available occasion, ever since I landed in Persia.'[57]

These early travellers to Iran were struck by its backwardness, in direct contrast to its splendid past. Malcolm wrote that 'Though no country has undergone, during the last twenty centuries, more revolutions than the kingdom of Persia, there is, perhaps, none that is less altered in its condition,'[58] and Lord Curzon later characterized Iran as 'remote and backward.'[59] Eric Chamberlin explains how this attitude to Persia was in part stimulated by the foreigners' reactions to the ancient sites of Iran and other Eastern countries:

The cultured tourist was obliged to indulge in a complex piece of mental gymnastics. He had come to admire the great monuments of the past – Baalbeck, Persepolis, the Parthenon, Ctesiphon, the Pyramids. Demonstrably, they were the work of a brilliant civilization: equally demonstrably, they could have no relationship with the feckless, unwashed, immoral, poverty-stricken 'natives' who lived near, and only too often on, these glorious monuments. Therefore, the present inhabitants of the country housing these monuments must themselves be not only decadent, but interlopers.[60]

To the European travellers, the modern reality of Persia provided a stark contrast to the splendid monuments of its past, and the imagined picture inspired by the romanticism of Hellenic and biblical accounts.

This disconnection, many European travellers reasoned, was brought about by the Arab invaders, whom they saw as brutish and uncivilized, or at the very least different and threatening. Some Europeans saw the advent of Islam as a direct cause of Persian depravity since their fall at the hands of the Arab invaders. Indeed, Malcolm writes that Islam was a prominent factor 'in retarding the progress of civilization among those who have adopted his [Mohammad's] faith ... The History of Persia from the Arabian conquest to the present day may be adduced as proof of the truth of these observations'.[61] Zia-Ebrahimi notes that

> a certain distaste for Islam and anything Islamic was deeply ingrained in European writings on the Orient; it is therefore no surprise that Orientalists held the period before Islam in higher esteem. Secondly, many Orientalists looked at their subjects from a classicist perspective, through sources in Greek and Latin. Therefore, as Classicists, they had an aversion to Islam, seen as the phenomenon that put an end to western antiquity.[62]

While it is questionable that Westerners in general had an aversion to Islam, for most Europeans, there was a vast difference between Ancient Persia and Islamic Persia. While the former inspired great interest, the latter was, in general, met with indifference. The Western penchant for ancient things was not confined to Persia. Between 1810 and 1910, nearly all minor and major excavations by Westerners in the Islamic world focused on pre-Islamic sites such as Babylon, Khorsabad and Nippur.[63] Europeans felt that this history, in some way, belonged to them, and that Islamic history was not particularly valuable or relevant. In focusing on Ancient Iran as the basis of the Pahlavi state ideology in the 1920s, the regime was, therefore, appealing to a foreign as well as domestic base. The international focus of the regime's strategies for legitimization can be observed throughout the early Pahlavi period, most strikingly during the 1000th anniversary celebrations of the birth of Ferdowsi in 1935.

Reza Shah and the Ferdowsi celebration

Claims to the uniqueness and indeed superiority of Iranian culture, race and civilization, and the symbolism of monarchical rule, came to form the ideological basis of Reza Shah's nationalism. Reza Khan chose an ancient Persian language, Pahlavi, as the name for his new dynasty and Achaemenid monuments were displayed on stamps throughout this period, remaining a dominant feature of Pahlavi iconography throughout the proceeding decades.[64] During the early years of Reza Shah's rule, old buildings in Tehran were demolished and, in their place, new buildings were erected, often designed in a classical style. The Bank Melli main office and police headquarters, for example, were constructed in neo-Achaemenid style and the Iran Bāstān Museum was designed after Sasanian era Ctesiphon.

During the same period, the state implemented a series of educational reforms, intended to propagate an official version of Iranian history. Like Atatürk in Turkey, Reza Shah sought to create a modern nation and to unite state and society under the standard of a distinct national culture. Intellectuals such as 'Isā Sadiq, 'Ali Asghar Hekmat and Hasan Pirniyā were tasked with implementing policies aimed at promoting the nationalist treaties of Jalāl al-Din Mirzā, Ākhundzādeh and Kermāni, as well as the articles contained within *Kāveh* and *Irānshahr*.[65] The educational policies of the early Pahlavi period reflected, therefore, according to Marashi, 'the state's desire to reconcile the dual interests of modernity and nationalism'.[66] Through the development of a curriculum and the writing of historical textbooks, the state sought to produce an official narrative for mass dissemination. Pirniyā, a notable political figure of the period, wrote a *History of Ancient Iran* in four volumes and in 1922 became one of the founders of the Society for the National Heritage, an organization that aimed to safeguard and promote Iran's national heritage.[67]

On 22 April 1925, Arthur Upham Pope, the famous American art dealer and scholar, gave a lecture in Tehran titled 'The Past and Future of Persian Art'. In attendance were the cabinet ministers of the Majles and the man who would soon become shah, Reza Khan. During the lecture, Pope evoked images of the great Iranian kings such as Cyrus and Ardashir, and he concluded his speech with an appeal to Iranians to appreciate their vibrant heritage.

> So instead of worshiping at the Peacock Throne, Persians can do much better to study thoughtfully the work of their own true artists. One page of the work of Mir Ali Qazvini is worth a hundred Peacock Thrones in the judgement of at least one student of Persian art. At least the principle that it is not wealth and display that make art but something more fundamental and noble, that cannot be challenged.
>
> If by instruction and by example these wrong theories, that retard the revival and development of real artistic sense can be corrected, then with the government's energetic support of practical measures, the future of Persian art is secure ... The government and the people together must do everything possible to bring art again to life in Persia.[68]

The idea of a Persian renaissance appealed to the modernizing ideologues of the period, and according to the historian Laurence Elwell-Sutton, it was this event that stimulated the first Pahlavi monarch's personal enthusiasm for Iranian heritage.[69] Donald Wilber agreed, noting that 'there can be no doubt of the lasting impact of what he had heard on this occasion. More than ever he was convinced that the heights reached by Iranians in the past must be scaled again'.[70] This analysis is supported by the fact that the speech was widely distributed 'for the use of teachers all over the country'.[71] Furthermore, the principal suggestions for the revitalization of Persian art stated in the speech were carried out by the Society for the National Heritage, as the words of Pope, according to 'Isā Sadiq, 'kindled fires within us like magic. We became proud of ourselves'.[72] Pope said nothing truly groundbreaking nor did this event represent any real break in the government's position on Iranian heritage, but the fact that these words were uttered by a foreign scholar legitimized, in a sense, the Persian cultural renaissance that was already taking place.

The celebration held to mark the 1000th anniversary of the birth of Ferdowsi in 1935 was part of the Society for the National Heritage's push for the revival of Iranian art. Pope was involved in the organization of the event and according to one of his former colleagues, Rex Stead, the celebration would 'have never succeeded without the efforts of Professor Pope'.[73] The celebration was held between 4 and 14 October and for the first four days an International Congress of Orientalists took place, attended by forty-five delegates from eighteen different countries.[74] They included such renowned scholars as Henri Massé, Jan Rypka, Arthur Christensen, Vladimir Minorsky and Sir Edward Denison Ross.[75] According to Marashi, the scholarly congress 'was presented as an affirmation of Iran's national culture by the world'.[76] After a brief stop at Omar Khayyam's grave in Nishapur, where scholars read excerpts from Khayyam and made a toast with wine in his memory, they arrived in Tus on 12 October, where the Shah inaugurated the new mausoleum built for Ferdowsi.[77] Stressing the revivalist attitude of the Pahlavi ideologues, Grigor observes, 'Morphologically, the structure was a synthesis between the Parthian mausoleum buildings and Cyrus's tomb as examples of Iran's pre-Islamic architecture'.[78] By modelling Ferdowsi's tomb on Cyrus the Great's, he became a national hero alongside Cyrus and Iranians were provided with 'a site on which collective history could be experienced at an exact place and time'.[79]

The anniversary of Ferdowsi's birth attracted attention around the world. In London, for example, the British Museum organized an exhibition of manuscripts of the *Shāhnāmeh*,[80] Sir Percy and Lady Cox exhibited Persian maps at the Royal Geographical Society, the Persian Club held a special event under the auspices of the Persian ambassador Hoseyn 'Alā, and a symposium on matters concerning Ferdowsi was held at the School of Oriental and African Studies.[81] Western scholarship was an important tool for Reza Shah in his promotion of Iranian civilization as a dominant cultural force in the region and the world. In the construction of historical narratives, however, Iranian scholars had, to a degree, been dependent on the West. When Pirniyā and Foroughi attempted to utilize modern historiographical methods in the study of their country, for example, their works relied heavily on Western scholarship.[82] The Ferdowsi celebration was part of a transformation that was occurring during this period, in which there was a concerted effort on behalf of the Iranian regime to work actively with foreign scholars, deciding research priorities and enthusiastically encouraging studies on certain aspects of Iranian history, culture and civilization. The politicization of culture during Reza Shah's rule played a part in this, but it was also stimulated by an increase in dialogue between academics in Iran and academics from outside. Underpinning the celebration was a striving for legitimacy as Reza Shah's ideologues, reflecting modern nationalist trends, used the *Shāhnāmeh* and the mausoleum of Ferdowsi to emphasize Iran's culture as distinct from Arab culture, and link the Pahlavi regime to the long line of Persian kings, mythical or otherwise.

Cyrus the Great

The initiation of the tomb of Ferdowsi in 1935 created a place in which the great poet could be venerated as a national hero. A similar *lieu de memoire* was created in 1971 when the Shah's regime sought to establish the tomb of Cyrus as an important site of collective remembrance for all Iranians. The question remains: how did Cyrus become the obvious choice as the figure to whom the Shah's regime would turn as the basis of its national ideology? Cyrus the Great was born between 600 and 590 BCE and ruled from 559 BCE until his death in 530. During his reign, he defeated the three regional powers of Media, Lydia and Babylonia to forge the largest empire the world had known, and laid the foundations for his successor Cambyses II's addition of Egypt to this domain. His apparent benevolence towards conquered rulers and his respect of local religions was exceptional in a typically violent region, accustomed to the brutality of the Assyrian kings.[83] Whereas these had tended to wreak destruction and inflict horrific violence on the peoples they conquered, Cyrus not only spared the great cities of the territories that he seized but also allowed their kings to live, usually sending them into retirement on an estate within his empire.[84] Proving that benevolence is not equal to weakness, he created a political system that stretched from the Hindu Kush in the east to the Hellespont in the west, a system that would remain intact for two and a half centuries.

Cyrus's supposed benevolence earned him legendary status in the ancient world. Herodotus of Halicarnassus, in his *Histories*, written in 440 BCE, ninety years after Cyrus's death, called Cyrus a 'father' who 'was gentle, and procured them [his subjects] all manner of goods'.[85] In Herodotus's account, Cyrus achieved freedom for his people by overthrowing Astyages, ruler of the Medes. The work is, however, in part a philosophical exploration of human nature and the character of kingship, and includes colourful and morally questionable characters such as the greedy Croesus, the tyrannical Cambyses and the deceitful Ephialtes. Herodotus guides us to appreciate the virtues of Cyrus in so far as it is possible to appreciate a king, for Cyrus ultimately succumbs to his ambition and dies in a bloody battle while fighting a Scythian tribe.[86]

Xenophon's philosophical study *Cyropaedia*, written around seventy years after Herodotus's *Histories*, presents Cyrus as the ideal king, compassionate, thoughtful and valiant. In Xenophon's account, Cyrus is also presented as a father figure to his people:

> [T]his is not the first time I have had occasion to observe that a good ruler differs in no respect from a good father. Even as a father takes thought that blessings may never fail his children, so Cyrus would commend to us the ways by which we can preserve our happiness ... Of one thing we may be sure: Cyrus will never put us to any service which can make for his own good and not for ours. Our needs are the same as his, and our foes the same.[87]

As an historical account it is questionable, but it impresses upon us the high regard in which Cyrus was held in the ancient world. Xenophon's work remains an influential source on Cyrus and the philosophy of leadership, and Thomas Jefferson later wrote to his son that *Cyropaedia* was the first book he should read in Greek.⁸⁸ The idea of the king as a father was an important aspect of the conceptualization of the monarchy in the Pahlavi period too, particularly under Mohammad Reza Pahlavi after the initiation of his White Revolution.

Other Greek philosophers and playwrights discussed the admirable qualities of the Persian king. Plato, for instance, wrote that Cyrus allowed for 'full liberty of speech' and that in his Persia 'there was freedom and friendship and communication of mind'.⁸⁹ According to Diodorus Siculus, Cyrus 'possessed exceptional qualities' and was 'the greatest man of his time'.⁹⁰ In many of these works, Cyrus was a convenient and accepted model onto whom the ideals of the civilized Greek world could be projected. Alexander the Great apparently shared a deep respect for Cyrus. When he saw Cyrus's tomb at Pasargadae, he was moved by the majestic simplicity of the monument, and was later so perturbed at finding the tomb vandalized and robbed that he ordered a 'thorough repair'.⁹¹ That Alexander, as a well-educated Greek, would have respect for Cyrus is perfectly understandable; however, it is possible that there was a more pragmatic motivation for his tribute to Cyrus, connected to his attempts to legitimize his rule as the new king of Persia. Aware of the reverence in which Cyrus was held by his people, Alexander sought to bypass the impossibility of relating himself through blood to the Achaemenids and rather present himself as a spiritual successor to the conquered dynasty.⁹² Two thousand three hundred years later, Mohammad Reza Pahlavi would employ a similar strategy in his attempts to legitimize his rule.

Reverence for Cyrus was not confined to the Greek world. After he released the Jews from captivity in Babylon, where they had been held since Nebuchadnezzar II's conquest of Jerusalem at the end of the 7th century BCE, Cyrus's actions were lauded by the Jewish chroniclers. According to Ezra, Cyrus issued a decree calling for the rebuilding of the temple of Jerusalem⁹³ and for this Isaiah refers to him as the 'Lord's anointed'.⁹⁴ Therefore, the modern perception of Cyrus going into the 19th century could be said to be an amalgam of Greek and biblical tradition. Just as Xenophon used the Greek perception of Cyrus to create his ideal king, Cyrus became convenient to the Pahlavi ideologues as one who appeared to encapsulate the ideals, and indeed represent the origins, of modern European political thought. This certainly contributed to the presentation of the Cyrus Cylinder in the 20th century as the first bill of human rights.

The idea of Cyrus's ideal government explicitly expressed by the Greeks became an increasingly important aspect of Persian nationalism at the end of the 19th century. Of Cyrus the Great, Kermāni writes: 'His government was based on justice and equality, and for this reason history baptised him as a "prophet". His personality became so notable because he never abused his power and treated the defeated monarchs as his political allies. The reign of Kurosh [Cyrus] was based on social justice and on the freedom of expression and faith'.⁹⁵ To Kermāni, religious fanaticism and the despotism of rulers were two of the worst evils in human society.⁹⁶ Cyrus, as presented by Kermāni, was the antithesis of these ills and in his society 'justice' and 'freedom' prevailed. The memory of Cyrus's ideal government also served as a spiritual and political rallying call:

> Oh sons of this chaotic Iran: the people in the world have successfully freed themselves from the chains of ignorance and slavery, going towards progress,

freedom and equality. While we transformed the 'ideal reign' (of Kurosh) to a dark cemetery. We are a sleepy nation, while others are awake. Look at how the spirit of freedom, justice and constitutionalism has already spread throughout the world. Then wake up and commit yourselves to realising a new political government, to make a free and dignified Iran.[97]

Not only did the government of Cyrus mark a high point of Iranian history, but Kermāni argued that Iranians could once more return to prominence.

An abridged version of the first volume of Hasan Pirniyā's history of Iran titled *Irān-e Qadim* was widely distributed in the late 1920s and became a standard textbook for young Iranian students.[98] In it, Pirniyā broadcast the romantic history of Ancient Persia and the legend of Cyrus the Great to a wide audience. Of Cyrus, he wrote that 'historians believe that he was a king with resolve, prudence, wisdom and clemency.'[99] Stressing the exceptional nature of Cyrus, he writes, 'In difficult situations he favoured reason over brute force, and unlike the kings of Assyria and Babylon and others, he was generous and kind to the people he defeated.'[100] In this context, Pirniyā argues, 'This great king caused a kind of moral revolution (*enqelāb-e akhlāqi*) in the ancient world.'[101] According to the narrative put forward in the state-commissioned literature at this time, Cyrus was not an ordinary king but an Iranian hero and a revolutionary, who set the standard for just and moral kingship.[102]

Standing in front of the tomb of Cyrus the Great in 1971, the Shah pledged to the spirit of Cyrus, in language similar to that of Kermāni cited previously, that his Iranians were now awake, and always would be. His regime's adoption of Cyrus mirrored the writings of Xenophon in that it presented Cyrus as the ideal king, a model for political leaders. It also mirrored Kermāni and Pirniyā, in that it claimed Cyrus had presided over an ideal government, in which justice and freedom flourished. In a significant publication for the Anniversary Celebrations, Shojāʿ al-Din Shafā quoted at length from a 1951 book by René Grousset, in which he spoke of the 'profoundly humane' nature of Iranian civilization: 'At a time when UNESCO, to save the world from chaos and hatred, has appealed to all mankind, to all people of goodwill, Iranian civilization provides a great historical example, for the common task a great spiritual force, for the common effort total support.'[103] The opinions of such scholars were endorsed and promoted in this period by the Pahlavi regime in order to reinforce the official state narrative. For example, at the beginning of his *Enqelāb-e Sefid* (White Revolution), the Shah cited Arthur Christensen: 'A real king in Iran is not only a political ruler but is first and foremost a teacher and sage; one who does not only build roads, dams, bridges and canals (*qanāts*), but also guides their spirits, thoughts and hearts.'[104]

In 1960, Arthur Upham Pope also stressed the moral importance of the Achaemenid Empire. He wrote that

> for the first time in history an empire was built on an *ethical foundation* with not only a superb political organisation (the Assyrians were competent in this field also), but also primarily because new principles, particularly those of *religious and racial tolerance*, were put into effect to build an empire that could command the

loyalty and enthusiasm of its subjects by reason of the *human dignity* conferred. [Emphasis added][105]

In the Shah's *Mission for My Country*, published in 1961, he echoed the sentiments expressed by these historians. He wrote that Cyrus was 'one of the most dynamic men in history'[106] and that 'wherever Cyrus conquered, he would pardon the very people who had fought him, treat them well, and keep them in their former posts ... While Iran at the time knew nothing of democratic political institutions, Cyrus nevertheless demonstrated some of the qualities which provide the strength of the great modern democracies'.[107] The enlightenment might have occurred in Europe in the 18th century, but according to the Shah, some of its principal ideas had been embraced by Cyrus over 2,000 years earlier. The Shah further observed that 'the empire founded by Cyrus the Great was not based on territorial acquisition alone, but also on international tolerance and understanding. The rights of all the subject nations were upheld, and their laws and customs respected. Indeed, I see in our first empire something of the United Nations of nearly 2,500 years later.'[108] This understanding of history is, of course, highly subjective and is illustrative of the Pahlavi ideologues' presentation of their history through both the prism of both modern Western philosophical tradition and the romantic nationalism which developed in Iran from the middle of the 19th century.

Having identified Cyrus as one of the great heroes of Iranian history, a modernizer in his own time and intellectually progressive, the Pahlavi ideologues set about presenting the Shah as his spiritual successor, thereby legitimizing the Pahlavi Dynasty in the context of a 2,500-year-old monarchical tradition. A passage from a commemorative bibliography of Iran published on the occasion of the Shah's coronation in 1967 expresses this sentiment clearly: 'It has been said that what Xenophon wrote of Cyrus the Great in 401 B.C. could equally well have been written of Mohammad Reza Shah Pahlavi.'[109] Another book that was published to coincide with the coronation in 1967 titled *Tājgozāri-ye Shāhanshāhān-e Irān* (The Coronation of the Kings of Iran) provided a history of coronation ceremonies throughout Iranian history, beginning with Cyrus the Great, the emergence of whom was described as 'one of the most important world events', and concluding with the coronation of Mohammad Reza Pahlavi.[110]

Publications in Persian at the time of the Celebrations also stressed the similarities between the progressive policies of Cyrus the Great, and the progressive policies of the current king. Some books featured in the introductory pages a gold-lettered translation of the text of the Cyrus Cylinder, alongside text of the Shah's White Revolution, clearly linking Cyrus with Mohammad Reza Pahlavi.[111] The organizers of the Imperial Celebrations reproduced these texts, engraved in Persian and cuneiform on stone slabs, and displayed them in many different towns and cities across Iran.[112] Newspapers, too, clearly made this comparison. In the pro-regime daily *Keyhān*, on 11 October, the day before the opening of the Celebrations, for example, a headline read 'The Immortality of Imperial Iran'. On the left side of the page was a picture of Cyrus the Great, on the right, the Shah in full coronation regalia. At the bottom of the page was text of the Shah's White Revolution alongside text of the Cyrus Cylinder.[113] The official programme for the Celebrations also implicitly makes the comparison between Cyrus and the Shah. It states that Cyrus was 'strong and magnanimous, just and humane ... a man of high ideals who lived up to his belief that no man was fit to rule unless he was the most capable man in the kingdom'.[114] The same page refers to the 'far-sighted leadership' of Mohammad Reza Pahlavi. It can be seen, therefore, that the presentation of the Shah as a successor to Cyrus gained political capital throughout the 1960s, reaching a climax during the Celebrations in 1971.

The connection with Cyrus also served to present the Pahlavi regime as rooted in a long and ancient tradition of kingship. The idea of the continuity of monarchy was to show that Iran had always had kings, and that the glory of its past had been due to the strength of the monarchical institution. In this way, the regime made, as Mostafa Vaziri noted, 'patriotism synonymous with cherishing the monarchy and the monarch'.[115] As a tribute to the historical monarchical tradition in Iran, the Anniversary Celebrations sought to encourage people to equate their love for their country with their love for the king.

The Cyrus Cylinder was an important cultural symbol that the regime adopted during this period and which became, in a sense, a tool of legitimization. It was a tangible evidence of the narrative of Cyrus promoted by the regime. By the time of the Celebrations in 1971, scholars spoke of the 'message of Cyrus', enshrined in the Cylinder, which had 'transcendental power'. In his presentation to the Congress of Iranology, Argentine scholar Ismael Quiles said,

> It is certain that Cyrus believed in a transcendent divine order, which goes above human and temporary events and governs the destinies of men, and which constitutes a guarantee of moral order for human relations. And that seems to us to be a fundamental and clear point in Cyrus' message, which gives great power, transcendental power, to his historical declaration of human rights made 2,500 years ago.[116]

The Pahlavi regime was successful in promoting the Cylinder as an ancient declaration of the rights of man. It became the centrepiece of the official logo of the Celebrations, which appeared on all literature and featured the artefact in a blue halo, with the Pahlavi coat of arms above, surrounded by Persepolitan-style flowers. Lowenthal observed that 'manipulating antiquities refashions their appearance and meaning' and we see clear evidence of this in the Pahlavi appropriation of the Cylinder.[117]

***

The concept of an Iranian homeland and an Iranian national identity developed from an intellectual movement from the middle of the 19th century into a political movement and ultimately state ideology in the Pahlavi period. Ancient Persia was refashioned by the Pahlavi ideologues to form the basis of this ideology, serving to accentuate the successes of pre-Islamic Iran and to look to a future as glorious as the past. Although, over the centuries, Iran had suffered repeated invasions, it had never lost its cultural identity. In this sense, as Zia-Ebrahimi writes, modern Iranian nationalism 'transmuted the Iranian nation into a phoenix, which rises time and again from the ashes of foreign invasion'.[118]

The first Pahlavi monarch, Reza Shah, sought to acquire legitimacy from the Persian monarchical tradition and the glories of Ancient Persia, rather than from the previous Qajar dynasty that had ruled for nearly 150 years. He ruled Iran as a strongman, putting an end to years of humiliation at the hands of the British and Russians, who had shown a disregard for Iranian sovereignty. Despite this, he was forced to abdicate by the British and Russians, and his son and successor, Mohammad Reza Pahlavi, was left to consolidate his rule in the turbulent post-war period. By the 1960s, he had gained confidence domestically and internationally and was able to seek to secure Iran's position as an influential and commanding global power. Through reforms such as the White Revolution, and events such as the coronation ceremony in 1967, the Shah sought to legitimize his rule by presenting the fortunes of Iran as dependent on the strength and fortitude of the monarchical institution. By comparing himself to Cyrus, he was appealing to a global and domestic audience. Cyrus was presented not only as an Iranian hero but also as a historical figure on whom modern European philosophical ideas could be projected.

Pierre Nora has written that history can be used as a way of 'figuring out what we are from what we are no longer'.[119] In his memoir, Shafā writes that during the Qajar period, Iran 'had declined to the level of an underdeveloped state', therefore, he continues:

> By holding this international celebration, we sought to remind the public that Iran is the same proud country, a producer of civilization (*tamaddon āfarin*), with 3,000 years of history that they had studied in history lessons at school, that had a prominent role in the ancient world, and fought against the Greek and Roman empires … and by reconnecting with its glorious past it is ready to accept responsibility for ensuring the same prosperity in the future as a dynamic and constructive nation.[120]

The Celebrations, therefore, marked the resurgence of Iran and its return to the centre of global politics. As it had fought against the Greek and Roman Empires, so it could challenge the industrial and military powers of the world to become a serious force on the international stage. While romantic nationalists presented Iran's return to pre-eminence as the natural result of historical forces, the underpinning message of the Celebrations was that this return was dependent on the strength and wisdom of the King of Kings, Sun of the Aryans, Mohammad Reza Pahlavi.

2

'The World's Centre of Happiness'

From the late 1960s, the Pahlavi state developed a strong political ideology, which is sometimes referred to as Pahlavism, after the series of books published by Manuchehr Honarmand.[1] Two central aspects of this ideology were designed to convince the world that Iran belonged to the Western family of nations, namely the employment of the Aryan myth to place Iranians in the same race as Europeans, and the appropriation of the pre-Islamic past. This demonstrated, first, that Iran was not, in essence, an Islamic country, and second, that Iran's ancient past was at least as glorious and civilized as Europe's. The Celebrations offered the regime an opportunity to promote both these aspects of Pahlavism to a domestic and global audience. As the previous chapter has shown, the adoption of the Aryan myth by the Pahlavi ideologues at the beginning of the 20th century was driven in large part by a desire to be viewed as more closely related to the modern Europeans than to Iran's Arab neighbours.

The idea of race as a determining factor in shaping identity was subtly expressed during the main ceremonies in Iran and also more overtly elsewhere. For instance, four children were chosen from around the world as representatives of different races – 'one each from the black, yellow, white and red races' – to receive scholarships from the Iranian government to cover their education up to university.[2] The 'black' child was a citizen of Kenya, the 'yellow' child Japanese, the 'red' child Canadian and the 'white' child Iranian. Each of the recipients was exactly 2,500 days old on the day the Celebrations began on 14 October 1971. This racial diversity was said to 'symbolize the values of equality and freedom which were proclaimed by Cyrus the Great'.[3] The Canadian speaker of the senate declared it 'a great honour, too, that a young Canadian, Roland Dominique, a Montagnais Indian from Schefferville, Quebec, was chosen to represent the red race'.[4] The choice of Iran as representative of the 'white' race, while a Canadian was a representative of the 'red' race, indicates the extent to which the Celebrations were used to stress both Iranian exceptionalism and its similarities with the West.

The second aspect, the Pahlavi appropriation of pre-Islamic Iran, likewise had its roots in the late Qajar period and was in part influenced by the West's deference to Ancient Persia. For a domestic audience, this was about identity and legitimacy, rooting the monarchy in an ancient historical tradition. For a global audience, the Celebrations represented an opportunity to underscore Iran's affinity with the West through its un-Arabness and its pre-Islamic past, even more ancient and glorious than that of Italy or Greece. It was hoped that Iran would be transformed in the eyes of the world from a traditional Islamic country to a modern, industrial and even secular state, far more palatable to Western politicians. Domestically, the appropriation of Ancient Persia showed that the Shah could modernize along European lines, while remaining true to Iran's ancient heritage. Later, when the Shah spoke of his Great Civilization, he essentially envisioned Iran as a Western state but with the trappings of ancient Persian culture.

During the 1960s, the Pahlavi state adopted several measures to contribute to the ideologizing of the crown, which increased in regularity and intended impact towards the end of the decade. On 15 September 1965, for example, the Majles granted to the Shah the title *Āryāmehr*. Sādeq Kiyā explained the meaning of the term and the reason for it being given to the Shah in a commemorative volume published on the occasion of the Shah's coronation in 1967: '"*Āryāmehr*" means the "Sun of Aryans" (*khurshid-e āryā*) and is befitting such a king, who is purely Iranian in essence, and who has worked with all his might and has done brilliant things for the comfort, development and pride of Iranians.'[5] The employment of terms such as *Āryāmehr* and *Shāhanshāh* were thus intended to emphasize the supremacy and Iranianness of the king and to honour his achievements.

The coronation itself sought to link the Shah to an ancient tradition, which, according to one work published for the occasion, 'strengthens the foundations of the relationship between the king and the people'. The author continues, 'By performing the ceremony of the coronation, great kings such a Kurosh, Dāryush, Ardeshir-e Bābakān, Khosrow Anushirvān, Shāh Ismāʿil Safavi, Shāh ʿAbbās, Nāder Shāh Afshār and Rezā Shāh Kabir, have become ever closer to the people.'[6] Several other commemorative works published to coincide with the coronation also made this point, while the ceremony itself marked the Shah's readiness to take his place in this illustrious company.[7] The Imperial Celebrations were the most blatant attempt to inculcate the population with the state ideology, but they were part of a broader process of ideologization that included the coronation. The coronation was initially intended to take place at the same time as the Celebrations, and although the two events differ in scale and monumentality, in terms of narrative, they were remarkably similar.

This chapter examines the Celebrations, investigating the planning and implementation of the official events, and thereby providing essential context to the analyses of Chapters 3–7. It will look at the Celebrations from their original conception in 1958 to the main ceremonies themselves in 1971, examining not only the ideological impact the organizers sought to create but also the practical and logistical problems that either hindered or facilitated their work and ultimately shaped their decisions.

Planning and implementation

The idea to hold a celebration honouring Cyrus the Great was put forward by Shojāʿ al-Din Shafā in 1958. Shafā was one of the leading ideologues in the Pahlavi Court and was well versed in the romantic nationalist discourse of the 19th century. Indeed, in his *Pas az 1400 Sāl* (After 1400 Years), published from exile in the early 2000s, Shafā regularly quotes the works of Ākhundzādeh and Kermāni.⁸ Much earlier, in January 1942, Shafā had started his own political party with a group of friends, namely Kāzem ʿEmādi, Majid Yektāʾi and ʿAli Jalāli, called *Mihan Parastān*, the Patriots.⁹ The party had its own daily newspaper with the same name, of which Jalāli was the licensee.¹⁰ The stated goal of the party was to 'defend Iranian nationalism and its cultural and historical values in the face of the psychological effects of Soviet, British and German propaganda' and to promote a moderate discourse given the re-emergence of 'religious fanatics' after the departure of Reza Shah.¹¹ It later merged with the Unite Party (*Hezb-e Vahdat*) to form the Iran Party (*Hezb-e Irān*).¹²

Shafā was also a widely respected scholar, having translated a number of Italian and French works into Persian, beginning with the poems of Lamartine, of which he produced a translation at the age of 18.¹³ In recognition of his translation of Dante's *Divine Comedy*, he was presented with a gold medal by the city of Florence in 1971, as an expression of appreciation for his 'great contribution of thought and doctrine' to the 'universality of the work and image of Dante'.¹⁴ Shafā held positions in the cabinets of Mohammad Mosaddeq and Hoseyn ʿAlā before his appointment to the Imperial Court in 1957 at the request of ʿAlā, who had recently become Court Minister.¹⁵ According to Shafā, the Celebrations were one of his first proposals to the court.¹⁶

Shafā had considerable influence in the Pahlavi Court and, in addition to proposing the Imperial Celebrations, he served as the Shah's primary speech-writer and ghostwrote a number of the Shah's books, including *Enqelāb-e Sefid* and *Beh Su-ye Tamaddon-e Bozorg* (Toward the Great Civilization). Shafā was a major force behind the drive to establish Iran's reputation internationally as culturally progressive, and he played a key role in the cultural programs initiated by the Imperial Court throughout the 1960s and 1970s. In a document about the Anniversary Celebrations, he wrote of Cyrus: 'Such a vast empire was founded by Cyrus the Great on the principles of liberty and tolerance; freedom of individuals and nations to practice any religion, freedom of expression and freedom of national habits and customs. This is the greatest gift that Iran has given to human society.'¹⁷ When discussing the role of ideology in the Pahlavi period, then, it should be noted that these ideas were driven not necessarily by the Shah himself, although he was clearly the chief mouthpiece, but primarily by members of his regime, such as Shafā.

Ehsan Naraghi has claimed that Shafā was inspired to propose a celebration honouring Cyrus the Great by a scholarly event held in Israel marking Cyrus's liberation of the Jews.¹⁸ Mokhtār Hadidi also makes reference to such an event, which he states took place in 1340 (1961).¹⁹ These analyses are supported by Shafā himself, who, in an interview, gave the following account:

> I remember one time a Jewish representative, non-official of course since they [Israel] did not have official representatives, came to the court to see me because of the cultural works I was involved in about Jewish history, and said that we want this year to be the year of Cyrus. I said, 'why?' He said, 'because in that year Cyrus took Babylon and freed the Jews to return to their homeland. He ended our Babylonian captivity, [and] for this reason his name appears in the Torah as the

Lord Messiah (*masih-e khodāvand*). This is the only time that a non-Jewish person appears in the Torah as Lord Messiah.' Until this time, I did not know of this matter in the Torah ... Cyrus freed everyone, everyone was free to practice their own religion, everyone had freedom of thought in life, and it came to my mind, why do we not do this [commemorate Cyrus] ourselves today?[20]

Commentators have frequently asserted, rightly, that the year 1971 had no real historical significance in the context of a 2,500-year anniversary. The year 1961, however, marked 2,500 years since Cyrus the Great's conquest of Babylon in 539 BCE, which was the original inspiration for the commemoration. This explains this chronological problem.[21]

Shafā's idea to commemorate Cyrus, therefore, had its roots in regional developments, but it was also in part inspired by UNESCO. Since 1954, UNESCO had been encouraging member states to hold commemorations of events or people of significance, and published a list of proposals annually. Listed events included occasions such as the 100th anniversary of the birth of Anton Chekhov (1960), the 1000th anniversary of the founding of the city of Luxembourg (1963) and the 100th anniversary of the Emancipation Proclamation (1963).[22] Shafā had a close affiliation with UNESCO and considered it important for Iran's emerging position in the world and the United Nations community that it nurtured these ties. In this context, in 1965, he spearheaded Iran's UNESCO-supported campaign to end illiteracy worldwide, hosting a congress in Tehran and giving talks around Europe.[23]

UNESCO responded positively to the initial idea for the Celebrations, which proposed to commemorate 'the start of the expansion of a culture whose arts, science and literature have been central forces in the artistic and intellectual development of both Orient and Occident'.[24] At the General Conference of 1960, UNESCO urged the world to join in the commemoration of Cyrus: '[The General Conference] recommends to Member States and interested non-governmental organizations that they associate themselves with the celebration of this event at the cultural level, in whatever way they deem most suitable; [and] invited the Director-General to take appropriate measures to co-operate with the Iranian authorities in this commemoration.'[25] Cultural dissemination through commemoration was within the framework of what UNESCO was attempting to achieve at the time, and the occasion proposed by Shafā would seek to contribute to this effort.[26]

On 22 December 1958, the Iranian press announced that these Imperial Celebrations would take place as early as 1959 and a group was set up to investigate the matter. The group consisted of Court Minister Hoseyn 'Alā, 'Ali Asghar Hekmat, Ahmad Farhād, Sayyed Hasan Taqizādeh, Mohammad Hejāzi, Sādeq Rezāzādeh Shafaq, Sa'id Nafisi, General Amānollāh Jahānbāni and Shojā' al-Din Shafā.[27] The official press release stated that 'the Ministry of Court will take action as soon as a Royal Command is issued'.[28] Shortly after having approved the idea, the Shah thus issued a *farmān* declaring that the event would actually take place in Autumn 1340 (1961).[29]

A more extensive organizing committee was established shortly after, which was called the *Shurā-ye Markazi-ye Jashn-e Shāhanshāhi-ye Irān* (Central Council of the Imperial Celebrations of Iran). It consisted of thirty-three members, with Hoseyn 'Alā as chairman, Javād Bushehri, a prominent government official and uncle of Mehdi Bushehri,[30] as vice chairman and Shafā as secretary general. From the outset, important ministers and other political figures were involved in the development of the project, such as the foreign minister, the interior minister, the minister of culture and art, the head of the police and the governor of Fars. There were eight subcommittees: finance, implementation, publications, culture, arts, ceremonies and receptions, military and sports, and communications.[31] It is clear from the published communications that 'Alā took on more of a ceremonial role and Bushehri was effectively in charge of the committee.

The Celebrations were planned to take place in 1961 but were delayed until 1962 due to the 'difficulty of providing adequate communications and hotel facilities by the earlier date'.[32] However, in a letter to the prime minister in January 1962, 'Alā wrote that the Celebrations would have to be postponed again: 'With the financial difficulties of the state, there is no other way but to accept the suggestion to delay the Imperial Celebrations for one year.'[33] In summer of 1963, in a letter to 'Alā, the minister of roads and head of press and radio, Nosratollāh Mo'iniyān, outlined some of his frustrations with the organization of the Central Council. 'For four years the Council for the Imperial Celebrations has been meeting irregularly', he wrote, 'and because the programme provided for the celebrations was developed without careful study and without taking into consideration the facilities of the state, as you know it encountered many problems.'[34] The original programme by the council may have been appropriate, Mo'iniyān argued, but subsequent proposals added by both members of the council and people outside the council, most of which were approved, meant that the programme risked becoming impossible to implement.

According to Mo'iniyān, the programme was also developed 'without calculating the cost'. The government eventually agreed to give around 25 million tomans to the council, but these funds were not handled effectively.

> Every government organization that somehow contributed to this issue added a new proposal on top of this and divided the amount between them. Because the government that pledged the money collapsed and the government that followed was in financial crisis, the council would not be able to receive the required amount and to fund the work on the Celebrations. Therefore, a lot of time was devoted to imaginary and impractical work that did not yield any results.[35]

Throughout the rest of the 1960s, the Central Council continued to suffer from organizational and financial difficulties. A new date to hold the Celebrations, 1965, was decided upon, however, shortly before then, in September 1964, an announcement was made, which stated: 'Given the importance of the matter, it is necessary that the Celebrations are implemented in a well-ordered fashion, worthy of the ancient and glorious Persian Empire. Therefore, it was ordered by royal decree that the firm date of the Celebrations will be officially shifted to Ābān 1346 (October 1967).'[36] Javād Bushehri then asked Minister of Foreign Affairs 'Abbās Ārām to inform embassies around the world of the postponement.[37] In these early years, there was little planning of the actual ceremonies, and the organizing council instead focused on the publication of books, signing contracts with film studios and arranging for work to be carried out at the ancient sites in Fars.

One thing that had been agreed was that heads of state would be invited. In 1960, 'Alā had informed the Dutch ambassador in Tehran that he thought it unlikely that heads of state would be invited, as the press had reported, due to lack of facilities in Iran for a fitting reception.[38] By 1964, however, the plan had firmly been set to invite all the heads of state of member states of the United Nations and preparations thereafter were accelerated towards providing adequate facilities.[39] From the outset, it had been intended for the Celebrations to coincide with the Shah's coronation and according to British sources, the Imperial Court had made informal inquiries as to whether Queen Elizabeth II would be able to attend the coronation, the answer to which was negative because of 'a convention that reigning Sovereigns are not invited to attend the Coronation of another'.[40] The potential exclusion of reigning sovereigns from this dual celebration contributed, therefore, to the decision to hold the two events separately. In addition to matters of protocol, Iran was infrastructurally unprepared in 1967 to hold two large-scale national celebrations together. Despite the fact they were ultimately held separately, the ideological message of the two events was very similar, legitimizing the Shah's position in the context of Iran's historic monarchical tradition and promising a future for Iran as glorious as its past. The coronation was held first, and set the tone for the Anniversary Celebrations, in the sense that every available means was used to broadcast and emphasize the philosophy behind the event.

The coronation

The Celebrations took some thirteen years to organize, from their conception in 1958 to the event itself in 1971. The coronation, on the other hand, was put together a little more hastily, in a matter of months. On 4 Esfand 1345 (23 February 1967), a *farmān* was issued to order the establishment of an organizing committee, called the *Shurā-ye 'Āli-ye Tājgozāri* (High Council for the Coronation),[41] which consisted of fourteen subcommittees, each charged with executing specific aspects of the ceremony itself and accompanying events held around the country.[42] The head of the Council was General Mortezā Yazdānpanāh, who had held high positions under both Pahlavi shahs, including minister of war, general adjutant, senator and director of the imperial inspectorate, and was said by one historian to be 'the oldest and most venerated general of his time'.[43] The organizing committee appears to have been based on the organizational structure of the Central Council for the Imperial Celebrations, which illustrates how the two events were interlinked, conceptually and tangibly. The document outlining the duties of each subcommittee was authored by Javād Bushehri, for instance, and some $3 million was taken from the budget of the Celebrations to fund the coronation.[44] One of the main works in Persian published for the coronation, *Tājgozāri-ye Shāhanshāhān-e Irān*, was compiled by the Central Council for the Imperial Celebrations.[45]

Although the coronation ceremony itself generally followed the precedent set by the Shah's father in 1926, there were some significant differences. During Reza

Shah's coronation, seventeen pieces of coronation regalia were brought before him by members of the political and military elite, including the armour and sword of Shāh Ismāʿil, the sword of Shāh ʿAbbās, the Nāderi bow and sword, the Kiyān crown of the Qajar shahs and the Pahlavi crown, made specially for the new dynasty.[46] In the second Pahlavi coronation in 1967, only five pieces of regalia were presented to the Shah: the royal cloak (*shenel-e aʿlāhazrat shāhanshāh*), the royal sword (*shamshir-e saltanati*), the royal sceptre (*ʿasā-ye saltanati*), the golden belt (*kamarband-e zarrin*) and finally the Pahlavi crown (*tāj-e Pahlavi*).[47] While Reza Shah had to follow, to a certain degree, precedent set by the preceding Qajar dynasty, in order to stress continuity, his son did not. He employed fewer Qajar symbols, and although the ceremony took place in the Golestān Palace, there was some discussion about future Pahlavi coronation ceremonies taking place at Persepolis.[48]

Notwithstanding the apparent simplicity of the ceremony, it reveals a lot about Pahlavi ideology. Zhand Shakibi has written that one of the purposes of Pahlavism was to serve as 'a substitute for religion and, more importantly, clericalism, as a mechanism for inculcating a common political culture and establishing new sources of legitimacy'.[49] This aspect of Pahlavism can clearly be seen in the coronation ceremony itself, which featured very few religious elements, aside from the Shah kissing a Quran and a short sermon delivered by the Friday Imam of Tehran.[50] This particular Quran was even referred to in letters as the *Qurān-e Āryāmehr*.[51] The Shah's self-crowning, meanwhile, served to show that the Shah did not depend on religious institutions for legitimacy, emphasizing the separation of church and state.

Throughout the coronation, the Shah presented himself as both the guardian of an ancient and glorious monarchical tradition, and its most fervent reformer. The Shah's regime, for instance, placed great emphasis on the fact that for the first time in its long history, Iran was crowning a Queen.[52] The crowning of Queen Farah was presented not only as recognition of the emancipation of women in Iran but also as a reflection of the wisdom of the Shah for bestowing such an honour on his wife. According to one official Iranian publication, for instance, on the 1963 reforms to electoral law, 'It was the Shah and not the feminists who struck the next blow against inequality'.[53] In other words, if Iran was to modernize, it had to rely on the throne, not political movements against social inequality. The enfranchisement of women was said to be 'not only a humanitarian gesture but a brilliant political move. With the wind taken out of their sails of protest, women were forced into positive activity'.[54] This fed into the narrative of the Shah as a revolutionary monarch, who would preserve ancient tradition, while modernizing and granting rights.

After the Shah had crowned himself, speeches were given, first by Prime Minister Amir ʿAbbās Hoveydā, president of the Senate Jaʿfar Sharif-Emāmi, Speaker of the Majles ʿAbdollāh Riāzi, and finally Professor Lotfʿali Suratgar of Tehran University, who offered thanks from the scholars and cultural personalities of the country and delivered a specially composed ode to the Shah.[55] It is interesting that these people were not court ministers or generals in the army, but figures one would associate with a modern democracy – the message was that the Shah was a 20th-century king, who derived legitimacy from both the traditional monarchical structure and the modern political structure.

As with the 2500th Anniversary Celebrations, the programme for the coronation also included cultural events, parades and sporting displays. For example, on the evening of the coronation ceremony itself, 26 October, the Rudaki Hall concert venue was inaugurated by the Shah and his newly crowned queen, and over the following days several foreign and local groups performed there, including the Grand Ballet Classique de France, the Los Angeles Philharmonic Orchestra, the Virtuosi di Roma, the Beethovenhalle Orchestra of Bonn and the Iranian National Ballet Company.[56] The next day a military parade took place, and two days after the coronation a grand sports event was held at the Amjadieh Stadium.[57] Other organizations arranged their own programmes; the Women's Organisation of Iran, for instance, organized a street carnival, published a picture album showing the status of women in society over the past fifty years, released a commemorative gold medal, and arranged a picture exhibition on women in the period between the coronations of the two Pahlavi monarchs.[58] Showing that they also took their religious responsibilities seriously, as part of the coronation programme, the imperial couple travelled to Mashhad for the Mab'ath.[59]

On 2 November 1967, in a fitting conclusion to the coronation programme, a memorial plaque produced with 5 kilograms of 18-carat gold by the Organization for Military Industries was placed in the foundations of the Shahyād Āryāmehr Tower (*Borj-e Shahyād-e Āryāmehr*).[60] Construction on the site began a few months later and it was inaugurated on 16 October 1971 during the Imperial Celebrations. During the coronation, efforts were made to stress the inclusive nature of the event. In the gardens of Golestān Palace itself, for instance, seating platforms were erected with space for 5,000 people, and the imperial couple's carriage rode through streets that were lined with cheering crowds.[61] Similar attempts were made to stimulate public participation in the Imperial Celebrations too, but due to security concerns and logistical limitations, these plans would prove more difficult to implement.

Organizing the Celebrations

One year after the coronation, in late 1968, Iran announced that the Celebrations would now take place in Autumn 1971.[62] However, little substantial preparation had taken place since the establishment of the Central Council ten years earlier. A number of books had been published, a design for a memorial building, the *Borj-e Shahyād*, had been chosen, and some of the proposed infrastructure projects, particularly roads and railway lines, had been carried out, but that was all. By 1969, still little had been organized, and in an attempt to rejuvenate the project, the Shah issued a *farmān* to promote twenty-six people to the Central Council, including Minister of Foreign Affairs Ardeshir Zāhedi, Minister of Finance Jamshid Āmuzegār, Minister of Culture Mehrdād Pahlbod and Director of the Plan Organisation Mehdi Sami'i.[63]

In September 1970, Javād Bushehri left his role as head of the Central Council to receive treatment for cancer, whereupon Mehdi Bushehri was promoted in his place. Mehdi Bushehri was, however, busy leading the *Maison de l'Iran* in Paris, so 'Abdolrezā Ansāri, who worked for the Pahlavi Foundation, was invited by Princess Ashraf to act as the deputy head of the Council (*qā'em maqām-e ra'is*).⁶⁴ Ansāri noted at this time that the purpose of the Celebrations was to initiate 'the reawakening of the history, civilization, and culture of Iran and creating awareness among the peoples of the world'.⁶⁵ In order to achieve this aim, a number of projects had already been discussed, including an international congress of scholars to be held in Shiraz; the reprinting of significant works on Iran; the production of books on Iranian history and culture by scholars; the construction of a monument and museum reflecting 2,500 years of Iranian civilization; and the hosting of exhibitions, conferences and festivals in Iran and around the world.⁶⁶ Some of these projects were, as noted, already underway, however, the organizing committee suffered from poor central leadership and financial organization.

Court Minister Asadollāh 'Alam blamed the lack of progress during the previous decade on Javād Bushehri, whom he apparently disliked.⁶⁷ In a diary entry at the time of Bushehri's death in 1973, he wrote, 'Senator Javād Bushehri has died. He was a miserable, strange and greedy man. Ten years as head of the committee for the Celebrations and he had done nothing, until finally the Shah told me to do it and it was done.'⁶⁸ It is perhaps harsh to attribute the failure of the organizing council at this stage solely to Bushehri; however, it was clear at the time that many doubted it would be possible to implement the event on a large scale. Without the direct involvement of the Imperial Court, Ansāri told 'Alam, the Celebrations might never be ready in time.⁶⁹

After consulting with the Shah, 'Alam announced that from October 1970, the Central Council for the Celebrations would act as a consultative body, and a new High Executive Committee (*Hey'at-e 'Āli-ye Ejrāi-ye Jashnhā-ye Shāhanshāhi*) would be established which would work full-time on the Celebrations. As Shafā outlined in a letter to the Dutch ambassador:

> This High Executive Committee has assigned different aspects of the work within this country and abroad to various sub-committees each of which has a separate managing director and is composed of the representatives of various government organizations in accordance with their fields of specialities.
>
> The channel of operation is such that each managing director of a sub-committee reports to the director of that High Executive Committee, who in turn, if necessary, discusses these reports in the committee meeting and informs each sub-committee of decisions reached.⁷⁰

The High Executive Committee consisted of the following eight members: Asadollāh 'Alam, minister of the Imperial Court; Mehdi Bushehri, head of the Council of the 2500th Anniversary Celebrations; Mehrdād Pahlbod, minister of culture and art; 'Abdolrezā Ansāri, deputy head of the High Council of the Celebrations; Hormoz Qarib, chief of protocol of the Imperial Court; Shojā' al-Din Shafā, deputy minister of the Imperial Court; Cyrus Farzāneh, head of the Tourist Organization; and Amir Mottaqi, director general of the Ministry of the Imperial Court.

Subcommittees were led by the following: cultural and art committee, Mehrdād Pahlbod; international committee, Shojā' al-Din Shafā; press and information committee, Javād Mansur; communication committee, Mansur Ruhāni; health committee, Manuchehr Shāhqoli; security committee, Ne'matollāh Nasiri; protocol committee, in charge especially of the entertainment of the guests at Persepolis, Hormoz Qarib; special committee for accommodation of heads of state in Persepolis, 'Abolfath Ātābāy; person in charge of Shiraz and Persepolis affairs, General 'Ali Akbar Zarghām; and person in charge of Tehran affairs, Manuchehr Nikpey.[71] The subcommittee for international affairs, headed by Shafā, was responsible for coordinating the international events held around the world, and included representatives from the Ministry of Foreign Affairs, the Ministry of Culture and Art, the Ministry of Information, the Tourist Organisation and the Central Council for the Celebrations.[72] Shafā had complained to 'Alam in May 1970 that during a trip to Europe, he noticed a lack of activity among the international committees that had been set up in countries around the world, which he attributed to the absence of a central organization in Iran. The establishment of this particular subcommittee, therefore, was a response to this problem.[73]

Ansāri records that the Executive Committee met once a week at the Ministry of Court under the chairmanship of 'Alam and once a fortnight at Niyāvarān Palace under Empress Farah's supervision.[74] The decision to place the Celebrations under direct supervision of the Imperial Court allowed the Executive Committee to implement the plans that were already in place and meant that its members would now be held accountable for their actions, which had not previously been the case. There were to be no excuses for failure and the importance of the occasion was made abundantly clear to those involved. The governor of Fars, for example, had been left to supervise progress of preparations in and around Shiraz, which included the construction of the Darius Hotel at Persepolis and the Cyrus Hotel in Shiraz. He had previously assured the Celebrations' organizers that everything was on schedule. However, when the committee members visited the province less than a year before the Celebrations were due to take place, they found the construction of the Cyrus Hotel still in progress and that of the Darius Hotel barely under way. The committee members were disappointed, particularly 'Alam, who berated the gathered officials. 'I'm telling you, once and for all', he warned,

> that the staging of these celebrations is a national priority, and what is at stake is Iran's honor in the eyes of the world. If there is to be the slightest error in the work that has been assigned to you and if the ceremonies are not conducted to the highest expected standards, I will personally take my pistol and shoot every one of you before taking my own life! From today you know what has to be done and be warned that no excuses will be tolerated.[75]

'Alam's dramatic outburst illustrates the frustration of the committee and its understanding that there was a huge amount of work to be done in a short space of time.

The hotels in Fars appear to have eventually been completed with little time to spare. On 14 September 1971, less than a month before the Celebrations were due to take place, the Dutch ambassador observed that the Darius Hotel at Persepolis was still not finished,[76] however, ten days later he reported that it was finally completed, adding perhaps sarcastically that 'the cold water tap in one of the rooms was even running'.[77] The hotel fiasco is perhaps a reflection of the entire project, planned for over a decade yet hastily put together in a little under two years. However, by October 1971, all was completed. An advertisement for the hotels from 1971 proudly reads: 'Introducing the hotels that took 2500 years to build ... Each with a style even Cyrus the Great would have loved.'[78] Despite the public facade of confidence, the organizers clearly had their concerns about the preparations, and as late as March 1970 there were informal soundings from the Imperial Court that the Celebrations would have to be postponed again. A letter from the Dutch embassy to the Ministry of Foreign Affairs read, 'Protocol told me confidentially, repeat, confidentially, that it is possible that a decision will be made very soon to further postpone the celebrations "because Iran with the exception of Tehran is not ready" for these festivities.'[79]

Until 1970, the emblem of the Anniversary Celebrations had featured a circle with a border marked with twenty-five black triangles, symbolizing twenty-five centuries, and an eagle at the centre.[80] Above the circle was the Pahlavi crown. However, some months prior to the Celebrations, the Iranian ambassador in Cairo sent a letter to the Executive Committee to raise concerns that the symbol might be misinterpreted as ancient Egyptian, rather than Persian.[81] To avoid such misunderstandings, the Executive Committee ordered the Ministry of Culture and Art to devise a new emblem, which should, it ordered, be unequivocally Persian. The chosen design was put forward by Shafā and featured a circle of twenty-five flowers, inspired by those in the reliefs of Persepolis' monuments, with the royal coat of arms at the top.[82] In the middle was the Cyrus Cylinder against a blue backdrop.

From October 1970 onwards, we see the Celebrations taking their form and considerable progress being made in their organization. The extensive programme developed by the Executive Committee at this time included a ceremony honouring Cyrus the Great at Pasargadae, a congress of scholars in Shiraz, a military parade, a light show at Persepolis, seminars in Iran and around the world, and the publication of books, including a reproduction of the *Shāhnāmeh-ye Bāysonghori* manuscript.[83] Committee members worked on the details of the programme over the following year and, in this manner, as 'Abdolrezā Ansāri writes, 'the celebration of the 2,500th anniversary of the founding of the Persian Empire, which had until now been semidormant, came to life'.[84]

The tent city

Two of the main tasks facing the Executive Committee were the issues of where to accommodate VIP guests and dining arrangements. In his memoir, Ansāri records that the decision to build tents to accommodate guests was taken by the Executive Committee. It was apparently by chance that 'Alam met with the director of the Swiss interior design firm of Jansen while on a trip to Europe in 1970.[85] 'Alam then negotiated a price for a city of tents, which was proposed to the rest of the Executive Committee.[86] It is likely, however, that the decision to accommodate guests in tents was instead nearly as old as the decision to hold the event itself. In 1960, Arthur

Upham Pope, the highly respected and influential American academic and arts dealer, made some suggestions to the Iranian organizers as to how the Celebrations should be carried out. They should be organized on a large scale, he asserted, in order to stress that 'it is not merely an episode in Persian history, but a very great event in the history of civilization'.[87] To achieve this, Pope suggested the construction of a great library in Iran to rival the Library of Congress,[88] a military parade at Persepolis, a light display at the ruins which should 'be done on a very large scale with tremendous effect', and tented accommodation which should 'err a bit on the luxurious side for the sake of foreign visitors'.[89] Pope may have made a similar suggestion earlier, too, for in September 1959, the British embassy reported that the 'idea at present is not to build large numbers of hotels in Shiraz, which would merely become white elephants, but to lodge distinguished guests in tents on the plain round the tomb of Cyrus'.[90]

The tent city complex provided accommodation in private apartments for heads of state or their representatives, and also included a large dining hall. The apartments each consisted of a sitting room, two bedrooms, two bathrooms and a service room, and were spaced out along five lanes branching out from a central fountain, with each lane named after a different continent.[91] Each tent was designed in a unique style, spread with Persian carpets and intended to be 'elegantly but not extravagantly decorated'.[92] In the sitting room, each head of state found their own portrait against the backdrop of Persepolis on a silk carpet, which they were able to take away as a souvenir.[93] Suggestions that bathrooms were built using marble were strongly refuted by a spokesperson for Jansen.[94] Indeed, some reporters who were allowed inside the tents were keen to point out that 'the bathrooms are beautifully done, but there are no marble tubs'.[95] Much of what was written about the opulence and extravagance of the tent city appears to have been based on hearsay. The Dutch ambassador noted this in a report: 'The same goes for the supposed excessive (and not actually existent) luxury of the tent city, which unfortunately was described by someone as being like the camp set up for the Battle of the Golden Spurs, after which everyone started claiming it was made of gold brocade'.[96] The decadence of the site was certainly overstated by some sections of the foreign media, but it is clear that the organizers went to great lengths to provide a comfortable atmosphere which gave the impression of luxury.

Apartments were equipped with the finest French toiletries, including Guerlain shaving preparations for men and Joy eau de cologne for women, while the linen and towels were supplied by Porthault of Paris.[97] By providing such small luxuries, the organizers attempted to assuage the concerns of foreign ambassadors about the facilities that would be available to their heads of state. For example, at a meeting of foreign diplomats, the Spanish ambassador raised the issue of the need for hairdressing facilities.[98] To answer these concerns, the Iranian chief of protocol organized for fully equipped salons to be set up, and for renowned hairdressers flown in to be at the service of guests. The Iranians even circulated a questionnaire to guests beforehand, in which they were asked, among other things, to indicate dietary requirements, preferred meals for breakfast, and 'preferred type and brand of beverages, cigars and cigarettes'.[99] It was particularly important, given that the Celebrations were partly inspired by the desire to showcase Iran's progress, that guests were treated in the manner to which they were accustomed.

The Celebrations presented Iran as a land of stability and prosperity. It had, according to the official narrative, been dragged from destitution into modernity by the two Pahlavi monarchs and was a truly emerging power. To enforce this presentation, the event organizers were careful to hide signs of poverty. For example, ʿAbdolrezā Ansāri wrote to the mayor of Tehran to ask him to remove a homeless camp from the view of a major highway on which foreign guests would be travelling.[100] In Fars province, walls were built to hide slums, villages were whitewashed to look, according to one diplomat, 'quaint instead of grubby'[101] and plans were made to construct 200 houses to accommodate the homeless in Shiraz.[102] The Celebrations were a declaration of Iran's emergence as a global power and it was important that the foreign guests saw only signs of progress.

This also explains why the Executive Committee decided to order catering from France rather than use Iranian chefs. ʿAbdolrezā Ansāri had made enquiries with Iranian caterers as to whether they would be able to provide dinner for such an occasion. He was told by the head of the catering department of the Imperial Court, ʿAbolfath Ātābāy, who was experienced in entertaining dignitaries, that catering for such numbers at Persepolis was far beyond Iran's capabilities. Ansāri received further negative assessments from Hoseyn Maqsudi, head of a group responsible for running a number of luxury hotels, and Taqi Emāmi, head of the National Tourist Board, although the former agreed to cater for the journalists and academics staying in Shiraz.[103] The Iranian restaurant sector simply lacked the experience and personnel for such a huge event and at relatively short notice it would have been impossible to develop these industries to the desired standard. To give an idea of the scale of the operation, in addition to the 150 heads of state and other special guests dining in the main banqueting hall, the Iranians also had to arrange a separate full dinner service for their entourage in a separate dining hall, with places set up for 600 people.[104]

The decision not to serve Iranian food at the royal banquet was difficult for some to accept, since the Celebrations were, above all, a commemoration of Iranian heritage and culture. Even important Iranian figures voiced their criticism. Foreign Minister Ardeshir Zāhedi, who served on the Central Council, later asked why, at the foot of one of the world's most inspiring ancient cities, guests could not be served Iranian dishes such as *kabab kubideh* or *ab-gusht*?[105] Empress Farah later recalled that she recognized at the time that this might be a problem. 'We've waited twenty-five hundred years', she said, 'we can wait a few more.' However, it was inconceivable at this point that the Celebrations would be delayed any further, so 'practically speaking', she concluded, 'it was too late'. Empress Farah also supposed that the press would come to criticize the event for this: 'Knowing what journalists are like, I suspected that they would latch on to these foreign contracts as a pretext to criticize.'[106] It was eagerness to impress the guests gathered from around the world that led to the controversial decision, as the Shah argued after the event, 'What am I supposed to do, serve them bread and radishes?'[107] Moreover, the choice of Maxim's, one of the most famously luxurious restaurants in the world, as caterer, further fed the foreign press' appetite for gossip. One British tabloid journalist excitedly wrote, 'There'll be 18 kinds of cheeses. The bill for the *saucisson* alone is reckoned to be £500. And somebody has ordered 50 kippers. Who's the kipper maniac on the list?'[108]

One of the main criticisms of the Celebrations is that normal Iranians were left out of the main festivities. There were logistical and security reasons for this, which will be discussed in Chapter 6, but aside from the main festivities, there was an elaborate programme of activities around the country, and provincial committees were established to direct regional events. Activities organized by these provincial committees typically included the erection of statues and commemorative plaques,[109] exhibitions, parades, parties and other cultural events.[110] Additionally, negotiations were held with the minority Zoroastrian, Jewish, Armenian and Assyrian communities about their participation in the festivities.[111] In response to this call for support, the Jewish community in Hamadan restored and expanded the site of Esther's tomb in the city.[112] Inside and outside the tomb underwent thorough repairs and a visitor centre was constructed. Other contributions from the Jewish Council for the Celebrations included the illumination and decoration of synagogues around the country, with special prayers held there during the principal ceremonies; a special wreath laid at the tomb of Reza Shah; music and dance performances; the expansion and development of the Cyrus the Great hospital in Tehran; the construction of a school for girls, also called Cyrus the Great; and the expansion and development of the Jewish Industrial College.[113] Regional committees also prepared books for publication. The committee of Hamedan published a work titled *Naqsh-e Hamedān dar Tārikh-e Dohezār o Pānsad Sāleh-ye Shāhanshāhi-ye Irān* (The Role of Hamedan in the 2,500-year History of Imperial Iran), the committee of Kerman published *Yādi az Gozashteh-ye Irān* (Remembering Iran's Past) and the Tehran committee published a work on cooperatives titled *Bahsi Darbāreh-ye Sherkathā-ye Ta'āvuni*.[114]

The organizers also sought to reach out to the general public through the media of cinema and television. Rezā Qotbi, head of National Iranian Radio and Television, arranged the live screening of the festivities around Iran and the world and Mehrdād Pahlbod, minister of culture and art, commissioned the production of *Forugh-e Jāvidān* (Eternal Flame), the official film of the Celebrations. It was directed by Farrokh Golestan, with music written and conducted by the Iranian composer Loris Tjeknavorian, and the English version of the film, titled *Flames of Persia*, was narrated by Orson Welles. The film, which premiered in October 1972 to coincide with the anniversary of the Imperial Celebrations, was shown five times a day for five days in thirty-one cinema houses across Tehran and forty around the country, and was subsequently distributed by Iranian embassies in foreign countries.[115] Another film released internationally around this time was *Tales from a Book of Kings* (1974), which was produced by Time-Life Inc. in the United States, and was based on poems of the *Shāhnāmeh*. The film ends with a caption thanking the Iranian ambassador in Washington and was declared to be 'in commemoration of the 2500th Anniversary of the Founding of the Persian Empire by Cyrus the Great and the First Declaration of Human Rights'.[116]

There were also talks with foreign film studios about producing a film about Cyrus the Great.[117] This idea was enthusiastically promoted by Arthur Upham Pope, who wrote in a letter in 1960, 'I suppose the possibility of a general moving picture of the birth and early history of the Achaemenid Empire has been discussed. There are immense possibilities and an enterprising company could do something almost as impressive as *Ben Hur* for one-quarter of the price, and it would be a marked contribution to the culture of our time.' In the letter, Pope goes on to make some suggestions as to how the film could be structured: 'The interest for a while should concentrate on the boyhood and education of young Cyrus, his feats of horsemanship, his being taught to use the bow and speak the truth. One might devise some George Washington-and-the-cherry-tree episode that would show Cyrus resolutely standing up for the truth contrary to inclination or advantage.'[118] The film was ultimately never produced, though there were some discussions with French film studios, but the fact that it was discussed so enthusiastically by some illustrates the wide variety of media and cultural tools that were considered to promote the key tenets of the Celebrations and the Pahlavi state ideology domestically and internationally.

In the months prior to the Celebrations, daily and weekly newspapers were published, with the mission of acquainting readers with the aims of the Celebrations, the glories of Iranian history and the White Revolution. These periodicals also included practical information, including details of events in Iran and around the world and membership lists of international committees.[119]

In spite of the slow start in preparing the Celebrations, by October 1971, all the plans and facilities were in place. On 19 September, the Shah inspected Cyrus's tomb at Pasargadae, the Darius Hotel and Persepolis, to ensure that they were ready.[120] Journalists from around the world had been issued their press passes, invitations had been sent out to the world's eminent Iranologists, and each foreign mission in Iran was prepared to receive its country's representative. After thirteen years of erratic preparations, as one pro-regime daily newspaper enthusiastically wrote, 'Irān āmādeh-ye bargozāri-ye bozorgtarin jashn-e tārikh-e khod shod' – 'Iran is ready to hold the biggest celebration in its history.'[121]

The Glorification of Cyrus the Great

The Celebrations were inaugurated with a ceremony officially titled the Glorification of Cyrus at Pasargadae on Tuesday 12 October, which, in the words of one journalist, 'set the tone of deadly seriousness which the Shah and his Ministers want to maintain'.[122] The British Institute of Persian Studies had led the first major excavations at Pasargadae in October 1961 and in the first major publication of the excavation's findings, the institute's director, David Stronach, declared his hope that the excavation would contribute to the planned Celebrations, and stressed that as a major site for the occasion it was important that work there should be carried out.[123] In preparation for the occasion, much to Stronach's dismay, column drums surrounding Cyrus's tomb, marking the presence of a congregational mosque constructed in the 13th century, were removed by the organizers in order to smarten up the area.[124] The removal of Islamic-era features also reflects the regime's attempts to stress the glory of Ancient Iran to the detriment of the Islamic era.[125] Cyrus the Great was an Iranian hero, who represented a time when Iran was a major global power; he was not to be associated with Islam.

Guests invited to the ceremony included Iranian ministers, officials, representatives of religious bodies, Iranologists, journalists, Iranian academics, representatives of the

Revolutionary Corps, and representatives of the Imperial Army.[126] The ceremony was brief and simple, lasting just 45 minutes, but was charged with emotion and served to express the significance of the ancient king Cyrus. The official programme records the following lines with which the Shah opened the event:

> Twenty five centuries ago, in a world where ruling was based on threats, terror and fear, and where the conquerors [sic] beliefs were imposed on the conquered, the Iranian Empire was founded by Cyrus the Great on the highest human principles of mutual understanding among nations and religious freedom. The moral and spiritual life of my people has been based on these principles.[127]

There was little doubt that the event was a dedication to a significant ruler, the father of the Iranian nation and a modernizer whose empire was built on moral principles. The memory of this great king was employed to support the Shah's modernist policies and by putting the Pahlavi monarchy in the context of the first king of the Persian Empire, the Shah attempted to legitimize his position and that of his dynasty.

The Glorification of Cyrus ceremony began with the arrival of the Shah, Shahbanou and Crown Prince by helicopter at 11.00 am, after all the guests had arrived and taken their seats. The Shah entered a royal tent at 11.30 am, emerging 10 minutes later to the sound of the national anthem and the firing of a 101-gun salute. The imperial family then approached the 'imperial arena', just short of Cyrus's tomb. The Shah stepped forward and placed a wreath at the foot of the tomb, returning after a minute's silence. At 11.36 am, he gave his grandiloquent speech to the tomb. In a voice shaking with emotion, the Shah read a tribute which included the following lines:

> Cyrus! Great king, king of kings, Achaemenian king, king of the land of Iran, on my behalf as king of Iran, and from my nation, I offer you greetings. In this glorious moment of Iranian history, me and all Iranians, descendants of this ancient kingdom that was founded by you 2,500 years ago, praise you before your tomb, and vow to preserve your legacy ... Cyrus, hero of Iran and the world, rest in peace, for we are awake and will always be awake.[128]

Asadollāh 'Alam recalled that this was the most emotional that he had ever seen the Shah and that he was 'so emotional that he had to stop for a second' to gather himself.[129] Some of those in attendance were equally moved. The statesman and scholar 'Isā Sadiq, for instance, wrote in his memoir that during the speech, 'my heart started to beat hard and tears of passion flowed from my eyes'.[130] The event was screened around the world and the Shah was fully aware that he was not merely speaking to a domestic audience but also a global one. Many who were there spoke about the presence of a whirlwind of desert sand that appeared during the speech and which added a certain eeriness to the occasion.[131] One article even describes the wind as keeping a 'respectful distance',[132] although the guards who were charged with keeping the audience quiet during the speech were frustrated by the noise caused by the flags blowing in the wind.[133]

The Shah was later mocked for the speech, the 'rest in peace', or 'sleep calm' line receiving particular attention. In one joke, a man is so excited at reading about the speech in a newspaper that he rushes home early to tell his wife, whereupon he finds her in bed with their neighbour, Cyrus. Overcome with emotion, the man raises his hand and says, 'sleep easily Cyrus, for we are awake.'[134] Others, taking advantage of the opportunity to attack the Shah's policies, simply mocked the Shah: 'Sleep calm, we're ruining the country. Sleep calm, we're spending the oil money. Sleep calm, we're pissing away all the wealth.'[135] At the time, however, the Shah was evidently pleased with the speech. It had been written by Shojaʿ al-Din Shafā, as were all of the speeches for the Celebrations, and was accepted by the Shah with only minor alterations.[136] Unlike other speeches, which the Shah usually practised just once beforehand, the Shah, aware of the speech's 'publicity-value', spent some time practising the text, 'discovering the intonations he liked'.[137] Responding to praise for the speech from an interviewer later, the Shah said, 'Thank you for the tribute, which I do not deserve. However, I need hardly assure you that we are awake and we shall for ever stay awake to guard Iran's precious heritage.'[138] Word of the public ridicule of the speech had perhaps not reached the imperial ears.

The speech encapsulated the ethos of the Celebrations, which presented Cyrus as a king at the cradle of the ideals of European intellectual history. The Shah's promise to 'preserve forever the traditions of humanism and goodwill, with which you founded the Persian Empire' illustrates this fact. Meanwhile, the Shah was presented as Cyrus's spiritual successor. This idea was understood by those in attendance. Roger Savory, who was one of the scholars present, wrote, for example: 'We are celebrating this anniversary because the present Shahanshah of Iran sees himself as being, in a very real sense, the heir of Cyrus the Great and the inheritor of his empire. No one, I think, who was present at the dignified and moving ceremony at the tomb of Cyrus, could doubt this for one moment.'[139] This presentation was made more credible by the attendance of foreign academics, who had dedicated their lives to the study of Iran. In evidence of the high esteem in which they were held, Elwell-Sutton commented that scholars were accorded a prominent position in the order of precedence, with only religious representatives and members of the cabinet enjoying a higher standing.[140]

The Second International Congress of Iranology, organized as an important part of the Celebrations, took place at the Pahlavi University of Shiraz from 13 until 15 October, and will be discussed at length in Chapter 5. The Iranian press claimed that the congress was the biggest congress of Iranian studies ever held and the official programme records that 275 scholars from 38 countries participated, including 24 from the USSR, 22 from the United States, 18 from Germany, 17 from India, 15 from Britain, and 14 from France.[141] Of the twenty-five papers presented, five were delivered by Iranian scholars and twenty by foreign scholars.[142] The scholars had a similar programme to the heads of state, although they were not permitted to enter the tent city. They attended the *son et lumière* on a different day, took part in a number of receptions and were invited to the parade at Persepolis, as well as the events in Tehran.

Heads of state or their representatives began to arrive from 12 October, landing in Shiraz from where they were transferred by helicopter or car to Persepolis. As they arrived at Persepolis, the Shah, who drove around the site in his open Rolls-Royce, was there to greet them.[143] In all, sixty-two heads of state or their representatives attended, fifty of whom were accommodated at the tent city. Among the fifty were Prince Philip and Princess Anne representing Queen Elizabeth II of the United Kingdom; King Hussein of Jordan; Prince Bernhard representing Queen Juliana of the Netherlands; President V. V. Giri of India; President Nikolai Podgorny of the Soviet Union; Cardinal Maximilian von Fürstenberg representing the Vatican; vice president of the United States Spiro Agnew; and Emperor Haile Selassie of Ethiopia, who held a prominent position during the Celebrations as the longest-serving monarch and one of the Shah's oldest friends.[144] For guests who arrived on 12 October, an informal lunch and dinner were prepared, and for the following two days, guests could take part in a number of activities. A questionnaire provided to guests outlined the possibilities:

> Please indicate which of the following activities are preferred: Visit to Naghshe Rostam, Pasargadae (the Palace and tomb of Cyrus the Great), Persepolis (the Palace of Darius), the Camp of the World Welfare Legion, The Aryamehr pilot farm, the Darius Dam, games such as mini-golf etc. or is it preferred to have meetings with the other Heads of States.[145]

Many trips to local sites took place. The British representatives, Prince Philip and Princess Anne, for example, were taken on a tour of Pasargadae by archaeologist David Stronach of the British Institute of Persian Studies, followed by a trip to the Royal Stables.[146]

A SAVAK report makes reference to Baha'i students of Pahlavi University, who were chosen to act as tour guides for foreign visitors while they were in Fars.[147] The Shah had been condemned by the international community in the mid-1950s for sanctioning an attack on Baha'i centres in Tehran and elsewhere in the country, which 'Alam claimed the Shah had been blackmailed into ordering by dissenting clerics.[148] The participation of Baha'i students, therefore, would enforce the perception that the Shah's Iran was a progressive and inclusive society, in which religious minorities enjoyed the same freedoms as the rest. After the Celebrations ended, there were opportunities for foreign dignitaries to travel further afield. Cardinal von Fürstenberg, for example, travelled to Rezāiyeh, in West Azerbaijan, Prince Moulay Abdallah of Morocco travelled to Mashhad, and governor general of Canada Roland Michener visited Rasht, Bābolsar, Bābol, Bandar Pahlavi and Rāmsar.[149]

The gala dinner

The evening of 14 October culminated in the royal banquet, which took place in the dining hall at the tent city. Guests at the banquet included Iranian government ministers and other dignitaries, foreign guests and ambassadors, and members of the Pahlavi family. The Shah opened the occasion with a speech, in which he said:

> I take the present assembly of the great personages of the world at Persepolis, the historic birthplace of the Persian Empire as a good omen, because I feel that in our gathering this evening, past history is linked with the realities of today. Naturally such a bond of past and present, achieved by understanding and friendship, is to

be taken as a good omen ... Distinguished friends, if we have been eager to invite you to the greatest festival in our history, it is because we thought that the occasion was one which merited the trouble you have taken to come here, for this festival is, above all, in honour of Iranian cultural heritage which belongs to humanity as a whole. In fact, your host this evening is 'History' itself rather than ourselves.[150]

The Shah was eager to stress that the Celebrations were first and foremost a commemoration of Iranian cultural heritage, a heritage which belonged to all mankind. The Shah was also keen to present himself as a serious political leader.

We all know that man is still grappling with many problems. We are aware that a large part of the population of the world still suffers from poverty, ignorance, hunger and all kinds of discrimination. Every day, in some corner of the world, we hear the whistling of bullets and come across various manifestations of violence and hatred. On the other hand, we also know that if man has thus far failed to eliminate disorder and prejudice, there is no cause to despair, for man's eternal and changeless mission is constant progress towards perfection. In order to follow the true path in fulfilling this mission, each one of us must try as hard as possible, as much as circumstances allow, to turn the world into one of love, peace and cooperation for mankind, a world in which every person may enjoy to the full the amenities of science and civilization.[151]

Against the backdrop of Persepolis, the ceremonial capital of an empire which the Shah's regime had presented as based on values of tolerance and human rights, the message presented the Shah as a progressive, willing to take the lead in solving the problems of the world. The speech was answered by Emperor Haile Selassie I of Ethiopia, who said, 'These celebrations show how to use history positively – not for false glorification or idle self-congratulations, but for new strength and revitalisation.'[152] Not all those who watched the recording of the speech on their television sets, or read the reports in newspapers, agreed with this assessment, or were so generous in their praise.

The subsequent criticism of the banquet was understandable. It was extremely expensive, with most of the food, equipment and staff flown in from Europe.[153] According to reports, the most significant Iranian contribution to the banquet was 300 pounds (136 kg) of caviar, but such figures are difficult to verify.[154] Guests were served a meal which included dishes such as quail eggs with Iranian caviar, mousse of crayfish tails, champagne sorbet and imperial peacock. Drinks included sixty-year-old champagne, the finest French wines and vintage cognac.[155] The dinner was reported by one journalist to be 'an expression of the most absolute luxury ... and the most complete refinement. It was the greatest of all the parties of the twentieth century and it is very possible that a similar one is never organised again'.[156] Despite some clearly exaggerated reports on the dinner, one must conclude that it was particularly lavish. Additionally, as critics were keen to stress, this celebration of Iran was distinctly lacking in Iranian flavour.

The lack of Iranian cuisine at what was one of the principal events of the Celebrations was clearly a public relations failure. It should be noted, however, that Iranian food was served on the second night, which was a more informal affair. At this event, guests were offered a buffet with a selection of Iranian dishes alongside international dishes, with Iranian hostesses on hand to explain what the dishes were. Iranian chefs were also chosen to assist the foreign chefs in preparing the Iranian food.[157] If this was done on the second night, could it not have also been done for the gala dinner? This was a missed opportunity and perhaps reflects a loss of nerve on behalf of the organizers, unsure as to what the foreigners' reactions to Iranian cuisine would be.

Following the royal banquet, the guests moved out to the ruins of Persepolis where they watched a *son et lumière* display and fireworks. Greek avant-garde composer Iannis Xenakis's latest work was premiered. The ruins were brought to life as actors dressed in traditional Achaemenid dress walked solemnly around them, while projected luminous patterns evoked the Zoroastrian symbolism of Ancient Persia and the voices of actors playing Achaemenid kings echoed around the once-great ceremonial capital.[158] The firm charged with installing the lights at Persepolis was reputable, and had already been employed on similar projects at sites such as the Palace of Versailles.[159] The event organizers were eager to make sure that the light show would be an impressive display, not out of place at any of the world's great historical sites.[160] Talinn Grigor has pointed out that this magnificent high-tech spectacle at the ancient ruins further enforced the impression that the Shah could transcend Orientalist traditions and modernize, while at the same time remaining true to Iran's cultural heritage.[161]

The parade at Persepolis, 15 October

The parade at Persepolis, a march of soldiers dressed in costumes representing the various epochs of Iranian history, was another important event in the programme of the Celebrations, and one of the events most vividly remembered. The organization of the parade was entrusted to a separate committee, the *Komisiyon-e Arteshi-ye Jashn-e Shāhanshāhi-ye Irān* (Military Committee of the Imperial Celebrations of Iran), headed by General Abulhasan Sa'ādatmand.[162] The *Komisiyon-e Arteshi* met frequently throughout the 1960s. By January 1969, they had already met 340 times, and between then and March 1970, they held 105 more meetings, during which they inspected samples of ancient military uniforms and equipment.[163] The design of the costumes was presented as a scholarly operation, the culmination of around twelve years of study, which had incorporated a wide variety of sources 'to ensure the greatest authenticity possible'.[164] Members of the *Komisiyon-e Arteshi* included, for instance, scholars such as art historian Yahyā Zokā', archaeologist Mohammad Taqi Mostafavi and the curator of the military museum of Tehran Professor V. Romanowski de Boncza, alongside military figures such as Amānollāh Jahānbāni.

The influence of scholarship on the parade is reflected in the works published in conjunction with the event. The main work was the *Rāhnamā-ye Rezheh* (Guide to the Parade; English title, *Parade at Persepolis*), published by the *Komisiyon-e Arteshi*, which contains detailed illustrations of the soldiers from the various epochs and includes Persian, French and English descriptions.[165] Yahyā Zokā', who served on the council, authored two works, *The Army of Imperial Iran from Cyrus to Pahlavi* and *Background* to *Pageants and Parades in Iran*,[166] and another council member, V. Romanowski de Boncza, wrote *Les Costumes Militaires de L'Empire Perse depuis sa Fondation*, which was published in Greece.[167] The artist Jalil Ziyā'pur produced a volume titled *Garments of the Achaemenids and Medes at Takht-e Jamshid*, which included illustrations and descriptions of the various soldiers depicted on the reliefs at Persepolis.[168]

These published works helped to legitimize the parade as an authentic representation of the continuity of Iran's military strength. They also underlined the fact that the event was more than mere pageantry; it was intended to have lasting cultural, as well as immediate symbolic, value. The historian Eric Chamberlin, for instance, noted that the costumes were created with a 'mixture of rigorous scholarly research and practical experiment'.[169] The detailed illustrations contained in the official volume *Rāhnamā-ye Rezheh* have been reproduced in recent scholarly works, signifying their lasting value.[170] Although the Celebrations are still demonized by the Islamic Republic, twenty-five mannequins dressed in the costumes of the parade, complete with standards and artificial beards, are on display in a prominent position in the military museum at the Sa'dābād Palace complex in Tehran.

The parade began at 3.00 pm, lasted nearly two hours and showcased over 2,500 years of Iranian military history, through soldiers dressed in historical costumes. Once again, the Shah gave a speech in which he sought to merge the past with the present:

> Today, after 25 centuries, Iranian soldiers once again will march past the pillars which stand upright in this vast plain as monuments of the age-old grandeur and glory of Persepolis. But these soldiers, like the soldiers of Achaemenid times, revere as the sacred goal the combination of national sovereignty and moral standards of twenty-five centuries ago, in an inscription which is only a few paces away from us now, and in which Darius the Great recorded the victories of his army, he also said these words: 'I love truth and abhor evil. I do not wish the strong to oppress the weak in my kingdom. I do not wish one to cause loss to another out of wickedness.'[171]

The Shah was presenting himself again as heir to the ancient Iranian kings, in this case Darius, whose typical Zoroastrian typology he cited. These ancient kings, according to his narrative, ruled fairly and justly and their soldiers were inspired to act according to the moral conviction of their ruler. The participation of the modern Iranian armed forces and the Revolutionary Corps in the parade enforced the idea of continuity, both moral and ethnic. But it was also a show of military strength. The event, which was apparently watched by millions around the world, indicated Iran's ability to reinvent itself throughout the ages. The message was that Iran had always played an important regional role which it had assumed with responsibility and moral courage over the past twenty-five centuries. The Shah was announcing to the world Iran's readiness to take back its rightful place among nations.

The parade was attended by royalty, political figures, academics, journalists and private guests. It began with soldiers dressed as pre-Achaemenid warriors, followed by soldiers in various costumes of the Achaemenid, Parthian, Sasanian, Saffarid, Deylamite,

Safavid, Afshar, Zand and Qajar periods, culminating in the Pahlavi period with the march of the Revolutionary Corps.[172] The Achaemenid section included additions such as reconstructions of triremes and siege equipment, and it has been alleged that for added authenticity some of the 3,500 soldiers participating in the procession were banned from shaving in the weeks leading up to the event.[173]

On the evening of the military parade, the guests were served a more informal dinner at the banqueting hall of the tent city. The Executive Committee had decided that Iranian food would be served on this occasion in order to 'present an opportunity to advertise our national culinary tradition as equal to those of China, Italy, India and France'.[174] Guests were advised not to wear short dresses, since they would be sitting on the floor or on low seats, in traditional Persian fashion.[175] The entertainment for the evening was also Iranian, with traditional dancing and music. As Empress Farah recalls in her memoirs, 'We had brought in artists and artisans from all the regions of the country for this event.' She continues: 'Musicians, painters, weavers, and cooks responded to our invitation; this dinner was designed to show everyone the cultural richness of Iran, beginning with its cuisine and its crafts. One of our ambitions was to get this sector flourishing again, especially the export of village-made carpets.'[176] However, this dinner received far less attention in the press than the gala dinner and was overshadowed by the parade which took place earlier in the day. The documentary *Decadence and Downfall* failed to mention the informal dinner at all, although footage of it exists in Farrokh Golestan's *Forugh-e Jāvidān*.

The Pahlavi regime was committed to the promotion of native art, a cause taken especially to heart by Empress Farah. The initial primary objectives of her Shiraz Arts Festival (1967–1977), for example, were the promotion of traditional Iranian music, and to provide a platform for the presentation of theatrical performances devised by native artists.[177] Throughout the Celebrations, therefore, attention was paid to traditional arts and crafts. The official invitations were sent out in special wooden boxes, designed by Hāji Eslāmiyān, head of the Culture Ministry's miniature design workshop. The finished products were worked on by twenty artists at the workshop, along with ten specialist Isfahani artists, and were meant as an example of Iranian art to be kept as a souvenir by the invitees.[178]

Tehran, 16–17 October

On 16 October, the day after the parade, guests were flown to Tehran to attend the inaugurations of the Shahyād-e Āryāmehr Tower and the Āryāmehr Stadium, as well as a wreath-laying ceremony at the tomb of Reza Shah. The name Shahyād means 'remembrance of kings', but during the early planning stages, it was referred to as *Darvāzeh-ye Kurosh* (Gate of Cyrus)[179] and *Darvāzeh-ye Shāhanshāhi* (Imperial Gate).[180] The name Shahyād was eventually chosen by scholar of ancient Iranian languages Bahrām Farahvashi, who argued that the monument should not only commemorate the Pahlavi era but also stand as a reminder of the achievements of all the former kings of the Iranian empire.[181] The Central Council for the Celebrations had asked Amir Nosrat Monaqqah, a prominent Iranian architect, to put forward a proposal for the design of the monument. Despite it being, according to Faryār Javāheriyān, 'a unique, impactful, memorable and ultimately symbolic' design, it was rejected by the Shah, under the influence of Generals Morteżā Yazdānpanāh and Amānollāh Jahānbāni, because it was lacking in grandeur.[182]

It was then decided that the design of the monument would instead be chosen through a nationwide competition, which was officially announced on 1 September 1966.[183] The only requirement was that the submitted designs must be no higher than 45 metres.[184] Twenty-one designs were submitted, and the winner was selected at Saʿdābād Palace by a panel of judges, which included Mohsen Forughi, Mohammad Karim Pirniyā and Mohammad Taqi Mostafavi.[185] The winner of the competition was Hoseyn Amānat, a young graduate of Tehran University, whose design successfully encapsulated the synthesis of past and present. The monument was to be a symbol of the strength of the institution of monarchy in the face of dynastical change, and, in the words of Grigor, presented 'an excellent synthesis of Roman triumphal arches, Parthian fire temples (Chahar-taq), the Sasanian Ctesiphon Iwan, Seljuk tomb towers, Safavid muqarnas, and the various modernist architectural qualities of austerity, iconoclasm, axiality, and monumentality'.[186]

Several reputable foreign companies were involved in the planning of the monument, including the British firm Arup and Partners, while the construction itself was left to the Iranian MAAP Construction Company.[187] Inside was a museum space of 87,000 square feet with an 'art centrum' which would display the cultural and artistic history of Iran from 'at least the last 2,500 years'.[188] The area immediately surrounding the monument was designed to be the centre of a public square. Its location, close to the airport, provided a further link to the modernization of the city and ensured that all foreign visitors who travelled from the airport to the city would pass by.[189] Conforming to the theme of cultural integrity in the face of modernization, the Celebrations' move from the ancient city of Persepolis to the modern capital of Tehran represented what Grigor describes as 'a conspicuous evocation of change and continuity – of ancientness and modernity'.[190]

During the first days after the museum's official opening, the Cyrus Cylinder was on display, on loan to Iran from the British Museum.[191] At the opening ceremony, a special plaque made with 14 kilograms of gold,[192] which featured on one side a message of appreciation for their Imperial Majesties and on the other the 12 principles of the White Revolution, was presented to the Shah by Tehran Mayor Gholāmreżā Nikpey.[193] A number of foreign military bands performed at the ceremony, including 79 members of a Jordanian band, 144 members of an Algerian band, 42 members of a Pakistani band, 133 members of a Swiss band, 19 members of a Romanian band and 99 members of a Kuwaiti band.[194] A 'most magnificent' fireworks display, which was clearly intended to impress, concluded the inauguration ceremony.[195]

Sport also appears to have been an important means through which the regime promoted the language of Pahlavi monarchism and Iran's modernization internationally. They held, for instance, an international football tournament called the Cyrus the Great Cup, in June and July 1971.[196] Although it was essentially a preseason friendly tournament featuring a curious mix of national and club teams, including the Turkey national under-23 team, the Austrian and Dutch amateur national teams,

FC Zbrojovka Brno of Czechoslovakia and Zamalek Sporting Club of Egypt, it was declared by *Kayhan International* to have launched 'a new phase in the nation's quest to become a world soccer power'. Congratulating the Iranian national team on their 1-0 victory over Romania's Fotbal Club Argeş Piteşti in the final, they wrote that the tournament was 'one of the biggest and best football tournaments ever held in the country'.[197] In evidence that some other countries in the region were convinced of Iran's emerging footballing status, Oman printed a special series of stamps to commemorate the Anniversary Celebrations, with illustrations of famous Iranian football players. Other sporting events included a tennis tournament, attended by the Shah, called the Āryāmehr Cup, held in May 1971 at the Imperial Sports Club in Tehran,[198] and the Cyrus the Great Polo Tournament held the same month.[199]

Enforcing the impression of Iran as a sporting power, one of the final events of the Celebrations was the inauguration of the 100,000-seat Āryāmehr Stadium on the afternoon of 17 October. The stadium had been designed by 'Abdol'aziz Farmānfarmā'iyān as part of the Olympic Village for the 1974 Asian Games, which were to be hosted by Iran, and later became an important part of Iran's bid to host the 1984 Olympic Games.[200] It took two and a half years to construct and was funded by the Plan Organisation at a cost of approximately $22.7 million.[201] As always, the Shah and the monarchy were everywhere in the stadium's structure – sports fans visiting the stadium would enter through the 'royal archway', passing a five-ton bronze statue of the Shah, before taking their seats.[202]

The inauguration, which took place after some of the foreign guests had already returned home, included traditional Iranian athletics, a parade and a dance spectacle.[203] Groups participating in the parade included sports groups from educational, military and charity organizations, and, as the procession marched into the stadium, one thousand members of various zurkhāneh clubs also entered 'for a mass display of traditional rhythmic exercises carried out to drum beats and religious chants'.[204] Towards the end of the day, according to the *Iran Tribune*, '2,500 balloons were released and a number of rockets were fired, releasing parachutes to which were attached the Iranian flag or pennants bearing the 12 points of the White Revolution. Spectators scrambled to catch one as a souvenir, but a light north-westerly breeze carried many of them beyond reach.'[205] Recording the inauguration event, *Keyhān* declared emphatically 'Injā, diruz markaz-e shādi-ye jahān bud' – 'here, yesterday was the world's centre of happiness'.[206]

The buildings inaugurated in Tehran during the Celebrations sought to reinvigorate the international image of Iran while injecting a degree of pride into the population. Naming the new buildings Āryāmehr (sun of the Aryans) and Shahyād (remembrance of kings) reinforced the central idea of the Celebrations; that the monarchy had been and always would be essential to the success of Iran. While the practical use of the sports stadium is clear, the Shahyād Tower attained a symbolic significance. It was referred to by foreigners at the time as the Iranian Arc de Triomphe and it became an emblem of modern Iran, even appearing on banknotes in the late 1970s. The vast square surrounding the monument became an important gathering point during the revolution and the monument came to symbolize the end of the monarchy that it was built to glorify.[207]

After the inauguration of the Āryāmehr Stadium, guests were invited to attend a ballet by the National Iranian Ballet Company, with music by the Tehran Symphony

Orchestra.[208] Following these events more guests began to leave, but those who remained were given the opportunity to visit attractions in Tehran, such as the crown jewels and the Golestān Palace, and to travel to Isfahan for more sightseeing.[209]

***

The Celebrations were initially conceived as a relatively modest cultural occasion, yet as this chapter has shown, from 1970, as they acquired a greater political significance, they became more elaborate. In the final year leading up to the event, as international interest in it increased, it became as much about international prestige as the commemoration of an ancient king. Had the Celebrations actually taken place in 1961, as originally planned, they would very likely have been small and quickly forgotten. By 1971 Iran's international standing was on the rise, the Shah had gained confidence through the successes of the White Revolution, and Iran had emerged from the 1960s as a land of economic opportunity. The Celebrations presented an occasion to showcase the Shah's modern Iran to the world.

The Celebrations became a grand expression of the political aspirations of the Pahlavi regime, expressing these aspirations through cultural activity and legitimizing them in the context of Iranian history. The organizers of the event were opportunists, ready to exploit the occasion for all its worth, and by focusing on culture and economic development, utilizing cultural symbols such as the Cyrus Cylinder, and investing heavily in the country's prestige, they presented the Shah to the world as an enlightened monarch rather than an oriental despot.

Throughout the main events of the Celebrations, the Shah had stressed links between the past and the present. As already stated, the presence of the Shah's creations such as the Revolutionary Corps and the Universal Welfare Legion, physical manifestations of his White Revolution, served as evidence of his progressive attitude. During their free time, guests were even invited to visit local Revolutionary Corps headquarters in Fars province before returning to their accommodations in the shadow of the ancient Achaemenid ceremonial capital.[210] Was this deliberate synthesis of past and present successful? The historian Eric Chamberlin believed so:

> 'preserving cultural values' ... 'marching forward into the future but preserving links with the past' ... One has learned to hear phrases like this with a certain sinking of the heart. But in this manner, Iran does seem to be using, consciously and successfully, the past as a vital ingredient of the present. The Shah made this point explicit. 'My hope is that we Persians may be able to merge into a new and harmonious form our antiquity and our modernity.'[211]

That the Shah was seen to be promoting Ancient Iran at the expense of Islam led to exasperation among sections of the *ulema*, expressed most explicitly by Khomeini in his speeches from Najaf.[212] But the pervasiveness of the Cyrus legend and of the glorification of the Achaemenid civilization, even among today's political establishment, in Iran and abroad, suggests that the promotion of this narrative was largely successful. The extent to which it helped secure Iran's reputation at the time as culturally progressive, politically stable and a regional authority, will be explored in the following chapter.

3

International diplomacy at Persepolis

Analyses of the Celebrations often present them as unsuccessful, not least because the Shah failed to attract President Nixon and Queen Elizabeth II. In this narrative, the Shah overstated his independence and importance, and the presentation of himself as a successor to Cyrus the Great was met by the international community with ridicule. This chapter will show, however, that the events of October 1971 stimulated political dialogue and trade discussions; in some cases, deals were sealed against the backdrop of the ancient ruins of Persepolis. There was a degree of cajoling involved from the Iranian side, but this is sometimes overplayed in the literature, too. In general, as this chapter will show, most guests were eager to attend, some felt obliged to attend, which says a lot about the inexorable rise of Iran at this time, and very few turned down their invitations. It is often argued that the Shah was aloof and out of touch, but by examining his diplomacy during the Celebrations we will see that he was in tune, at least, with the realities of global politics, and the Celebrations had the rich and powerful of the world paying tribute to him and his vision for Iran.

Iran's foreign relations from the 19th until the middle of the 20th century were shaped by the imperial competition between Britain and Russia.[1] Following a military defeat to Russia and the signing of the Treaty of Turkmenchay in 1828, Iran lost its remaining territories in the Caucasus and was forced to submit to a number of capitulations. After the Peace of Paris in 1857, which followed another humiliating Persian military defeat to the British, as Axworthy writes, 'the British and Russians interfered so insistently in Persian government that in some respects the shah's independence appeared merely nominal'.[2] The dividing of Iran into zones of influence in 1907, with Russia controlling the north and Britain the south, and the effective crushing of the constitutional movement further undermined Iranian sovereignty.[3]

British support of the coup that brought Reza Khan to power in 1921 was vital to its success, although the coup itself was carried out entirely by Iranian forces.[4] The British ambassador in Tehran, Sir Percy Loraine, encouraged British support of Reza Khan ultimately to keep Russia at arm's length, preserve British oil resources in Persia and prevent Russian encroachment in Iraq, the Persian Gulf and India. Reza Khan was backed as one who could engender a degree of stability in Persia, thereby furthering British interests.[5] The British ultimately did not benefit from the coup, though, and, as Zirinsky has written, instead merely gained 'the reputation of having been behind it, and that idea was proof to nationalists of England's perfidy'.[6]

Iranian political integrity was further challenged throughout the early to mid-20th century, most significantly in 1941 when, ignoring Iran's declared neutrality during the Second World War, Britain and Russia invaded and forced Reza Shah to abdicate. The BBC Persian Service broadcast derogatory stories about Reza Shah in an effort to legitimize this intervention,[7] and the blatant flouting of international law to invade a country that had stayed neutral during the war left Iranians with a sense of 'disbelief and revulsion'.[8] The rial was set at an unreasonable rate against the British pound, going from 68 rials to the pound to 168 in order for Iran to pay for the occupying British forces.[9] Bars frequented by foreign troops had signs at the entrances that read 'Iranians and dogs forbidden' and Iranian soldiers were made to salute British troops when passing them in the street. British soldiers were not expected to return the courtesy.[10]

It was against this backdrop that Mohammad Reza Pahlavi, then only 21 years old, took the throne. In 1943, Stalin, Roosevelt and Churchill held a congress in Tehran to discuss the opening of a second war front in Europe. Not only was the new shah not invited to take part in the discussion, but he was also largely ignored and not even informed of the meeting until the last moment.[11] The Shah was upset that Churchill, in particular, did not observe official protocol and pay a visit to the monarch. 'He didn't even bother to come and call on me at my residence', said the Shah, 'although I was King of the host country'.[12] The humiliation of both this personal snub, and the experience of being ruler of an occupied country, shaped the Shah's later thinking when it came to Iran's regional and global position. The British ambassador in Tehran during the Anniversary Celebrations felt that these humiliations were 'at the root of modern Iranian nationalism'. The ignominy of foreign intervention had inspired a sense of patriotism, for 'although the Iranian reaction to these humiliations was anti-Imperialist in sentiment, paradoxically they re-aroused Iranian national and imperial pride more than any successful conquest might have done'.[13]

Early in his rule, the Shah faced a territorial crisis in Azerbaijan and the oil nationalization crisis of the early 1950s assured him of the fragility of his position. The extent of British and US involvement in the events of 1953 is still fiercely debated,[14] but what is clear is that the coup that brought about the fall of Prime Minister Mohammad Mosaddeq typified, in the eyes of many Iranians, the incorrigible meddling of Britain and the United States, and the weakness of Iranians for failing to stand up to such foreign pressure. Since the end of the Second World War, the British had continually sought to influence Iranian affairs, however, in the years following the fall of the Mosaddeq government, the role of the United States became increasingly significant.

By the 1960s, as the Shah consolidated power, he became better able to assert his influence on the direction of Iran's foreign policy and ensure greater independence from the great powers. During his coronation ceremony, the Shah pledged to ensure 'the ever-increasing advancement of the country and nation of Iran … to preserve the independence and sovereignty of this country and bring Iran to the status of the most progressive and prosperous societies in the world … and restore its historical pride'.[15] He expressed similar ideas in private, too. In 1974, during a conversation with 'Alam, the Shah said, 'Still, I have higher aspirations. I have to bring the country to the status of the most powerful countries in the world, to be the first in the Middle East. There is no reason not to be, we have the means, power and raw materials. What have others done that we cannot?'[16] On an international level, one of the claims of the Pahlavi state ideology was that Iran had an inalienable right and historical duty to regional hegemony,[17] and at Persepolis, the Shah was eager to show that he could play a key role in tackling the major problems facing the world.

Guests staying at the tent city received a copy of a book titled *Iran, Philosophy Behind the Revolution*, in which the Shah's global vision was articulated through extracts from his books and speeches.[18] The book presented the Shah as an enlightened monarch, one whose policies were intended to benefit the world beyond his country's borders. In a quote from *The White Revolution*, for instance, contained in the book, he writes:

> I think that what has already been said clearly shows that our revolution is above any kind of selfishness or narrow-mindedness, and the progress it makes should not be confined within the boundaries of the country, but should help the advancement of all human societies… Today all the communities of the world are linked together like a chain; we cannot see basic social reforms being carried out in one part of the world without observing their repercussions on others.[19]

In a speech to Harvard University on 13 June 1968, also printed in the book, the Shah called for world peace and the establishment of a Universal Welfare Legion: 'I dearly wish that the countries of the world will take a decisive step toward final disarmament, and then place a part of the amount they thus save at the disposal of this international legion.'[20] In the Shah's speeches during the Celebrations, too, he was keen to stress his role as a unifier. He spoke of 'understanding and friendship' and of 'loving unity with the Iranian nation',[21] and at the parade on 15 October he said, 'It is my ardent wish that the great cause of understanding and friendship which has brought together in one place the distinguished representatives of so many countries and nations of the world may inspire all the people on earth to pursue the way that leads to real prosperity and human society.'[22] The period of Cold War détente had begun just two years earlier, so when the Shah spoke about peace and goodwill, he was aware that this language was in keeping with geopolitical realities. During this Cold War lull, it was possible to carve out a new direction for Iran, one in which the Shah could become a force for international unity.

While the Shah presented himself as belonging to an ancient Iranian tradition of kingship domestically, the attendance of other monarchs legitimized the Shah's claims to be a respected figure within the global monarchical tradition, too. Cyrus the Great was presented around the world as a figure of importance not just to Iranian but also European history. The Cyrus Cylinder became a relic of national significance, a tangible reminder of Iran's historic regional and global leadership. The loan of the Cyrus Cylinder from the collection of the British Museum for the Celebrations and the subsequent concerns from the Foreign Office offer clues as to how the Shah's developing regional position and his political ideology were perceived internationally.

Monarchy and protocol

The Celebrations offered an opportunity for the Shah to present his ideology and vision for the future of his country to a global audience. The presentation of monarchy as the ideal form of government was central to this vision, but was also partly a reaction to recent global political developments. The 20th century had been miserable for the monarchical institution; most of Europe's monarchies had been abolished at the end of the First and Second World Wars and from the 1950s onwards a number of Commonwealth countries had relinquished the British crown. In the Middle East, King Farouk of Egypt was toppled in 1952, Faisal II of Iraq lost his throne and life in 1958, and the monarchies of Yemen and Libya were abolished in 1962 and 1969 respectively. Therefore, according to Michael Axworthy, the Shah sought to 'assert the strength and enduring character of Iranian kingship, at a time when monarchy as an institution was menaced by republicanism and communism internationally'.[23]

In the Shah's mind, monarchy was a sort of worldwide fraternity, and its members were brought to Persepolis to legitimize the Pahlavi crown as part of this global institution. The Pahlavi monarchy had faced internal and external threats in its short history, but had survived. Governments might come and go, but the monarchy was permanent. When asked why the Shah's recently deposed and exiled friend King Constantine of Greece was at the Celebrations, an Iranian protocol officer declared, 'For us, the government is the king.'[24] When profiling royal guests, local newspapers were eager to draw attention to them as symbols of the permanence of monarchy as an institution. *Ettelāʿāt*, for instance, noted the fact that Denmark, represented by King Frederick IX, was 'the oldest monarchical country in Europe'.[25] Writing in an English-language publication for the Celebrations and stressing the central position of monarchy in Iranian history, Deputy Minister of Information Mohammad ʿAli Samiʿi wrote that 'monarchy was – and still is – the main factor in the survival of Iranian nationhood. The secret of Iran's unique ability to withstand the devastating forces of 2,500 years of history lies in the guidance from the throne.'[26] The attendance of foreign royals, some of whom represented centuries-old traditions, helped to legitimize this position.

Further signs of this attitude to monarchy can be observed in the strict adherence to rules of protocol established in the 19th century, according to which kings and emperors hold a higher status than presidents and prime ministers.[27] Iran's chief of protocol, Hormoz Qarib, travelled around Europe in 1971 in order to learn the finer details of these regulations,[28] and the British were called upon to resolve any confusion. In a letter to Qarib, the British ambassador wrote, 'Presidents, being Heads of State, take precedence after Monarchs but before Consorts and Crown Princes.' He continued:

> I am informed that Prince Philip takes precedence over Prince Charles. Although he is not officially called "the Consort", Prince Philip is in fact the Consort. Assuming, therefore, that Prince Bernhard of the Netherlands has been Prince Consort longer than Prince Philip, the former takes precedence over the latter. They both, of course, take precedence over the Crown Prince of Sweden.[29]

Adherence to these long-established rules of protocol was important in promoting the Pahlavi monarchy as part of the global and historical monarchical tradition. By observing these accepted diplomatic practices, moreover, the Shah was asserting his and Iran's sovereign equality to the crowned heads of Europe. The Celebrations stressed what could be achieved by an assertive king possessing a deep sense of morality and a spiritual relationship with his people, such as Cyrus the Great and Mohammad Reza Pahlavi.

Protocol did cause some practical problems, since non-royal guests did not want to be upstaged. This was the reason for French President Pompidou's late withdrawal from the event, as will be discussed shortly, which particularly displeased the Shah.[30] As a result, the event organizers went to great lengths to ensure that no guests felt underappreciated and the British were also on hand to help with practical matters relating to procedure. Ambassador Ramsbotham was approached by Qarib to help with the seating arrangements for the gala dinner at Persepolis. Qarib was keen that no guests should feel embarrassed by being placed too far from the Shah or being sat next to someone they considered of a lower status than themselves. Qarib told Ramsbotham, 'The English, we acknowledge, are better than anybody in the world at these things. We are new to this, Western style; we could do it, of course, our own way, but we are having everybody here. We would like you to advise on this.'[31] Together Ramsbotham and Qarib devised a system whereby the table was set out like a 'big snake', with 'five big sweeping points'. At the top of each point was seated a member of the Pahlavi family; either the Shah himself, Empress Farah, the queen mother, or one of the princes and princesses. It did not matter too much who sat where because each guest would be sat close to someone of honour and the layout made it difficult to determine whether one person was better placed than another, so as to cause minimal offence.[32] Iran was keen to prove that not only could it hold such a huge event, but it could do it successfully, while demonstrating its understanding of international procedure and protocol.

The Celebrations presented an opportunity to underscore Iran's similarities to the West, with a focus on its pre-Islamic past. It was hoped that Iran would be transformed in the eyes of the world from a traditional Islamic country to a modern, industrial and even perhaps secular state, far more palatable to the West. The Pahlavi ideologues were keen to push this shift in perception at any available opportunity. In one example of this attitude, the Dutch Foreign Ministry proposed to send a carillon to Iran as a gift for the Celebrations.[33] A prominent Dutch Islamic scholar, Hanna Kohlbrugge, was consulted about the issue and advised that it might be considered insensitive to send an essentially Christian symbol to the ruler of an Islamic country.[34] The Dutch ambassador, Hendrik Jonker, nevertheless put the proposal directly to Asadollāh 'Alam, who thought it a 'splendid idea', even suggesting that it could be placed at Persepolis.[35] When Jonker relayed his ministry's fears over the appropriateness of the gift, 'Alam urged the ambassador not to worry. After all, he responded, 'we are not real moslims [sic], we are shi'ites'.[36]

One British diplomat commented that the Celebrations were 'proof that the Pahlavi Dynasty was frivolous; it was not serious'.[37] It is, of course, the gift of hindsight that gives such statements credibility, for at the time of the Celebrations, although foreign powers did not necessarily buy into the Pahlavi ideology, they did not hesitate to employ it to improve their relations with the Shah. Although individuals may not have taken the ideology seriously in private, in official correspondence they were careful not to challenge it. On a state visit to Iran in 1969, for example, British Foreign Minister Michael Stewart was given a private tour of the ruins of Persepolis, after which he commented on the wisdom of Cyrus, Darius and Xerxes, adding, 'I think your current shah shares characteristics with each of these three great kings.'[38] The minister's statement perhaps amounted to little more than flattery, but it is nevertheless evident that the state ideology had become a useful tool in negotiations with the Pahlavi regime. Furthermore, foreign governments and academics acknowledged the importance of this ideology to the Shah, as shown by the loan of the Cyrus Cylinder from the British Museum to Iran to coincide with the Celebrations.

The Cyrus Cylinder

The Cyrus Cylinder was discovered during Hormuzd Rassam's excavations at Babylon on behalf of the British Museum in 1879 and was subsequently purchased by the British Museum in 1880. The Cylinder itself has always been an item of historical significance, but it was not until the 1960s that it began to take on a different meaning. Its original function had been to record building work carried out at the Babylonian temple following Cyrus's invasion in 539 BCE. Far from being a unique declaration, this was standard practice, for as Amelie Kuhrt writes, 'Such pious acts of temple work were part of a standard process of legitimisation in Babylonia, and thus follow conventional forms.'[39] The Cylinder also sought to present the foreign invader Cyrus as a liberator who would respect Babylonian gods and free its people from a tyrant. According to Josef Wiesehöfer, the Cylinder 'fits into the framework of the ideological conflict between the new and the old king, and says less about Cyrus's character than about his efforts at legitimisation and his ability to use local traditions and modes to serve his own purposes'.[40]

A. T. Olmstead, in his 1948 publication *History of the Persian Empire*, wrote that the Cylinder was merely a 'model of persuasive propaganda',[41] while Richard Frye in his *The Heritage of Persia*, published in 1962, makes no mention of any special qualities of the Cylinder, noting rather that the inscription is 'characteristic of older conquerors in the Near East'.[42] By the time the political manipulation of the artefact reached its peak in 1971, P. R. Berger from the University of Münster, announcing the identification of a fragment belonging to the Cylinder, stressed that the find should 'emphasise the essential character of the Cyrus Cylinder as not a general declaration of human rights or religious toleration but simply a building inscription'.[43] Taken out of a political context, therefore, the link between the Cylinder and human rights is tenuous.

Pierre Nora wrote that 'the less memory is experienced from within, the greater the need for external props and tangible reminders of that which no longer exists qua memory'.[44] The Cylinder, as an ancient relic, served as material evidence of the idea of Cyrus that the Shah wished to project. These types of historical artefacts are generally amenable to change and reinterpretation. According to David Lowenthal, relics can undergo two types of transformation, physical (location, enhancement or iconoclasm), and conceptual (interpretation and appreciation).[45] The Cylinder underwent such a conceptual transformation, evolving from a building inscription found beneath a temple in Babylon into a national symbol, tangible evidence of the supposed humanitarian values of an ancient king and an important part of the British Museum's collection.

As early as 1968, Iran had been contacting embassies around the world to request loans of Iranian artefacts to be exhibited in Iran during the Celebrations.[46] A request to borrow the Cyrus Cylinder was relayed through the British ambassador to the Foreign Office on 20 August 1971.[47] The request was rejected by the Foreign Office on the grounds that it would 'merely arouse Iranian cupidity'[48] and 'would cause immense complications for us if we ever wanted to get it back to Britain'.[49] The merits of such a loan to the Iranians were clear; after all, the Cylinder, surrounded by Persepolitan-style flowers, was the emblem of the Celebrations. It served as physical proof of the benevolent character of Cyrus and symbolized the endurance of the Iranian monarchy. There was even a suggestion that the Cylinder should be presented to the Shah as a gift, to placate him during Britain's negotiations over its withdrawal from Abu Musa and the Tunbs.[50] Moreover, it is perhaps a measure of the emerging influence of the Shah that the British were so concerned that they would be powerless if the Shah refused to give the Cylinder back.

As it happened, and unbeknown to the Foreign Office, the British Museum's Board of Trustees had already agreed to an unofficial request from the Iranian ambassador to allow Iran to have the Cylinder for the duration of the Celebrations.[51] As soon as Ramsbotham heard of the planned loan, he attempted to warn the British Museum against it, but by that point the Cylinder was already in Iran. Richard Barnett, keeper of Western Asian Antiquities, had been invited to take part in the Congress of Iranology in Shiraz and was asked to bring the Cylinder with him, an arrangement which was approved by the Board of Trustees in July 1971.[52] It was apparently common knowledge at the time that Barnett's eagerness to attend the Celebrations facilitated, perhaps even prompted, this arrangement.[53] Neither the Iranian embassy in London nor the British Museum informed the Foreign Office and when they found out, the Foreign Office became concerned that if Iran attempted to exert pressure on the British Government to give them the Cylinder, this might result in a rather uncomfortable diplomatic incident. These worries were not unfounded, and one Iranian newspaper suggested that Iran 'might take the opportunity afforded by the centenary celebrations and ask the British Museum to let Iran keep the cylinder for good'.[54]

The request came shortly after Barnett's arrival in Iran, when he was invited to a meeting with Minister of Culture and Art Mehrdād Pahlbod. At the meeting, as expected, Pahlbod put forward the idea of an extension of the loan, perhaps even to a permanent arrangement. Barnett, however, explained that the Cylinder was required back in London for the British Museum's commemorative *Royal Persia* exhibition, and drew from his pocket a leaflet advertising the event.[55] Another request was expected to come at the opening of the Shahyād Tower, where the Cylinder was on display in the museum. Ramsbotham was concerned that the Shah could put a request directly to Prince Philip, who, being put on the spot, might find it difficult to refuse. To ensure that such a request was not made, Barnett chaperoned Philip for the entire event, keeping him as far away from the Shah as possible.[56] The Cylinder left Iran safely on the evening of 19 October, stored, as it had been when it arrived, in Barnett's sports holdall.[57] The loan had been a success, in part due to Barnett's 'tactful handling'[58] of the situation, but more outspoken advocates of giving the Cylinder to Iran came from Britain when the artefact was safely back in the British Museum.

Former Attorney General Lord Hartley Shawcross, Liberal MP Jeremy Thorpe, newspaper tycoon Vere Harmsworth, Conservative MP Sir Clive Bossom and former MP and head of the Iran Society Sir Peter Agnew, all respectable British establishment figures and private guests of the Shah at the Celebrations, supported the idea of a permanent loan of the Cylinder. Bossom wrote directly to Prime Minister Edward Heath: 'I feel that by allowing this cylinder to be on permanent loan it could greatly smooth the way before next year's problems arise.'[59] Shawcross, a highly respected and decorated figure, also wrote to the Prime Minister:

> The four of us [Jeremy Thorpe, Clive Bossom, Vere Harmsworth and himself] unanimously agreed (before we had seen the place given to the Cylinder in the Museum) that we should strongly recommend to you that the Cylinder should be presented to Iran … in view of the serious disputes which exist between Britain and Iran which will soon come to a head, we have no doubt that a decision to make the gift to Iran (and naturally the sooner the better) would immensely improve the atmosphere of our relations. I believe that our Ambassador shares this view.[60]

The idea that the Cylinder could become a bargaining tool in the issue of Britain's potentially awkward retreat from the Persian Gulf was apparently not without merit, and is reflective of the significance of the Cyrus ideology in Iranian diplomacy.

It was clear to those involved that the Cylinder could become, if it was not already, a powerful diplomatic tool which could both hinder and improve British relations with Iran. Even Ramsbotham, having fought to keep the Cylinder in the British Museum's possession, supported the idea of another loan in the future. 'The Iranians' readiness to let the tablet slip through their hands this time suggests', he argued, 'that we ought to be able to hold them to an understanding of any loan.'[61] The British Museum, however, was adamantly opposed to any further agreement, in particular the Foreign Office's proposal that the Cylinder could be displayed in Iran every third year. The Museum's chairman Lord Trevelyan argued that it would be 'incredibly unlikely that the Iranians would ever return the Tablet to the British Museum at the end of the first year's loan'.[62]

An Icelandic member of the Congress of Iranology wrote to Shafā after the Celebrations, stating his belief that the Cylinder was 'not just an archaeological remnant, but a symbol of the existence of the Persian Empire … a holy symbol, historically, culturally and nationally'.[63] The British Foreign Office was well aware of the power of this 'holy symbol'. The Foreign Office was clearly expecting a more robust challenge to the British Museum's ownership of the Cylinder and one draft report has a note scribbled in pen that 'it looks as though the Iranians may develop a campaign about this, and we will be in for a long tussle'.[64] It is for this reason that Prime Minister Heath was forced to intervene personally, writing to Shawcross to urge him not to make public his opinion that the Cylinder should be given to Iran.[65] The Foreign Office was advised that if the Iranian ambassador should bring up the question of a permanent agreement, then they should respond that, while appreciating the importance of the Cylinder to Iran, 'it forms too important a part of the British Museum collection for the Trustees to be able to agree to a permanent loan to Iran; they had already made a major concession in permitting it to leave the Museum for the Celebrations'.[66] There was a romance attached to the Cylinder, which was historically, in large part, stimulated by the Cyrus legend in the West. One finds it hard to imagine such a campaign to repatriate the Ardabil Carpet from the Victoria and Albert Museum, for example. There was a particular aura surrounding the Cylinder, which was encouraged by the Shah and which fuelled the Pahlavi ideology.

In addition to the loan, replicas of the Cylinder were displayed in the United Nations buildings in New York and Geneva in an effort to accentuate the message of Cyrus and the Anniversary Celebrations.[67] On 14 October, in New York, Princess Ashraf presented a replica Cylinder to UN Secretary-General U Thant, who declared that 'in creating the ancient Persian Empire twenty-five hundred years ago, Cyrus displayed the wisdom of respecting the civilizations and peoples whom he "unified" under his sway'.[68] Additional casts were made by the British Museum and were distributed among dignitaries who attended the festivities in Iran,[69] as well as scholars such as 'Ali Sāmi of the Persepolis Museum[70] and Richard Barnett.[71] As a result of the Pahlavi campaign to promote the Cylinder as a national symbol, the artefact retains to this day a special importance to Iranians and is still mentioned in terms of human rights. Speaking at her Nobel Prize lecture in 2003, human rights lawyer Shirin Ebadi, for example, said that 'the Charter of Cyrus the Great is one of the most important documents that should be studied in the history of human rights'.[72]

The Shah's presentation of himself as Cyrus's successor is generally viewed with some scepticism. His speech at the tomb of Cyrus became a source of mockery within Iran and William Shawcross suggested that the presented connection constituted a 'complete divorce from reality'.[73] The Cylinder loan is clear evidence, however, that foreign governments were more than willing to speak to the Shah in his own language and use his ideology to further their own interests. The idea that the Cylinder could become a bargaining tool during Britain's withdrawal from the Persian Gulf is reflective of the importance the Iranians attached to the Cylinder within the context of the Pahlavi state's ideology. Even if the international political establishment did not take the Shah's comparison of himself to Cyrus seriously in private, in public they toed the official line. The fact that leaders and diplomats from around the world familiarized themselves with and used this narrative is illustrative of the Shah's emerging role as a serious presence on the international stage during this period.

Iran's political and economic standing

There was clearly something to gain by presenting oneself as understanding, accepting and in some cases promoting the historical narrative presented by the Shah's regime. The prize was more than merely a personal relationship with the Shah himself, and included access to lucrative Iranian markets. Throughout the 1960s, Iran's economy expanded considerably, boosted in large part by increased oil revenues. Gross national product (GNP) nearly tripled between 1959 and 1970, from $3.8 to $10.6 billion.[74] By the late 1960s, Iran offered one of the Middle East's most lucrative prospects for foreign investors, with vast natural resources and, due to its recently acquired financial clout, considerable purchasing power. Realizing the potential of this growing market, foreign powers scrambled for influence in Iran and the Celebrations, in some respects, became an elaborate business fair, with many countries competing for contracts, trade deals and political leverage. Furthermore, dealing with Iran required a certain savoir faire and success depended as much on whom one knew and how one presented oneself, as what one could offer. Business leaders were included on the international committees for the Celebrations and many companies launched special advertisements to show their support for the occasion.[75] Being involved with the Celebrations brought high-level exposure which companies were naturally glad to take advantage of. A number of firms even took part 'in an honorary capacity', offering their services for free, such as the famous hairdressing salons of Carita, Alexander and Elizabeth Arden.[76]

Other firms competed for lucrative contracts. One British firm, for example, won an $864,000 contract to supply street lights for Tehran and Shiraz.[77] Spode produced commemorative dinner plates for £5,000 ($12,150), a comparatively modest sum, but with considerable prestige.[78] The Swedish company Sporrong was commissioned to make commemorative gold medals, men's bronze brooches and women's pins,[79] and the Dutch electrical company Philips won the contract to supply lights at Shahyād and Persepolis.[80] But the main short-term beneficiaries were the French, whose jewellers produced jewellery for the imperial family, interior designers provided furniture for the tents, and whose chefs provided food for the main receptions. Using the international interest in the Celebrations to promote their new model, from 11 until 23 August the car manufacturer Citroën even sent a brigade of 600 cars to tour Iran, with 1,400 passengers and a 29-man strong media crew.[81]

There were also long-term commercial opportunities on offer for those who managed to win favour. The success of this courtship became naturally linked to political representation. For example, British and French competition to win the rights to mine copper at Kerman became 'inextricably linked with the presence or absence of President Pompidou at the celebrations'.[82] Furthermore, directly as a result of Pompidou's snub, the Shah 'cancelled all the big orders given to the French and for a number of years the French were in the doghouse'.[83] According to Ramsbotham, despite concerns over human rights, President Heinemann of West Germany was persuaded to attend the event 'for the sake of Germany's extensive commercial interests in Iran'.[84] Facing criticism at home over the plight of political prisoners in Iran, Heinemann argued that 'When a state maintains ties to another state, in international understanding that implies neither judgement of its form of government nor the politics of that state.'[85] In an open letter to his country's young socialists, Heinemann noted Iran's regional political and economic power as justification for his decision to take part in the festivities.[86] Similarly, a member of the Swiss delegation accompanying president of the Swiss Confederation Rudolf Gnägi declared that his mission was 'not very pleasant', but necessary since 'international customs and commitments simply cannot be ignored'.[87] Economic alignment was widely presented as justification for engagement, despite widespread concerns in some European states over issues such as human rights.

The Shah was troubled by the negative presentation of the Celebrations in the Western press in the months leading up to the festivities. At the end of July, he complained about the issue to Prime Minister Hoveydā, who ordered the minister of information to Paris to assess the situation.[88] European states were evidently aware of the offence that negative articles could cause in their relations with the Shah. Consequently, in order to inspire more positive articles in Germany, the German Federation of Advertising paid the newspaper *Die Welt* 80,000 Deutschmarks (around $22,000) to produce some flattering articles about the Celebrations.[89] There were later concerns that other German papers, such as *Süddeutsche Zeitung*, *Der Spiegel* and *Stern* might demand similar payments, otherwise they would continue to make 'false claims' about the Celebrations. The British ambassador also made an offer to 'Alam to 'try to inspire a constructive article in one of our leading newspapers'.[90]

In the Netherlands, the Foreign Ministry was forced to defend Iran in public in order to maintain good relations during this important period, narrowly avoiding a scandal in the process. After an Iranian carpet dealer living in the Netherlands refused an order from the Iranian ambassador to give discounts during the Celebrations, his passport was revoked and he was ordered to return to Iran 'as soon as possible'.[91] The implication in the press was that this was a punishment for his disobedience and the issue was debated in the Dutch House of Representatives, with House members asking whether the ambassador overstepped the mark with his 'unacceptable behaviour'.[92] Minister of Foreign Affairs Norbert Schmelzer, in defence of the ambassador, argued that 'it should not be seen as uncommon that on occasion of special events or for other reasons compatriots should be asked to lend their support to such a manifestation'.[93] Schmelzer declined to take the ambassador to task over the allegations, even when faced with hostile journalists who were, in general, critical of the Shah and the Celebrations. Criticizing the conduct of an Iranian ambassador, particularly at this time, would have had broader political implications and Schmelzer's defence is telling.

The Shah was aware of the fact that the foreign delegations at the Celebrations were competing for his favour and encouraged this competition. In a press conference held shortly after the Celebrations, the Shah said to a German reporter, 'You are exporting to us 10 times more than what you buy from us. If we stopped trade with you, you would be the losers not us. We can buy what you sell to us elsewhere.'[94] The message was clear: you need us more than we need you. This position encouraged competition for the regime's favour and with it a good measure of flattery. A commemorative edition of *Anglo-Iranian Trade* was published by British Industrial Publicity Overseas, for example, with the gushing tribute printed on the cover 'British Industry Salutes Their Imperial Majesties Mohammad Reza Pahlavi Aryamehr Shah and the Shahbanu Farah of Iran and Their Nation on the Historic Occasion of the 2500th Anniversary of the Founding of the Persian Empire by Cyrus the Great: Long Live His Imperial Majesty the Shahanshah Aryamehr!'[95] One British diplomat was struck by the 'outrageous flattery' that was the norm during this period in general, and the Celebrations in particular saw expressions of admiration that bordered on sycophancy.[96] The Apadana reliefs at Persepolis depict representatives from each quarter of the Persian Empire waiting to pay homage to their king, and to a certain degree the Celebrations were a 20th-century manifestation of this ancient practice.

The realization that one's attendance could be viewed in the context of flattering the Shah in the hope of better economic and political relations was a factor in Queen Elizabeth II's refusal to attend the event. Appearing to be submissive to the Shah, particularly as Britain was going through a troubling departure from the Persian Gulf, was not palatable to the British monarchy. Denis Wright recalled that he wondered 'why should we, having all this abuse hurled at us in the press, bring our Queen out just to please the Shah?'[97] Conversely, this was also cited as a reason why some in the Foreign Office thought that the queen *should* attend the Celebrations. In a letter dated 10 September 1968, J. R. Rich wrote to Sir Denis Allen:

> I recommend that the Foreign Office should advise that Her Majesty the Queen should accept the invitation from the Shah ... the attendance of Her Majesty The Queen would clearly be a great feather in the Shah's cap, would give him great satisfaction and could be expected to be beneficial to Anglo/Iranian relations. If the Queen can agree to go and if Anglo/Iranian relations come under some strain because of Persian Gulf affairs or indeed other issues the Queen's attendance at the Shah's celebrations would clearly have to be reconsidered. The prospect of this might serve to act as a restraining influence on the Shah in so far as differences between his government and Her Majesty's Government were concerned.[98]

Allen wrote at the end of the letter in pen, 'I support this recommendation.' When the British ultimately informed the Shah that the queen would not be attending, they were careful not to politicize the rejection, informing the Shah that as a general rule 'the Queen does not go on international jamborees'.[99] Moreover, to soften the blow when the Shah's second choice, Prince Charles, declined his invitation, the queen was encouraged to write a personal letter to the Shah since he 'will regard refusal as a personal slight'.[100] In this letter, the queen addressed the Shah as 'Sir My Brother', and wrote that she was 'deeply conscious of the disappointment' caused.[101] There was clearly some concern over the implications of the queen's and the prince's rejection for British interests in Iran.[102]

Much has been written about the refusal of other world leaders to attend the Celebrations. One journalist wrote mockingly at the time, 'You just weren't important if you weren't invited; but you couldn't have been that important if you actually showed up.'[103] Some had practical reasons for not attending. German President Gustav Heinemann had intended to go, as discussed above, but was kept away by a 'sudden – and real – eye disease',[104] President Nixon had agreed to attend but later declined due to security concerns[105] and Emperor Hirohito of Japan cited old age as a reason not to attend.[106] Leaders also faced domestic pressures to accept or reject their invitations. For instance, the rulers of some of Iran's neighbours, such as Mohammed Zahir Shah of Afghanistan, sent medium-level representatives, for fear that their attendance would embolden the fanatics in their own countries.[107] Amid intense criticism of the Shah and the Celebrations from opposition groups such as the Confederation of Iranian Students, backed by figures such as Jean-Paul Sartre and Simone de Beauvoir, who called for a boycott of the Celebrations, some Western governments may also have feared the political ramifications of attending.[108] This international campaign clearly had some success. Princess Beatrix, heir to the Dutch throne, for example, declined to attend the Celebrations to avoid offending her country's socialists.[109]

It appears that only Pompidou publicly declined his invitation. To the annoyance of the Dutch ambassador, Pompidou 'decided that it was more important to be too busy to attend than to accept his place, as dictated by protocol, *after* the King of Lesotho'.[110] Responding in the press, Pompidou added that he would probably be mistaken for just another French waiter anyway.[111] Despite the Shah reassuring Pompidou's replacement, Prime Minister Chaban-Delmas, that the 'great desert wind and the blue sky of Persepolis have swept away the alleged clouds between us and France', he was clearly annoyed by the rejection.[112] There were perhaps other factors that persuaded Pompidou not to attend the Celebrations. In September 1971, he had received a letter from the overseas-based opposition organization Free Iran, urging him to stay at home. It is not clear whether this pressure influenced his decision, but Free Iran were delighted at the snub.[113]

There was also a degree of cajoling involved from the Iranian side. The Shah apparently sent a personal message to the Romanian president, Nicolae Ceaușescu, 'almost pleading with him to attend next year's junketings in person'.[114] Grand Master of Ceremonies Hormoz Qarib, meanwhile, summoned the Dutch ambassador to inform him 'in fairly strong terms' that Queen Juliana was expected at the Celebrations. Qarib was not satisfied with the ambassador's suggestion that Princess Beatrix could go in her place; 'the Iranians expected crowned heads'.[115] The tone of the cajoling may have been slightly overstated in the British records. One report from an Iranian diplomat describes how he approached the chief of Royal Court 'in a friendly manner' to find out whether Queen Juliana intended to attend the Celebrations.[116]

The Shah's inability to persuade certain heads of state to attend, particularly Queen Elizabeth II, President Nixon and President Pompidou, was undoubtedly a disappointment and undermined to some extent the image he wished to promote of himself as a serious figure on the international stage. However, these rejections should also be seen in the broader context of both public opposition to the Shah's rule in the West and the security situation, and did not necessarily reflect the governments' position on the Shah and his regime, as evidenced by a number of the absentee heads of state visiting Iran in state visits shortly after the Celebrations, most notably President Nixon in 1972. Rumours circulated after the event that Ardeshir Zāhedi was removed from his post as foreign minister partly as a result of his failure to persuade these figures to attend are unsubstantiated, not least because Zāhedi was not entirely responsible for invitations.[117]

To emphasize the significance of the occasion on an international level, a number of 'Cyrus the Great Committees' were set up years before the Celebrations, in countries around the world, typically chaired by heads of state.[118] When Arthur Upham Pope was charged with forming the American committee in 1960, it was hoped that Kennedy and Eisenhower would serve as patrons, an indication of the perceived international importance of the occasion even at this early stage in its development.[119] General De Gaulle was installed as chair of the French committee, King Baudouin led the Belgian committee and General Franco acted as head of the Spanish committee.[120] By the time the Celebrations were underway in 1971, there were seventy such committees around the world and there was even a suggestion that they could remain functioning after the event as 'Friendship Committees'.[121] The regime took these committees quite seriously and British Ambassador Peter Ramsbotham records that he was repeatedly pressed about the vacant role of head of the British committee. The Iranians viewed this as an illustration 'of the British Government's anti-Iranian policy'.[122] When Prince Philip was eventually chosen to chair the committee, it was because 'the Iranians want a Royal personage to take part', thus underlining both the significance of these foreign committees to Iran and the willingness of foreign governments to acquiesce to Iranian demands.[123]

In the months leading up to the Celebrations, Iran relayed a message to attending delegations to inform them that gifts were not expected.[124] During other events of international significance, such as the Shah's coronation in 1967, gifts had been offered,[125] but the regime was eager not to present this event too overtly as a homage-paying trip. Some ignored this instruction and did bring gifts. President Tito brought a gift of a bronze statue of four figures engaged in a traditional Yugoslav dance[126] and as mentioned the Dutch also brought a gift. This was presumably to compensate for their 'totally inadequate' offering at the coronation, when the Shah was presented with flower bulbs in cartons.[127] It is clear that some countries went to significant lengths to ensure that their friendship with the Shah was properly expressed.

Tent city diplomacy

The Celebrations represented a coming of age for the Shah. No longer would foreign states abuse his country's sovereignty, nor would heads of state like Churchill come to Iran and ignore him; he was now a key player on the international scene. In the imperial competition of the Cold War, the Shah could create a role for himself as mediator, able to solve the major problems facing the world. Dialogue was promoted, with time set aside during the days at Persepolis for informal meetings and discussions, and many of these took place. South African State President Jacobus Fouché, for example, was invited to the Indonesian tent for cocktails, and similar informal meetings were held in his own tent with, among others, King Moshoeshoe II of Lesotho.[128]

Those attending the event were aware of the political ramifications of their visit. In his briefing for Vice President Spiro Agnew ahead of his visit as representative of President Nixon, Henry Kissinger wrote:

> Your visit to Iran is essentially an expression of our respect and friendship for the Shah. The 25th Centenary Celebrations are a symbolic assertion that Iran, under the leadership of the Shah, is assuming the full promise of its ancient heritage. Your participation in these events is intended to identify the United States with these accomplishments and the Shah's leadership.[129]

The relationship between Iran and the United States had developed during this period in such a way that Iran was no longer a subservient country, but a partner. In this context Agnew was given a list of issues to discuss with the Shah, one of which was the escalating tension between India and Pakistan over the situation in East Pakistan, considered 'the subject at the top of our priority list'.[130] Agnew was to set out the US position on the issue and inform the Shah of his appreciation of anything that he 'might be able to do along these lines'.[131]

In order to underline his credentials, therefore, and show the United States that he was a worthy partner, the Shah attempted to mediate talks between India and Pakistan during the Celebrations. Outside of Iran such a meeting with president of the Soviet Union Nikolai Podgorny, president of Pakistan Yahya Khan and President V. V. Giri of India in one place would have been impossible, but here they all stayed in the tent city together, which, according to Ramsbotham, substantiated 'the Shah's claim to be an independent world leader'.[132] The Pakistani delegation considered the meeting a relative success, with the Soviets assuring them of their commitment to the preservation of Pakistan,[133] although for his efforts the Shah received little more than a stern warning from Podgorny not to supply weapons to Pakistan.[134] Seemingly undeterred by his failure to conclude peace talks, the Shah pledged to do 'all in our power' to avert military confrontation, 'even if our preliminary efforts do not prove as fruitful as we would like them to be'.[135]

The Shah's intervention in this matter should not merely be seen in the context of his desire to serve American interests. He often spoke of his foreign policy objectives and of achieving influence in his own region. During an extensive interview published as *The Mind of a Monarch*, he discussed his vision for an 'economic union under a common market of all Indian Ocean countries', stretching from Africa to Iran and South Asia.[136] The Shah's vision for his country's role in the modern world was not confined to its relationship with the United States and the Soviet Union; he wanted to carve out his own sphere of influence. At Persepolis, many of the countries that would be involved in his Indian Ocean initiative were represented, giving the Shah the chance to present himself as a respected world leader. Critics mocked the Shah for failing to secure Nixon and Pompidou – indeed, one article in *Newsweek* stated that 'he invited virtually everybody who was anybody – but mostly nobodies showed up'.[137] In the context of his broader foreign policy objectives, however, the attendance of these 'nobodies' was just as important, if not more so. The participation of South Africa's President Fouché was significant in this regard, particularly since his invitation was viewed in South Africa as a contrast to the general international isolation that the country experienced at this time.[138]

In an effort to extend his influence in Africa, the Shah also held a meeting with Senegalese President Léopold Sédar Senghor. During this meeting, the ambitious idea was first raised to establish a large petrochemical and industrial complex along with a new town and port, 80 kilometres north of the capital Dakar, with Iranian assistance.[139] The plan was to construct a city with a population of 200,000 people, mostly working in the industrial complex. As part of a deal with Iran, 'tankers would deliver Iranian oil for refining, and return with loads of phosphate fertilisers'.[140] The new city was to be called Keur Farah Pahlavi and Empress Farah travelled to Senegal herself in 1976 to lay the foundation stone.[141] According to a book on Moshe Safdie, the architect charged with executing the project, the detailed design and prototype units had been completed, but the 'development of the city was interrupted when the Khomeini regime in Iran discontinued its support'.[142]

One local pariah state with which the Shah wished to maintain good relations was Israel. Although Israel was not officially invited so as to avoid both an Arab boycott and offending Iranian public opinion, Israeli scholars were secretly housed in a motel on the outskirts of Shiraz so that they could attend the Congress of Iranology[143] and David Ben-Gurion contributed a chapter on Cyrus the Great to the first volume of *Acta Iranica*, a series initially established to publish the proceedings of the Congress.[144] Some in Israel were said to have been disappointed with the decision not to invite President Zalman Shazar to the Celebrations, but they also understood that the snub was purely political.[145] While it would clearly have been problematic to invite official Israeli representatives, the fact that efforts were made to include Israeli academics in the scholarly events shows the importance of Israel to the Shah both as a regional power and a fellow close ally of the United States.

The imminent departure of the British from the Persian Gulf presented Iran with an opportunity to take a leading role in Gulf politics, too. The emirs of each of the seven Trucial States attended the Celebrations, as did the emir of Bahrain, whose involvement as an independent head of state allowed the Shah to draw a line under his country's claims to the territory. On 16 October, during the Celebrations, Iran established diplomatic relations with Qatar, underlining the Shah's intention to play a significant part in the integration of the former British protectorates into the international community.[146]

The Shah also used the Celebrations to reach out to communist China, with which the United States had initiated talks. From 13 until 19 April 1971, Princess Ashraf visited China for a meeting with Premier Chou En-lai. During a toast at a banquet in her honour, she raised a glass to Chairman Mao, and said that 'Personal contact such as ours here today, inevitably leads to dialogue ... I know that, through this unpretentious visit, we already have taken the first step in that direction.'[147] Later that month Princess Fatemeh also visited, accompanied by Leylā Hoveydā, the wife of the prime minister. Fatemeh's visit coincided with the May Day celebrations and affirmed, according to the *Peking Review*, 'the atmosphere of friendship between the people of China and Iran'.[148] This effort contributed to the formal establishment of diplomatic relations between the two countries, signed on 16 August 1971.[149] The Chinese had intended to send the vice chairman of the Standing Committee of the National People's Congress, Kuo Mo-jo, to the Celebrations as China's representative, but he fell ill on the way, so China's ambassador to Pakistan, Chang Tung, was sent in his place. On 15 October, the Chinese delegation presented a letter from the Chinese government, which read:

> China's Special Envoy Kuo Mo-jo has been invited to pay a friendly visit to your country. We believe that with the joint effort of our two sides the relations between China and Iran based on the principles of mutual respect for sovereignty and territorial integrity, mutual benefit, and peaceful coexistence will develop

continuously, and the friendly contacts, and mutual understanding between the two peoples will be further strengthened.[150]

A day later, on 16 October, Prime Minister Amir ʿAbbās Hoveydā met with the Chinese representative to discuss the development of relations between the two countries.[151] In September 1972, just months after Nixon's historic visit to China, Empress Farah and Prime Minister Hoveydā led an Iranian delegation to China in order to develop relations further. Speaking on that occasion, Premier Chou En-lai noted China's presence at the Celebrations as an example of the growing friendship between the two countries.[152] The Celebrations were evidently successful in helping Iran to develop relationships, expanding its global influence in the process.

The absence of negative reports from foreign dignitaries suggests that the Shah's message of 'friendship' and 'unity' was appreciated rather than merely tolerated. The event was used to show off Iran's pre-eminence, while both strengthening and expanding bilateral relations, and in this regard, it appears to have been successful. The organisers' attention to detail and dedication to making guests feel comfortable and relaxed served to further endear the Shah to his guests and contributed to the positive atmosphere that the festivities sought to foster.

***

The evidence presented in this chapter has demonstrated that beyond the pomp and ceremony, the Celebrations largely achieved their international objectives. Despite the opposition to the event from sections of the foreign media, there was an unprecedented level of interest from global business and political and cultural figures to participate. According to Denis Wright, who served as British ambassador to Iran from 1963 to 1971, there was a general understanding from anyone engaged in Iran that the Shah was ultimately the man in charge. If one sought influence in Iran, then one had to pay the Shah the occasional lip service when the opportunity presented itself.[153] As the Shah's international status grew, it became more important to keep him content and the Celebrations provided many opportunities for flattery. The Celebrations successfully announced to the world the re-emergence of Iran as a full-fledged and independent power, free from the shackles of foreign imperialism that had overshadowed its modern history. The Celebrations were also political theatre, and the Shah was presented not only as the main focus for Iranian nationalism but also a major political figure of the global 1970s. The Shah had evolved from an uncertain, even timid, young monarch into a strong leader, convinced of his own destiny, becoming in the words of Ramsbotham, 'an oriental de Gaulle, but without the latter's saving grace of irony and humour'.[154]

The Shah's appreciation of his, and indeed his country's, change in fortunes can be observed in an entry in ʿAlam's diary from May 1973, when the Shah had received a request from Prince Philip to be elected to the governing committee of the Iranian Imperial Equestrian Society: 'The Shah laughed a lot. He said, "I remember in the past, if an Iranian politician was not invited to a cocktail party at the British embassy, it would have been a great misfortune for them, and now the request from the Queen's husband for membership of the equestrian society of Iran is a matter of little importance." '155 One way in which the Shah measured the progress of his country under his rule was by his treatment by other world powers. The Celebrations were part of the process by which the Shah became ever more confident in Iran's importance as a regional and global authority. 'Iran was once a great country', the Shah said, 'but fell upon difficult times. I see the celebrations as a sign to the rest of the world that Iran is again a nation to equal all others.'[156] Iran, under the Shah's leadership, would not just become a regional power, but a global force.

The Shah is often ridiculed for the Celebrations and the prevailing narrative contends that the event was a resounding failure. Some heads of state did not attend, but the fact that these decisions were taken after much high-level deliberation shows that the issue was not taken lightly. Foreign powers saw opportunities, both political and economic, in engaging with Iran, and the Shah was eager to accentuate and promote the image of Iran as a land of peace and possibilities. There has been a tendency for critics to focus on refusals by some heads of state to participate in the Celebrations as evidence that they were not taken particularly seriously. But the evidence presented here suggests that not only did foreign countries participate willingly, even eagerly, their support was fundamental in achieving the principal goals of the Celebrations.

4

The Celebrations and cultural policy

While the ceremonies at Persepolis, Pasargadae and Tehran helped to articulate aspects of the Shah's national ideology, so too did museum exhibitions, academic conferences and scholarly publications. According to the official *Ketābshenāsi-ye Jashn-e Shāhanshāhi-ye Irān* (Bibliography of the Imperial Celebrations), more than five hundred books were published, nearly four hundred of which were published in Iran.[1] Although the main ceremonies emphasized the glory of Cyrus the Great, the publications and wider events held in conjunction with the Celebrations drew attention to many different aspects of Iranian civilization and culture. The current chapter details the scholarly events organized in Iran, including the grand Congress of Iranology held during the main festivities, in order to understand how such events contributed not only to the ideologization of the monarchy but also to the regime's broader cultural and educational policies.

In an interview conducted shortly before the Celebrations, the Shah stressed that the event was a way in which Iran could draw attention to its history and culture.

> After all, apart from the great warrior-statesman Cyrus, who bequeathed to civilization its first humanitarian code, we contributed to it, also, the prophet Zoroaster, the scientist-philosopher Avicenna, the mathematician-poet Omar Khayyam, the astronomer Biruni, the alchemist Rhazes and the poets Ferdowsi, Saʿdi, Hafez and Rumi. Throughout the centuries Persia has stood as a bridge in geographical, historical and cultural exchanges between the great civilizations of Asia and Europe.[2]

Since the times of Cyrus, according to the narrative promoted by the Celebrations, Iran had contributed to the world in culture, science and humanities, and although the Achaemenids were celebrated as the epitome of Persian grandeur, they were not celebrated in isolation. After all, it was Shojāʿ al-Din Shafā, the Shah's cultural advisor, who came up with the idea for the Celebrations in 1958, and who played a key role in its execution. He was the driver of cultural policy at the Imperial Court and throughout the 1960s spearheaded a number of cultural initiatives that laid the groundwork for the programmes launched in conjunction with the Anniversary Celebrations.

In the early Pahlavi period, the regime put much effort into the construction of an official historical narrative, and the cultural organs of the state played a key role in its propagation. To illustrate this, between 1925 and 1935, the budget of the Ministry of Culture and Education increased sixfold.[3] The work constituted a nationalizing of Iran, to borrow Marashi's term.[4] During the 1960s and 1970s, Mohammad Reza Pahlavi's regime continued this tradition, investing considerable resources in culture, academia and education for the purpose of advancing its historical narrative. The cultural initiatives devised by the Imperial Court included the Imperial Cultural Council (*Shurā-ye Farhangi-ye Saltanati*), the Pahlavi Library (*Ketābkhāneh-ye Pahlavi*), and the Committee for Authoring the History of Iran (*Komiteh-ye Ta'lif-e Tārikh-e Irān*). These organizations each played a role in the construction and dissemination of educational materials, both in Iran and around the world. The cultural movement the Celebrations stimulated can thus be viewed as the culmination of a decade of work by Shafā at the Imperial Court.

Education and modernization

One pertinent example of how the Celebrations contributed to projects already underway was the plan to construct 2,500 commemorative schools to coincide with the event. This plan was rooted in the work of the Literacy Corps, which was established in 1963 as part of the Shah's White Revolution. From 8 until 19 September 1965, Iran had hosted a congress in Tehran as part of a UNESCO-sponsored campaign to eradicate illiteracy worldwide. In a speech presented at the end of the congress, written by Shafā, the Shah had said,

> The battle against the spectre of ignorance has always been one of my major concerns. The concrete results of the Unesco Congress which has just terminated its work, encourages me to launch on the occasion of the 20th anniversary of the Organization in this great forum a new appeal in order that all governments set about for a general mobilization of available human and material resources for the purpose of waging a final battle against ignorance. This crusade is one of the noblest and heaviest tasks that man has ever ventured upon for his own true emancipation, and for world peace.[5]

The congress was said by UNESCO to be 'decisive and of world importance', and it helped substantiate Iran's claim to be a leading member of the organization.[6]

While the Literacy Corps sought to eradicate illiteracy within Iran's boundaries, Shafā sought to present its work internationally by founding the Committee for the International Fight Against Illiteracy (*Komiteh-ye Peykār-e Jahāni bā Bisavādi*), which was to be chaired by the Shah, with Princess Ashraf acting as vice-chair and Shafā as general secretary.[7] The initiative played a central role in the Tehran Congress of 1965 and the subsequent presentation of Iran as a world leader in the battle against illiteracy. A film was produced by the Iranian Oil Operating Companies about the work of the Literacy Corps, which was recorded in English, French and Persian, and Shafā travelled around Europe to promote the campaign and attend film screenings.[8] He gave a speech about the 1965 congress in London arranged by the Iran Society, for instance, which was attended by hundreds who were, according to Shafā's report, so enthused that it took him an hour to answer the many questions that were put to him afterwards.[9]

To underline and draw international attention to his dedication to the cause of ending illiteracy, the Shah pledged the equivalent of a day's budget of the Iranian armed forces to the campaign and urged other nations to make a similar pledge. He also stated that Iran was prepared to extend its efforts internationally 'for the benefit of peoples everywhere'.[10] To coincide with Cyrus the Great Year, another short film was produced about the Literacy Corps, commissioned by the Committee for the International Fight against Illiteracy. It began with shots of the degradation and ignorance of rural Iran; shopkeepers managing accounts by notches on a stick and 'illiterate country folks' signing documents prepared by a scribe with a fingerprint. Then follows the creation of the Literacy Corps by the Shah, the graduation ceremony and the work of the corpsmen and women, building schools, and teaching the once-poor and ignorant to read and write. Music from Beethoven's first and ninth symphonies provided the soundtrack, chosen by its director Rāmin Gohariyān, because 'it is imbued with hope – hope that the gallant start will continue until its logical conclusion'.[11] The choice of music suggests, too, that the film was produced not only for domestic but also for foreign consumption. While the proclaimed successes of Iran's literacy campaigns helped to boost the image of Iran internationally as intellectually progressive and pioneering in educational development, the Celebrations presented opportunities to underline these credentials.

It was in this context that the establishment of 2,500 commemorative schools was announced, to mark the beginning of a 'cultural renaissance'. Building on the work of the Literacy Corps and the Committee for the International Fight Against Illiteracy, the schools would represent 'lighting 2,500 torches of knowledge'.[12] This idea originally came from ʿAbdolrezā Ansāri, who, in his role as governor of Khuzestan during the celebration for the Shah's twenty-fifth year on the throne, had encouraged people to build schools in rural areas that lacked proper educational facilities. The project was so successful that Ansāri suggested to the Executive Committee that it be replicated for the Imperial Celebrations.[13]

After deliberations with a number of officers from the Plan Organization, the Ministry of Education and the Ministry of Housing and Development, Ansāri concluded that the schools would cost around 30,000 tomans ($4,000) each to build, including the cost of desks, chairs and other teaching equipment. A special account was set up at the Bank Melli where the public could donate money to build the schools. Anyone who donated 30,000 tomans would be given the opportunity to name a school. Many schools were named after historical figures, royal family members and political personalities; one school, for example, was listed as having been funded by the students of Alborz Highschool (*dāneshāmuzān-e Dabirestān-e Alborz*) and was named 'Shojāʿ al-Din Shafā'.[14] Setting an example for others to follow, Empress Farah contributed to fifty schools, six of which were to be named after members of the royal family.[15] Names of contributors were read out on local radio stations in order to encourage more people to participate in the programme, but the majority of contributors appear to have been major businesses and government agencies.[16] According to the list published in *Keyhān*, Iran Air, Bank Melli and the Plan Organization funded several schools, and the National Iranian Oil Company funded at least ninety-six schools.[17] The project was designed to stimulate the participation of Iranian citizens in the festivities and resulted in a widespread campaign that should be seen in the context of the education programmes already underway.[18] The construction of the schools, for example, was overseen by the deputy secretary general of the Committee for the International Fight Against Illiteracy, Farhad Ganje'i.[19] The scheme ultimately led to the construction of around 2,700 schools, exceeding the original target.[20] On 27 June 1971, in the village of Sohbān, the first school, which was named after Cyrus the Great, was opened in a ceremony attended by Princess Ashraf.[21]

Cultural programmes at the court

Shafā was instrumental in several other cultural initiatives throughout the 1960s, the first being the *Shurā-ye Farhangi-ye Saltanati* (Imperial Cultural Council). The council was an executive body established to evaluate cultural projects undertaken by the Imperial Court, explore potential opportunities and to direct cultural operations concerning Iranian studies worldwide.[22] It was established by imperial decree on 5 December 1962 and consisted of thirteen eminent Iranian scholars. These included Ebrāhim Purdāvud, Sayyed Hasan Taqizādeh, Mohammad Hejāzi, 'Ali Asghar Hekmat, Parviz Nātel Khānlari, 'Ali Akbar Siyāsi, Fakhr al-Din Shādmān, Sādeq Rezāzādeh Shafaq, 'Isā Sadiq, Hoseyn 'Alā, Badi' al-Zamān Foruzānfar, Sa'id Nafisi and Shafā.[23] Six of the thirteen members were part of the original nine-man advisory council for the Celebrations, discussed in Chapter 2.

With the help of the Ministry of Foreign Affairs and Iranian embassies abroad, the council was kept au courant with all events, initiatives and publications related to Iranian studies internationally.[24] Shafā, in his role of secretary general of the council, contacted cultural centres in sixty-two countries in an effort to assure 'wide collaboration on a global scale' and to maintain 'close relations with hundreds of different scientific centres and universities which carry out research in different fields related to language, literature and Iranian civilization'.[25] This was seen as an important task because these international scientists 'often did not feel like they were contributing to a collective oeuvre', and as such the council sought to be the 'point of contact between the Iranologists, who in this way are kept up to date with the work of their colleagues'.[26] This was the first state-sponsored programme that sought to take a leading role in the development of Iranian studies both in Iran and in other countries. It ultimately contributed to the Imperial Court's objective to promote Iran internationally as progressive and committed to intellectual development.[27]

In a further effort to establish Iran as an international base for Iranian studies, the Pahlavi Library was established on 17 October 1965.[28] It was to be 'the core of all research studies' into Iranology internationally[29] and its goal was to gather all literature on Iran in one place to provide 'the vastest source of documentation on the Iranian culture and civilization, for the benefit of those who study such matters all around the world as well as in Iran itself'.³⁰ This was tangentially linked to the planning of the Imperial Celebrations. In a letter to the Central Council of the Imperial Celebrations on 16 February 1961, 'Isā Sadiq wrote that a special library for the study of Iranian history and civilization should be completed at the National Library in Tehran, to mark the occasion.³¹

The Imperial Cultural Council served as the board of trustees and its duties included approving plans for work on the library, selecting management and members of the advisory board and seeking financial backers.³² Shafā was the managing director of the library and one of his duties was to contact the cultural organizations identified by the Imperial Cultural Council.³³ The purpose of these communications was not only to investigate which manuscripts, books, documents and other materials the library needed to obtain, but also to ensure close collaboration. In a three-page letter sent to international institutions outlining the aims of the library, Shafā wrote,

> To start a close collaboration (knowing your interest in this subject as well as your being a worthy friend of the Iranian Culture) I would highly appreciate it if you would be kind enough to send me your ideas, suggestions and remarks on this subject so that we would be able to accomplish the task given to us by His Imperial Majesty the Shah's good will and generosity.³⁴

From this early stage, Shafā was keen to show that the library was an international project and that the Iranians were willing to work with their international colleagues to ensure its success. Scholars and librarians from all over the world responded enthusiastically, offering advice and cooperation. The Pahlavi Library attempted to establish a fluid exchange of knowledge, and scholars around the world were encouraged to seek support from it. Professor Felix Tauer of the Charles University in Prague, for example, offered the Pahlavi Library copies of his and other Czech books in exchange for periodicals published in Iran which were inaccessible in his country.³⁵ This shows that already in 1965, the Pahlavi Library had begun fulfilling its role as an international hub for Iranian studies.

As well as seeking to build its collection and develop strong relations with other cultural institutions, the library also arranged publications and financially supported academic conferences. Two months after the creation of the Pahlavi Library, a committee of Iranian and foreign scholars and officials was formed, called the *Komiteh-ye Ta'lif-e Tārikh-e Irān* (Committee for Authoring the History of Iran). The purpose of the committee was to compile a complete history of Iran, 'based on all the documents that the "Pahlavi Library" would reunite'.³⁶ The focus was not merely on providing a piece of scholarship but also on educating the Iranian youth in the history of their country. Members of the committee included headmasters, regional secretaries of schools, provincial educational representatives (*namāyandeh-ye āmuzesh va parvaresh*)³⁷ and the deputy director of publications of the *Sepāh-e Dānesh* (Literacy Corps)³⁸ in addition to scholars from universities across Iran.³⁹ Marashi has observed that in the formative years of the Pahlavi state, educators were tasked with constructing an official history and a special committee was established to oversee the production of books, called the *Anjoman-e Ma'āref* (Commission on Education).⁴⁰ In the late Pahlavi period, too, organizations such as the Committee for Authoring the History of Iran, although dedicated to, in the Shah's words, 'compiling a comprehensive history ... in all fairness, far from arbitrariness and partiality',[41] were tasked with producing works that complemented official narratives.

Another significant project which exemplifies this atmosphere of international cultural cooperation, initiated in and focused on Iran, in which Shafā also played a key role, was *Jahān-e Irānshenāsi* (World of Iranology), an encyclopaedia of Iranian studies programmes.[42] The initial idea for the encyclopaedia can be dated to the founding of the Imperial Cultural Council in 1962, which identified the need for such a resource.[43] Universities and cultural institutes from around the world were asked to provide details of their programmes relating to Iran which were then translated into Persian and included in the volume. The correspondence connected to this work reveals the vast network that Shafā had built up over his years in office.[44] Rouhollah Ramazani of the University of Virginia, for example, wrote a detailed letter to Shafā outlining his teaching experience and publication history. He wrote, 'I am personally honored to know of your interest in our program as it relates to Iran and would be happy to see our teaching, research and writing activities on Iran recounted in your Encyclopedia.'[45] By all accounts, academics were very forthcoming in providing information for the publication. It is a measure of the position of Shafā within the scholarly community that he was able to command such a response. He was recognized as a central figure in the cultural initiatives of the Pahlavi state and a facilitator, and scholars wrote personal notes to him requesting anything from books to conference funding.[46] With the publication of the World of Iranology and the founding of the Pahlavi Library, the Pahlavi regime sought to gain ownership of scholarship on its own history and to endorse studies of its own country.

The Second International Congress of Iranology

In October 1971, while the world's elite gathered at Persepolis for the Anniversary Celebrations, a group of scholars took part in the Second International Congress of Iranian Studies, held at the Pahlavi University in Shiraz. The First Congress had been held five years earlier in 1966, with two hundred scholars from thirty-two countries taking part.[47] Its purpose had been to gather the 'most outstanding Iranologues' of the world to 'exchange views, researches, experiences, ideas and suggestions'.[48] This had been designated as a priority by the Imperial Cultural Council two years earlier.[49] As usual at such state-organized cultural occasions, the Shah gave an inaugural address, which was followed by a speech from the minister of culture and art, Mehrdād Pahlbod. The congress took place at the Iran Bāstān Museum, was accompanied by a number of exhibitions, including one on recent archaeological discoveries at Marlik, and several receptions were held, one of which was hosted by Pahlbod himself.[50] To underscore the political significance of the event, a stamp was commissioned to commemorate the congress, depicting a find from Marlik.[51]

The participants travelled from Tehran to Isfahan and then on to Shiraz, where the conference continued at the Pahlavi University, inaugurated there with a message from

Empress Farah.⁵² The political attention this event received demonstrates the important role of Iranian studies in the regime's cultural policy. In all, 94 papers were presented at the conference in Persian, French, English, German, Russian, Italian, Arabic and Turkish, which were then collected by the Pahlavi Library in a 3,000-page volume.⁵³ At the closing of the congress, an international committee had been established by the Pahlavi Library, called the International Union of Iranologists (*Etehādi-ye Jahāni-ye Irānshenāsān*), which would direct future congresses.⁵⁴ At the meeting, a resolution (*qat'nāmeh*) was passed declaring the Pahlavi Library to be the official international centre for Iranian studies.⁵⁵

The hosting of a major international scholarly conference in Iran in conjunction with the Imperial Celebrations had long been designated a priority by the organizers. As early as 1959, Hoseyn 'Alā had informed foreign diplomats that 'according to present plans, the central point of the celebrations would now be an international archaeological congress in Iran'.⁵⁶ When 'Abdolrezā Ansāri became involved in the organization of the Celebrations in 1970, he too recognized that the principal goal of the Celebrations was to bring about 'the reawakening of the history, civilization and culture of Iran and creating awareness among the peoples of the world'.⁵⁷ Some of the ways in which this goal would be achieved included publishing books, constructing a national monument and museum, hosting exhibitions and seminars, and 'the formation of an Iranian and International Congress of Iran Scholars to be held in the city of Shiraz to examine various aspects of Iran's culture and civilisation and its influence in the world'.⁵⁸ These goals were broadly in line, too, with the cultural policies of the Pahlavi Court, and sought to contribute to the projects already discussed.

According to the official programme, scholars from thirty-eight countries attended the Second Congress of Iranology, not including Israelis, who, as discussed earlier, were officially excluded from the programme, but who did attend.⁵⁹ The list of attendees included scholars from a wide variety of academic and geographical backgrounds. Among those who attended were Felix Pareja of Spain, a Jesuit professor of Islamology and Arabic, and director of the *Instituto Hispano-Arabe de Cultura* in Madrid; the great Hungarian scholar János Harmatta, who was responsible for the decipherment of the Parthian ostraca and the papyri of Dura Euopos; and the Austrian theologian Cardinal Franz König, whose research concentrated on Iranian influence upon Judaism. Other notable attendees were Phyllis Ackerman, Persian art scholar and wife of Arthur Upham Pope, as well as Ehsān Yārshāter and Henri Corbin. Scholars were also invited from countries less widely known for their tradition of Iranian studies, such as Argentina, Brazil, Syria, Ceylon (Sri Lanka) and Indonesia. Five Japanese archaeologists were invited, including Namio Egami from the University of Tokyo, who had led expeditions to Iran during the 1950s and 1960s. Iran was represented by no fewer than seventy scholars, including 'Isā Sadiq, 'Abdolhoseyn Zarrinkub, Iraj Afshār and Sādeq Kiyā.⁶⁰

There is little evidence that scholars were pressured into attending the event, and it appears as though there was a general eagerness to take part. Invited scholars were established academics in their fields with notable publications and considerable influence. The British academic delegation, for instance, consisted of Richard Barnett of the British Museum; John Boyle of Manchester University; Hubert Darke and

Ilya Gershevitch of Cambridge University; the former keeper of Oriental antiquities at the British Museum Basil Gray; archaeologist with the British Institute of Persian Studies John Hansman; Bernard Lewis of the School of Oriental and Asian Studies in London; the historian Laurence Lockhart; George Morrison of Oxford University; the retired former professor of the Pahlavi University in Shiraz Reverend Norman Sharp; director of the British Institute of Persian Studies David Stronach; and Laurence Elwell-Sutton of Edinburgh University. In examples of the enthusiasm of many academics for the conference, Elwell-Sutton took the opportunity to travel to Iran with his wife and later wrote a favourable account of his experience,[61] and Bernard Lewis declared himself 'delighted to receive an invitation'.[62] As mentioned in the previous chapter, it was common knowledge at the time that the loan of the Cyrus Cylinder was facilitated by Richard Barnett's eagerness to be invited to the Celebrations.[63]

Another scholar who was thrilled to be invited was Norman Sharp, who arrived in Iran in 1924 as an Anglican missionary and subsequently founded churches in Yazd (1928), Shiraz (1938), Qalat (1944) and Bushehr (1944).[64] Sharp was well respected as an academic as well as a minister of the church. In 1954, he was appointed to a lectureship in Old Persian at the University of Shiraz.[65] He designed the University arms and their replacement when it changed names in 1962 to become the Pahlavi University, and also the academic robes for a visit to the University by the Shah.[66] He had already contributed to the Celebrations with his book *The Inscriptions in Old Cuneiform of the Achaemenian Emperors*, which was published in 1966, as well as a short booklet in Persian titled *Theories about Ancient Persian Inscriptions*.[67] He had earlier translated three of the works of 'Ali Sāmi into English, namely *Pasargadae: The Oldest Imperial Capital of Iran*, *Persepolis* and *Shiraz*. Respect for him in Iran was such that he was asked in 1978 by the Society for the Protection of National Monuments to translate any work of his choice from Persian into English, in light of 'his archaeological attainments and translations during his long residence in Iran'.[68] Writing in the preamble to this volume, Hushang Nahāvandi declared himself 'sincerely appreciative of the efforts and services of this Iranologist and friend of Iran, for whom the Divine favour is sought'.[69]

Sharp also contributed to the Celebrations by preparing an inscription in Old Persian cuneiform on a stone tablet, sourced from the original quarry which had produced the marble for the palaces of Cyrus near Sivand, to be displayed in the Shiraz Church. The inscription read, 'God chose Cyrus, and made him king in this earth. May this land of Cyrus be always happy! Honoured be the good name of Cyrus!'[70] In 1970, however, Sharp had retired back to the United Kingdom and despite his contributions to the occasion he felt that it would 'be a case of out of sight out of mind'.[71] By September 1971, Sharp still had not received his invitation and wrote to his friend Paul Gotch, 'I won't get an invitation, for there are so many the Government must ask, and there can't be room for the many who would give anything to be present'.[72] His excitement was palpable in his next letter on 9 October, when he wrote: 'Almost at the last moment the Persian Government have included me among their guests, and with a group of Iranologists, as they are called, I fly direct to Shiraz from Paris on October 11th in a special Iranair plane'.[73]

There were many reasons why scholars participated. Some may have identified with the Shah's ideology; some may have merely been happy to take advantage of an expenses-paid trip to Iran. Others may have recognized the value of the regime's efforts to support scholars engaged in Iranian studies, and for this reason were pleased to be involved. In his report of the event, Elwell-Sutton makes a special reference to the scholar Gustave von Grunebaum, who, although was suffering from the illness that would shortly take his life, 'was conveyed from one event to another in a wheel-chair'.[74] The Dutch scholar Hanna Kohlbrugge apparently left her dying sister's bedside to attend what she considered to be a hugely significant event in the history of Iran.[75]

There were, however, some notable absentees, such as Ann Lambton, who had fallen out with the Shah over his White Revolution after drawing attention to the shortcomings of his reforms.[76] The Shah did not appreciate these criticisms.[77] Robert Zaehner at Oxford University also rejected his invitation. He was close to Lambton, having worked with her during the Second World War and in the early 1950s, during the oil nationalization crisis, so it is possible that he followed her lead. Another prominent British figure who declined to attend was Peter Avery. His was apparently a rejection of the ideology behind the Celebrations. Speaking nearly fifteen years after the event, he said,

> A lot of this flew very much in the face of Islamic tradition as well as in the face of historical accuracy. It was a party to which I was invited, but which I did not go to because I couldn't believe that it would be correct for anybody who thought of himself as a historian of Iran to support a so unhistorically, unauthentic event, in terms of history ... And for those of us who did know what it was about did, in fact, know who Cyrus was and what the history was and, of course, realized that it was phoney history.[78]

There may have been other scholars who held such opinions at the time, but there were perhaps few with the reputation to press the point.

It should be noted that although Peter Avery chose not to attend the event, he did contribute an article to UNESCO's special publication and alluded to one of the Celebrations' ideological principles that stressed cultural integrity in the face of foreign incursion. In the article titled 'Iran: Cultural Crossroads for 2,500 Years', he wrote:

> Seekers of the solutions to the world's problems could have no more generous and perfect hosts than the Iranians, whose courtesy is rightly proverbial and has been almost since time began; but whose long experience as guardians of civilization against the encroachment of desert sands, of rapacious enemies, of chaos and disorderliness makes them more than generous hosts.[79]

In this quotation, Avery is careful not to endorse the philosophy behind the event, but does stress the idea of cultural continuity through many centuries of adversity and even the most zealous of Pahlavi ideologues would have been pleased with the line 'guardians of civilization'.[80] Notwithstanding Avery's purported opposition to the event, the fact that he contributed with this publication, illustrates that there was so much happening in terms of publications, exhibitions, seminars and conferences, not to mention the main ceremonies in Iran, that there were few scholars who did not take advantage of the opportunities the Celebrations presented.

A number of scholars from other countries, too, declined their invitations. In Italy, for instance, three of the ten invited scholars turned down the request to attend. Enrico Cerulli, a scholar and diplomat who had previously served as Italian ambassador in Tehran, declined due to old age and work commitments at the Accademia dei Lincei, where he served as president. Giuseppe Tucci, the famous Italian archaeologist and adventurer, who headed the Italian committee for the Celebrations, personally informed Shafā that he could not attend. Finally, Gianroberto Scarcia declined because of work commitments at the University of Venice where he taught.[81] There is no indication that hostility to the regime played a part in any of these rejections and indeed, Italian scholars made a significant contribution to the Celebrations in other ways. The light and sound show at Persepolis, for instance, was developed under the supervision of Giuseppe Tucci in his role as president of the Istituto Italiano per il Medio ed Estremo Oriente (IsMEO).[82]

The Asia Institute, meanwhile, which had been founded in 1928 by Arthur Upham Pope, and had been re-established as part of the Pahlavi University in Shiraz in 1966, also contributed.[83] Richard Frye, who took over as head of the institute following Pope's death in 1969, bemoaned in 1971 that the institute's budget had been plundered to fund the event and that it was 'fighting for rials now, not toumans ... Everyone is working on the 2500 celebrations and it is like a sickness'.[84] Frye worked alongside his Iranian colleagues to organize the Congress of Iranology and was also expected to help in other ways, such as by finding translators for dignitaries and media personalities.[85] Organizations such as the Asia Institute relied on the support of the Iranian government, financially and logistically, therefore, their support in the Celebrations was expected.

The Western Iranologists who accepted their invitations were flown from Paris to Iran on 11 October by Aer Lingus, the Irish airline, which, according to Donald Wilber, who was present as part of the American delegation, 'was hired in the scramble to find enough planes for all of the passengers'.[86] Despite the 'unsettling discovery' that the flight crew had never actually flown to the Middle East before, the flight arrived safely in Shiraz, after a short stop in Rome to pick up more scholars.[87] The scholars were put up in university accommodation and hotels, rather than the comparatively sumptuous tent city which was reserved for political representatives. Their programme began on 12 October, with the Shah's speech to the tomb of Cyrus the Great, which effectively served to open the Celebrations. Noteworthy here is that the dignitaries staying at the tent city were not invited to this particular event, but the foreign academics were, alongside their Iranian colleagues. Indeed, as noted in Chapter 2, they were given a prominent position in the order of precedence.[88]

The Congress of Iranology began the next day, on 13 October, with the national anthem, followed by a message from the Shah, echoing his speech to the 1966 congress, delivered by Minister of Court Asadollāh 'Alam.[89] It read:

> The worthiest of our armies have, over the millennia, been those men and women who have kept the torch of knowledge and culture alight in the face of the storms of time and passed it on to posterity with growing brilliance. True victory to us

lies in the recognition of this truth, for geographical and military ascendancy is inevitably followed by regression and decline, whereas intellectual and spiritual values never perish in the face of any force.[90]

The speech claimed that the successes of Iran's past were due to the durability of its cultural achievements, rather than its military might. It also made clear the 'exceptional significance' of the congress, since 'the Anniversary Celebration is, above all, the celebration of Iranian history, civilization and culture'. For this reason, it was 'only natural that the eminent scholars who have devoted their lives to research on the various aspects of our culture and history take a special place in this Celebration and in the hearts of the Iranian people'.[91] Following the speech by 'Alam, Shafā read out the programme, after which the Iranologists were invited to offer their best wishes for the occasion.[92] The theme of the conference was 'The Continuity of Iranian Civilization and Culture' and in the following days twenty-five papers were scheduled to be delivered on a wide variety of subjects, although papers focusing on the Achaemenid period received special attention. The whole event took place in the Pahlavi Auditorium of the Pahlavi University.[93]

The first delegate to address the congress was the Iranian scholar and vice chancellor of Tehran University, Sayyed Hoseyn Nasr, followed by Henri Corbin who discussed Islamic philosophy, and H. S. Nyberg who presented a paper titled 'History and Religion under Cyrus'.[94] David Stronach presented 'Median and Achaemenid Architecture', George Cameron devoted his paper 'Cyrus and Babylonia' to an analysis of Herodotus's account of Cyrus's campaign of Babylon, and Richard Frye presented a paper titled 'Continuity of Iranian History'.[95] An additional half-day was added after the congress' formal closing, in order to accommodate additional papers. There was also a book display exhibiting a number of titles that were published to commemorate the Celebrations.[96]

The gathering was productive in the sense that it gave scholars with expertise on varied subjects and from different countries the opportunity to engage with one another. On one occasion during some free time, for example, David Stronach arranged for a group of scholars to visit a nearby archaeological site. John Hansman of the British Institute of Persian Studies had recently been excavating at Maliyān, which lay on the fertile plain of Bayzā and which he proposed to be the site of the ancient city of Anshan.[97] Stopped at road blocks, the group of scholars, which included Stronach, Hansman, Roman Ghirshman, Ilya Gershevitch and Richard Frye, claimed to security forces that they were a group of waiters on their way to Persepolis.[98] They were allowed to pass and investigated the site together. Maliyān is now the accepted site for the city of Anshan, birthplace of Cyrus the Great.

Besides the scholarly conference, the Iranologists took part in an elaborate programme of activities. In the late afternoon of 12 October, following the ceremony at Pasargadae, the Iranian and international scholars, together with members of the news media, had an audience with the Shah and Empress Farah during an afternoon tea and cocktail reception at Bāgh-e Eram in Shiraz. A reporter for the *New York Times* observed that 'One by one Iranologists from abroad approached the Shah, offering him scrolls and pictures as mementos of the 2,500th anniversary of the Persian Empire.

He greeted each as personally as if he were in a private salon, switching easily from French to German and Persian to English.'[99] After this reception, the Iranologists were taken to Persepolis, where they watched a *son et lumière* performance, the same performance the heads of state would later observe.[100] The Iranian hosts' attention to detail on this occasion was remembered fondly by Elwell-Sutton, who wrote, 'Further reminders here of the Iranian reputation for imaginative hospitality – not only the standard welcoming refreshment, but also blankets to ward off the chilly night air, and miniature bottles of brandy and whisky to keep by one in case the effects of earlier potations should wear off too soon.'[101]

Other events included a 'splendid banquet' hosted by the governor general of Fars, which featured a display of traditional dancing.[102] Following the parade at Persepolis, the Iranologists were served another fine dinner at the Darius Hotel at which, 'in contrast to the delicious Persian fare provided on other occasions, the guests were confronted with a magnificent spread in the best French style'. Elwell-Sutton speculated that these may have been leftovers from the gala dinner of the previous evening, however, he concluded, 'there were no peacocks'.[103] The Iranologists' schedule also took them to Tehran along with the rest of the guests on 16 October. On 18 October, they were received by the Shah at Saʿdābād Palace, where the venerable French scholar Roman Ghirshman expressed his gratitude to the Shah on behalf of the Iranologists.[104] For those who were still in Iran, a day trip by plane to Isfahan was arranged on 19 October, which included another impressive meal at the Shāh ʿAbbās Hotel. On the following day, the date of departure, each Iranologist was presented with a bronze commemorative medal.[105]

It is clear that the Iranologists enjoyed a level of prestige during the Celebrations. Like the politicians staying at the tent city, the scholars were given the opportunity to network and form new relationships on Iranian turf, which cast the Iranians in the role of facilitators, a role they relished in the academic as well as political arena. The attendance of scholars at the Celebrations allowed for such engagement, while also underlining Iran's new position as the international centre for Iranian studies and legitimizing the central points of the Pahlavi national ideology expressed at the Anniversary Celebrations. The media in Iran boasted that the most eminent scholars of the world had taken part in the congress, who between them were said to have published over 4,000 books and articles.[106]

Following the congress in Shiraz, a committee was established to publish the papers that had been presented. In 1972, five members of this committee – Henri Corbin, Roman Ghirshman, Geo Widengren, Giuseppe Tucci and Jacques Duchesne-Guillemin – met to discuss the planned publication. It was decided that the youngest of the group, *le plus petit des cinq grands*, Duchesne-Guillemin, would head the project.[107] The resulting *Acta Iranica* book series, published by the Pahlavi Library and Brill, the first volume of which was titled *Hommage universel: actes du congrès de Shiraz 1971, et autres études rédigées à l'occasion du 2500e anniversaire de la fondation de l'empire perse*, was one of the most important publications of the Celebrations. In addition to papers presented at the congress, additional chapters were published by such figures as British historian Arnold Toynbee, former prime minister of Israel David Ben-Gurion, Arthur Upham Pope and British scholar John Hinnells.[108] The work was hailed by *Keyhān* as 'the greatest publication on Iranian studies in the world' and 'the primary publication of the Pahlavi Library'.[109] Hundreds more books were published in Iran and abroad to coincide with the Celebrations, many of which were directly commissioned by the Central Council, regional committees or universities.

Publications in Iran

During the preparations for the 2500th Anniversary Celebrations, a special subcommittee was established as part of the Central Council. It was called the Historical Committee of the Imperial Celebrations (*Komisiyon-e Motāle ʿāt-e Tārikhi-ye Jashn-e Shāhanshāhi-ye Irān*) and was headed by Khān-bābā Bayāni, a professor of history at the University of Tehran. Its purpose was to direct the cultural events that took place as part of the commemoration, in a manner 'worthy of the traditions of the past'.[110] By July 1966, the Historical Committee had met 309 times,[111] and by September 1970, it had met 886 times, an average of almost three times a week over the four-year period.[112] Even when the Anniversary Celebrations were repeatedly delayed throughout the 1960s and their future was uncertain, the Historical Committee kept meeting and authorizing publications to coincide with the event.

The Historical Committee was naturally connected to similar organizations, such as the Committee for Authoring the History of Iran, and its members included representatives from the Ministry of Education.[113] This is important to note, since one purpose of the publications, as with the Committee for Authoring the History of Iran, was to educate the Iranian youth and the general public on the history of Iran, or rather the Pahlavi version of history.[114] The 500 titles published for the Celebrations covered a broad range of topics and included books that one imagines might have been published anyway, such as annual reviews of the work of various sectors, as well as titles that were quite clearly published in order to contribute to the promotion of the Celebrations' ideological message.

The main commissioners of books for the Anniversary Celebrations were the Central Council and its cultural subcommittee, the Cultural Committee of the 2500th Anniversary Celebrations of Imperial Iran (*Komiteh-ye Farhangi-ye Jashn-e Dohezār o Pānsadomin Sāl-e Shāhanshāhi-ye Irān*). They published at least sixty-eight books and pamphlets in Persian and included works that sought to trumpet the underpinning philosophy of the Celebrations, such as Nāser al-Din Shāh Hoseyni's *The Connection Between the Shah and the Nation of Iran*, Eqbāl Yaghmā'i's *Why We Love the King and the Monarchy*, and ʿAbbās Parviz's *Iranian Uprising on the Way to the Revival and Glory of Iran*.[115] Other works included editions of the *Shāhnāmeh*, works by Hafez and Saʿdi, and scholarly works on history, which stressed cultural, political and religious continuity. The Central Council also translated works into foreign languages, including Shirin Bayāni's *Cyrus the Great* and *Darius the Great*, ʿAbbās Parviz's *The Society and Civilization of the Parthians* and *The Society and Civilization of the Sasanians*, and Malekzādeh Bayāni's *The Fine Arts of Iran in the Sasanian Period*. The authors were directly commissioned by the Central Council to produce the works, and they were printed in English, Persian, Russian, Spanish and French.[116]

Publications normally began with a dedication to the auspicious event. This is the case in, for example, *12 Articles: On the Occasion of the Celebrations of the 2500th Anniversary of the Founding of Imperial Iran*, published by the college of literature and foreign languages.[117] The author introduces the work with the following words: 'Divine exaltation and the heavens instilled in the great King of Kings of Iran Āryāmehr, with the wisdom and creativity to hold the Celebrations of the 2500th Anniversary of the Founding of Imperial Iran.' According to the author, the stated purpose of the Celebrations was to 'draw attention to Iran's contribution to the world' in the fields of literature and human culture. 'The greatness of this wonderful and creative initiative cannot yet be understood', the text continues, '[but] imagine in the coming centuries, how much spiritual pleasure the Iranian children will get in learning of such an event in history, and how proud they will be.' The introduction ends with a poem about the Shah, which reads:

> Artist king (*shāhanshāh-e honarvar*), Āryāmehr
> Lord of justice, Āryāmehr
> Read the stories of times past
> See the situation of other shahs
> From the time of Cyrus to Reza Shah
> There has never been such wise kingship
> Shāhanshāh, that with divine grace
> Does not follow any path, but the path of benevolence.
> Able to bestow strength upon his army
> To maintain calm in his country.

The poem continues in this vein for another page, stressing both the important role the monarchy has played in the annals of Iranian history, and the exceptionalism of the current shah.

During the preparations for the Celebrations, regional committees were set up, which commissioned publications of their own. These regional committees often published only one or two works, which were usually either general information booklets on the Celebrations, or regional histories in relation to either Ancient Iran or the Pahlavis. These included titles such as *The Contribution of the People of Khorasan to the Survival of Imperial Iran*, Birām Qalij Āqcheh-li's *The Face of Gonbad Qābus in the Period of the Glorious Pahlavi Dynasty*, and Mohammad Ali Tāheriyā's *6,000-Year-Old Damghan*.[118] One exception was the East Azerbaijan Committee, which published nearly twenty works, not including works published by the University of Tabriz, which also established a special committee. Works in East Azerbaijan were particularly lavish in their praise of the Shah and the historical narrative promoted by the Pahlavi regime. They included Hoseyn Ahmadipur's *The Ancient History and the Glorious Past of Imperial Iran, from the Perspective of Shāhanshāh Āryāmehr, Azerbaijan During the Period of Construction and Revolution* and *The Role of Azerbaijan in the 2500-Year History of Imperial Iran*.[119] Ahmadipur also wrote *The Heart That Beats for the People and the Nation*, which was an eloquent endorsement of the Shah.[120] The first chapter of the work, titled 'Parcham-e enqelāb bar dush-e yek pādeshāh' (The flag of the revolution on the shoulders of a king), sets the tone of the work, which places the Shah at the centre of the achievements of the past thirty years of his reign.

Some of the principal academic publications for the Celebrations in Iran were arranged in part by members of the aforementioned cultural organizations. Sa'id Nafisi, a former professor of Persian literature who served on the Historical Council, contributed to the University of Tehran's *Atlas-e Tārikhi-ye Irān* (Historical Atlas of Iran).[121] The project began when the Celebrations were first announced and accelerated to completion when the exact date for the occasion was confirmed.[122] Other universities in Iran also contributed to the Celebrations through publications. The University of Tabriz, for example, had a committee of professors that arranged publications. Some of these were translated into other languages, such as *Le Rôle de l'Azerbaïdjan au cours de XXV siècles d'histoire de l'empire d'Iran*, which was donated to the committee in 1965 and translated to coincide with the Celebrations in 1971.[123] Other Persian language contributions from universities included:

- *Folk Culture or Interpreting Persian Idioms and Proverbs*, University of Isfahan.
- *The Textile Industry of Iran from Ancient Times to Today*, Tehran Polytechnic University.
- *Education in Iran from the Ancient Era to Today*, Jondishapur University, Ahvaz.
- *Rituals in Ferdowsi's Shāhnāmeh*, University of Tabriz.
- *The Capital Cities of Achaemenid Iran (Shush and Ecbatana)*, Pahlavi University, Shiraz.
- *Articles on Town and City Planning*, National University of Iran, Tehran.
- *Khorasan and Imperial Iran*, University of Mashhad.

Some universities published multiple works. The Pahlavi University, for instance, published at least seven books and universities also had their own committees that arranged publications to coincide with the Celebrations. Universities also held exhibitions, such as the University of Tehran's library, which held a display of manuscripts.[124]

In addition to original works, there were also translations of major Western texts. For instance, two of the works of Arthur Christensen were translated: *Keyāniān* (The Kayanids) and *Kārnāmeh-ye Shāhān dar Revāyāt-e Irān-e Bāstān* (Record of the Kings in the Tradition of Ancient Iran). Christensen was, as previously mentioned, frequently cited by the regime in official literature. He was quoted by Shafa at length in one of the official guides to the Celebrations, in a passage introduced as 'one of the best definitions of the moral significance of the monarchy in Iran'.[125] The same book reproduces a lengthy (five-page) passage from Rene Grousset, which was said to have 'strikingly reflected all of the factors that serve as the ideological basis' of the Celebrations. Quoting such eminent Western scholars added a certain authenticity to the Pahlavi regime's ideological messages. The works of other prominent Western scholars were also translated,[126] as were some classical texts; no fewer than three works of Xenophon appeared, for instance.

The Central Council had some control over what was published, and commissioned authors were expected to alter their texts in line with requests from the Central

Council. One unfortunate example was a book written by Sylvia Matheson, titled *Treasures of 25 Centuries*. Having worked on the manuscript for some months, making 'every change and addition [the Central Council] recommended', and having received the informal approval of the Council, Matheson became concerned at the hesitancy of the authorities to agree formally to the project. Although the work was to be published by a British publisher, the contract depended on the Council agreeing to purchase a certain quantity. In a letter to the Council, dated 23 April 1970, Matheson appealed to the Iranians' 'sense of justice', and sought a 'speedy and satisfactory conclusion', adding that 'naturally I shall be happy to make any further modification or change to the manuscript that might be required'.[127] In response to the letter, Matheson was informed that the Council no longer intended to support the publication of her work. 'Abdolrezā Ansārī informed Matheson that the reason for the rejection was 'by way of retaliation for the Iranian Government's disapproval of the fairly recently published Cambridge History of Iran'.[128] Whether this was the genuine reason or not – the British embassy in Tehran thought it unlikely – this episode illustrates that the Central Council had some degree of control over the content of commemorative publications.

In light of this, it is perhaps unsurprising that many of published works largely conformed to official narratives. One important example was *Persia: Immortal Kingdom*, which was the most expensive book directly funded by the Central Council at 47,616,720 rials ($635,000).[129] In addition to English, it was also published in Russian, Spanish and French editions and included three chapters on ancient, medieval and modern Iranian history. Roman Ghirshman, who was one of the leading scholars of his generation, authored the first chapter on Ancient Iran. His characterization of Cyrus the Great largely follows the Pahlavi reading of history:

> Thus died Cyrus the Great, who conceived Iran as a state, and turned that concept into a reality ... Few kings have left so noble a reputation as Cyrus. A great captain and leader of men, he was generous and benevolent. He had no thought of forcing conquered countries into a single mould, and had the wisdom to leave unchanged the institutions of each kingdom he attached to the Persian Crown.[130]

The text of the Cyrus Cylinder, he argues, 'was a true reflection of his aim of bringing peace to mankind'. The Celebrations carried the message that the Achaemenids had constructed a monarchical ideology based on moral, social and economic values, an argument that was strengthened by works such as Ghirshman's, which glorified the early Achaemenid kings. Since the middle of the 19th century, one key aspect of the romantic nationalist discourse was to discover the 'real' Iran, as it existed in ancient times, before it was contaminated by foreign influence.

The other sections of the book, too, present a glorified image of Iranian history. When discussing Nāder Shāh's invasion of Delhi, for example, Vladimir Minorsky notes that 'rioting led to the death of some 3,000 Persian soldiers', after which Nāder Shāh 'ordered reprisals'. Minorsky then praises Nāder Shāh for his command over his troops, for 'when he called a halt to the killing and looting, his command was instantly obeyed'. Minorsky quotes 'Abdolkarim Kashmiri that Nāder Shāh's command of his troops on this occasion was 'one of the most wonderful things in the world'.[131] This was one of the most brutal episodes in the history of Nāder Shāh and while Minorsky notes the Persian deaths (which more likely numbered hundreds rather than thousands), he fails to mention, even in passing, the fact that Nāder's obedient troops had slaughtered between 20,000 and 30,000 Indians before he called for order.[132] This whitewashing of history perhaps reflects Nāder Shāh's status under the Pahlavis.[133] In 1959, the Shah ordered that Nāder Shāh's remains be exhumed and placed in a new tomb,[134] and to mark the Shah's coronation in 1967 the Malek Library in Tehran published a new edition of the *Zafar Nāmeh* (Book of Conquests).[135] Such selective historiography also conforms to the general narrative of the Iranian kings that the Celebrations promoted; they were thoughtful and valiant, rather than violent and ruthless.

Perhaps unsurprisingly, Ramesh Sanghvi's chapter on the modern period is a curious amalgam of exaggeration and misinformation. Of Mosaddeq, Sanghvi observes that he and his supporters 'wanted only to protect and preserve the economic and social privileges accruing to themselves from the old system of land tenure ... his hatred of Reza Shah stemmed from the fact that the new monarch symbolised the future of modern Iran. In fact, he went to the extent of stating that Reza Shah's policy of modernisation was equivalent to treason'.[136] According to Sanghvi, the Shah was accused of being a communist, to which he responded, perhaps as a nod to the Russian edition, that 'if his progressive social policies were to be thought of as communism, he was willing to be considered a communist'.[137] Sanghvi makes little mention of oil, but rather characterizes the period as a clash over the Shah's policies of modernization and land redistribution.

> The clash between the Shah and Mossadeq began with the Shah's decision to hand over Crown lands to the government for distribution among the landless peasants. It intensified with the Shah's insistence on a planned economy ... When he realised that the Shah was unlikely to give in, he determined to stage a coup d'état, with a view to overthrowing the Pahlavi dynasty.[138]

Sanghvi repeatedly states that Mosaddeq sought the overthrow of the Pahlavi regime, but, in reference to the events of August 1953, asserts that the Shah defeated Mosaddeq 'with the people's backing'.[139] Given that the first two chapters of this work were written by serious historians, Sanghvi was perhaps a surprising choice to cover the modern period. However, although not a historian per se, Sanghvi had established himself as one of the Shah's more diligent literary cheerleaders in recent years and his chapter in *Immortal Kingdom* was his fourth work published on the Shah in just four years.[140]

The second most expensive book funded by the Central Council was a reproduction of the *Shāhnāmeh-ye Bāysonghori*, a manuscript from the 15th century preserved in the Imperial Library in Tehran, copies of which were handed out as gifts to guests. They were produced at a cost to the Central Council of 10,448,960 rials ($140,000), nearly half of which was reimbursed by the Imperial Organization for Social Services.[141] The plans to reproduce the 'most exquisite *Shāhnāmeh* in the world' for the Celebrations had been announced as early as July 1959, but despite the obvious intention to produce a work of exceptional value, the quality of reproduction has been criticized by art historians.[142] At least fourteen other books were published dealing with aspects of the *Shāhnāmeh*, with titles such as *The Shah and the Army According to Ferdowsi's Shāhnāmeh*, *The Great National Epics: Shāhnāmeh, the World's Greatest Masterpiece* and *Women of the Shāhnāmeh*.[143] Ali Ansari has commented that the *Shāhnāmeh* had 'not been invited to the celebrations',[144] which is correct to a degree – there was certainly no mention of the *Shāhnāmeh* in the principal ceremonies – however, the fact that so much money was spent on the *Shāhnāmeh-ye Bāysonghori* and that other works on the *Shāhnāmeh* were published, indicates that it was not entirely forgotten in the accompanying literature.

***

While the ceremonial aspects of the Anniversary Celebrations were concluded within three days, the cultural aspects of the event were longer lasting. As this chapter has shown, the Celebrations were part of a concerted effort on behalf of the Pahlavi regime to improve education and scholarship in Iran. Iran did not merely seek to be a partner to the Iranologists of the world, but it sought to be a leader. During the First International Congress of Iranology in 1966, for example, each panel of specialists was purposefully chaired by an Iranian scholar.[145] Through these events Iran was eager to show that it could be the central hub of Iranian studies worldwide, producing academics who could work alongside their international counterparts. When Richard Frye spoke to the Shah about the fourth volume of the *Cambridge History of Iran*, for instance, the Shah expressed his delight that there were Iranian contributors, unlike in previous editions which were dominated by non-Iranian scholars.[146]

This was an effort that began before the Celebrations and continued afterwards. Another International Congress of Iranology was held in Tehran in September 1972 and each year thereafter, and many other conferences took place in the years that followed. The production of books to commemorate special occasions in Iran was also a tradition that began before the Celebrations and continued after. On the occasion of the fiftieth anniversary of the coronation of Reza Shah in 1976, the Pahlavi Commemorative Reprint Series was launched, comprising fifty titles in sixty-three volumes of rare and important books on various aspects of Iranian culture and history, some of which had been out of print for centuries. Another ninety books were published for this commemoration, including Reza Shah's *Safarnāmeh-ye Māzandarān* (Mazandaran Travelogue), which 'Alam noted sold particularly well.[147] The publication of works to commemorate such national events had become an important means through which the state could project its particular understanding of history onto the Iranian public and contribute to the ideologization of the monarchy that was at the heart of Pahlavism.

Iran's impressive economic development throughout the 1960s and 1970s was a sign that the Shah's policies were achieving success, but the Shah sought to improve Iran's standing in the world and consolidate power not only through economic growth but also through culture and academia. By making Iran the nodal point of Iranian studies around the world, by ensuring that international conferences were held in Iran, that Iranian scholars participated in major scholarly events, by arranging publications and organizing exhibitions at museums around the world, the Shah's regime was indicating to a domestic and global audience that Iran was now a major power that no longer needed to rely on foreign expertise to lead the research on its own history. Programmes such as the Imperial Cultural Council, the Pahlavi Library and ultimately the cultural events held as part of the Anniversary Celebrations, articulated this change.

Throughout the 1960s and 1970s, the Pahlavi regime used a wide variety of means to promote knowledge of Iranian culture and civilization domestically and abroad. This had a very clear political purpose, as the regime sought to promote the central themes of the Pahlavi ideology, based on the strength of the monarchical institution and the continuity and uniqueness of Iranian culture over many centuries. This effort constituted a cultural movement that encouraged the participation of academics both international and domestic. The success of this enterprise was facilitated by Shojā' al-Din Shafā, who used his position as the Shah's cultural counsellor to build up a vast network of contacts around the world, which included individuals and institutions. While some of the commemorative events of the Celebrations were transient, the cultural activities were extensive and had long-term benefits. The primary purpose of such work was to bolster the ideological fabric of the Pahlavi state, but in many instances, they also served a genuine scholarly purpose, notably the *Acta Iranica* series, developing understanding of Iranian culture and civilization, not just domestically, but internationally too. The extent to which these efforts were replicated internationally and the success of this endeavour will be explored in the following chapter.

5

International cultural activity

While Iran was eager during the Celebrations to stress its role as the international centre of Iranian studies, other countries also contributed with their own cultural activities. Culture can play an important soft power role in international relations and the organizers of the Celebrations encouraged states around the world to express their friendship with Iran through cultural activities. Concurrently with the Celebrations, exhibitions were held in museums around the world dedicated to aspects of Iranian civilization. According to published figures, 143 exhibitions, 326 congresses, seminars and other academic proceedings were held, and 131 books on various aspects of Iranian civilization and culture published.[1] Over forty committees were established internationally, typically chaired by the head of state of the country. These committees were called 'Cyrus the Great Committees', and their purpose was to ensure that each country developed a significant programme of events, and to coordinate with the Central Council in Iran. One of the reasons Iran encouraged such events was, as *Keyhān* reported at the time, 'to make Iran better known around the world'.[2] To maximize the soft power exerted through these events, many were designed to feed into the principal theme of the Celebrations, which stressed over 2,500 years of Iranian cultural integrity in the face of multiple foreign incursions and to demonstrate awareness of Iran's state ideology as well as an appreciation of Iranian culture.

Previous chapters have shown that UNESCO played a part in the initial conception of the Imperial Celebrations and remained a supporter of the event throughout. Shojāʻ al-Din Shafā, in his role as cultural counsellor to the Imperial Court, was able to build up a vast international network of institutions and individuals engaged in Iranian studies, and he was duly appointed the head of a separate subcommittee directing international operations. Iranian engagement with established cultural institutions from around the world served to strengthen the Shah's internationalist policies, which were at the centre of the Celebrations. By placing Iran within a global cultural and historical context, and by ensuring cooperation with major global institutions, Iran was asserting its position as a significant part of the international community, not merely an economic power but also civilized and appreciative of Western intellectual tradition. The sheer scale of international interest in the Celebrations confirmed the Shah's growing international prestige. In 1959, in response to Iranian encouragement for events to be held in other countries for the Celebrations, one British diplomat had written that 'the Iranians seemed to be in danger of over-estimating the general interest in foreign countries in a rather esoteric anniversary'.[3] By 1971, there was huge international interest in the Celebrations and Iranian history, stimulated by, as this chapter will show, the Iranians, foreign governments and individual cultural institutions.

Exhibitions, conferences and international committees

The Pahlavi regime was keenly aware of the usefulness of culture to strengthen bilateral relations and create awareness of Iran worldwide. At the opening of an exhibition titled *Seven Thousand Years of Art in Iran* in Washington in 1965, the Shah said, 'This exhibition is undoubtedly the best cultural ambassador we have ever sent to our North American friends. This messenger of culture, I am sure, will be instrumental in establishing spiritual understanding between our two nations and in bringing us closer together.'[4] Other states were also aware of the good publicity that these events could bring. For example, in 1961, the US State Department recommended that Mrs Kennedy should fly to Paris to see the same exhibition, arguing that the publicity generated 'would be highly favourable to us in Iran, whose orientation and destiny are of great importance to us, and in the entire Arab world, especially if the trip were presented solely in the context of Mrs Kennedy's interest in art and history, and not of the cold war'.[5] The exhibition had, incidentally, been organized in conjunction with the 2500th Anniversary Celebrations, which were at this point planned for 1961. In the accompanying volume, President Charles de Gaulle declared France 'proud' to arrange this 'human and national testimonial' in the year of the planned festivities.[6] There was some discussion about dedicating a similar exhibition in the Netherlands to the Celebrations in 1962, but the Dutch organizers felt that this would be problematic, since it began to emerge around this time that the Celebrations would be postponed.[7] Conversely, in Britain, an exhibition on the *Turkomen of Iran* in 1971–72 was listed by the British committee as being organized as part of their contribution to the Celebrations, even though it had nothing whatsoever to do with the festivities.[8] There was clearly considerable political capital to be gained in arranging these types of cultural activities and the Celebrations presented many opportunities.

The planning of cultural events thus became the principal way in which foreign countries contributed to the Celebrations. From very early on, Shojaʿ al-Din Shafa was working with cultural institutes worldwide, promoting the Celebrations and encouraging them to take part. Even in the long periods of uncertainty during the 1960s when there was no fixed plan for the Celebrations, Shafa was promoting them around the world as an opportunity to develop understanding of Iranian culture. On 19 June 1964, for example, Shafa attended a dinner in his honour in Rome, at which Professor Giuseppe Tucci expressed his appreciation for Shafa and his interest in 'any initiative relating to cultural exchanges between Iran and Italy'. The Italian scholars who were present used the opportunity to publicly pledge their support for the Anniversary Celebrations.[9] Indeed, as stated in Chapter 2, UNESCO explicitly encouraged member states to engage with the Celebrations on a cultural level and until around 1970 when it became clear that large numbers of foreign dignitaries would be attending, the Celebrations were intended to be primarily a cultural occasion.

The international committees, which were established from the early 1960s, typically consisted of business leaders, political figures and academics. For example, the original French committee, established in 1960, included Minister of Cultural Affairs André Malraux and Minister of Foreign Affairs Maurice Couve de Murville, alongside renowned scholars Henri Massé and Roman Ghirshman, with Jacques Jaujard, famous for preserving the Louvre's collections during the Second World War, acting as president.[10] This committee was the first to be set up and to mark its creation it published an information booklet listing its members and outlining the work it intended to carry out. In an introduction addressed to the Shah, Malraux offered the monarch 'best wishes for the growing greatness and prosperity of Iran, a country which has not ceased to develop, over the course of the centuries, a magnificent oeuvre of human civilization, and which today continues its high spiritual mission according to the traditions of a genius three thousand years old'. Stating the purpose of the committee, he continues, 'The French committee, basing its activities on the friendship which has united our two countries for so long, undertakes to make even better known the civilizing history of Iran as well as the achievements of modern Iran.'[11] Commenting on the plans of the French committee in a letter, the head of the Africa and Middle East section of the Dutch Ministry of Foreign Affairs stated that it 'demonstrates in which direction the thoughts go and what tasks await the future Dutch committee'. Moreover, the minister recommended that 'because of the excellent relations between the Netherlands and Iran it seems advisable to meet Persian demands in this regard to the extent possible'.[12]

The French committee evidently provided a model for others to follow and the committees that were later established contained a similar mix of political, cultural and business figures. For example, among the members of the British committee were lead barrister at the Nuremburg trials Lord Hartley Shawcross, media tycoon Vere Harmsworth, chairman of BP David Steel, former ambassadors to Iran Sir Denis Wright and Sir Roger Stevens, alongside academics including Sir Max Mallowan, John Boyle and Bernard Lewis.[13] The German committee consisted of Bundeskanzler Willy Brandt, Minister of Foreign Affairs Walter Scheel and President Gustav Heinemann, along with director of the Oriental Seminars at the University of Wurzburg Professor Wilhelm Eilers and director of the University Library in Hamburg Dr H Braun.[14]

The Italian committee consisted of fifty members serving in an honorary capacity, with fifteen of those serving on the executive committee. This executive committee was headed by Professor Giuseppe Tucci and nine of the remaining fourteen were also scholars, highlighting the significance of scholarship to the committee.[15] The Pakistani committee contained the heads of all major universities and various government ministers, and consisted of a central committee as well as separate committees for the provinces of Sindh, Balochistan, Punjab, the North-West Frontier and the provincial government of East Pakistan.[16] Programmes organized by these international committees were primarily cultural, yet often served a political agenda. The *Gāhnāmeh-ye Panjāh Sāl-e Shāhanshāhi-ye Pahlavi*, a chronology of Pahlavi Iran commissioned as part of the commemoration of the fiftieth anniversary of Pahlavi rule in 1355 (1976–77), records the establishment of every single committee in the months leading up to the Celebrations, indicative of the importance the regime ascribed to them.[17]

Despite the initial enthusiasm that led to many committees being established, some committees appear to have suffered from lack of leadership. Early in 1970, Shafā travelled around Europe to discover the progress being made internationally. He concluded that although countries had been quick to establish committees, since that time 'little positive work has been done'. Although Shafā found, through 'personal acquaintance with members of committees in most countries', that academics had shown 'great interest and willingness to participate', they suffered from a lack of central direction.[18] It should be remembered that from the time the Celebrations were first announced, they had been postponed four times. It might have been difficult to maintain enthusiasm for ten years. Despite these problems, by October 1971, each committee had put together a programme of events.

Programmes arranged abroad by the international Cyrus the Great committees included exhibitions, publications, parades, academic conferences and much more. For example, in Pakistan along with street parades lauding the Shah,[19] an illustrated catalogue was published titled *Iran and Pakistan: The Story of a Cultural Relationship Through the Ages*.[20] The Canadian committee, headed by Jean-Paul Deschatelets, president of the Senate, organized a week of cultural activities in June 1971, which was initiated by Empress Farah during her visit to Canada that month.[21]

At the 28th International Congress of Orientalists in Canberra, Australia, in January 1971, congress members were invited to give the Celebrations 'all their support in the cultural domain by giving lectures and organizing exhibitions in their own countries'.[22] Scholarly events were indeed held around the world, and formed an important part of the international contributions. The Canadian committee, for example, sponsored a conference titled *Iranian Civilization and Culture* at the University of Toronto, organized by Professors Roger Savory and Charles Adams.[23] From 27 to 30 September in Leningrad, there was a conference on Iranian history and culture, and further academic events were held in Moscow and other cities in the USSR.[24] A conference in Moscow was organized in conjunction with the Imperial Court's cultural office and was attended by Shafā.[25] At least two conferences were held in India: in New Delhi[26] and in Bombay.[27] A series of special lectures was held at Addis Ababa University in Ethiopia on Iranian history and culture along with a series of publications on the subject,[28] and the University of Tunis established a chair of Persian language to coincide with the Celebrations.[29]

These were scholarly events, yet often with a clear political agenda. To illustrate this, in the forewords of the publication of a German academic conference on Iranian history titled *Festgabe Deutscher Iranisten zur 2500 Jahrfeier Irans* (A Commemorative Publication of German Iranologists for the 2500th Anniversary of Iran), President Gustav Heinemann stressed the importance of German contributions to the field of Iranian studies and the ambassador to Germany, Hossein-Ali Loghman-Adham, echoed the claim that 'it has always been the German scholars who have done the pioneering work in the area of Iranian Studies'.[30] Bundeskanzler Willy Brandt, also writing in the preamble to the work, said:

The work that you have in front of you bears testimony to the open-minded interest of the German Iranologists in the past and present of the Iranian Empire. They have thereby made an important contribution to the deepening of our understanding of the history of Iran and its development into a modern state. For our Iranian friends, this work can serve simultaneously as a demonstration of the respect we have for their country, and as an expression of our will to maintain and stimulate the traditional German-Iranian friendship.[31]

Opening an exhibition titled *2500 Jahre Kaiserreich Iran* at the Museum für Völkerkunde in Vienna, President Franz Jonas similarly stressed the unique 'bond of friendship' between Iran and Austria:

Austria and Iran have never been enemies. The Austrians may be proud of the fact that the treasures of Iranian culture, which our country looks after, never came into Austrian possession as trophies of armed conflict, but instead were often gifts for highly-placed guests, which were gladly given and gladly received. Despite the great geographical distance, Iran and Austria have always been connected by a bond of friendship. In both countries, people live and work who love peace and are open to the great labours of the mind.[32]

During another event held at Vienna's Institut für Orientalistik, former chancellor Alfons Gorbach gave a speech on the history of Imperial Iran.[33] Similarly, the proceedings of the congress in New Delhi included messages from President V. V. Giri, Prime Minister Indira Gandhi and Iranian Minister of Culture Mehrdād Pahlbod, who stated that India with its 'longest and sincere' relations with Iran 'has a right and proper place to celebrate this occasion with great gusto and zeal'.[34] An exhibition in Pakistan was said to be a 'symbol of the bonds of love and affection which have existed between the people of Pakistan and Iran through the ages, and which continue to grow closer and stronger day by day'.[35]

In the Netherlands, a ceremony was held at the Hall of Knights in The Hague on 14 October to coincide with the main festivities in Iran. That the ceremony was held in such a location, where the monarch opens parliament every year and official delegations are received, indicates its political significance. Professor Arie Kampman delivered a lecture on Cyrus the Great to the six hundred guests, which included Queen Juliana, Princess Beatrix and Prince Claus, along with the Iranian ambassador and the ambassadors to the Netherlands of forty other countries. Queen Juliana was presented with a special edition of the Society Holland-Iran journal *Persica*, and a film was shown about Iran chosen by the *Maison de l'Iran*.[36] The event was an interesting synthesis of cultural and political activity, as well as royal ceremony, and it is a measure of the growing international influence of Iran that it was able to inspire such high-level political interest.

The British Cyrus the Great Committee also made a notable contribution. Among the events held in Britain was a lecture by Max Mallowan to the Iran Society about Cyrus the Great,[37] and a seminar on Iran at Beveridge Hall in London, with talks by the Iranian ambassador to UNESCO Fazlollāh Rezā, John Boyle of the University of

Manchester and art historian Basil Gray.³⁸ One seminar at the University of London was hosted by the Royal Asiatic Society, with its president in the chair.³⁹ Exhibitions also took place at the British Museum and the Ashmolean Museum in Oxford.⁴⁰ Writing in the preamble to the British Museum's exhibition that ran from 29 October 1971 until 30 January 1972, Sir John Wolfenden, the museum's director, stated:

> This present exhibition is offered to His Imperial Majesty The Shahanshah and his people as the British Museum's contribution to this historic occasion ... We hope that it will be taken as illustrating some of the events in Persia's long history and the achievements of her most illustrious rulers in the execution of their kingly office and in the fostering of learning and the arts.⁴¹

The British committee also wrote to the Bodleian Library in Oxford to invite it to hold a special exhibition but was rejected since the library would be hosting the Sixth International Congress of Iranian Art and Archaeology the following year.⁴² The BBC arranged a poetry competition in which people were invited to submit poems based on the theme of 'Iran's Cultural Heritage', as part of a Festival of Poetry to mark the Anniversary Celebrations. The winners of the competition, Iranian poets Ahmad Kamāl and Mehdi Hamidi, were invited to Britain at the behest of the BBC for a ten-day visit in order to read their poems on air.⁴³

The most extensive programme of exhibitions and events was held in the United States. In writing to the Iranian embassy in Washington in 1960, the renowned Iran expert Arthur Upham Pope argued that 'it is of outstanding importance that the presentation to the American people of this occasion should stress the fact that it is not merely an episode in Persian history, but a very great event in the history of civilization'.⁴⁴ In order to achieve this, Pope was charged with forming the American committee,⁴⁵ which was eventually chaired by First Lady Pat Nixon, and had more than 200 members in total, including all ministers and governors, and more than 100 cultural and artistic personalities.⁴⁶ It was the largest of any international committee and Shafā noted that the 'enthusiasm with which the Americans participated in the Celebrations was unprecedented'.⁴⁷ The exhibitions held were numerous and contributing museums included the Metropolitan Museum of Art in New York, which displayed miniatures from Shāh Tahmāsp's *Shāhnāmeh*; the Boston Museum of Fine Arts, which gave a display of Iranian dishes, tiles and textiles; Walters Art Gallery in Baltimore, which presented Iranian handicrafts; the Philadelphia Museum of Art, which presented its collection of Iranian carpets and other Islamic art; the Museum of the Oriental Institute of the University of Chicago, which held a special exhibition on Iranian civilization; the Nelson-Atkins Museum of Art, which displayed its collection of ancient Iranian statues and sculptures; the M. H. de Young Museum in San Francisco, which exhibited art from the Islamic period; the Detroit Institute of Arts, which exhibited its collection of Persian miniatures; and the Seattle Art Museum in Washington State, which displayed its collection of Iranian textiles, handicrafts and vessels.⁴⁸ The Corning Museum of Glass in New York held an exhibition in the spring and summer of 1972 in honour of the Celebrations, titled *A Tribute to Persia: Persian Glass*,⁴⁹ and the Textile Museum in Washington, DC held one titled *From Persia's Ancient Looms*.⁵⁰ It appears that any museum that owned any Iranian artefacts was encouraged to host a special exhibition at this time.

Events with Persian food and music were also arranged in various cities across the United States; these were called Persepolis Nights. The state of Utah even named 22 July 1971 'Iran Day', following a motion which was passed in the Senate.[51] Other events took place at universities across the country. At New York State University, for example, an eight-week programme of activities was launched which included lectures, slide shows, discussions and films on Iranian history and culture.[52] The Iranian embassy in Washington was eager to stress its approval of these cultural contributions. Writing a letter to the University of Pennsylvania to congratulate it on its publication of a series of articles on Iranian archaeology, Ambassador Aslān Afshār stated that the 'outstanding publication ... will play a leading role in the United States commemoration' of the Celebrations. He further stated his wish that the Celebrations would 'renew and reaffirm the great friendship between Iran and the United States'.[53] The Iranian embassy, for its part, donated Persian language textbooks to universities with special Persian language courses, such as Princeton, Chicago, Pennsylvania and Texas.[54] As a gesture of goodwill, Ambassador Afshār was given an honorary doctorate by the University of Utah, as well as a key to the city of Los Angeles, Tehran's sister city.[55] At the October festivities in Iran, the mayor of Tehran, Gholāmrezā Nikpey, accepted a gold medallion from the mayor of Los Angeles, Sam Yorty, bearing the image of Cyrus the Great and the official emblems of Iran and the United States.[56]

Among other exhibitions held around the world were one on Persian carpets organized by the Museum für Kunst und Gewerbe in Hamburg;[57] one on Persian art that toured Japan in September and October 1971;[58] one on 2,500 years of Iranian coinage at the National Gallery in Prague;[59] one at the Royal Museum of Art and History in Brussels that ran from 10 to 19 December 1971, titled *De Iraanse kunst in de Belgische verzamelingen* (Iranian Art in Belgian Collections);[60] one on early Iranian art at the Musée de l'Homme in Paris;[61] and an archaeological exhibition held in Madrid in November and December 1971.[62] Not every exhibition held in conjunction with the Celebrations necessarily promoted their message, which stressed 2,500 years of unbroken continuation of monarchy, but they did propagate the idea of Iran as a distinct cultural space. Most of these exhibitions were arranged by institutions with the support of their governments, however, Iran sometimes offered support. The Iranian government itself organized an exhibition in Montreal, which included precious objects and books from the National Museum of Iran, the Imperial Library, the Jewellery Museum, and from private collections.[63] Expenses for the exhibition, which amounted to nearly $680,000, including transport costs and the preparation of the site, were borne by Iran. One ʿAli Akbar Dibāj was chosen to oversee the mission.[64]

The Iranians were also keen to loan items from their collections to other exhibitions, including one at the Hermitage in Leningrad, and a special quota of items was arranged for any European committee that intended to organize an exhibition on Iranian fine arts and handicrafts.[65] Items would first be sent to the headquarters of the European committees for the Celebrations at the *Maison de l'Iran* in Paris and distributed from there.[66] The Ministry of Culture and Art prepared a slideshow of 37,200 slides in 60 series of monuments and artefacts of Ancient Iran, to be distributed to Iranian embassies and cultural centres around the world.[67] Mehrdād Pahlbod stated that the purpose of such initiatives was to help Iranians living abroad to educate local populations about 2,500 years of Iranian culture and recent political developments in Iran.[68] The Iranian embassy in Washington even launched a publication titled *Vox Persica* to inform American readers about Iranian culture and civilization.[69]

One interesting case of Iranian support for scholarly activities abroad was the Congress of Mithraic Studies held in Manchester from 13 to 20 July 1971. It had long been planned by John Hinnells and Professor Sir Harold Bailey, yet almost at the last minute Shojāʿ al-Din Shafā, who had become aware of the plans through Richard Frye, offered Iranian support.[70] This support included funding trips for the delegates to go to Mithraic sites on Hadrian's Wall and two receptions during the conference, plus a grant for the publication of the proceedings through the University of Manchester Press.[71] The sole conditions for the funding were that the Iranian ambassador Amir Khosrow Afshār be invited, and that the proceedings be dedicated to Empress Farah as part of the 2500th Anniversary Celebrations, both of which the organizers were happy to go along with.[72] Hinnells recorded his gratitude in the conference proceedings:

> It is my personal pleasure to record formally the deep gratitude of all involved in the First Congress to the Imperial Pahlavi Library for bestowing upon that Congress the honour of official incorporation into the Twenty-fifth Centenary Celebrations of the founding of the Persian Empire by Cyrus the Great ... Without such support the venture could not have proceeded as it did or have achieved whatever success it did.[73]

With the success of the first congress, the organizers were invited to convene the second congress in Tehran in September 1975 under the patronage of Empress Farah, who personally addressed the members of the congress and received them at the imperial residence.[74] The Imperial Court even funded the publication of the *Journal of Mithraic Studies*, which ran successfully until the revolution. One might suppose that the regime's support of any project on Ancient Persia would seek to strengthen the regime's ideological connection to Cyrus the Great's empire, however, this was clearly not always the case. What this episode makes clear is that the Celebrations were used as an opportunity to engage with and support cultural and academic initiatives, and in doing so firmly establishing Iran as the natural nodal point of Iranian studies around the world.

In addition to the activities in their own countries, some governments expressed interest in arranging events inside Iran during the Celebrations. There were preliminary discussions by the Dutch government to have the Concertgebouw Orchestra perform in Iran, and the Berliner Symphony Orchestra and Vienna Symphony Orchestra were also suggested by their respective governments.[75] There were many such offers and it appears that were it not for some logistical and financial limitations then the Celebrations might have been implemented on a much larger scale. In general, however, foreign contributions to the programme were kept to a minimum, with a small number of exceptions. For instance, in April 1969, the Protocol Department of the Iranian Ministry of Foreign Affairs invited army musical bands to participate in the festivities.[76] As a result a number of foreign military groups performed at the opening of the Shahyād Tower and at the inauguration of the Āryāmehr Stadium.[77]

Participation in the Celebrations was, in part, driven by competition and each foreign committee tried hard to make a noteworthy contribution that stressed its dedication to Iran. The Germans, as already mentioned, emphasized the importance of their unique contributions to Iranian studies. The Dutch were also eager to stress that the type of event that took place at the Hall of Knights formed a 'unique contribution to the commemoration outside Iran'.[78] Pakistan declared a national holiday to mark the Anniversary Celebrations, symbolizing its friendly relations with Iran,[79] while the Italian committee named a street in Rome after Cyrus the Great.[80] A number of countries, including Belgium, Italy, Oman, the UAE, Turkey and Tunisia, produced special commemorative stamps to mark the occasion. The government of South Africa inaugurated the Reza Shah Museum in Johannesburg on 13 October to coincide with the main festivities in Iran.[81] In the Vatican, a conference was held on the subject of 'Cyrus the Great and 25 centuries of Iranian civilization', attended by around 500 cardinals and political figures.[82] In Rabat, a programme of Iranian music and dancing was organized,[83] and in Indonesia a competition was held inviting participants to compose a song for the Celebrations and a text about Cyrus the Great.[84] In France, a group of department stores declared September 1971 to be 'Iran Month', during which shops were decorated with Iranian art and customers given the opportunity to taste Iranian food.[85] It is clear that there was something to gain by making a contribution to the Celebrations, the more enthusiastic and imaginative the better.

The British Council contribution

The British Council's contribution to the Celebrations provides a clear example of the politicization of cultural activity. The British Council was founded in 1934 by the British Foreign Office, with the aim of countering German and Italian propaganda through its own programme of cultural activities abroad.[86] The stated purpose of the council was to promote English language and culture overseas in order to develop 'closer cultural relations between the United Kingdom and other countries, for the purpose of benefitting the British Commonwealth of nations'.[87] The British Council has a rather distinct status; its primary source of funding is the Foreign Office, yet it is deemed autonomous on an operational level. The perceived independence of the organization is important to how it functions. As Robert Phillipson has noted, 'The ideological significance of the notion of autonomy is that it serves to strengthen the myth that the Council's work is non-political.'[88] In spite of the claim of independence, the council simply could not function 'unless it was attuned to the needs of government and to relevant sectors of private business'.[89]

The primary focus of the British Council has been to influence local populations through the promotion of the English language. Sir Reader Bullard, Britain's ambassador to Tehran during the Second World War, wrote that promoting English 'give[s] us contact with the younger generation and an opportunity to influence them in a pro-British direction'.[90] Though the council was primarily a cultural organization, it remained closely tied, particularly through direct funding, to the Foreign Office and, as such, there was a clear political dimension to its activities. The Imperial Celebrations provided a good opportunity for the council to advance British cultural and political interests in Iran; an opportunity that it was eager to take advantage of.

The British Council had intended to send the London Symphony Orchestra to perform during the festivities and the composer Sir Arthur Bliss had initially accepted a commission of $1,000 from Iran to compose a special piece for the Celebrations, but he later pulled out, citing as his reasons old age and lack of inspiration.[91] The Oil Consortium contributed £2,500 to the proposed concert, but the British Council was unable to afford to pay the orchestra the 'customary fee' of £6,000. Ambassador Denis Wright wrote to Iranian Minister of Culture and Art Mehrdād Pahlbod, asking if Iran would pay this fee.[92] Pahlbod responded that while Iran was willing to support foreign performers while staying in Iran, 'payment of the fees … is not possible'.[93] He did, however, offer to invite the orchestra to Iran at a future date to perform at the Rudaki Hall.

In the lead-up to the Celebrations, the Iranian Ministry of Culture and Art invited several countries to organize exhibitions in Iran as part of the occasion. It was decided that the British Council would arrange two exhibitions, including one of the works of Henry Moore, which toured the main centres of the council before the Celebrations, 'so that it would not be overshadowed by the actual celebrations in October'.[94] Henry Moore was chosen as a subject for the exhibition because apart from a few museums in Tehran, 'little was known about the facilities for showing original works of art in Iran'.[95] Despite a 'most successful' opening two weeks in Tehran, from 5 until 23 May, the rest of the tour, in Isfahan (12 to 24 June) and Shiraz (23 August to 4 September) suffered from 'dismally low' attendance figures.[96] There was clearly little enthusiasm for Henry Moore's art in Iran and one report describes the guests as 'baffled' by the works on display.[97]

The council's second exhibition was *British Contributions to Persian Studies*, which opened at the Iran Bāstān Museum on 19 October 1971, and thereafter toured the country until spring 1972. The opening of the exhibition was made memorable by an address by 'Isā Sadiq, who 'evoked memories of E. G. Browne and other noted British scholars'.[98] To have Sadiq speak at the opening of the event offered it legitimacy. As an educator, he had helped to establish Tehran University in 1935 and Tabriz University in 1947, was involved in the renovation of Shiraz University in 1964, served as Minister of Education for six terms and held a lifetime appointment to the Iranian Senate.[99] In addition, he was a distinguished scholar and had worked at Cambridge University during the First World War, under the supervision of Browne.[100] Several British scholars who were in Iran to take part in the Congress of Iranology also attended the opening event, including Laurence Elwell-Sutton, Basil Gray, John Boyle, Laurence Lockhart and David Stronach.[101]

The exhibition consisted of a series of 50 panels charting the contributions Britain had made to the study of Iran over the past 400 years.[102] It included panels on numismatics; travel, history and the pioneer archaeologists; and ancient history and modern archaeology. It also included sections on academic institutions in Britain, namely those at Cambridge, Oxford, Manchester, Durham, Edinburgh and SOAS.

A book was published in cooperation with the British Institute of Persian Studies to accompany the exhibition, which included articles by Sir Max Mallowan, David Stronach, David Blow, Basil Gray and Gavin Hambly.[103] The propaganda purposes of such a publication were clear and in tune with the council's *raison d'être*.

Along with the main centres of the council, the exhibition also travelled to Ahwaz. It was opened there on 11 March 1972 by the British Council Deputy Representative and the director of Management Services of the Iranian Oil Exploration and Production Company. Also in attendance was the governor general of Khuzestan province.[104] Ahwaz was expanding rapidly during this period, benefiting from the expansion of the Iranian oil industry, and the British Council had identified it as a potential location for the establishment of a new council centre. The population of Ahwaz at the time was around 300,000, but it was expected to reach half a million within a matter of years and within a decade was expected to overtake Tabriz as the second most populous city in Iran.[105] With growing foreign investment in Khuzestan province, the merits of advancing the English language in the region were obvious. In this context, the *British Contributions to Persian Studies* exhibition sought to endear the local political establishment to the idea of a new council centre, developing relationships that would facilitate the operation.

How successful were these exhibitions in realizing the political and cultural objectives of the British Council? The showing of original British art in the Henry Moore exhibition certainly fit within the framework of the dissemination of British culture, although the local population's response was somewhat underwhelming. Despite this, at the opening of the exhibition in Tehran, Empress Farah did purchase one Henry Moore piece and her attendance ensured enthusiastic publicity in the local media.[106] The *British Contributions to Persian Studies* exhibition appears to have been more successful overall and was certainly more in tune with what other countries were doing. Italy, for example, arranged a similar touring exhibition in 1971, consisting of a photographic display of Italian excavations and restorations in Iran.[107] Ramsbotham's 1972 report on the activities of the council stressed that it had been 'particularly important for the British Council's reputation that some special activity should be mounted … to mark the 2500th Anniversary of the Persian Monarchy by Cyrus the Great'.[108] He goes on to say that both exhibitions were 'a distinct success' and recommended similar events in Iran in the future. It is clear that the British Council was able to attract a degree of interest from high-profile figures for the exhibitions, but despite Ramsbotham's confident tone, it is probable that their success lay in the political capital gained, rather than their popularity with the Iranian public.

Publications

In addition to exhibitions and conferences, hundreds of articles, brochures and books were published in conjunction with the Anniversary Celebrations. Publications included conference proceedings, such as the ones already mentioned published in Canada, India and Germany, museum programmes, scholarly studies and general histories. Examples include Banri Namikawa's Japanese publication *The Legacy of*

Cyrus the Great, Jayad Haidari's edited volume on literature titled *Iran: In Celebration of the 2500th Anniversary of the Founding of the Persian Empire by Cyrus the Great*, a bibliography of books in Turkish on Iran, published in Ankara and several books published in Portugal on various aspects of Iranian history.[109]

The greatest number of titles was published in Pakistan: upwards of twenty works in total. Official publications sponsored by the Pakistan committee included editions of Persian poetry, language guides, books on the historical relationship between Iran and Pakistan, and works based on Persian manuscripts.[110] The honorary secretary of the Pakistan Committee, Mumtaz Hasan, stressed the importance of Persian language and literature in South Asia, and its 'vital influence on the growth of Urdu and Bengali'. Thus, he continues, 'the cultural relations between Pakistan and Iran and rooted deeply in the historic past'.[111] Iran was Pakistan's key strategic ally in the region, so its enthusiastic support, demonstrated in part through the number of commemorative publications it commissioned, was a way in which it could underline its friendship with the Shah. Scholarly publications were a way of showing that not only was the relationship between Iran and Pakistan strategic, but it also had historic, cultural and linguistic roots.

Many officially sponsored books featured introductions by political figures. In the introduction to *Imperium Persicum*, the Austrian president, Franz Jonas, wrote:

> The name of this ruler [Cyrus] is connected to the human rights proclaimed by him, through which he replaced prejudice with tolerance and made a stance for the equality of all subjects independent of religion, race and origin. Challenged time and again by tyrants, this lodestar of these high ideals may have been temporarily obscured, but was never extinguished. For this reason, the remembrance of this wise ruler, who was far ahead of his time in terms of his national political thinking, is meaningful not just for Iran, but has worldwide perspectives.[112]

An anonymous author of the final chapter of the work describes the national miracle (*Staatswunder*) that had taken place since Mohammad Reza Pahlavi had taken the throne. They continue, 'Who could be surprised that the Iranians are throwing a global party for their country, which has been a monarchy for 25 centuries? Today, as it was 2,500 years ago.'[113] The political implications of this outward acceptance of the narrative of the Celebrations were clear and many other books published internationally contain similar dedications from political leaders, lauding both Iranian history and the Shah's place in it, and drawing attention to cultural or political links between their countries and Iran.[114]

Cultural organizations arranged their own publications, such as Terre D'Europe's *Iran*, which included a chapter by Louis Vanden Berghe titled 'Cyrus le Grand et la Rayonnement de la Civilisation Iranienne', and UNESCO's *Iran: Cultural Crossroads for 2,500 Years*, which included chapters by Peter Avery and Sayyed Hoseyn Nasr.[115] Academics were also encouraged to contribute outside of these special publications. IsMEO, for instance, invited scholars to enter papers into a competition, with a $4,000 prize for the best submission, to be judged by its Board of Examiners.[116] As a result of this effort, a number of works published by the Italian Committee in conjunction with

IsMEO emerged, for instance, Alessandro Bausani's *L'Iran e la sua tradizione millenaria* and Giuseppe Tucci's *Ciro Il Grande*.[117] Academics were seemingly eager to engage with the event, whether motivated by political or purely scholarly factors. Carlo Paoloni, in a publication on the sacred fires of Ancient Persia, declared that his motivation for the publication was directly a result of

> the decision of the Iranian nation, to celebrate in October 1971 the 2500th anniversary of the foundation of the Persian Empire by Cyrus the Great, with the noble intention to spread this great celebration to all regions of the world, calling on the participation of all forces who love the beauty and the greatness of the past of the Iranian nation, thus opening a passage to Peace and International Friendship.[118]

There may be a temptation to see such a dedication and dismiss the work as a sort of pseudo-scholarship, but despite the flamboyant dedication, the publication contains no further mention of the Celebrations, or their historical context. The content does not intend to glorify the image of Cyrus the Great, nor draw any similarities between the ancient king and the present shah. It was apparently scholarship for the sake of scholarship and the Celebrations provided opportunities for academics to publicize their work.

Other works, though, did pay homage to the Shah and Cyrus the Great in ways that were evidently intended to flatter. An edited volume published by the Iran Culture House in Bombay contains essays with titles such as 'Cyrus the Great and the Glory of Ancient Iran', 'Cyrus the Great – a Paragon of Rulers', and 'Was Cyrus the Great a Vegetarian?'[119] In the latter article, the author, Ervand Peer, states, 'Many historians have written about the various aspects of this great king, Cyrus, but a few have cared to mention his immense love for animals latent in his glorious heart.'[120] In an article on the concept of monarchy in classical Persian poetry, contained within another Indian publication, B. M. Gai writes of the 'justice and generosity of the Iranian monarchs' and concludes his piece with the following passage: 'In the benevolent rule of the present ruler of Iran, Shahanshah Aryamehr Muhammad Reza Pahlawi, who has followed the healthy and progressive rule of his late father, we find happy reminiscences of the glorious rulers of the Sassanid Iran, of whom Firdawsi has sung eloquently in his *Shahnama*.'[121] The articles in these volumes may have been academically sound, but some of their authors were clearly aware of the political benefits of registering one's support of the Pahlavi historical narrative, and happy to exploit this opportunity.

The many books and articles published abroad in conjunction with the Celebrations evidently differed in both relevance and quality. In many cases, however, the funds and publicity provided at the occasion of the Celebrations contributed to works already underway, which the preface to *Indo-Iran* illustrates:

> Since its inception the [Indo-Iran] Society has carried on its work with zeal and vigour and has succeeded in enlisting the cooperation of the intelligentsia of this country. The Cultural Department of the Imperial Embassy of Iran had also done some spade work in this direction and wished to organise a function

where scholars of various disciplines could gather together to talk on Indo-Iranian relations through the ages.

Then came the occasion of the Celebrations of the 2500th Anniversary of the Founding of the Monarchy in Iran. The Indo-Iran Society came forward to organise a Congress of Iranologists and Indologists to commemorate the occasion in a befitting manner.[122]

These scholarly events and publications, therefore, should be seen within the broader context of the cultural policies of the Pahlavi state, which stressed greater intellectual cooperation between Iran and the world. The Celebrations merely provided extra impetus and exposure.

***

In his 1983 publication *Ancient Persia*, J. M. Cook wrote, 'In the last ten years or so, thanks partly to the interest aroused by the 2,500 year anniversary of Cyrus the Great and the publication of the Persepolis Fortification tablets, the modern literature on the Achaemenids has doubled itself.'[123] The publication of the Fortification Tablets, incidentally, came initially in the form of Richard Hallock's groundbreaking article contributing to volume two of the *Cambridge History of Iran*, first published in 1971 'as a token of what is to come, to mark an anniversary unique in the history of the course of which the Board were set up to survey'.[124] While the events at Persepolis, shown on television sets around the world, drew attention to the ancient heritage of Iran, the exhibitions, conferences and publications provided greater exposure to all periods and aspects of Iran's history and culture in line with the promotional efforts of the regime.

Alongside the publications that were officially declared to have been published as part of the Celebrations, many authors and publishers were keen to take advantage of the publicity generated and released, translated, or reprinted their own books on Iran.[125] Jean Perrot, who was one of the Iranologists present in 1971, wrote in the introduction to his 2013 publication *The Palace of Darius at Susa* that the Celebrations sparked a renewed interest in Achaemenid archaeology, which led to the relaunch of investigations at Susa, bringing the city to life 'in all its greatness'.[126] It is clear that the Celebrations made a significant contribution to the field of Iranian studies, not merely through the projection of Persepolis and Pasargadae on television screens across the globe but also through the extensive and far-reaching cultural programmes organized by cultural institutions from around the world.

This chapter has shown that despite the political motivations of the international activity, it also had genuine cultural and scholarly merit. The British Council used the Celebrations to promote Britain in Iran, stressing its scholarly contribution to understanding of Iranian civilization, but it also promoted modern British art. This cultural activity also indicated, through the council's participation in the Celebrations, its support of the regime. The holding of exhibitions and conferences around the world, as well as the publication of books, served to highlight friendly governments' support for the principal message of the Celebrations, as promoted by the Shah's regime.

Writing in a letter to the Imperial Court in June 1971, Shojā' al-Din Shafā declared that a comprehensive list of cultural programmes would be made available to all embassies, foreign committees, cultural centres and media outlets around the world. Shafā stated his belief that the supplied list proved the Celebrations to be the 'largest and most extensive global operation in the service of culture and art that the world has seen to date'. Any criticisms of the Celebrations, he said, therefore, were 'unfounded, malicious and stupid in every sense'.[127] While it is clear that some of the cultural programmes initiated served a political agenda, they also contributed to the promotion of Iranian culture. This work carried out by Shafā throughout the 1960s in his role in the Imperial Court, explored in Chapter 4, laid the groundwork for the cultural operation that was set in motion for the Anniversary Celebrations. As noted in Chapter 3, the emergence of Iran as a powerful player on the international scene meant that states were eager to develop closer relations with the Shah's government. Shafā took advantage of this position and was able to ensure that the cultural aspects of the event found international participation on a large scale. The culture of international collaboration was to play an important part in the development of other projects initiated by the Pahlavi regime throughout the 1970s. Meanwhile, the promotion of Iranian culture had material benefits, as will be made clear later, in Chapter 7, which explores the development of the tourism sector in the period of the Celebrations.

6

Criticizing the Celebrations

In the lead up to the Celebrations criticism was levelled at their organizers, in Iran and internationally, for their over-reliance on foreign services, alleged corruption, spending and the ideological incongruity of the event. The organizers were criticized by students in Iran and abroad, as well as by the Shah's political opponents, most significantly Khomeini. As this chapter will show, however, these criticisms were directed as much at the Shah himself and the system he represented as at the Imperial Celebrations and their ideological message – the event merely provided a focal point for disparate groups to voice their opposition to the regime. Khomeini saw the Celebrations as part of the Pahlavi strategy to discredit the traditional Islamic class, which was true to a certain degree. However, his opposition to the Shah can be traced back to the time before his exile in 1964, and his criticism should be seen in this context rather than as a spontaneous outburst at the event itself. This chapter will examine opposition to the Celebrations, consider to what extent the criticisms were valid and discuss how these criticisms reflected a changing social and political environment.

This book has thus far outlined the strategies employed by the Shah's regime to articulate its ideology and express its political goals. The principal purpose of the Celebrations on a conceptual level was to reinforce the Pahlavi state ideology, built around the institution of monarchy in Iran, Iran's Aryan roots and the glory of Iran's pre-Islamic past. However, many in Iran and abroad rejected this message. In his *Gharbzadegi*, published in 1962, Jalāl Āl-e Ahmad wrote of the hypocrisy of Iran to celebrate its monarchical tradition, while its people were struggling to survive and the country was over-reliant on foreign capital.[1] He resented the regime's 'mania for showing off in front of strangers, for competing in boasting vaingloriously and stupidly of Cyrus and Darius'.[2] Many intellectuals with him were unconvinced by what they perceived as the regime's self-orientalizing exploitation of its ancient history.

In *Gharbzadegi*, Āl-e Ahmad offered a powerful critique of both the regime's policy of rapid modernization and the secular intellectuals, whose ideas, he argued, had no roots in Iranian culture.[3] From the outset, the Celebrations were an establishment intellectual project and by focusing on modernization, foreign tastes and pre-Islamic civilization, and largely ignoring Islam, they encapsulated much of what Āl-e Ahmad considered was wrong with Iran's experience with modernity. One should remember, for instance, that the first organizing council consisted of modernist intellectuals and politicians such as Mohammad Hejāzi, Sādeq Rezāzādeh Shafaq, Shojāʿ al-Din Shafā, Hoseyn ʿAlā, ʿAli Asghar Hekmat and Sayyed Hasan Taqizādeh. Referring to his work *On the Service and the Treason of the Intellectuals*, Mehrzad Boroujerdi writes that Āl-e Ahmad 'criticized secular Iranian intellectuals for their isolation from the masses, their superficiality, their rejection or ignorance of the majority's beliefs, and the ease with which they were often co-opted by the ruling classes'.[4] The Celebrations were essentially driven by secular intellectuals linked to the Pahlavi court and the types of works published in conjunction with the event, and the subjects of the conferences and exhibitions, largely conformed to the situation derided by Āl-e Ahmad.

The critics of the Celebrations received considerable exposure in the press, both in Iran and worldwide, and the tendency of the regime to shrug off their criticisms rather than robustly challenge them for a sustained period contributed to the prevailing negative impression of the event. Of course, that is not to say that some of the criticisms were not valid, but the regime had the resources to challenge them and could have done more to promote a positive view of the occasion. The SAVAK reports show that the security services were aware of the perception of corruption and overspending among the Iranian population, as indeed was the organizing committee. Viewed in this light, the official presentation of the Celebrations was severely damaged by what must be considered a public relations failure on behalf of the regime. To gain a more complete picture of the Celebrations, therefore, it is important to understand that despite the efforts of the regime, their positive message was not received or accepted by all Iranians, and indeed, that even if some were enthused by the opulence of the occasion, many more were turned off.

Religious opposition

In a SAVAK report dated 10 Shahrivar 1350 (1 September 1971), it was argued that religion was an important factor in opposition to the Celebrations and an order was issued to use all available means to tackle this threat.[5] The single most vociferous critic of the Celebrations was the dissident cleric Ruhollah Khomeini, who argued that the event and the glorification of the monarchy flew in the face of Iran's Islamic tradition. The Celebrations presented the pre-Islamic empires as the foundation of the Iranian character, a view that Khomeini believed was dangerous to the future of the *ulema*'s standing. His concern was justified. Shafā later admitted that one of the goals of the Celebrations was to remove support for the religious factions and encourage Iranians to relate to the monarchy rather than Islam as the source of their national identity.[6] This clash between the ambitions of the Pahlavi modernists and the *ulema* did not, however, have its roots in the Celebrations. Instead, the Celebrations provided a focal point for long-standing grievances that galvanized many of the Shah's political opponents, particularly Khomeini.

In Iran's modern history, Islam has been a constant and vocal critic of political authority, and has been able to rouse popular support. This was evident during the late Qajar period, notably during the protest over the Tobacco Concession (1891–92) and during the Constitutional Revolution (1905–11).[7] The ability of clerics to draw widespread support came, in large part, from their popularity among the traditional bazaari class. This support base remained loyal throughout the 20th century. During the early Pahlavi period, Reza Shah introduced a number of secular reforms that directly challenged the *ulema*'s authority. Such policies included the outlawing of traditional dress for all other than state-recognized clergymen in favour of Western clothing, and the banning of the veil for women. These policies led to protests in Mashhad in 1935 during which hundreds of protesters were massacred at the Imam Reza shrine by troops with machine guns.[8] Reza Shah attempted to replicate the modernizing policies of Atatürk in Iran, though he failed in his efforts to declare Iran a republic. His nationalist ideology took its inspiration from Ancient Iran, which was also unsettling for the traditional classes, who strongly identified with Islam. The Reza Shah period thus marked, as Gheissari and Nasr have noted, 'an end to the age-old conceptions of Shia realm that was built on an alliance between the shahs and the *ulema*'.[9]

Reza Shah's fall in 1941 gave rise to the restoration and expansion of the religious expression that had been suppressed under his rule.[10] In the open social space created by the resulting power vacuum, modernist ideas were challenged by the resurgent religious class. In 1946, Ahmad Kasravi, an anti-clerical modernist intellectual, was assassinated by the *Fadāiyān-e Eslām*. Two years earlier, Khomeini had urged the *ulema* to rise against the ideas perpetrated by people such as Kasravi.[11] In the political turmoil of the following decades, religious organizations were able to mobilize popular and often radical support. The attempted assassination of Mohammad Reza Shah by a gunman posing as a reporter for an Islamic publication and Prime Minister 'Ali Razmārā's assassination at the hands of the *Fadāiyān-e Eslām* demonstrate the emergence of militant Islam during this period.

As Mohammed Reza Shah consolidated his power in the 1960s, he continued the modernization efforts of the Reza Shah years. This, coupled with the regime's increasing interest in pre-Islamic history, was seen by the *ulema* as an attempt to marginalize the religious institutions. The riots of June 1963, which ultimately resulted in the deportation of Khomeini, formed a key episode in this period of growing animosity between the royal house and sections of the *ulema*. The protests were triggered by the land reforms that had been introduced as part of the Shah's White Revolution and which would threaten the *ulema*'s land holdings, as well as the law granting women the right to vote, but on a deeper level they revealed the general clerical disquiet at the rate of modernization.[12] The protests were led by Khomeini and supported by a coalition of bazaaris and clerics.[13] 'Alam, who was serving as prime minister at the time, with characteristic assertiveness crushed the rebellion, giving the mullahs 'the screwing they'd been asking for'.[14] There is little doubt that 'Alam considered the mullahs permanently pacified. Indeed, he later said to the US ambassador, 'The only possible way they [the clergy] could make a comeback would be if HIM were rendered powerless and you and the British promoted the clergy as a bulwark against communism'.[15]

Khomeini was deported one year later following his criticism of a new law granting American citizens immunity from prosecution, which had been granted, he claimed, by the Mansur government in exchange for a $200 million loan. From his residence in Qom, Khomeini said: 'Our dignity has been trampled underfoot; the dignity of Iran has been destroyed ... The government has sold our independence, reduced us to the level of a colony, and made the Muslim nation of Iran appear more backward than savages in the eyes of the world!'[16] Despite Khomeini's deportation, the Shah failed to sever his ties to the Iranian masses, and exile turned him into a sort of martyr and an ideal figurehead for political opposition, while placing him beyond the Shah's reach.[17] Indeed, as Ali Ansari has written, the episode marked 'the gradual transformation of Khomeini from a recalcitrant cleric to a national leader'.[18]

In the weeks prior to the coronation in 1967, Khomeini wrote a two-page open letter to Prime Minister Hoveydā, in which he complained about exile, rallied against the coronation, and urged students at the madrasas to forfeit their exams in protest.[19] In the madrasas themselves, students speculated as to the cost of the coronation, and one Hoseyn Musavi claimed to have documents showing that the office of post and telegraph alone had spent 19,000 tomans ($2,500) on the coronation. One student suggested that for that money a factory could have been built and the generated capital would have been enough to fund the whole coronation ceremony.[20] Meanwhile, three clerics, listed in a SAVAK report as Montazeri, Rabbāni and Makārem, met each night in Khomeini's library in Qom 'until as late as 9.30 or 10pm' to collate information about the cost of the coronation for distribution on the day of the event itself.[21] This strategy was employed during the Imperial Celebrations too.

In the run-up to the Celebrations in 1971, Khomeini publicly and explicitly announced for the first time his desire for the overthrow of the monarchy. For this reason, some have pointed to this period as pivotal in the revolutionary movement.[22] In a speech on 22 June 1971, he stated that 'king of kings is the vilest of words', and that sovereignty belongs to God alone,'[23] but this was not the first time he expressed his distaste for monarchy. A year earlier, his *Velāyat-e Faqih* was published, a theological treatise which called for the establishment of political rule by a cleric and thus was fundamentally at odds with the monarchical institution. Rather than the event at Persepolis having led Khomeini to reassess his theological convictions, it seems that it merely provided an opportunity to attack the regime. Khomeini was a shrewd and calculated opponent who was attentive to the political mood of the Iranian population. The Celebrations should not, therefore, be seen as a turning point in Khomeini's thinking, but rather as a point at which he took advantage of the negative perceptions of the Celebrations and of the global spotlight shone on Iran to consolidate opposition against the Shah.

Khomeini's criticisms of the Celebrations reached a large audience in Iran. His speeches and letters, in which he urged Iranians to mobilize and fight against the regime, were broadcast on the Persian language section of Baghdad radio and were subsequently distributed in Iran on tapes and in pamphlets.[24] Pamphlets by student opposition groups, distributed on university campuses, outlined Khomeini's ideas and helped to cement his position as a key opposition figure against the Shah. In order to stop the distribution of tapes, SAVAK ordered the arrest of people involved and imposed more stringent border controls.[25] In spite of these efforts, Khomeini's speeches against the Celebrations were still transmitted in Iran in Persian through Iraqi radio stations. One SAVAK agent reported seeing people gathered at an ice-cream shop listening to reports on the radio from Iraq criticizing the Shah and the Celebrations.[26]

In Najaf, the head of one madrasa warned students that if they participated in the Celebrations, their scholarships would be cut and they would be considered enemies.[27] After a service at Hedāyat Mosque in Tehran after the Celebrations, led by Ayatollah Mahmud Tāleqāni, a number of people criticized the Shahyād Tower, calling it a 'Baha'i symbol'[28] and arguing that 'it is wrong for this faith to have so much power in an Islamic country'.[29] A group had planned to protest in Tehran over the issue, but were persuaded not to by their peers as they believed it would have led to a police crackdown.[30] It was evidently not merely Khomeini who objected to the event, as many protesters in Iran were clearly inspired by his opposition.

From the middle of the 1960s, 'Ali Shari'ati, considered by many to be an important ideologue of the revolution,[31] emerged as one of the fiercest critics of the state and society of Pahlavi Iran. While it was primarily the traditional classes who followed the *ulema*, Shari'ati espoused an Islamic discourse that had broad appeal among the educated middle class.[32] Like Āl-e Ahmad, he opposed the blind following of Western intellectual thought. He described the West as having 'metamorphosized' Iranian history, 'and when we look[ed] at our own new portrait we hated it. Consequently we began to run towards our "metamorphosized" past and religion, as well as towards European school and culture'.[33] In this context, he objected to the regime's appropriation of pre-Islamic history. 'Our people do not find their roots in these civilizations', he wrote in *The Return to Ourselves*. 'Our people remember nothing from this distant past and do not care to learn about pre-Islamic civilizations.'[34]

Shari'ati gave a series of lectures around the time of the Celebrations that included thinly veiled criticisms of the occasion, which served, as Lafraie has noted, as an 'indictment of the Shah's regime'.[35] One such lecture titled *On the Plight of the Oppressed* was clearly aimed at the Shah's appropriation of ancient civilization, his oppression of his people and his arrogance. Addressing a fictional slave who built the pyramids, he wrote:

> My friend, you have left this world, but we are carrying the loads for the great civilization, clear victories, and heroic works. They came to our homes at the farms and forced us, as beasts, to build their graves. If we could not carry the stones or complete the task, we were put into the walls with the stones! Others took the pride and credit for the work that we did. No mention had ever been made of our contributions.[36]

The inference here is that the Shah and the historic system he represented took all of the 'pride and credit' for the blood and toil of the people. Instead of 2,500 years of glorious monarchical tradition, Shari'ati spoke of 5,000 years of 'deprivation, injustice, class discrimination and repression'.[37]

There was opposition, too, from long-time political opponents of the Shah. Mozaffar Firouz, a Qajar prince and former diplomat, wrote a strongly worded critique of the Celebrations and the Shah, titled *L'Iran face à l'imposture de l'histoire*, from Paris, where he had lived in exile since 1958. He claimed to be 'guided by the desire to present Iran and the Iranian people to the western world as they really are' and wrote:

> While we welcome with pleasure the glorification of the great Iranian and Aryan people and the contribution which they have made to civilization and humanity, we think that the entire conception which was suggested to us is based on a fundamental historical error, and we regret that millions of dollars from an underdeveloped country, a poor and needy nation, will be wasted on celebrations which have nothing to do with historical facts and the true interests and traditions of the Iranian people.[38]

The Celebrations were, according to him, little more than a 'political gaffe and a clumsy action, which go against historical truths',[39] and he frequently referred to the 'personality cult' of the Shah.[40] Firouz also objected to the concept of celebrating just 2,500 years of history. The number 2,500, according to him, had 'no national significance or historical justification whatsoever, as the history of Iran, of the people and monarchy is much older'.[41] Whereas Khomeini criticized the Celebrations for looking too far into the past and neglecting the Islamic period, Firouz criticized them for not stretching far enough into Iran's ancient past. There was clearly a political subtext to Firouz's cynical analysis of the Celebrations, for he was known to have desired the fall of the Pahlavi dynasty,[42] and the work illustrates how useful the Celebrations were as an opportunity to oppose the Pahlavi regime from all sides, secular and religious.

Student and militant opposition

By the middle of the 1960s, 'Alam considered the traditional clerical opposition and the National Front to have been permanently pacified, but the regime faced threats from militant groups and student opposition groups both in Iran and abroad. In his 1961 annual report, the British ambassador in Tehran wrote:

> The greatest danger to the regime comes not from them [the National Front], but from their children, the students, of whom there are now 14,000 in the University of Tehran alone. Their number, swollen by several thousands who are being educated in universities abroad, greatly exceeds the capacity of the country to absorb them ... Their frustrations and the uncertainty of their future naturally impel them towards rebellion against authority. The politically active minority is largely influenced by the National Front, and to a lesser degree by Communism, and has a capacity for mischief out of all proportion to its members. The risk is ever present that the agitation in the University may spread beyond it.[43]

The type of opposition the regime faced by the end of the 1960s was multifaceted and different to what they had encountered before. Moreover, greater global interconnectedness in this period meant that student movements and civil protests in the United States, Europe and the Third World had a direct impact on protest movements in Iran.

During the 1960s, due to significant improvements in education and a young population, every place at the University of Tehran was contested by some twenty applicants, which led many students to move abroad to study. While in 1955 there had been around 6,000 Iranian students studying abroad, mostly in West Germany, by 1960 there were 20,000, and by 1972 there were 30,000, one-third of whom were based in the United States and Canada.⁴⁴ As Matthew Shannon writes of the experience of Iranian students studying in the United States:

> While nation building and modernization efforts compelled states to invest in educational programs, the postwar networks of globalized education provided unprecedented opportunities for individual students to pursue their own academic interests and establish relationships with Americans who saw rights – rather than development – as the most important priority for the international community.⁴⁵

Concepts such as human rights and democracy, therefore, were at the core of student opposition to the Shah from the 1960s. Although the Shah presented himself as a defender of human rights, from abroad, student opposition groups saw this as a charade. In early 1960, the Confederation of Iranian Students in Europe was formed by representatives from West Germany, the United Kingdom and France. Two years later, this group merged with the Iranian Students Association in the United States to form the Confederation of Iranian Students National Union. The confederation was an umbrella organization mainly comprising of student organizations outside of Iran, but it also included the Organization of Tehran University Students.⁴⁶

During the 1960s and into the 1970s, as Michael Axworthy has written, Iranians studying in the West 'were exhilarated by the fashionable enthusiasm for Marxism and Maoism, for revolution and against the Vietnam War'.⁴⁷ In convincing non-Iranian leftist groups that the Shah's regime was as ruthless and repressive as the military junta in Greece and apartheid South Africa, Iranian opposition groups abroad, such as the Confederation of Iranian Students, helped to usher in a period of aggressive opposition to the Pahlavi regime around the world.⁴⁸ Wherever the Shah travelled in the West, he was met with crowds protesting his rule. On 2 June 1967, while the Shah was attending a performance of Mozart's *The Magic Flute* at the Deutsche Oper in Berlin, clashes between pro- and anti-Shah groups led to the shooting by the police of a student, Benno Ohnesorg. The event was an important moment in the radicalization of the left in Germany, and the formation of the Baader-Meinhof Group. Such episodes further illustrate, as Axworthy writes, 'the interlinked nature of international and national politics at this time'.⁴⁹

These foreign opposition groups became more organized and confrontational in their opposition to the Pahlavi regime towards the end of the 1960s. Events of national significance were naturally convenient rallying points. In 1967, for instance, during the run-up to the coronation, a California-based organization called *Goruh-e Māziyār* issued an edict, addressed to Iranian security services, the ministry of foreign affairs, embassies and consulates, forbidding, in strong terms, any celebrating of the coronation, warning that 'violators will be punished most severely'.⁵⁰ When it became clear that events would take place in San Francisco, the group urged all Iranians studying or residing in California to demonstrate.⁵¹ On 25 and 26 October, protests took place outside the Iranian consulate in San Francisco. On the first day, there were only eight demonstrators present, who held placards and were described as 'quiet and peaceful'. The tone changed the following day, when twenty-five protesters demonstrated, chanting anti-regime slogans and throwing potatoes and tomatoes at the consulate walls. They were removed by the police after they attempted to storm the building.[52]

On 14 October 1971, the day of the gala dinner at Persepolis, a bomb exploded at the same Iranian consulate in San Francisco, in an apparent protest against the events that were taking place in Iran. Although there were no fatalities, the blast was so powerful that it shattered windows several blocks away, injured four people and caused one million dollars' worth of damage.[53] As a result, security was increased at Iranian official premises in the United States, where demonstrations were expected during the days of the Celebrations.[54] The day following the blast, a march took place in San Francisco organized by the Confederation of Iranian Students. Over the course of two hours, the protesters walked from the Federal Building on Golden Gate Avenue to the damaged Iranian consulate. They held up signs that read 'a hungry nation does not need a 2500-year celebration' and many wore brown paper bags on their heads in order to shield their identities from SAVAK spies. One protester was heard to refer to the Celebrations as an 'extravagant orgy'.[55] Student activists in the United States also attempted to disrupt academic events held at campuses in conjunction with the Celebrations. An article appeared in *The Stanford Daily*, for example, calling on students to join a planned protest at a conference at Stanford University against 'Iran's oil-rich butcher king'.[56]

Similar protests occurred in other cities of the United States and in Europe, and the campaign by the Confederation of Iranian Students against the occasion attracted support from academics and political activists from around the world. A letter signed by figures such as Jean-Paul Sartre, Simone de Beauvoir and fourteen British Members of Parliament referred to the 'oppression and misery to which the Iranian masses have been subjected' and argued that the regime's focus on its Aryan roots was 'an ideology borrowed and propagated by the Pahlavi Dynasty from Hitler's Germany'. The letter called for an international boycott of the Celebrations:

> participation in effect, would be tantamount to sanctioning all the crimes and oppression with which the Iranian monarchy is associated in the last 25 centuries; it would as well be an approval of the countless financial expenses directly or indirectly imposed on a people, a large majority of whom are deprived of most elementary needs for a human and dignified survival.[57]

The Popular Front for the Liberation of the Arab Gulf, a Marxist and Arab nationalist revolutionary organization based in the Persian Gulf Arab states, also offered their support for the campaign against the Celebrations and the 'oppressive regime which has subjected the Iranian people to the misery of humiliation, poverty, and under-development'.[58] A publication of the Committee for Free Iran, an opposition organization based in Washington, DC, stated,

Instead of bringing glory to the Persian Empire as it marks 2500 years of history, the Shah has created a land in which human lives have less value than the flies that disturb a growing number of political corpses, and natural resources are squandered and given away to provide fleeting pleasure for the royal family and the fawning favorites of his court.[59]

The French communist newspaper *L'Humanité* also contrasted the 'appalling and inhumane poverty of the masses' in Iran to the lavishness of the Celebrations.[60]

There was indeed poverty in Iran and large disparities in wealth existed between the urban middle class and the poor rural communities. All over the country people from all circles spoke of their disillusionment with the high cost of the Celebrations, which they speculated to be as much as 20 billion rials ($267 million). Some even suggested that due to the heavy financial burden of the Celebrations, some people in the south of Iran, which had suffered from drought, did not have water or bread, and some farmers and nomads lost their livestock.[61] There was also some grumbling amongst the bazaaris over increases in the taxes they paid, which they linked to the high government spending associated with the Celebrations.[62] For these reasons, many people found it difficult to feel any enthusiasm for the upcoming festivities.

The security services were eager that voices of dissent inside the country were muted. In April and May 1971, student protests were, in the words of the British ambassador, 'ruthlessly crushed' by the security forces.[63] These protests occurred on the campuses of Tehran University and Āryāmehr University, where hundreds of students demonstrated while shouting slogans against the Celebrations and the Shah. In both instances the authorities deployed riot police, who arrested hundreds of students from each campus.[64] The excessive response to these disturbances only added to students' disillusionment with the regime. Despite the crackdown, in the weeks prior to the event, students at various universities were still distributing pamphlets criticizing the Shah and the Celebrations. Protest leaflets were distributed at a technical college in Tabriz, for example, calling for students to refrain from participation in the Celebrations and not to decorate the campus for the occasion.[65] One SAVAK report suggested that when Iranian students who studied in the West returned home to visit their families, they were being recruited by subversive elements in Iran to act as their proxies abroad.[66]

One pamphlet titled *Jashn-e Zed-e Mardomi-ye Shāh* (The Shah's Celebration Against the People) was distributed on behalf of students at the faculty of economics of the University of Tehran to various dormitories, including those at Amir Ābād.[67] It began with a morbid assessment of the situation in the country:

> This year half of the people of our homeland have suffered from famine and hunger. Because of destitution, the nomads of Fars are committing suicide one after the other. Because of hunger, the people of Sistan and Baluchistan are forced to sell their children. The starving people in the famine-struck villages of Khorasan because of malnourishment have been forced to rob and steal.

The pamphlet goes on to criticize the Shah for the 'benefits and privileges' given to other countries to 'support his dirty work', claiming that Israeli experts were among the foreigners employed for the Celebrations. It continues: 'The various sections of our country who bear the financial burden, and the intellectuals who recognize the repressive nature of this crime [the Celebrations], declared their opposition to this puppet show from the beginning. But the tyrant regime of the Shah puts these people who demand freedom in chains.' The leaflet ends with a pledge to fight against the regime: 'Our oppressed people have begun their long struggle for liberation and as long as there is life in their bodies they will continue on this path.'[68]

Figures on numbers of political prisoners during the Pahlavi period tend to be exaggerated in foreign media, and the reporting on the crackdown during the Celebrations was no exception. Indeed, reports in the foreign media on the conduct of SAVAK sometimes resorted to outright sensationalism. According to one account, there were 10,000 arrests and writers were forbidden from publishing so they would not be able to express their criticisms of the Celebrations.[69] A report appeared in *Time* which argued that SAVAK, 'by ironic coincidence, arrested exactly 2,500 potential troublemakers'.[70] Amnesty International believed the numbers of arrests to be between 1,000 and 4,000,[71] though the organization was later criticized for accepting inflated figures for political prisoners directly from opposition organizations without appropriate scrutiny.[72] 'Abdolrezā Ansāri, citing General Nasiri, suggests a more conservative number, saying that 1,500 suspects were monitored during the Celebrations, and a smaller number of them subsequently detained.[73] Whatever the real number of detainees, the crackdown on protests did little to dispel the criticisms of Iran's human rights record internationally. In early 1972, US Congressman Parren James Mitchell wrote a letter to the Iranian ambassador, Amir Aslān Afshār, expressing concerns for the over 100 Iranians arrested during the Celebrations who were, he believed, being tried in secret military courts.[74] More appeals followed, some addressed directly to Prime Minister Hoveydā.[75]

During this period the threat from militant organizations in Iran was high. An attack on a military outpost in the village of Siāhkal, by a radical Marxist-Leninist urban guerrilla group named *Fadāiyān-e Khalq* (Martyrs for the Masses), on 8 February 1971, ushered in a new phase of opposition to the Shah's regime. Moreover, and alarmingly for the security services, the group made it one of their principal objectives to disrupt the Celebrations.[76] Around the time of the festivities, US Ambassador Douglas MacArthur was almost kidnapped by gunmen who ambushed his limousine, and a plan to kidnap the British ambassador, Peter Ramsbotham, was also uncovered.[77] More attempted kidnappings prompted an increase in security, as the Dutch ambassador explained in a report in early October: 'Considering the two recent failed kidnapping attempts of Eghbal followed by the very recent almost successful kidnapping in the centre of Tehran of the son of princess Ashraf the security measures have become extreme.'[78] SAVAK later claimed that sixty members of the Iranian Liberation Organization were charged with plotting to carry out kidnappings during the Celebrations.[79] Moreover, a plan by the Islamic militant organization *Mojāhedin-e Khalq* to blow up Tehran's main power station in order to disrupt the Celebrations was also foiled.[80]

In response to this growing threat from violent organizations, in the period leading up to the Celebrations, the country was placed in lockdown. Some tourists had difficulty gaining access to Iran during the week of the festivities as no one was to be given entry or transit visas without prior approval. Ramsbotham noted that in particular 'young student or hippy types will obviously have great difficulty securing Iranian visas during this period as intention seems to be to refuse entry to any possible trouble makers'.[81] The issue of security was discussed among the international community, which would be sending their representatives to Iran, at the highest level. President Nixon, for example, was said to have accepted his invitation at first, only to withdraw later due to the 'major problems' of 'security and logistics'[82] and security concerns were raised by other states, including Australia.[83] Security services around the world were undoubtedly aware of Iraqi support for militant activists who opposed the Shah and of their intention to disrupt the occasion. Indeed, a State Department report noted the intensification during the first three months of 1971 of violent activities by 'externally directed and supported subversive elements'.[84] This is supported by SAVAK reports, which note that Iraq, in conjunction with several other countries, intended to sabotage the Celebrations.[85] With the eyes of the world on Iran, any disruption would have caused huge embarrassment and dispelled the impression that was promoted through the Celebrations of Iran as a land of peace and opportunity. The severity of the actions of the security services in Iran should, therefore, be viewed in light of the heightened threat from militants and radical political activists in this period.

Security concerns led to the exclusion of large numbers of Iranian citizens from the Celebrations. Festivities did occur in cities, towns and villages all around the country, however, these were outshone by events such as the gala dinner, the commemoration at Pasargadae and the parade at Persepolis, at which ordinary Iranians were absent, able to watch only on their television screens. This was contrary to the advice of Arthur Upham Pope, who made the following suggestion in 1960: 'Of course there should not be a single person in Persia during this period who does not have the message of this significant event dramatically brought home to him. It can be a tremendous creator of morale and intense loyalty to the country and of a resolute home to build a future adequate to the promise of its beginnings.'[86] The military parade, he suggested, should travel from city to city, giving everyone the chance to observe the spectacle. Pope envisioned a celebration in which the country could come together in a moment of communal merriment. Instead, the security forces turned the area around Persepolis into something akin to a 'maximum security prison',[87] sealed off with troops from the gendarmerie, the airborne division and the Imperial Guards.[88] Even to diplomats staying in Shiraz, it was virtually impossible to gain access to what seemed to them like an 'impregnable fortress'.[89] There were 2,000 seats reserved at the parade at Persepolis for private Iranian citizens, over half of whom were already in Shiraz, and a further 800 who would fly to Shiraz from Tehran on the day of the event, but it must be said that this is a small number.[90] Given the security concerns and lack of space, it was perhaps felt that it would be difficult to accommodate any more than that.

Considering the state of high alert, it is understandable that the organizers of the event, in particular the head of SAVAK, General Nasiri, who was 'personally responsible' for security measures, were reluctant to take any chances.[91] This, however, left many

Iranians feeling left out at the expense of foreigners, for whom the Celebrations were not intended to be a matter of national pride. One person said, 'We, the people, knew nothing of it. We paid for it. It was in our name but we could not get within a mile of it. Literally. The road was blocked by soldiers – real soldiers, not walk-on operetta parts.'[92] The vast sums of money spent had been justified on the basis that they would benefit the Iranian people, but many felt excluded. They saw images of foreigners eating a splendid dinner of French food, paid for, as they believed, by state funds. To the regime the stringent security measures were necessary, but its overzealous approach contributed to discontent. The Economist Intelligence Unit, an independent analytical body, stated that it was 'a comment on the stability of the regime that its opponents were able to mobilise so little support at such a crucial time'.[93] It was perhaps rather a comment on the ruthless efficiency of the security forces that such opposition was rendered ineffective.

Corruption and the Pahlavis

Rumours of corruption damaged the perception of the Celebrations too. During one meeting of the Executive Committee, Shojāʿ al-Din Shafā delivered a report on his recent trip to Europe, detailing the harsh criticism in the European press of the contracts signed with Jansen and Maxim's. When he finished his report, Empress Farah complained that the corruption and malpractice of a few were damaging the reputation of the Executive Committee.[94] Incensed, ʿAlam, who was responsible for the contracts, withdrew from the meeting, threatening to resign.[95] Not only were the Celebrations considered wasteful, but the already rich and powerful were also believed to be benefitting from the wastefulness. This was not merely a criticism of the Celebrations but also of a political culture in which those in positions of authority became ever more rich and powerful. Whenever a lot of money was spent on a project, many people assumed that pockets were being lined. Rumours of corruption, therefore, contributed to dissatisfaction and, as Ramsbotham noted, 'although it was only the students who protested publicly, muttered criticism of the expense could be heard from almost every quarter'.[96]

Although there was no direct evidence of ʿAlam misappropriating funds, SAVAK had serious concerns about financial irregularities concerning another member of the Executive Committee. Cyrus Farzāneh, head of the Iranian National Tourist Organization, was, according to a report, 'known among the people as corrupt', and during the construction of hotels for the Celebrations, there were said to have been 'many discussions as to his misuse of funds'. Apparently, the report continues, a cheque of 2.2 million rials ($29,000) was sent from Queen Farah's office to the Tourist Organization, along with a letter asking for a confirmation of receipt. When the queen's office later contacted the Ministry of Information, which by then had absorbed the Tourist Organization, to find out what happened, no evidence of the letter or the cheque was found. After investigation, it became clear that Farzāneh had destroyed the letter and had cashed the cheque. When asked about the money later, Farzāneh claimed that he had given it to Mehdi Bahremand, deputy head of the Tourist Organization at the time, but, the report states, 'that was not the case and it is not clear what happened to the money'. The author of the report appeared frustrated that, although both the head of Farah's office, Karim Pāshā Bahādori, and the later minister of information and tourism, Gholāmrezā Kiyānpur, were aware of the issue, nothing was done and there was no serious investigation.[97]

It is difficult to assess properly the accuracy of this report, not least because it was published by the Islamic Republic in the form of a transcript of an undated document. But parts of the account ring true. Farzāneh was a member of the elite and, according to the same report, travelled with the Shah abroad on most of his trips, which perhaps explains the lack of investigation into the issue. In another example of this protection of people close to the Shah, Parviz Sābeti, the head SAVAK's internal security division, was threatened with a court-martial for writing a report critical of one of the Shah's friends.[98] Not only was such corruption commonplace among the political elite, but there was also no organization in place with the power to investigate. The report concludes that 'Farzāneh continued his corruption until 1355, when he had a heart attack and retired.'[99] In spite of question marks over the reliability of this story – SAVAK sources published by the Islamic Republic are customarily selected to elicit a negative perception – it does give a good impression as to the type of financial benefits the political elite were believed to have enjoyed.[100]

Meanwhile, local and foreign journalists continued to focus their reports on the extravagance of the Celebrations. Even after the student protests of early 1971, which clearly demonstrated popular anger at the purported high cost of the Celebrations, reports still appeared in the local press boasting of the spending. *Kayhan International*, for example, ran the story in June 1971 that a British firm had won an $864,000 contract to install decorative lights in Tehran and Shiraz.[101] The regime promoted this luxury expenditure as indicative of its success and was eager to show off these aspects of the event to the local and foreign media, but this only led to more rumour and conjecture. One student speculated that the lights from Mehrābād Airport to 24 Esfand Square alone cost one million tomans ($135,000) and that this was the source of people's unhappiness.[102] An opposition radio station stoked the anger of Iranians by suggesting that 'poor people's taxes have been poured into the pockets of the English firm'.[103]

From a public relations perspective, not only did the Pahlavi regime simply not do enough to counter the disapproval of the high cost of the Celebrations, even if some of it could have easily been justified in the context of Iran's economic development, but they also fanned the flames of protest. British Ambassador Peter Ramsbotham recognized both the positive aspects of the Celebrations and the regime's failure to present them convincingly, as they adopted the (unsuccessful) strategy of trying to divert attention away from any talk of expenditures: 'Even the luxury expenditure on the tent city (the "Claridges in the desert" aspect, pounced upon by the foreign press) was justified as necessary to attract foreign tourists and investment, although the Shah and the Empress tried to divert attention from it.'[104] The construction of the tent city was widely presented in the media as a waste of money, but it formed part of a strategy to develop tourism infrastructure and attract foreign tourists to Iran. This strategy was ultimately successful and benefitted Iran's economy, as will be discussed in the following chapter. Rather than make that case strongly in the media and tackle the criticism directly, the regime tended to distance itself from it and refused to address any subjects of criticism.

But with such vast resources and influence in the media, how did the Pahlavi regime allow the negative perception of the Celebrations to endure? The answer seems to be that the Pahlavis grew tired of the media condemnation and rather than fight it simply ignored it. Queen Farah, for instance, was involved in the organization of the Celebrations, and in interviews with the foreign media beforehand showed great enthusiasm for the event. However, one year later, when 'Alam suggested she attend the premiere of the official documentary of the Celebrations, she responded, 'Leave me alone, I do not want our names to be associated with the work of the Celebrations anymore.'[105] There was a sense that by this time the regime was eager to move on from the Celebrations and a number of initiatives planned to commemorate the occasion did not come to fruition. For example, funds had been set aside in the budget of the Central Council for the publication of a volume commemorating the Celebrations, titled *Yādnāmeh-ye Jashn-e Shāhanshāhi-ye Irān*. It was planned for publication in 1353, three years after the Celebrations had taken place, but the project was apparently abandoned.[106] A year after the Celebrations, a bibliography of works published for the event in Iran and around the world was issued, titled *Ketābshenāsi-ye Jashn-e Shāhanshāhi-ye Irān*, volume 1.[107] Volume 2, of which no mention can be found anywhere, but which would perhaps have included greater details concerning books published outside Iran, since this aspect of volume 1 was incomplete, was not published.

In October 1972, a ceremony was held at Pasargadae to mark the first anniversary of the 2500th Anniversary Celebrations. A wreath was laid at the tomb of Cyrus the Great by 'Alam in a ceremony reminiscent of the one held one year earlier, followed by the broadcasting of the Shah's speech at the tomb. 'Alam was accompanied by cabinet ministers, military officers and civilian officials. Other venues for similar commemorations included the Shahyād Tower and Rudaki Hall in Tehran, and schools, factories and national institutions around the country, while cinema houses arranged special film screenings.[108] An exhibition was held in Tehran, arranged by the Imperial Court and the Ministry of Culture and Art, detailing all of the publications from forty-seven countries that had been released to coincide with the Celebrations.[109] The commemoration was modest in comparison with the festivities of the previous year and did not receive much media attention. The Shah evidently did not consider it particularly important and went to Russia on a state visit while it was being held. The regime had intended to turn the date of the Celebrations into an annual holiday, but after one year this plan was also abandoned. Presumably, there was little interest from the Imperial Court and the regime shifted its focus on to the next celebration, the fiftieth anniversary of the Pahlavi Dynasty, which was held in 1976–7.

***

As has been shown, the wide exposure the Celebrations received gave the regime's opponents an opportunity to rally resistance against them and, by extension, the regime itself. The emergence of armed guerrillas in northern Iran at the beginning of 1971, meanwhile, is evidence of the radicalization of some of the groups opposed to the Shah that had been forced underground. In his report on the Celebrations, Peter Ramsbotham noted the historical context of the protests.

> Unlike the Coronation, which had been a popular occasion, little criticised, the preparations for the 25th centenary aroused some bitter opposition ... But it would be wrong to assume that the centenary extravaganza was alone responsible for provoking the increased discontent with the regime which has been evident over the past year ... Since 1967 there has been a sense of growing disillusionment and frustration, which the students first expressed in the bus riots of February 1970, long before the celebrations became a burning issue. Undoubtedly the celebrations offered opponents of the Shah a perfect target on which to focus popular discontent.[110]

It is easy to take a simplified view of the hostility to the Celebrations, but those engaged in Iranian politics at the time understood the complexities of political opposition. There were some valid criticisms of the Celebrations, but there was also a general trend, as Ramsbotham noted, of 'growing disillusionment and frustration' developing in this period. The Celebrations provided a convenient focal point but were not the sole source of popular discontent.

Jahāngir Āmuzegār observed that during the Pahlavi period in general, 'the opposition had a systematic and elaborate plan for discrediting him [the Shah] and the regime where the impact was greatest', but the regime, in contrast, had no such organized and efficient public relations mechanism in place. The effectiveness of the opposition against the Shah was, therefore, 'partly the result of the wide gap in competence and sophistication between his own poor public relations' apparatus and that of his enemies'.[111] The international attention the Celebrations received allowed for the consolidation of disparate groups with varying political ideologies into a unified opposition to the Shah. Abbas Milani referred to the Celebrations as a 'propaganda bonanza' for the Confederation of Iranian Students, and certainly the same could be said of other groups both in Iran and abroad.[112] The perception of the Celebrations even today is overwhelmingly negative, indicative of the effectiveness of the opposition to them. It is the victor who writes the history, it is said. In today's Iran, the events of 1971 are referred to as *bazm-e ahriman*, the devil's feast.

Khomeini's opposition to the Celebrations through his speeches from Najaf, which were relayed into Iran by radio and in written reproductions, and subsequently quoted in opposition pamphlets distributed around universities, made him a figurehead of opposition to the Shah's rule. Khomeini attacked the Pahlavi historical narrative, the ideology of Pahlavism and by extension the very legitimacy of the Pahlavi regime itself, which the Celebrations were supposed to reinforce. In a sense, the religious opposition constituted a clash of narratives, with one side promoting the idea that Iranian kingship had brought success and glory to the country, and the other side arguing that Iranian kings had enslaved the people, bringing them misery and destitution. This view was most clearly expressed by Khomeini, but as this chapter has shown, opposing narratives were also promoted by other influential figures such as Shari'ati, while students in Qom objected to the Shahyād Tower in Tehran which they considered to be an un-Islamic symbol.

Meanwhile, the regime did not do enough to counter the negative perception of the Celebrations, and rather than attempt to answer the concerns of protesters with a positive message, they locked them up and adopted more rigorous security measures. This left many Iranians feeling angry at being left out. They were largely excluded from the principal ceremonies in Persepolis and Pasargadae, and in their place were foreigners, experiencing the Shah's sumptuous hospitality at a supposedly enormous cost to the national budget. The regime would justify such spending as contributing to Iran's economic development by encouraging international investment and inspiring foreign tourists to visit Iran, but these arguments failed to pacify its detractors. Ali Ansari has written that the Pahlavi regime tended to prioritize Iran over Iranians themselves, a criticism that could be levelled against the organizers of the Imperial Celebrations.[113] It is clear that domestically the regime took for granted the passivity of its citizens and while individual acts of dissent were dealt with decisively by the security forces, the underlying causes of discontent were not given much scrutiny.

7

The cost of the Celebrations

The Imperial Celebrations formed the highlight of a year-long commemoration of Cyrus the Great. During his 1350 Nowruz speech, the Shah said: 'The best gift which we can certainly offer to this (Cyrus the Great) immortal hero at the beginning of such a year is the existence of a proud, progressive and prosperous Iran who, drawing on her magnificent past heritage is looking up to a yet more magnificent future.'[1] During the Cyrus the Great Year, the regime placed great emphasis on economic development: dams, industrial complexes and hotels were constructed and airports and roads were expanded. Reflecting on the period, Hushang Nahāvandi, then chancellor of the Pahlavi University, wrote: 'These were just some of the projects, among hundreds of others, which made the Year of Celebration a "great leap forward" for Iran, demonstrating its economic vitality and dynamism and showing its will to draw upon new sources of collective imagination and creativity, while renewing its millennial traditions.'[2] Despite the commonly held belief that the Celebrations were 'squanderous', therefore, there is a case to be made that a significant part of the spending associated with the occasion should be considered investment. This is important to consider when discussing the costs incurred, for although many projects were completed in conjunction with the Celebrations, and the spending associated with them was included in estimates for the total cost of the event, they were not funded by the organizing committee but by other agencies, such as the Plan Organization. Moreover, most of these projects were not implemented for the enjoyment of the foreign attendees of the Celebrations in October 1971 but were intended to provide widespread and lasting benefits to the Iranian nation.

Much has been written about the Celebrations' expense and wild speculation as to the cost could be heard not only on the streets of Tehran and on university campuses but also in the foreign press. The presentation of the Celebrations as lavish and wasteful has largely gone unchallenged since the time of the occasion in 1971. Critics, international and domestic, at the time commented on the unsuitability of Iran to hold such an event, while some of its people still lived in abject poverty. A report in the *Washington Daily News* called the Celebrations a 'vain, pompous, vulgar show of wealth'[3] and *Newsweek* wrote that the event was 'a mixture of pomp and pomposity, of regal splendor and petty carping'.[4] The Iranian Liberation Front, a foreign-based organization opposed to the Shah, declared that 'the Puppet regime wants to have the most expensive celebration in human history'.[5] According to Andrew Scott Cooper, as mentioned earlier, reports such as these 'presented a devastating portrait of conditions inside Iran and helped define the Shah as a corrupt, cruel dictator'.[6] The Celebrations have become such a crucial part of the characterization of the extravagance of the Pahlavi court that they are considered beyond vindication. Even more favourable accounts in the secondary literature conclude that they were overpriced and ultimately counterproductive.

The heightened media attention introduced an element of sensationalism to the event, particularly with regard to the cost, that has persisted to this day. In a recent interview, Abulhasan Banisadr, former president of the Islamic Republic, said, 'I haven't made a detailed study, but I heard that it [the cost] was $650 million.' In the same television programme, a Swiss waiter declared confidently that the equivalent of the annual budget of Switzerland had been spent on the occasion.[7] In fact, depending on which source one reads, the estimated cost of the Celebrations fluctuates from the official figure of $16.8 million stated by Asadollāh 'Alam at the time to $300 million,[8] $1 billion,[9] and even $4 billion.[10] Herein lies the problem: when discussing the costs associated with the Celebrations, do we include infrastructural development, or merely the entertaining of guests over five days in October 1971? If the latter, then state spending was closer to 'Alam's estimate than Banisadr's. If the former, then even Banisadr's was perhaps too conservative. The regime can take some blame for this. Throughout the year 1350, they were keen to link spending on huge projects to the Celebrations and the Cyrus the Great Year, fostering the impression that vast amounts were spent on 'the Celebrations'.

One important sector that benefitted both from the exposure generated by the main ceremonies and from infrastructural development was tourism. The basic objectives of tourism planning, as set out by the Plan Organization, were threefold: first, to make Iranian culture better known; second, to improve the facilities for foreign and domestic tourists; and third, to attract a larger number of foreign tourists to Iran.[11] Each of these points was covered during the planning and implementation of the Celebrations, with positive results. The industry saw huge investment, and tourism figures increased significantly in the years following the Celebrations. This chapter evaluates the cost of the Celebrations, emphasizing the distinction between costs directly associated with the principle ceremonies and those related to infrastructure and industry.

The Plan Organization and the Celebrations

In the late 1940s, it was decided that Iran's economic planning should be carried out by a new government agency. This agency, named *Sāzemān-e Barnāmeh*, the Plan Organization, was established in 1949. It was designed to be semi-autonomous, thus removing it from the 'soggy mess', as Khodādād Farmānfarmā'iyān termed it, of the Iranian government bureaucracy, and it had its own finances earmarked, which it had the authority to dispense as it saw fit.[12] For example, all of the country's oil revenues were set aside for the First Plan (1949–55), which, due to the oil nationalization crisis in the early 1950s, ultimately led to a halt in its progress.[13] Abulhasan Ebtehāj, who headed the Plan Organization from 1954 until 1959, explained the rationale behind such government planning efforts:

> Some degree of national planning is essential to the high rate of investment that is required if undeveloped countries are to break the vicious circle of poverty and stagnation. The government must be planner. But the government will only be an originator of new activities, the chief engine of growth, a major source of innovation, and a large scale enterpriser to the extent that private investors and businesses fail to recognize, or to exploit their myriad opportunities for expansion.[14]

In other words, private businesses held the key to Iran's economic development, but it should be the responsibility of the government to kick-start this development and create a sophisticated plan. The Third Plan (1962–68) was the first real comprehensive development plan and oversaw more directly productive results.[15] Its principal objective was to achieve a minimum gross national product (GNP) growth of 6 per cent annually, which it exceeded by 2 to 3 per cent.[16]

The Fourth Plan (1968–73), which covered the period of the Celebrations, sought to increase GNP at an average annual rate of around 9 per cent. One of the ways in which it would achieve this was through industrial development, by 'gradually increasing the importance of industry, raising the productivity of capital, and using advanced techniques of production'.[17] To help it accomplish this goal, 92 per cent of the $10.8 billion assigned to the Fourth Plan was financed domestically, primarily through oil revenues.[18] When we discuss the high costs associated with the Celebrations, it must be understood that much of what was spent fell under the remit of the Fourth Plan. Of course, the Plan Organization was also one of the consultative bodies involved in the organization of the Anniversary Celebrations from the late 1950s onwards.[19]

As Iran entered the 1970s and the Celebrations began to take shape, it became clear that they presented opportunities to further the Plan Organization's strategy in developing key infrastructure. In his Nowruz message, Prime Minister Amir 'Abbās Hoveydā pointed out that the budget for 1350 (1971–72) was the biggest yet, made possible through the recent increase in the price of oil.[20] To take advantage of the momentum generated, many projects overseen by the Plan Organization were accelerated so that their completion could coincide with Cyrus the Great Year. Among the many projects completed during this year were six dams across the country (named Darius the Great, Cyrus the Great, Aras, Shāh 'Abbās Kabir, Shāpur I and Sangarsavar)[21] and a number of television stations, notably in Kurdistan, Baluchistan and Khorasan.[22] These television stations were a part of a larger $225 million project of national telecommunications, which was established in this year and which also sought to provide 14,000 kilometres of transmission lines.[23] The Ministry of Co-operatives and Rural Affairs announced the establishment of 2,500 cooperatives throughout the country, which would be inaugurated during the Celebrations.[24] This scheme can be linked to both the third phase of the land reform programme initiated as part of the White Revolution, and the Fourth Plan.[25]

At a meeting of the Iran Novin Party on 5 May 1971, Hoveydā, answering criticisms of the spending associated with the Celebrations, argued that without them 'many projects, among others the steel factory (in Isfahan) would not have been finished'.[26] According to the regime, this steel factory was part of a $450 million complex, which, like many other projects, was already underway, but the Celebrations provided an extra impetus to finish it.[27] In effect, as the Shah argued, during Cyrus the Great Year, due to the increase in productivity, 'nearly a whole year's extra work was performed'.[28] The regime tended to exaggerate their achievements and the Shah's statement that an extra year's work was performed is perhaps misleading. What is clear, however, is that the spending associated with the Cyrus the Great Year has often been conflated with spending associated with the ceremonies in Persepolis, Pasargadae and Tehran, which is partly to blame for the inflated estimates as to the overall cost.

Much attention has been paid to the foreign businesses that benefitted from the Celebrations, most notably the French. However, Iranian companies also profited from both the exposure generated and from lucrative contracts directly associated with the occasion. Iran Air, for example, was declared the 'official airline of the celebrations'[29] and used the event to promote itself as a competitive global airline.[30] In the years that followed, it became one of the fastest-growing airlines in the world. Iranian construction companies were also involved in many of the building projects. For example, a company called Pre-Fab Inc. supplied the precast concrete benches for the Āryāmehr Stadium, which was directly funded by the Plan Organization.[31]

One of the industries that benefitted most from the Celebrations was tourism. The positive effect on this sector was not merely a convenient by-product; the Celebrations were part of an overall strategy to develop a potentially lucrative industry that would bring foreign capital to Iran and create jobs. The sites of Persepolis and Pasargadae have always held an allure for travellers to Iran. Despite this, there was no real infrastructure in place to deal with any significant number of tourists visiting the country. In the case of Persepolis, the roads linking the site with Shiraz were of very poor quality, making the 70-kilometre journey long and uncomfortable. The 135-kilometre journey from Shiraz to Pasargadae was even more uncomfortable. Furthermore, there was a general shortage of hotels in the region. The Celebrations were thus intended to act as a catalyst to help the Fars region in particular and the country in general to achieve its tourism potential.[32]

Tourism

In her memoir, Cynthia Helms, the wife of the US ambassador to Tehran, Richard Helms, claims that the idea to hold a national event in Iran was first suggested to then Prime Minister Asadollāh 'Alam by the chairman of the Israeli Government Tourist Association, Teddy Kollek, who would later become mayor of Jerusalem. Kollek argued that the site around Persepolis should first be developed with hotels, roads and new vehicles, and then an event should be organized to attract visitors. According to Cynthia Helms, Kollek never imagined that his suggestion would result in such a huge nationalist spectacle.[33] This story is not entirely true, not least because 'Alam did not become prime minister until 1962, four years after the Celebrations had been conceived. However, though the Celebrations were not originally held with tourism promotion specifically in mind, the organizers were quick to realize that the event could help to bring visitors to Iran and develop the tourism sector.

In the 1950s, fewer than two thousand tourists had visited Iran each year, a figure that rapidly increased throughout the decade to reach around fifty thousand by 1962. In that year, Asadollāh ʿAlam, who was then prime minister, noting the potential of this industry, announced a 200 million rial ($2 million) plan for tourism promotion, and in early 1963 the Iranian National Tourist Organization (INTO) was set up to direct the development of the sector.[34] The organization invited foreign experts to Iran who suggested rather optimistically that within ten years the tourism sector should be able to compete with the oil sector as a source of national revenue.[35] Between 1344 (1965–66) and 1345 (1966–67), the number of visitors increased from 181,498 to 211,824.[36] The Economic Review of 1348 (1969–70) recorded that in that year, numbers had risen to 300,000.[37] Over a third of these foreign visitors arrived from Pakistan, Afghanistan and the Arab world, with another third from the more lucrative markets of United States and Western Europe.[38] It was the latter group that INTO sought to attract in greater numbers.

By 1971, the tourism industry was generating $43 million per year, making it the country's fourth largest industry, behind oil, carpets and raw cotton, in terms of foreign currency earnings.[39] There were clear indications that tourism would soon overtake the other non-petroleum-based industries. Between 1344 (1965–66) and 1349 (1970–71), for instance, the value of exports from carpets rose from $45.4 million to $53.9 million, an increase of 19 per cent, and earnings from raw cotton increased by 13 per cent. During the same five-year period, earnings from tourism saw a 113 per cent increase. A pamphlet published by INTO shortly after the Celebrations stated,

> the industry is still on the threshold of its large potential ... Preparations for the 2500th Anniversary Celebration accelerated those developments to the point where Iran now feels ready to invite the world to her doorstep. The immediate goal is to raise tourist income above the famous Persian carpet and highly valued Persian cotton to take second place behind the export earnings of Iran's massive oil exports ... the country is preparing itself for a mass tourist invasion.[40]

Significant investments in tourism and transport infrastructure included the asphalting of roads, amounting to around $40 million,[41] which had been discussed by the organizers of the Celebrations as being of considerable importance to the occasion as early as 1961.[42] Other significant developments in transport infrastructure included the completion of airports at Abadan, Sanandaj, Kerman, Hamadan, Tabriz, Isfahan and Mashhad, as well as the expansion of the Mehrābād Airport in Tehran and Shiraz Airport,[43] and the inauguration of the railway line between Iran and Turkey.[44] The Van-Kotur-Sharafkhāneh train service began operations on 27 September 1971, and was intended to alleviate administrative problems associated with travel through the Soviet Union, and to benefit both Iran and Turkey economically. According to the *Railway Magazine*, 'Iran, in particular, will divert a large part of her import and export traffic, at present carried by ship to Persian Gulf ports, to the land route.'[45]

A number of tourism pamphlets were published in conjunction with the Celebrations by the Ministry of Information, the Tourist Organization and Iran Air.[46] Books were also published by organizations abroad. The Touring and Automobile Club of Turkey, for instance, published *Türkiye/Iran Transit Route*, a 43-page booklet offering practical travel advice for tourists driving by car through Iran and Turkey.[47] Other books were published abroad for the occasion which sought to increase international exposure of Iran's ancient heritage, such as *Iran of the Master Builders*, published in Switzerland,[48] and the Japanese photographer Banri Namikawa's *Iran*,[49] which included photographs from the parade at Persepolis.

The construction of hotels was also considered as a long-term investment for Iran's tourism infrastructure. The economic report for 1348 (1969–70) announced the building of a ten-storey hotel in Shiraz at a cost of 500 million rials ($6.7 million), for example, and the earlier 1346 (1967–68) report makes it explicitly clear that such spending should be viewed in the context of the Fourth Plan.[50] The tourism budget during this five-year period was set out as follows: construction and installations, 3.6 billion rials ($48 million); education and training, 60 million rials ($800,000); and advertising, 200 million rials ($2.7 million).[51] The 5.5 per cent of the total budget for advertisement was small in comparison to that of construction, which contributed to a supply and demand problem, for although hotels were being built, there was not yet the demand to fill rooms. It was thought that if the construction of hotels could be made to coincide with international events such as the coronation and the Imperial Celebrations, 'if properly utilized' this could help to alleviate this problem.[52]

Three hotels were opened during the Celebrations that had been built specifically with the October festivities in mind: the 160-room Cyrus Hotel in Shiraz; the 180-room Darius Hotel at Persepolis; and the 13-storey Inter-Continental in Tehran with over four hundred rooms. These were collaborative efforts in which INTO had a majority interest. For example, the Inter-Continental cost $13 million, with INTO providing 50 per cent of the capital. Equal parts of the remaining 50 per cent came from the Inter-Continental Corporation and an individual investor, Prince Sadruddin Aga Khan.[53] Although the hotels were built initially to deal with the guests arriving to take part in the Celebrations, particularly the two in Fars, their construction should be viewed also in the context of the development of the tourism industry as part of the Fourth Plan.

The tent city, too, was handed over to the Tourist Organization and was intended to be turned into luxury accommodation, 'a sort of Club Meditarranée for millionaires prepared to pay for the joys of sleeping in the same bed as Princess Grace'.[54] Shortly after the Celebrations, it was rented out for 'a princely sum' for the annual Bal des Petits Lits Blancs and more such events were expected.[55] INTO was charged with developing the area around Persepolis into a grand tourism resort. In a report written four months after the Celebrations, head of INTO Cyrus Farzāneh described his vision for the area:

> A resort with a casino, shows and an evening orchestra at the hotel and the large tent (*shādervān-e bozorg*) in the tent city, should be designed. In addition to that, facilities should include sports and recreational clubs, such as a country club, swimming pool, riding, tennis etc. The next stage is to consider a suitable location near to Persepolis for the construction of a tourist village, with villas and cheap

accommodation, a centre for handicrafts, an artificial lake, a venue for ceremonies and folklore performances, and the starting point for hunting, picnicking, mountain climbing and hiking.[56]

Casino du Liban expressed interest in investing in the project. They wrote to Farzāneh, 'Persepolis, because of the richness of its ancient monuments, has gained increasing praise, especially in light of the 2500th Anniversary Celebrations of Cyrus the Great. It can [therefore] be a centre for tourist attraction.'[57]

INTO, keen to attract further interest from investors, outlined in a booklet on tourism investment opportunities in Iran:

> Near Persepolis is a complex of approximately 50 structures which were designed to house visiting heads of state during the celebrations of the 2,500th Anniversary of the Founding of the Persian Empire, along with the dining and recreation facilities. The buildings are in the form of tents, to evoke the exotic ambience of the country, but in fact they are permanent structures equipped with all modern facilities. This complex could be converted into a unique and appealing ultra-luxury tourist facility and is available to any well-established hoteliers who wish to do so.[58]

Despite these efforts, in a letter to 'Alam after the Celebrations, Farzāneh explained the difficulties in finding serious investors.[59] According to the letter, a number of companies, including Pan American, Intercontinental and Hilton declined the opportunity to invest in the tents. Club Meditarranée offered to take control of the tents, but were only prepared to pay INTO the meagre sum of $3 a night per guest, so INTO rejected the offer. A number of other options were explored, including turning the tents into a museum or country club and putting them up for general sale to the Iranian public, but in the end, it appears that plans to turn them into permanent accommodation were put on hold.

Responding to criticism of the building projects in Fars province, Empress Farah said to a reporter in Europe, 'We would have had to do that at some point anyway, and now we've had to do it a bit quicker. In time the tourists will bring us back the money.'[60] This shows that at least this part of the money spent on the Celebrations was intended as an investment. The fact that the head of INTO, Cyrus Farzāneh, was involved in the planning committee further demonstrates the importance of tourism for the occasion.[61] In addition to infrastructural development, there was a clear and demonstrable effort on behalf of the Celebrations' organizers to promote tourism in Iran, which was made explicit in the months leading up to the event. In a report on the projected effects of the Celebrations on the tourism industry, Farzāneh stated that the '2500th Anniversary Celebration may well be regarded as one of the most rewarding tourist promotion developments of the 20th century.'[62]

The tourism industry was also important as a creator of employment. In 1349 (1970–71), the industry directly employed 23,030 people, with a further 266,200 people employed in construction related to tourism, and 44,381 in restaurants.[63] By 1350 (1971–72), the employment figures were certainly greater, especially given the volume of construction projects underway, particularly in Fars province. In his report, Ramsbotham argued that 'it was good for decentralisation that so much money should be spent outside the capital'. He continued: 'In fact, it was fortunate for the drought-stricken province of Fars that so much money should be poured into it this year: many of the Qashqai nomads who had lost all their flocks, were employed in the celebrations instead of being left to die. Indeed, without the celebrations, Fars might have been a sorry sight.'[64] So, although the regime was criticized for spending money on the Celebrations while people suffered from drought, the attention on the area of Fars actually helped to create employment. As the tourism figures show, the investment was not short term and the projects that were initiated had the potential to provide jobs into the future, as well as bring foreign capital to the area.

The growth of the tourism industry in the immediate period following the Celebrations was considerable. According to official figures, in 1973, 415,000 tourists visited Iran, over a hundred thousand more than in 1970.[65] These tourists spent up to $60 million in the country, representing 14 per cent of the total foreign currency earnings for that year.[66] These figures steadily increased throughout the 1970s into the Fifth Development Plan. By 1975, the number of tourists had increased to 628,000, reaching 690,550 by 1977, with an increase in earnings over the two-year period from $123 million to $152 million.[67] The 10 per cent increase in tourist numbers alongside a 24 per cent increase in generated income during this period suggests a degree of success from INTO in attracting wealthier visitors, as well as effectively harnessing the industry's profitability. It was the aim of the Fifth Development Plan to reach the ambitious figure of 925,000 tourists by 1978, with a budget increase from four billion rials ($53.3 million) at the beginning of the Fourth Plan to 13.6 billion rials ($181.3 million).[68] A later figure proposed that the tourism investment figure for the Fifth Plan would actually reach 23 billion rials[69] and the number of tourists would surpass one million by 1978.[70] A number of initiatives contributed to the increase in the number of tourists throughout the 1970s, including, for example, the introduction of visa-free travel for many countries.[71] But the initial increase of around 35 per cent in tourist figures from 1970 to 1973 suggests that the Celebrations were successful as an exercise in tourism promotion. Moreover, the development of infrastructure to help deal with the projected increase in tourist numbers over the following decade reinforces the argument that a large part of the spending for the Celebrations could be considered as vital investment that ultimately came back through foreign capital.

The cost

At the time of the Celebrations, a large number of Iranian citizens were living below the poverty line, and though the events were partly intended to stimulate the economy, this became one of the principal sources of criticism of the event and the reason many international newspapers focussed their reports on the excessive spending.[72] One Dutch newspaper, for example, reported it as 'fantastic (but true)' that the Celebrations 'will cost a billion dollars in total … [which] serves only to obscure how badly Iran is actually doing … Even in the official statistics the employment rate in the country is estimated at just 29 per cent'.[73] The overseas-based opposition publication *Iran Free Press* wrote: 'Men of conscience, the world over, will either laugh – or cry – at the presumptuousness of an illiterate despot who will wantonly squander 600 million dollars to bedazzle a handful of ineffective or second rate plenipotentiaries while his own people wallow and die in their own filth just beyond the smelling distance of his opulent tables'.[74] As mentioned previously, estimates of the total cost of the Celebrations vary from the official figure of $16.8 million stated by Asadollāh ʿAlam to $4 billion.[75] How can there be such a vast disparity? It is striking that in the literature on the Celebrations, few primary sources are cited as evidence of the cost of the festivities. For example, James Bill states in *The Eagle and the Lion* that the Celebrations cost $200 million, which he admitted is a 'personal estimate based on an examination of various sources'. He does not directly reference any of these 'various sources'.[76]

Shortly after the Celebrations, ʿAlam gave a press conference at which he made a statement regarding the cost of the occasion. The British Foreign Office transcript of this conference underlines, in supposed disbelief, ʿAlam's claim that the Celebrations 'cost no more than 16.8 million dollars'.[77] He confirmed that work associated with the Fourth Plan should not be taken into account since the projects in question 'would have been constructed in any case'.[78] According to ʿAlam, the cost of entertaining heads of state was $2.3 million, the tents at Persepolis cost $6.3 million, the Shahyād Tower cost $6 million and the cost of the parade, the printing of books and transport completed the spending.[79] It should be noted that some of the foreign firms offered their services for free, presumably eager to showcase their wares and services at such a high-profile gathering.[80]

An important consideration is who exactly was responsible for costs associated with the principal festivities in October 1971. According to official sources, the private sector covered the cost of the tent city, the Maxim's dinner,[81] as well as other costs, such as the purchase of fifty cars which were placed at the disposal of foreign heads of state and were donated to the government following the festivities.[82] In another example, in the months leading up to the Celebrations, people were heard to say of the Shahyād Tower things such as 'how many of Iran's poor could be given a better existence with the money spent on that?'[83] Answering this question at a meeting in May 1971, ʿAlam revealed that money had been put aside for the construction of the monument, when suddenly the private sector found out and offered to pay for the whole project.[84] 'Those who oppose the celebrations because of the cost, therefore', he stated in typically robust language, 'cannot be considered Iranians'.[85]

Published documents from the period show that the private sector covered at least some costs. In July 1971, for example, ʿAlam listed donations that he had received amounting to 427,094,750 rials ($5.7 million).[86] The extent to which these donations were 'voluntary' is questionable. The land redistribution of the White Revolution had forced former rich landowners towards the industrial sector, and there was an awareness among the new industrial rich that the regime could, at any time, make things very difficult for their businesses.[87] In the case of the Rezai brothers, in February 1971, the regime, without warning, nationalized their mines, which were worth an estimated $1 billion.[88] At the time of the coronation in 1967, a money changer (*sarof*) from Shiraz was arrested and sent to prison, apparently, his family thought, because of his refusal to contribute financially to the local festivities.[89] There were obvious benefits in keeping the regime on one's side and if businesses had been invited to pay up for a common cause, then it would have been unwise to refuse. The large number of Iranians who bought shares in the commemorative schools for the Celebrations illustrates the extent to which the rich were willing, or persuaded, to contribute. There is also evidence that foreign firms contributed financially, including British banks.[90]

Though much of the spending on the Celebrations can be viewed as investment in Iran's economy, it must be stressed that this was not the case for all costs incurred, and some of the spending was certainly extravagant. Jewellery was made for the imperial family specially for the occasion, using rough diamonds and pearls from the treasury and platinum, with costs covered by the Imperial Court.[91] To give an idea of how much this cost to make, when a relatively minor royal, Princess Pari Simā,[92] declared her intention to attend, a tiara made with diamonds and necklace and earrings made with diamonds and pearls were produced at a cost of 3,582,400 rials ($47,800).[93] The cost to the Imperial Court for this particular occasion, given that all of the imperial family were present as representatives of the monarchy, was potentially considerably high.

Other costs included the purchase of 11,000 commemorative medals, which were ordered from the French firm Arthus-Bertrand at a cost of nearly 200,000 francs ($36,000).[94] In addition to these special medals, commemorative coins were minted by the Central Bank in gold, silver and bronze, and were mostly offered as gifts to guests at Persepolis.[95] The cost of arranging exhibitions could also reach a considerable amount. An exhibition sent to Canada, for instance, cost upwards of $677,800,[96] and the production of books was more expensive than one might imagine. The publication of the aforementioned *Persia: The Immortal Kingdom*, for example, cost 47,616,720 rials ($634,890)[97] and 32 million rials had been budgeted ($426,700) for the planned commemorative volume about the Celebrations (*Yādnāmeh-ye Jashn-e Shāhanshāhi-ye Irān*).[98]

Notwithstanding these costs, often-stated figures between $100 and $300 million are evidently incorrect, though the exact cost is nearly impossible to determine. The reasons for this situation are fourfold. First, as stated above, money came from different sources, and some of the money spent on the Celebrations came from the existing budgets of ministries. In a letter to Bushehri in December 1969, 'Alam makes this point clear. In response to a request from the Ministry of Natural Resources for a budget of 2.5 million rials ($33,000) to cover costs for the Celebrations, and a request from the Police Force asking for 15.3 million rials ($200,000) to buy 100 police motorcycles for use during the Celebrations, 'Alam said that the funds should come from their existing budgets. He told Bushehri to 'please inform these institutions [Ministry of Natural Resources and Police] and all other government agencies and ministries that this is a national celebration and that it is the duty of every individual to do whatever they can to help'.[99] Rather than wait for an order from the Central Council, all government and non-government agencies were advised that funding should come out of their own budgets and they should not seek extra money from the Imperial Court. Supposedly annoyed by such requests, 'Alam ended the letter by discouraging frequent correspondence along these lines. Funds allocated by ministries to the Celebrations were relatively modest, particularly given the large figures associated with the event. A document from December 1970, for instance, states that the Ministry of Finance had agreed to spend 30 million rials on the Celebrations the following year, around $400,000.[100] One of the problems with trying to come up with a satisfactory sum for the total cost of the Celebrations, therefore, is that some of what was spent was covered by the budgets of different government ministries and therefore did not appear in the final accounts of the Central Council.

Second, as argued earlier in this chapter, some of the money spent on the Celebrations could be said to have contributed to Iran's long-term economic plan. Since tourism promotion was an important aspect of the Celebrations, anything that contributed to this exercise could, arguably, be justified as viable investment, including, for instance, the construction of the tent city. Even if the Central Council had agreed to pay for the 100 motorcycles requested in the letter to 'Alam cited above, this could also have been considered as a long-term investment. The ephemeral aspects of the event are often overstated in many historical accounts of the Celebrations, but by studying the available documentary evidence, we see that there was a clear focus on providing lasting benefits and that there was comparatively little waste.

The third problem with citing such huge sums is that they do not consider the fact that spending was spread over a number of years. Part of the spending for the Shahyād Tower, for instance, amounting to around $2.5 million, was spread evenly over three years, from 1347 (1968–69) to 1349 (1970–71).[101] Furthermore, the accounts for the Central Council show that between Mehr 1339 (September 1960) and Esfand 1349 (February 1971), the purchases of the council amounted to 422,494,290 rials ($5.6 million), in 1350 (1971–72), 579,941,476 rials ($7.7 million) and in 1351 (1972–73), 344,071,090 rials ($4.6 million).[102] There were additional expenditures on top of this, but these figures clearly show that spending was spread over a period of time. James Buchan argues in his *Days of God* that $300 million amounted to a third of Iran's oil revenue in 1970, so had such a sum been spent for a three-day event then 'Iran's civil servants, armed forces and public creditors could not have been paid and the country would have been bankrupt'.[103] He has a point, and the suggestion that there was a huge strain on the economy for just one year to fund only the ceremonies and banquets of the Celebrations is misleading.

Finally, the final reports from the accounting office of the Central Council reveal no evidence of the spending of hundreds of millions of dollars that has been widely speculated about. The largest outlays were as follows:

- Costs associated with the Shahyād Tower: 441,529,405 rials ($5.9 million).
- Catering in Isfahan, Tehran, Persepolis and Shiraz, and related costs: 217,852,489 rials ($3 million).
- Plan for the 'camp tourism facility': 113,746,569 rials ($1.5 million).
- Repair of Persepolis, with funds allocated to the Ministry of Culture and Art: 77,062,237 rials ($1 million).
- Aviation costs including ground hospitality, allocated to the transport committee and the national airline, Iran Air: 60,214,630 rials ($800,000).
- Dining service by the Imperial Court: 11,150,431 rials ($148,672).[104]

Total costs borne by the Central Council were calculated at 1.8 billion rials ($24 million), which includes $3 million taken out of its budget to fund the coronation in 1967.[105] The main financial contributor to the council was the Imperial Court, which gave 1,342,648,702 rials ($17.9 million), but it also received receipts from the National Oil Company ($800,000) and the Plan Organization ($1.3 million for the design of the camp).[106] If hundreds of millions of dollars were spent on the Celebrations then the money certainly did not come directly from the Central Council.

When discussing the cost of the Celebrations in his memoirs, 'Abdolrezā Ansāri says that a garden in east Tehran, Bāgh-e Javādiyeh, was purchased by the council for use during the Celebrations. He also noted that the council had a budget of around $7 million and that daily expenses were covered by interest.[107] The final accounts support his recollections and show that the purchase and furnishing of Bāgh-e Javādiyeh cost 64,808,754 rials ($864,117). The interest on loans received by the council between 1340 and 1351 amounted to $1.4 million and Bagh-e Javādiyeh was later sold for $1.3 million, a considerable profit.[108] Ansāri's account is by far the most detailed and, when judged against the published financial records, the most accurate, too. Ansāri also records a meeting he held with 'Alam after the press conference in which he stated the cost of the Celebrations to have been $16.8 million. Ansāri asked 'Alam why he used a different figure to the one he offered. 'He replied that his figures were based on the report issued by his financial department', Ansāri recalls.[109] The records show that the receipts from the Imperial Court until Esfand 1350 (March 1972) amounted to approximately $17.9 million, just over $1 million more than 'Alam stated in the press conference. 'Alam's conference was held in October 1971, so it is possible that the extra money represented funds missed by the Imperial Court's accounting at the time, or outstanding payments. So, while at first glance 'Alam's $16.8 million estimate seems disingenuous, it is possible that there was some factual basis to his statement, though he referred solely to the cost to the Imperial Court rather than the overall spending.

***

In the absence of paperwork from individual ministries and contributing businesses, it is impossible to come up with an irrefutable figure for the cost of the main ceremonies. At the same time, it is clear that the high sums often quoted with the spending on the Celebrations are not backed up by the available documentary evidence. Even the documents published by the Islamic Republic in *Bazm-e Ahriman* with the express intention to incriminate the organizers of the Celebrations do not provide this information.

Was the attempt to use the Celebrations to stimulate the economy successful? Looking at the tourism industry alone, it seems it was. The industry generated less than $45 million per year in the three years leading up to 1971 but would generate $152 million by 1976. As well as direct investment in the sector through the construction of hotels and development of roads, the Celebrations were extremely successful at promoting Iran around the world and bringing foreigners to the country. The regime's promotion of the Pahlavi state ideology, which drew attention to Iran's rich culture and civilization, and the exhibitions and special events held in countries around the world, also supported this effort. Moreover, restoration work carried out at the ruins of Persepolis was of long-lasting benefit to the tourism industry, as was the equipment for the light and sound show installed at the ruins, which made the ancient Achaemenid city only the fourth major tourist attraction in the world to have such a feature.[110] The British ambassador, Peter Ramsbotham, who became the ambassador to the United States later in the 1970s, argued that the Celebrations 'put Persia-Iran on the map'. He continues: 'When I was in the United States afterwards, people knew about it – "Oh, gee, were you at Persepolis?" They actually knew where Persia was. They never knew before. It was a successful way of putting Persia on the international map.'[111] If this was one of the purposes of the Celebrations, as this chapter has argued it was, then they certainly achieved a degree of success.

It is tempting to dismiss the building projects initiated during the Celebrations as vanity projects. But although the Shahyād Tower could be viewed as such, many of the projects were of considerable importance in the context of the programme of the Plan Organization. In a review of the Iranian economy for the year 1349 (1970–71), the author stated: 'It is significant of modern and resurgent Iran that the ephemeral elements in the celebration of this anniversary are being kept to a minimum and that His Imperial Majesty is placing great emphasis on the advancement and completion of projects of permanent value to the country.'[112] The evidence presented in this chapter suggests that this observation was accurate, at least to a degree. This chapter has shown that one of the purposes of the Celebrations was to stimulate the economy and encourage foreign investment. The regime is often criticized for the stringent security measures taken during the Celebrations, discussed in the previous chapter, however these were vital to present Iran as a land of stability and opportunity. The Celebrations were similar to an international sporting event, such as the Olympic Games, in that such events are essentially held to demonstrate the achievements of the host country. They require a sophisticated security apparatus, high-quality infrastructure and considerable political clout. By demonstrating progress in these areas, Iran was asserting its place among the community of nations as a modern and rapidly developing country, worthy of attention and investment.

Conclusion

This book began with a quote from Professor Laurence Elwell-Sutton, who in 1973 called for 'an objective assessment' of the Imperial Celebrations, which he believed was necessary in view of the 'discourteous tone' of many of the reports from foreign journalists. In spite of Elwell-Sutton's remark, such an impartial assessment had hitherto not been undertaken and thus the perception of the Celebrations in the literature on Pahlavi Iran has been overwhelmingly negative, effectively since the time of the event in 1971. As recently as 2017, for example, the historian Christopher de Bellaigue described the Celebrations as an 'unfeasibly silly party'.[1] This book has made the case that the Celebrations, though aspects might be described as 'silly', achieved many of their objectives, primarily in terms of economic development, international relations and cultural policy.

The Celebrations were part of a cultural movement that began when Shojāʿ al-Din Shafā became head of the Imperial Court's culture office in the late 1950s. As one of the key architects of the regime's cultural policy, Shafā helped to ensure that the work of organizations with which he was involved, such as the Imperial Cultural Council, the Pahlavi Library and the Committee for Authoring the History of Iran, both influenced the Celebrations and benefitted from them. Many of the cultural initiatives served to promote the Pahlavi state ideology, which argued that the monarchy was central to the past and future success of Iran, but many also sought to stimulate genuine scholarly inquiry. The positive impact of not only the Celebrations but also the regime's patronage of scholarship initiated what should be considered an unsurpassed golden era for Iranian studies. Many international academic initiatives survived solely due to support from the Pahlavi court, such as the *Journal of Mithraic Studies*, which was subsidized by the court from 1976 and was disbanded immediately following the revolution. The revolution left a significant funding hole that, in many cases, was left unfilled.

The promotion of a 'Hellenocentric' view of Ancient Persia served the Pahlavi regime's ideological interests, allowing them better to broadcast the narrative of the paternal and humanitarian Cyrus. Though in certain cases this may have encouraged lazy scholarship, it also prompted debate. At the time of the Celebrations, for example, an announcement of a recently identified fragment of the Cyrus Cylinder was made ahead of publication 'in view of the interest in the Cyrus Cylinder aroused by the recent celebrations of Cyrus's 2500th anniversary ... [to] emphasize the essential character of the Cyrus Cylinder as not a general declaration of human rights or religious toleration but simply a building inscription'.[2] In the 1980s, a series of workshops was organized by Heleen Sancisi-Weerdenburg and Herman Wallinga, with the aim of correcting the Hellenocentric approach to the history of Achaemenid Persia by bringing together scholars from diverse fields such as Assyriology, Egyptology, Classics and Old Testament studies.[3] In 2005, John Curtis and St John Simpson argued that 'Achaemenid Studies have undergone a revolution in the last 30 years', which they connected 'perhaps with a period when large-scale foreign excavations in Iran have not been possible and scholars have had the opportunity to undertake a radical review of the whole subject'.[4] The Pahlavi regime's cultural policy, which promoted all studies in Ancient Iran by supporting conferences, exhibitions, excavations and publications, played a role in this too.

While scholars reassessed their approaches to the Achaemenid period partly in response to the cultural policies of the Pahlavi regime, a rebranding was also attempted by militant clergymen in Iran. Shortly after the revolution, Sādeq Khalkhāli, nicknamed the 'hanging judge' for the callous ruthlessness he displayed in his role as chief justice of the revolutionary courts, portrayed Cyrus the Great as a wicked sodomite in his 57-page booklet *Kurush-e Dorughin va Jenāyatkār*, The False and Criminal Cyrus (published 1360). In the work, Khalkhāli was eager to show that the Pahlavi presentation of the Achaemenid king was a distorted one. Far from being a great king, he 'like all other kings and powerful men of history, of all God's gifts, only had brute force and the sword, and with a barbaric logic that by force of arms others would submit to their control' sought to achieve dominion over the world.[5] Moreover, and in Khalkhāli's eyes perhaps more damning than his supposed brutality, Cyrus had a Jewish mother, so 'at the age of 12 Cyrus had read the Torah and was familiar with the Jewish language and script'.[6] According to Khalkhāli, it was Cyrus's mother who ordered him to attack Babylon, in order to release her and, by extension, his people from captivity. 'The Jewish race today', Khalkhāli continues, 'has been introduced as criminal, and an enemy of humanity'.[7] From a historical perspective, Khalkhāli's account was complete nonsense, but, as Ali Ansari has noted, his work did address the fact that 'Cyrus was much more prominent in Judeo-Persian literature than in its concomitant Islamo-Persian texts, where the principal aim had been to reconcile the histories and mythologies of the *Shahnameh* with those of Islam'.[8]

Hushang Nahāvandi has argued that if 'it had not been for the camp at Persepolis and the banquet at Maxim's ... and if it had not been for the two hundred waiters from *Potel et Chabot* ... then Iranian opinion would scarcely have been upset by the event'.[9] While Nahāvandi certainly has a point, even if the Celebrations had been considerably more modest, the likes of Khomeini and the militant opposition would most likely still have used them as a rallying point against the Shah. Indeed, in his speech from Najaf, Khomeini did not mention Maxim's, nor the tent city at Persepolis, and was less concerned with the vast expenditure than with rumours of Israel's participation. 'Experts have been invited from Israel to take care of the arrangements', he said; 'from Israel, that stubborn enemy of Islam and the Qur'an ... which is at war with the Muslims and plans to occupy all the lands of Islam up to Iraq and (God forbid) to destroy the noble shrines of Islam!'[10] The decision to use foreign firms such as Maxim's clearly caused problems for the organizers, but on a conceptual level, it was the regime's adoption of a pre-Islamic, thus non-Muslim figure, praised in the Torah as the Lord's anointed, and lauded by pagan Greek playwriters, historians and philosophers, that provoked the anger of clerics like Khomeini and Khalkhāli.

Not only did the regime not attempt to reconcile the great figures of Ancient Iran with Islam, some members of the clergy suspected that they wanted to erase Islam. These suspicions were confirmed in 1976 when the regime substituted the Shamsi calendar for a newly invented imperial calendar. The idea for this initiative can be dated to 1346 (1967–68), when Mohammad Farahmand, political deputy at the Ministry of the Interior, proposed the change to his ministry.[11] According to 'Abdolrezā Ansāri, Farahmand reasoned that the Shamsi calendar, with its Islamic connection, served as 'a reminder of the Arab conquest of Iran and the cruel massacre of Iranians, the burning of libraries, the destruction of cultural centres, and the eradication of our rich and glorious civilisation and culture'. As a result, therefore, he concluded that it made no sense to use this period as the starting point of Iranian history. With the Imperial Celebrations drawing attention to Iran's pre-Islamic past, 'it was proper that the Shamsi calendar be reconsidered'.[12]

The proposal, which was given the blessing of the Shah, was sent to the University of Tehran for investigation. After further deliberations, the Central Council for the Celebrations decided that it would be better to delay the initiative. They also decided that when the change eventually took place, both the Shamsi and imperial calendar should be used together 'because the people of the country need time to familiarise themselves with the idea'.[13] In the run-up to the Celebrations, the issue was again considered, and an article appeared in the magazine *Khāndanihā* outlining imminent plans to replace the Shamsi with the imperial calendar. According to the article, this issue was 'a creative and patriotic one which would benefit our nation'.[14] It was also perfectly in keeping with the Celebrations' aims and messages. A SAVAK report on the issue outlined some of the problems inherent in the plan. Although Iranians were proud of their history and welcomed the Imperial Celebrations, they were equally proud of their Islamic tradition, thus, the report continued, 'even if the majority of the population support the plan, there will be cause for religious propaganda against it'.[15]

The report concluded that 'the issue is of the uttermost importance and worthy of careful consideration'.[16] In spite of advice to be cautious, four years later in 1976, on 30 Esfand, at 15.22 and 30 seconds, the year 1354 ended and the year 2535 began.[17] Local newspapers praised the change, as did Laurence Elwell-Sutton, who described it as a 'fitting epilogue' to the Imperial Celebrations.[18] The change backfired, however, as it proved to anyone who may still have been in any doubt that the Shah now wanted to replace Islam, rather than conveniently ignore it.[19] Michael Axworthy has written of the significance of 'dumping Islam as the point of reference in favour of a monarchical date',[20] and just two years after the switch, in 1978, during the unfolding crisis of the revolution, the government of Sharif-Emāmi reverted to the Shamsi calendar. Beginning with the Celebrations, up to the implementation of the imperial calendar, and *Etteʿlāʿāt*'s ill-conceived article on 7 January 1978 that painted Khomeini as a British stooge, the Pahlavi regime's actions more and more convinced the pious of their rulers' contempt for Islam.[21]

This book has shown that the regime was aware of the rising threat posed by religious opposition at this time; SAVAK reports show, for instance, that Khomeini's speeches were widely broadcast during the run-up to the Celebrations and also that the regime attempted to prevent this. The fact that SAVAK advised against changing the calendar, but the court pushed on regardless, indicates that SAVAK, or indeed security concerns in general, were not given much consideration in such matters. Thus, while the regime promoted the ancient period as one of glorious Persian supremacy, this allowed for the construction and dissemination of a powerful counter-narrative, denigrating the Pahlavis and the ancient monarchical system they presented in favour of Islam. This vilification gained traction with the lectures of Khomeini and Shari'ati, who were otherwise diametrically opposed and whose lectures were aimed at different audiences, but who converged in religious opposition to the evils of monarchy. In the revolutionary turmoil of 1979, Sādeq Khalkhāli reportedly led a team of bulldozers to destroy the ruins of Persepolis but was driven away by locals.[22] The Shah had encouraged people to associate ancient ruins such as those with the monarchy, thereby unwittingly endangering their survival during the revolution.

Notwithstanding the ultimate failure of the Pahlavi regime to convince Iranians of the virtues of Pahlavism, this book has made the case that the ideology was not entirely ill-conceived. Iranian intellectuals from the middle of the 19th century onwards had lauded the kings and culture of Ancient Iran, and both Pahlavi monarchs merely politicized these historical narratives. Political leaders in the Islamic Republic have continued to pay attention to Iran's ancient past, and, indeed could be said to have drawn legitimacy from it. In 1991, for instance, President Rafsanjani became the first statesman of the Islamic Republic to visit Persepolis. He said, 'Standing in the middle of those wonderful centuries-old ruins, I felt the nation's dignity was all-important and must be strengthened. Our people must know that they are not without a history.'[23] He clearly understood the ability of the ancient ruins to inspire national fervour. Similarly, President Hassan Rouhani, elected in 2013, published a photograph of himself at Persepolis with the caption: 'Persepolis is one of the invaluable and unique remains of the ancient history of this land, which demonstrates the antiquity of the civilization, the ingenuity, the wisdom, and the management skills of the great people of Iran, as well as their monotheism.'[24]

Perhaps the most deliberate re-enactment of the type of political spectacle one might associate with the Shah took place during the presidency of Mahmoud Ahmadinejad. In 2010, the Cyrus Cylinder returned to Iran for the first time since 1971 and during the opening ceremony of the exhibition at the National Museum in Tehran at which the artefact was displayed, Ahmadinejad referred to Cyrus as the king of the world and draped a Palestinian-style keffiyeh over the shoulders of an actor dressed as the ancient king.[25] One year later, in 2011, Ahmadinejad's chief of staff, Esfandiyār Rahim Mashāi, even proposed to celebrate Nowruz at Persepolis and invite regional heads of state and monarchs.[26] These acts reflect both the re-emergence of a Persian nationalism centred on Cyrus, and the readiness of political figures within the Islamic Republic to alter their political ideologies to incorporate new secular and nationalist trends in order to boost their popularity.[27]

The popularity of Cyrus the Great in modern Iran is reflected in the increasing attention for the International Day of Cyrus the Great, which is celebrated every year on 7 Ābān, and which in recent years has seen thousands gather at the tomb of Cyrus at Pasargadae to honour the ancient king. The 2010 loan of the Cyrus Cylinder to Tehran and the publicity it received is indicative of the perceived significance of the artefact as an accepted symbol of Iranian pride. Today a replica of the Cylinder is displayed outside the National Museum in Tehran to commemorate the 2010 loan, along with a plaque calling the Cylinder a 'symbol of wisdom ... freedom and justice'. Even to this day, Persian language course books published by government-sponsored programmes in Iran include chapters introducing foreign learners to the Cyrus Cylinder, Darius the Great and Persepolis. The legend of Cyrus also retains political significance outside of Iran. In 2015, the Croatian Speaker of Parliament Josip Leko claimed to his Iranian counterpart, 'Ali Lārijāni, that the name Croatia is derived from the name of the ancient king Cyrus.[28]

One important aspect of the Pahlavi regime's cultural policy was education, disseminating booklets informing Iranians about their ancient past, in line with the official historical narrative. The Celebrations were part of this cultural policy agenda and, as this book has shown, hundreds of books were published, schools built, and exhibitions and conferences held. Clearly one of the purposes of these events was to stimulate a common understanding of what it meant to be an Iranian in the modern, secular world, and they were intended to encourage pride in Iranian civilization and culture. It would be too easy to point to the revolution as proof that this effort was ultimately unsuccessful. After the turmoil of the revolution had subsided, political figures and ordinary Iranians still identified with Ancient Iran, which indicates that the situation is a little more complex.

Internationally too, the efforts of the Pahlavi regime created a hero out of Cyrus the Great and the Cylinder became a universally recognized symbol of tolerance. The Pahlavi regime actively promoted this recognition in efforts which reached a peak during the Imperial Celebrations. The Cylinder became the official symbol of the Celebrations and replicas of the relic were, and are still, displayed in the United Nations buildings in New York and Geneva. In 2013, the Cylinder travelled to the United States where it appeared in five of the country's top museums, with the director of the Metropolitan Museum of Art in New York commenting that 'the tolerance embraced by the Cylinder's text has been applauded throughout history'.[29] In addition, on 4 July 2017, a sculpture representing the Cyrus Cylinder was unveiled in Los Angeles, symbolizing how 'Los Angeles embodies diversity'.[30] In January 2018, during a debate on the protests that were taking place in Iran, the chairman of the US House of Representatives Foreign Affairs Committee referred to 'the first declaration of human rights – the Cyrus Cylinder' and to Cyrus's 'humanitarian values of freedom for all people, respect for culture and religious diversity, and recognition of the fact that it is better to be loved than be feared'.[31] One of the purposes of the Celebrations was to promote Iranian history around the world, in particular the legacy of Cyrus the Great, framing it in the language of the modern political, particularly enlightenment, philosophical tradition. The success of the propagation of this message can be observed by the reverence in which Cyrus and the Cylinder are held both in Iran and around the world, even today.

The Pahlavi regime clearly made many mistakes politically, but many of the building and infrastructural projects associated with the Imperial Celebrations contributed to economic and social development. The Āryāmehr Stadium had been built for Iran's hosting of the Asian Games in 1974, and the spectacle that marked its inauguration during the Celebrations was designed to broadcast Iran's claim to be a major sporting powerhouse. An article in *Iran Tribune* at the time perfectly articulates this sentiment:

> Described as the best equipped stadium west of Japan and the largest in the Middle East it will undoubtedly attract numerous international sports events which hitherto have not been held in the Middle East because of the lack of facilities suitable for handling large crowds … Football presents no problem, except that of coordinated transport, because in recent years it has become almost a mania among Iranians. Now the leader in Asian soccer, Iran has its eyes on the coveted world cup.[32]

In March 1974, with the Asian Games imminent, Iran was confident enough to approach Brian Clough, one of the most famous football managers in the world at the time, to manage the national football team.[33] In the late 1970s, Iran was even putting together a bid for the 1984 Olympic Games, so had the Pahlavi regime survived, then Iran would perhaps have become the first and only country in the Middle East to date to host the Olympics.

Although the Celebrations are often characterized as wasteful, this book has shown that much of the spending done was with a view to the future. The tent city is a good example, for while attempts to transform the area around Persepolis into a tourist resort were ultimately unsuccessful, it is conceivable that these plans would have later been reconsidered. It did remain an important site and was used for major political and cultural events, such as the meetings to approve the Fifth Development Plan (November 1972) held under the supervision of the Shah, the Second International Congress of Architects (September 1974) headed by Empress Farah, and the International Symposium for Literacy (September 1975) led by Princess Ashraf. The Islamic Republic has also considered utilizing the tents. As late as 2001, the director of the Fars Province Cultural Heritage Organization proposed to revive the tent city as luxury accommodation.[34] Unsurprisingly perhaps, given the decades-long demonization of the event by the Islamic Republic, this idea came to nothing. The fact that today, nearly fifty years after the Celebrations took place, the metal frames of the tents are still standing, indicates that they were built to last. The lights installed at the ruins of Persepolis for the purpose of the *son et lumière* also still function today, and one can see a light show there during the summer months.

The actual spending associated with the main ceremonies is also vastly inflated in many journalistic and historical accounts. One gets the impression from these sources that the regime was willing to spend whatever was necessary, which is not accurate. 'Alam records in his diary, for instance, that on 6 April 1970 he met with the Shah to discuss the plans for the dining tent. He records that he went to 'great trouble' to get the Shah to agree to the plan, and that the Shah eventually only agreed on the condition that the size and cost would be reduced to a quarter of the original proposal.[35]

More evidence of the regime's insistence on remaining within budget has been cited throughout this book. For example, the British Council's plan to have the London Symphony Orchestra perform in Tehran during the Celebrations was scuppered by the Iranian Ministry of Culture and Art's refusal to pay the customary fee. The spending associated with the Celebrations is often presented as evidence of the ostentatiousness of the Pahlavi Court, or the financial negligence of the regime, but this book has shown that the reality is a little more nuanced.

***

The positive impacts of the Celebrations were demonstrable, particularly in terms of cultural output and investment in the economy, but the regime failed to sell the message convincingly. The negative impression of the occasion is indicative, therefore, of a public relations failure on behalf of the regime. In the post-revolution period, the Celebrations became part of the revolutionary narrative in which, while many Iranians were struggling to get by, a megalomaniac Shah invited the world's elite to Iran to feast on the spoils of the people's oil wealth. Instead of marking the commemoration of a great hero, the Celebrations were characterized as the 'devil's feast'.

In many ways, the Celebrations marked a high point in Pahlavi Iran's international standing. Mohammad Reza Shah had gained confidence through his White Revolution reforms and the Iranian economy was growing rapidly. The Celebrations intended to show the world that Iran was no longer the plaything of imperial powers, as it had been for the previous 150 years, and could, under the guidance of the throne, carve out a new direction for itself. This book has shown that the Shah achieved some success in delivering this message. From the early 1960s, the Pahlavi regime had placed emphasis on education and culture, domestically and internationally. Much of this had a political focus, whether used as a tool in international diplomacy or to encourage Iranians to identify with the monarchy as a historical source of national unity.

This book has provided the type of sober analysis Elwell-Sutton called for and has looked in considerable detail at the many different aspects of the event, including cultural initiatives, international relations and attempts made by the regime to stimulate the economy. This is a contrast to the prevailing discourse, which presents the Celebrations as futile and ultimately counterproductive. By recording what happened and placing the events in their proper context, the book has argued that much of the Celebrations were part of a sophisticated long-term cultural and economic strategy. In an interview published after his death in 2010, Shojāʿ al-Din Shafā said that the Celebrations were 'a great source of pride for me and even the greatest honour of my life'.[36] One can argue, with some justification, that the underlying narrative ultimately contributed to the revolution, that the security clampdown helped to present the Shah as a cruel despot, or that the vast expenditure, whether real or rumoured, helped to characterize the regime as corrupt and wasteful. Beyond the pomp and splendour of the tent city, however, as this book has shown, was a huge operation, which successfully promoted Iran domestically and around the world as a distinct cultural space, a significant prospect for economic investment and an important regional power.

Notes

Acknowledgements

1 Robert Steele, 'Pahlavi Iran on the Global Stage: The Shah's 1971 Persepolis Celebrations', in *The Age of Aryamehr: Late Pahlavi Iran and Its Global Entanglements*, ed. Roham Alvandi (London: Gingko Library, 2018), 110–46.

Introduction

1 John Manuel Cook, *Ancient Persia* (London: Dent, 1983), iii.
2 Jean Perrot, *The Palace of Darius at Susa: The Great Royal Residence of Achaemenid Persia* (London: I.B. Tauris, 2013), xii.
3 'Porshokuhtarin Meyhmāni-ye Tārikh', *Keyhān*, 24 Mehr 1350/ 16 October 1971, 13.
4 Marvin Zonis, *Majestic Failure: The Fall of the Shah* (Chicago: University of Chicago Press, 1991), 69.
5 Martin Clark, 'The Party', in *Celebration at Persepolis*, ed. Michael Stevenson (Bristol: Arnolfini, 2008), 28.
6 James Bill, *The Eagle and the Lion: The Tragedy of American-Iranian Relations* (New Haven: Yale University Press, 1988), 184.
7 Guy Rais, 'World's VIPs to See Shah's Spectacular', *Daily Telegraph*, 11 October 1971.
8 'Fun in the Sand: 2500 Year Celebration', *Washington Daily News*, 16 October 1971.
9 Loren Jenkins, 'Iran's Birthday Party', *Newsweek*, 25 October 1971, 33.
10 Andrew Scott Cooper, *The Fall of Heaven: The Pahlavis and the Final Days of Imperial Iran* (New York: Henry Holt, 2016), 171.
11 Ibid., 197.
12 Hendrik Jonker, '2500 year celebration Persian Monarchy', 3 November 1971, Nationaal Archief (Dutch National Archives, henceforth NA) 2.05.191/554.
13 Ibid.
14 Joseph Santa-Croce, 'Les attardés du XIXe siècle et le roi moderne', *Le Monde*, 24 November 1971.
15 Document number A 6452-3211-1, 31 October 1971, Iranian Institute for Contemporary Historical Studies. Available online: http://iichs.org/index_en.asp?id=2036&img_cat=126&img_type=1 (accessed 28 October 2016).
16 George Ball, *The Past Has Another Pattern* (New York: Norton, 1982), 435–6.
17 'Mosāhebeh-ye Chāp Nashodeh az Shojāʿ al-Din Shafā Darbāreh-ye: Jashnhā-ye Dohezār o Pānsad Sāleh' [Unpublished Interview with Shojāʿ al-Din Shafā About: The 2500th Anniversary Celebration], *Rahāvard*, 95 (2011), 184–5.
18 Ibid., 184.

19 'Shojāʿ al-Din Shafā az Zabān-e Khodash', in *Yādnāmeh-ye Shojāʿ al-Din Shafā*, ed. Claudine Shafa (Paris, 2013), 75–6.
20 Ibid., 76.
21 Walter Schwarz, 'A Kingdom Remembered – 2,500 Years on', *The Guardian*, 13 October 1971, 1.
22 William Shawcross, *The Shah's Last Ride* (London: Chatto and Windus, 1989), 47.
23 Ibid., 38.
24 Ibid., 47
25 Zonis, *Majestic Failure*, 69.
26 Nikki Keddie, *Modern Iran* (New Haven: Yale University Press, 2003), 224.
27 James Buchan, *Days of God* (London: John Murray, 2012), 56.
28 Roy Mottahedeh, *The Mantle of the Prophet: Religion and Politics in Iran* (Oxford: Oneworld, 2009), 326–7.
29 Fakhreddin Azimi, *Quest for Democracy in Iran: A Century of Struggle Against Authoritarian Rule* (Cambridge, MA: Harvard University Press, 2008), 282–90.
30 Martin Beglinger, 'The Most Expensive Party Ever', *Tages-Anzeiger*, May 2014. Available online: https://www.alimentarium.org/en/magazine/history/most-expensive-party-ever (accessed 30 January 2017). The claim has been repeated elsewhere. See Ishaan Tharoor, 'How Ancient Ruins Are Perfect Propaganda in the Middle East', *The Washington Post*, 6 May 2016. Available online: https://www.washingtonpost.com/news/worldviews/wp/2016/05/06/how-ancient-ruins-are-perfect-propaganda-in-the-middle-east/?utm_term=.c323be89e167 (accessed 22 October 2018). The documentary claims that these birds actually died from thirst because there was not enough water, though it should be pointed out that there was a huge water fountain in the middle of the tent city, as well as grass and trees around the site.
31 Robert Hardman, 'Princess Anne and the £1Billion Party That Lit the Fuse of Islamic Terror 45 Years Ago', *The Daily Mail*, 13 February 2016. Available online: http://www.dailymail.co.uk/news/article-3445017/Princess-Anne-1billion-party-lit-fuse-Islamic-terror-45-years-ago.html (accessed 7 February 2016).
32 Laurence Elwell-Sutton, '2500th Anniversary Celebrations', *Bulletin of the British Association of Orientalists*, 6 (1973): 24.
33 Gholam Reza Afkhami, *Life and Times of the Shah* (Monterey: University of California Press, 2008), 472.
34 Abbas Milani, *The Shah* (New York: Palgrave Macmillan, 2011), 323.
35 Murray Edelman, *Constructing the Political Spectacle* (Chicago: University of Chicago Press, 1987), 7.
36 Frank E. Manning, 'Cosmos and Chaos: Celebration in the Modern World', in *The Celebration of Society: Perspectives on Contemporary Cultural Performance*, ed. Frank E Manning (Bowling Green, Ontario: Bowling Green University Popular Press, 1983), 16.
37 Ibid.
38 'Payām-e Shāhanshāh Āryāmehr, dar Tārikh Sabt Shod' [The Message of the King of Kings Āryāmehr, Inscribed in History], *Rastākhiz*, 19 Mehr 2535 (1355)/ 11 October 1976, 12.
39 Naomi Barry, 'Feest in Persepolis, reclame zonder te betalen' [Party in Persepolis: Advertisement Without Paying], *Haagsche Courant*, 25 September 1971, 7.
40 'Jashnhā-ye Shāhanshāhi Seyl-e Jahāngardān rā Motavjeh-ye Irān Khāhad Kard' [The Imperial Celebrations Will Bring a Flood of Tourists to Iran], *Ruznāmeh-ye Jashn-e Shāhanshāhi-ye Irān*, 6 Mordād 1350/ 28 July 1971, 4.

41 Orlando Figes, *A People's Tragedy: The Russian Revolution 1891–1924* (London: Pimlico, 1997), 3.
42 Robert K. Massie, *Nicholas and Alexandra* (London: Head of Zeus, 2013), 236.
43 Richard S. Wortman, *Scenarios of Power: Myth and Ceremony in Russian Monarchy*, vol. 2 (Princeton, NJ: Princeton University Press, 1995), 439–40.
44 Ervand Abrahamian, 'Revolutionary Iran: A History of the Islamic Republic by Michael Axworthy', *The Times Higher Education*, 4 April 2013. Available online: https://www.timeshighereducation.com/books/revolutionary-iran-a-history-of-the-islamic-republic-by-michael-axworthy/2002873.article (accessed 23 October 2016).
45 Roham Alvandi, *Nixon, Kissinger and the Shah* (Oxford: Oxford University Press, 2014).
46 Cooper, *The Fall of Heaven*, 12.
47 Reza Baraheni, *Crowned Cannibals: Writings on Repression in Iran* (New York: Vintage Books, 1977), 101–2.
48 Tim McDaniel, *Autocracy, Modernization, and Revolution in Russia and Iran* (Princeton: Princeton University Press, 1991), 90.
49 Asadollah Alam, *The Shah and I: Confidential Diary of Iran's Royal Court, 1969–1977*, ed. Alinaghi Alikhani (London: I.B. Tauris, 1991), 245–6. See, for example, Cooper, *The Fall of Heaven*, 174; Talinn Grigor, '"They Have Not Changed in 2,500 Years": Art, Archaeology, and Modernity in Iran', in *Unmasking Ideology in Imperial and Colonial Archaeology: Vocabulary, Symbols, and Legacy*, ed. Bonnie Effros and Guolong Lai (Los Angeles: Cotsen Institute of Archaeology Press at UCLA, 2018), 139; and Farshid Emami, 'Urbanism of Grandiosity: Planning a New Urban Centre for Tehran (1973–76)', *International Journal of Islamic Architecture*, 3:1 (2014): 90.
50 Diary entry 18 Mehr 1351/ 10 October 1972, *Yāddāshthā-ye ʿAlam*, vol. 2 (Tehran: Ketābsarā, 2014), 363.
51 Kamran Scot Aghaie, 'Islamist Historiography in Post-Revolutionary Iran', in *Iran in the 20th Century: Historiography and Political Culture*, ed. Touraj Atabaki (London: I.B. Tauris, 2009), 260.
52 Ibid.
53 SAVAK report, 30 Farvardin 1350/ 19 April 1971, *Bazm-e Ahriman: Jashnhā-ye 2500 Sāleh-ye Shāhanshāhi beh Revāyat-e Asnād-e Sāvāk va Darbār* [The Devil's Feast: The 2500th Anniversary Celebrations According to SAVAK and Court Documents], vol. 4 (Tehran: Markaz-e Barresi-ye Asnād-e Tārikhi-ye Vezārat-e Ettelāʿat, 1378), 37.
54 SAVAK report, 3 Tir 1350/ 24 June 1971, ibid., 118–20.
55 The work is set out chronologically: volume one covers Esfand 1337 to Esfand 1342 (February 1959–February 1964), volume two covers Farvardin 1343 to Esfand 1346 (March 1964–February 1968), volume three covers Farvardin 1347 to Esfand 1349 (March 1968–February 1971), and volume four covers Esfand 1350 to Esfand 1351 (March 1971–March 1972).

1 Ideology and historical background

1 Pierre Nora, 'General Introduction: Between Memory and History', in *Realms of Memory: Rethinking the French Past*, vol. 1, ed. Pierre Nora, trans. Arthur Goldhammer (New York: Columbia University Press, 1996), 7.

2. See Richard S. Wortman, *Scenarios of Power: Myth and Ceremony in Russian Monarchy*, vol. 2 (Princeton, NJ: Princeton University Press, 1995), 439–80; Aristotle Kallis, 'Framing Romanità: The Celebrations for the Bimillenario Augusteo and the Augusteo-Ara Pacis Project', *Journal of Contemporary History*, 46:4 (2011): 809–31; Jan Nelis, 'Constructing Fascist Identity: Benito Mussolini and the Myth of "Romanità"', *The Classical World*, 100:4 (2007): 391–415; Kenneth James Ruoff, *Imperial Japan at Its Zenith: The Wartime Celebration of the Empire's 2,600th Anniversary* (Ithaca: Cornell University Press, 2010).
3. Elie Podeh, *The Politics of National Celebration in the Arab Middle East* (Cambridge: Cambridge University Press, 2011), 19–24.
4. David Kertzer, *Ritual, Politics, and Power* (New Haven: Yale University Press, 1988), 37–8.
5. See Babak Rahimi, *Theater State and the Formation of Early Modern Public Sphere in Iran: Studies on Safavid Muharram Rituals, 1590–1641 CE* (Leiden: Brill, 2012); Jean Calmard, 'Shi'i Rituals and Power II. The Consolidation of Safavid Shi'ism: Folklore and Popular Religion', in *Safavid Persia: The History and Politics of an Islamic Society*, ed. Charles Melville (London: I.B. Tauris, 2009), 139–90; Kamran Scot Aghaie, 'Religious Rituals, Social Identities and Political Relationships in Tehran Under Qajar Rule, 1850s-1920s', in *Religion and Society in Qajar Iran*, ed. Robert Gleave (Oxon: Routledge, 2005), 373–92.
6. Reza Zia-Ebrahimi, *The Emergence of Iranian Nationalism: Race and the Politics of Dislocation* (New York: Columbia University Press, 2016).
7. Helen Ting, 'Social Construction of Nation – A Theoretical Exploration', *Nationalism and Ethnic Politics*, 14:3 (2008): 454.
8. Jean-Jacques Rousseau, *Constitutional Project for Corsica* (1765). Available online: http://www.constitution.org/jjr/corsica.htm (accessed 6 March 2017).
9. Geoff Eley and Ronald Grigor Suny, 'Introduction: From the Moment of Social History to the Work of Cultural Representation', in *Becoming National: A Reader*, ed. Geoff Eley and Ronald Grigor Suny (Oxford: Oxford University Press, 1996), 7. For more on the 'functionalist' reading of nationalism, see John Breuilly, *Nationalism and the State* (Manchester: Manchester University Press, 2001).
10. Mohamad Tavakoli-Targhi, 'From Patriotism to Matriotism: A Tropological Study of Iranian Nationalism, 1870–1909', *International Journal of Middle East Studies*, 34:2 (2002): 218–19.
11. Pejman Abdolmohammadi, 'The Political Thought of Mirzā Aqā Khān Kermāni, the Father of Persian National Liberalism', *Oriente Moderno*, 94:1 (2014): 160.
12. Ibid., 149.
13. Ernest Renan, 'What Is a Nation?', paper delivered at the Sorbonne 11 March 1882. Available online: http://www.ucparis.fr/files/9313/6549/9943/what_is_a_nation.pdf (accessed 6 March 2017).
14. Tavakoli-Targhi, 'From Patriotism to Matriotism', 221.
15. Afshin Marashi, *Nationalizing Iran: Culture, Power, and the State, 1870–1940* (Seattle: University of Washington Press, 2008), 55.
16. David Lowenthal, *The Heritage Crusade and the Spoils of History* (Cambridge: Cambridge University Press, 1998), 176.
17. Marashi, *Nationalizing Iran*, 55.
18. Ibid., 59.

19 Abbas Amanat and Farzin Vajdani, 'Jalal-al-din-Mirza', *Encyclopaedia Iranica*, online edition, 2008. Available online: http://www.iranicaonline.org/articles/jalal-al-din-mirza (accessed 4 September 2018).
20 Abbas Amanat, *Iran: A Modern History* (New Haven: Yale University Press, 2017), 322–3.
21 Ibid., 321.
22 Quoted in Mohamad Tavakoli-Targhi, *Refashioning Iran: Orientalism, Occidentalism and Historiography* (Houndmill: Palgrave, 2001), 102.
23 Marashi, *Nationalizing Iran*, 72.
24 Tavakoli-Targhi, *Refashioning Iran*, 37.
25 David Motadel, 'Iran and the Aryan Myth', in *Perceptions of Iran: History, Myths and Nationalism from Medieval Persia to the Islamic Republic*, ed. Ali Ansari (London: I.B. Tauris, 2014), 124.
26 For this analysis of race in nationalism, see Ali Ansari, 'Iranian Nationalism and the Question of Race', in *Constructing Nationalism in Iran: From the Qajars to the Islamic Republic*, ed. Meir Litvak (Oxon: Routledge, 2017), 101–17.
27 Marashi, *Nationalizing Iran*, 75.
28 Homa Katouzian, *State and Society in Iran: The Eclipse of the Qajars and the Emergence of the Pahlavis* (London: I.B. Tauris, 2006), 324.
29 Ibid., 77.
30 On nationalism and the Constitutional Revolution, see Ali M. Ansari (ed.), *Iran's Constitutional Revolution of 1906: Narratives of the Enlightenment* (London: Gingko Library, 2016).
31 Ali M. Ansari, 'Mohammad Ali Foroughi and the Construction of Civic Nationalism in Early Twentieth-Century Iran', in *Iran in the Middle East: Transnational Encounters and Social History*, ed. H. E. Chehabi, Peyman Jafari and Maral Jefroudi (London: I.B. Tauris, 2015), 16.
32 Ali Ansari, *The Politics of Nationalism in Modern Iran* (Cambridge: Cambridge University Press, 2012), 105.
33 Ansari, 'Mohammad Ali Foroughi and the Construction of Civic Nationalism', 15.
34 Marashi, *Nationalizing Iran*, 125.
35 Mehrdad Kia, 'Persian Nationalism and the Campaign for Language Purification', *Middle Eastern Studies*, 34:2 (1998): 10.
36 Ibid., 23.
37 Quoted in Nematollah Fazeli, *Politics of Culture in Iran: Anthropology, Politics and Society in the Twentieth Century* (Oxon: Routledge, 2006), 36. See also Ansari, *The Politics of Nationalism in Modern Iran*, 55–65.
38 Pejman Abdolmohammadi, 'History, National Identity and Myths in Iranian Contemporary Political Thought: Mirza Fathali Akhundzadeh (1812–78), Mirza Agha Khan Kermani (1853–96) and Hassan Taqizadeh (1878–1970)', in *Perceptions of Iran: History, Myths and Nationalism from Medieval Persia to the Islamic Republic*, ed. Ali Ansari (London: I.B. Tauris, 2014), 31.
39 Marashi, *Nationalizing Iran*, 79–85.
40 For a discussion of the content and aims of the journal, see Afshin Matin-Asgari, *Both Eastern and Western: An Intellectual History of Modern Iran* (Cambridge: Cambridge University Press, 2018), 63–74.
41 Ibid., 71.
42 George Curzon, *Persia and the Persian Question*, vol. 2 (London: Longmans Green, 1892), 394–6.

43 Talinn Grigor, 'Orientalism and Mimicry of Selfness: Archaeology of the Neo-Achaemenid Style', in *L'Orientalisme architectural entre imaginaires et savoirs*, ed. Nabila Oulebsir and Mercedes Volait (Paris: Picard, 2009), 3. Available online: http://journals.openedition.org/inha/4911 (accessed 29 April 2019).
44 Ali Gheissari, *Iranian Intellectuals in the 20th Century* (Austin: University of Texas Press, 1998), 19.
45 Ali Mousavi, *Persepolis: Discovery and Afterlife of a World Wonder* (Boston: Walter de Gruyter, 2012), 144.
46 Nader Nasiri-Moghaddam, 'Archaeology and the Iranian National Museum', in *Culture and Cultural Politics under Reza Shah: The Pahlavi State, New Bourgeoisie and the Creation of a Modern Society in Iran*, ed. Bianca Devos and Christoph Werner (London: Routledge, 2014), 129.
47 Richard Frye, 'Persia in the Mind of the West', *Islam and Christian-Muslim Relations*, 14:4 (2003): 403.
48 Ali Ansari, 'Persia in the Western Imagination', in *Anglo-Iranian Relations since 1800*, ed. Vanessa Martin (London: Routledge, 2005), 10.
49 Lindsey Allen, *The Persian Empire: A History* (London: British Museum Press, 2005), 168.
50 For an account of the influence of the East on England during the Elizabethan period, see Jerry Brotton, *This Orient Isle: Elizabethan England and the Islamic World* (London: Allen Lane, 2016). For Shirley's exploits, 233–66.
51 Parvin Loloi, 'Portraits of the Achaemenid Kings in English Drama: Sixteenth-Eighteenth Centuries', in *The World of Achaemenid Persia: History and Society in Iran and the Ancient Near East*, ed. St John Simpson and John Curtis (London: I.B. Tauris, 2010), 34–40.
52 Which, due to the sudden death of the actor playing Cyaxares, was abandoned after just four nights. See Hugh James Rose, ed., *A New General Biographical Dictionary*, vol. 3 (London: Fellowes, 1841), 117.
53 St John Simpson, 'Pottering Around Persepolis: Observations on Early European Visitors to the Site', in *Persian Responses: Political and Cultural Interaction with(in) the Achaemenid Empire*, ed. Christopher Tuplin (Swansea: Classical Press of Wales, 2007), 347–51.
54 Von Kotzebue (1819), quoted in St John Simpson, 'Making Their Mark: Foreign Travellers at Persepolis', *Arta* 1 (2005): 12.
55 John Malcolm letter to his father from Shiraz, 17 August 1800, in John William Kaye, *The Life and Correspondence of Major-General Sir John Malcolm*, vol. 1 (London: Smith, Elder, 1856), 124.
56 John Malcolm, *The History of Persia from the Most Early Period to the Present Time*, vol. 1 (London: John Murray, 1815), v.
57 Quoted in Thomas Harrison, 'Reinventing Achaemenid Persia', in *The World of Achaemenid Persia*, ed. Simpson and Curtis (London: I.B. Tauris, 2010), 23.
58 Malcolm, *The History of Persia*, vol. 2, 621.
59 Curzon, *Persia and the Persian Question*, vol. 1, 634.
60 E. R. Chamberlin, *Preserving the Past* (London: J.M. Dent and Sons, 1979), 20–1.
61 Malcolm, *The History of Persia*, vol. 2, 622.
62 Reza Zia-Ebrahimi, 'Self-Orientalization and Dislocation: The Uses and Abuses of the "Aryan" Discourse in Iran', *Iranian Studies*, 44:4 (2011): 465.
63 Magnus T. Bernhardsson, *Reclaiming a Plundered Past: Archaeology and Nation Building in Modern Iraq* (Austin: University of Texas Press, 2005), 11.

64 Roman Siebertz, 'Depicting Power: The Commemorative Stamp Set of 1935', in *Culture and Cultural Politics under Reza Shah*, ed. Bianca Devos and Christoph Werner (London: Routledge, 2014), 156.
65 Marashi, *Nationalizing Iran*, 89.
66 Ibid., 92.
67 Talinn Grigor, 'Recultivating "Good Taste": The Early Pahlavi Modernists and Their Society for National Heritage', *Iranian Studies*, 37:1 (2004): 20-1.
68 For full text of the speech see Arthur Upham Pope, 'The Past and Future of Persian Art', in *Surveyors of Persian Art: A Documentary Biography of Arthur Upham Pope and Phillis Ackerman*, ed. Jay Gluck and Noël Siver (Costa Mesa, CA: Mazda Publishers, 1996), 93-110.
69 Laurence Elwell-Sutton, 'Reza Shah the Great', in *Iran under the Pahlavis*, ed. George Lenczowski (Stanford, CA: Hoover Institute Press, 1978), 37.
70 Donald N. Wilber, *Reza Shah Pahlavi: The Resurrection and Reconstruction of Iran* (Hicksville: Exposition Press, 1975), 98.
71 'Isā Sadiq, quoted in Grigor, 'Recultivating "Good Taste"', 33.
72 'Isā Sadiq in Gluck and Siver, *Surveyors of Persian Art*, 2.
73 Rex Stead in Gluck and Siver, *Surveyors of Persian Art*, 11.
74 Arthur Upham Pope, 'The Celebrations of the Thousandth Anniversary of the Birth of Firdawsi, Epic Poet of Persia', *Bulletin of the American Institute for Persian Art and Archaeology* 7 (1934): 39.
75 See A. Shahpur Shahbazi, 'Ferdowsi, Abu'l-Qāsem iv. Millenary Celebration', *Encyclopaedia Iranica*, 9:5 (1999): 527-30.
76 Afshin Marashi, 'The Nation's Poet: Ferdowsi and the Iranian National Imagination', in *Iran in the 20th Century: Historiography and Political Culture*, ed. Touraj Atabaki (London: I.B. Tauris, 2009), 105.
77 Ibid., 107.
78 Grigor, 'Recultivating "Good Taste"', 37.
79 Talinn Grigor, *Building Iran* (New York: Periscope Publishing, 2009), 75.
80 Joanna Bowring, *Chronology of Temporary Exhibitions at the British Museum* (London: British Museum, 2012).
81 Pope, 'The Celebrations of the Thousandth Anniversary of the Birth of Firdawsi', 42.
82 Zia-Ebrahimi, 'Self-Orientalization and Dislocation', 465.
83 For an example of the violence of Ashurnasirpal II (r. 883-859 BCE), see Karen Rhea Nemet-Nejat, *Daily Life in Ancient Mesopotamia* (London: Greenwood Press, 1998), 229.
84 The Lydian capital of Sardis was, however, brutally seized since its king, Croesus, had risen against Cyrus. Cyrus, it seems, was not averse to brutality when the situation demanded it. According to some sources, however, Croesus was spared and received an estate in the Median town of Barene, with a personal attachment of 5,000 cavalry and 10,000 light infantry. See Reza Zarghamee, *Discovering Cyrus: The Persian Conqueror Astride the Ancient World* (Washington, DC: Mage Publishers, 2013), 109.
85 Herodotus, *The Histories*, 3.89.
86 As Daniel Beckman noted, this failure by overreach is a recurring theme in Herodotus, since Cambyses, Darius and Xerxes fail in Ethiopia, Scythia and Greece respectively. See Daniel Beckman, 'The Many Deaths of Cyrus the Great', *Iranian Studies*, 51:1 (2018): 5.
87 Xenophon, *Cyropaedia*, 8.1-5.

88 'Cyrus Cylinder: How a Persian Monarch Inspired Jefferson', *BBC*, 11 March 2013. Available online: http://www.bbc.co.uk/news/world-us-canada-21747567 (accessed 7 September 2016).
89 Plato, *Laws*, 3.
90 Quoted in Shojaeddin Shafa, *Facts about the Celebration of the 2500th Anniversary of the Founding of the Persian Empire by Cyrus the Great* (Tehran: Committee of International Affairs of the Festivities, 1971), 11.
91 Arrian, *The Campaigns of Alexander*, 6.29–30.
92 Ali Mousavi, 'Pilgrimage to Pasargadae: A Brief History of the Site from the Fall of the Achaemenids to the Early Twentieth Century', in *Cyrus the Great: An Ancient Iranian King*, ed. Touraj Daryaee (Santa Monica, CA: Afshar Publishing, 2013), 29.
93 Ezra, 6.3–14.
94 Isaiah, 45.1. This appears not to have been an empty gesture, for indeed there is evidence that the rebuilding of the temple commenced as little as two years after the first exiles returned home to Jerusalem. See Zarghamee, *Discovering Cyrus*, 235.
95 Kermāni quoted in Abdolmohammadi, 'History, National Identity and Myths', 26–7.
96 Abdolmohammadi, 'The Political Thought of Mirzā Aqā Khān Kermāni', 153.
97 Kermāni quoted in Abdolmohammadi, 'History, National Identity and Myths', 27.
98 Marashi, *Nationalizing Iran*, 99.
99 Hasan Pirniyā, 'Qabl az Eslām', in Hasan Pirniyā, 'Abbās Eqbāl Āshtiyāni and Bāqer 'Āqeli, *Tārikh-e Irān* (Tehran: Nashr Nāmak, 1393), 81.
100 Ibid.
101 Ibid., 82.
102 Pirniyā's *Irān-e Qadim* can still be found in many bookstores in Iran, usually alongside a volume on Iran after the advent of Islam.
103 Quoted in Shafa, *Facts about the Celebration*, 7–9.
104 Mohammad Rezā Pahlavi, *Enqelāb-e Sefid* [White Revolution] (Tehran: Ketābkhāneh-ye Pahlavi, 1967), 2–3.
105 Arthur Upham Pope letter to H. Amir Ebrahimi, 4 December 1960, in *Surveyors of Persian Art*, 427.
106 Mohammad Reza Pahlavi, *Mission for My Country* (London: Hutchinson, 1961), 21.
107 Ibid., 164
108 Ibid., 21.
109 Ardeshir Zahedi, 'A Memoir of His Imperial Majesty Mohammad Reza Shah Pahlavi, Shahanshah of Iran', in *Bibliography of Iran*, ed. Geoffrey Handley-Taylor (London: Bibliography of Iran, 1967), xvii.
110 *Tājgozāri-ye Shāhanshāhān-e Irān* [The Coronation of the Kings of Iran] (Tehran: Shurā-ye Markazi-ye Jashn-e Shāhanshāhi-ye Irān, 1346), 1.
111 See, for example, *2500 Sāl Shāhanshāhi-ye Irān: Az Kurosh tā Pahlavi* [2500 Years of Imperial Iran: From Cyrus to Pahlavi] (Tehran: Vezārat-e Behdāri, 1971).
112 See Norman Sharp's letter to Paul Gotch, 13 August 1967, Paul Gotch Papers, BM (British Museum).
113 'Jāvidānegi-ye Shāhanshāhi-ye Irān', *Keyhān*, 19 Mehr 1350/ 11 October 1971.
114 *Celebration of the 2500th Anniversary of the Founding of the Persian Empire by Cyrus the Great* (Tehran: Ministry of Information, 1971), 7–8.
115 Mostafa Vaziri, *Iran as Imagined Nation: The Construction of National Identity* (New York: Paragon House, 1993), 198.

116 Ismael Quiles, 'La Philosophie sous-jacente au message de Cyrus', in *Acta Iranica*, vol. 1, ed. Jacques Duchesne-Guillemin (Tehran: Bibliothèque Pahlavi; Leiden: Brill, 1974), 23.
117 David Lowenthal, *The Past Is a Foreign Country* (Cambridge: Cambridge University Press, 1985), 263.
118 Reza Zia-Ebrahimi, 'Better a Warm Hug Than a Cold Bath: Nationalist Memory and the Failures of Iranian Historiography', *Iranian Studies*, 49:5 (2016): 839.
119 Nora, 'Between Memory and History', 13.
120 Shafā, 'Shojāʿ al-Din Shafā az Zabān-e Khodash', 74.

2 'The World's Centre of Happiness'

1 See Zhand Shakibi, 'Pahlavism: The Ideologization of Monarchy in Iran', *Politics, Religion and Ideology*, 14:1 (2013): 114–35.
2 Charles J. Adams in the introduction to his edited volume, *Iranian Civilization and Culture: Essays in Honour of the 2,500th Anniversary of the Founding of the Persian Empire* (Montreal: McGill University, Institute of Islamic Studies, 1973), xiv–xv.
3 Ibid.
4 Jean Paul-Deschatelets, 'Foreword', in *Iranian Civilization and Culture*, ed. Adams, x.
5 Sādeq Kiyā, *Āryāmehr* (Tehran: Vezārat-e Farhang va Honar, 1346).
6 *Tājgozāri-ye Shāhanshāhān-e Irān* (Tehran: Shurā-ye Markazi-ye Jashn-e Shāhanshāhi-ye Irān, 1346), preface.
7 See, for example, Zabihollāh Safā, *Āyin-e Shāhanshāhi-ye Irān* (Tehran: University of Tehran, 1346); and *Nāmeh-ye Tāj* (Tabriz: Dāneshgāh-e Adabiyat va ʿOlum-e Ensāni-ye Tabriz, 1346).
8 See Reza Zia-Ebrahimi, *The Emergence of Iranian Nationalism* (New York: Columbia University Press, 2016), 213–14.
9 Qāsem Tabrizi, 'Shojāʿ al-Din Shafā beh Revāyat-e Asnād-e Sāvāk' [Shojāʿ al-Din Shafā According to SAVAK Documents], *Faslnāmeh-ye Motāleʿāt-e Tārikhi* 60 (1397/2018): 126.
10 This newspaper continued irregularly from 1943 until 1945 and was briefly replaced by *Shahbāz* (The Falcon) in 1943. See Laurence Elwell-Sutton, 'The Iranian Press, 1941–1947', *Iran* 6 (1968): 91–9.
11 Shojāʿ al-Din Shafā, 'Shojāʿ al-Din Shafā az Zabān-e Khodash', in *Yādnāmeh-ye Shojāʿ al-Din Shafā*, ed. Claudine Shafa (Paris, 2013), 49.
12 Tabrizi, 'Shojāʿ al-Din Shafā beh Revāyat-e Asnād-e Sāvāk', 126.
13 See *Shojaeddin Shafa and His Literary and Research Works* (Tehran: Kayhan Press, 1972), 4–5.
14 Mayor of Florence Luciano Bausi to Shafā, 9 February 1971, Shafā Archives.
15 'Mosāhebeh-ye Chāp Nashodeh az Shojāʿ al-Din Shafā', 188–9.
16 Ibid., 189.
17 Shojāʿ al-Din Shafā, 'Jashnhā-ye 2500 Sāleh-ye Shāhanshāhi', undated document, 13, Shafā Archives.
18 Ehsan Naraghi, *From Palace to Prison: Inside the Iranian Revolution*, trans. Nilou Mobasser (London: I.B. Tauris, 1994), 26–7.
19 Mokhtār Hadidi, 'Pahlavi-ye Dovvom va Nemuneh-ye Andishehhā-ye Bāstāngarāyāneh: Negāhi beh Asnād-e Mahramāneh-ye Jashnhā-ye 2500 Sāleh-ye

Shāhanshāhi' [The Second Pahlavi and some Elements of Archaistic Thoughts: A Look to the Secret Documents Relating to the 2500th Anniversary Celebrations], *Tārikh-e Moʿāser-e Irān*, 2:5 (1377/1998): 103.

20 Marjān Mirghafāri, 'Mardom Jashnhā-ye 2500 Sāleh rā Farmāyeshi Midānestand: Goftogu bā Shojāʿ al-Din Shafā, Mobtakar-e Bargozāri-ye Jashnhā-ye Shāhanshāhi' [The People Knew the 2500th Anniversary Celebrations Were Ordered: Conversation with Shojāʿ al-Din Shafā, Initiator of the Imperial Celebrations], *Tārikh-e Irāni*, 11 Ābān 1395/ 1 November 2016. Available online: http://tarikhirani.ir/fa/news/53/bodyView/5631 (accessed 21 May 2019).

21 Incidentally, Cyrus's ascent to the throne in 559 BCE was exactly 2,500 years before Mohammad Reza Pahlavi's in 1941. This coincidence was not lost on the Pahlavi ideologues and was raised during discussions about the creation of a new imperial calendar. See ʿAbdolrezā Ansāri to Asadollāh ʿAlam, 12 Tir 1350/ 3 June 1971, *Bazm-e Ahriman*, vol. 4, 134–5.

22 'Commemoration of Anniversaries of Great Personalities and Events: The Living Past', Paris, 31 August 1962, UNESCO/MC/46.

23 There is a file dedicated to this project in the Shafā Archives.

24 'Commemoration of Anniversaries of Great Personalities and Events'.

25 UNESCO, Records of the General Conference 11th session, Resolution 4.723, Paris, 1960, 57.

26 This resolution was apparently written by Shafā himself. See Shafā to Asadollāh ʿAlam, 8 Khordād 1349/ 29 May 1970, 'Asnād-e Mahramāneh-ye Jashnhā', 156–9.

27 G. W. Harrison to Selwyn Jones, 1 January 1959, FO 371/140887.

28 'A Commemoration of Twenty-Five Centuries of Grandeur and Glory', FO 371/140887.

29 'Gozāresh va barnāmeh-ye jashnhā-ye 2500 sāleh-ye kurosh-e bozorg va bonyād-e shāhanshāhi-ye Irān' [Report and programme of the 2500 anniversary of Cyrus the Great and the founding of Imperial Iran], 24 Esfand 1337/ 15 March 1959, *Bazm-e Ahriman*, vol. 1, 1–5.

30 Mehdi Bushehri was to become the Shah's brother-in-law; he married Princess Ashraf in 1960.

31 'Dovvomin gozāresh-e motāleʿāt-e shurā-ye markazi-ye jashnhā...' [Second study report of the Central Council for the Celebrations...], c. January 1961, *Bazm-e Ahriman*, vol. 1, 96–104.

32 G. W. Harrison to Roger Stevens, 2 October 1959, FO 371/140887.

33 Hoseyn ʿAlā to ʿAli Amini, 17 Dey 1340/ 7 January 1962, 'Asnād-e Mahramāneh-ye Jashnhā', 125.

34 Nosratollāh Moʿiniyān to ʿAlā, 9 Mordād 1342/ 31 July 1963, Shafā Archives.

35 Ibid.

36 Letter from Javād Bushehri, 25 Shahrivar 1343/ 16 September 1965, *Zanān-e Darbār beh Revāyat-e Asnād-e Sāvāk: Farah Pahlavi*, vol. 2 (Tehran: Markaz-e Barresi-ye Asnād-e Tārikhi-ye Vezārat-e Ettelāʿāt, 1388/2009), 195.

37 Javād Bushehri to ʿAbbās Ārām, 22 Shahrivar 1343/ 13 September 1964, 'Asnād-e Mahramāneh-ye Jashnhā', 127–8.

38 H. J. Levelt to Minister of Foreign Affairs, 2 May 1960, NA 2.05.191/42.

39 A. H. Hasselman to Minister of Foreign Affairs, 23 September 1964, NA 2.05.191/42.

40 J. R. Rich to Sir D. Allen, 28 August 1968, FCO 57/69.

41 *Jashn-e Tājgozāri: Beh Revāyat-e Asnād-e Sāvāk* [The Coronation: According to SAVAK documents] (Tehran: Markaz-e Barresi-ye Asnād-e Tārikhi-ye Vezārat-e Ettelā'āt, 1385), 35.
42 Ibid., 58–69.
43 Marvin Zonis, *The Political Elite of Iran* (Princeton, NJ: Princeton University Press, 1971), 65.
44 Bushehri to 'Alam, 4 Shahrivar 1347/ 26 August 1968, 'Asnād-e Mahramāneh-ye Jashnhā', 128.
45 *Tājgozāri-ye Shāhanshāhān-e Irān* [The Coronation of the Kings of Iran] (Tehran: Shurā-ye Markazi-ye Jashn-e Shāhanshāhi-ye Irān, 1346/1967).
46 'Bedin Guneh Rezā Shāh Pahlavi Tāj-e Shāhanshāhi rā Bar Sar Gozāsht' [In this way Reza Shah Pahlavi Placed the Crown on his Head], *Rastākhiz*, 4 Ordibehesht 1355/ 24 April 1976, 12–13.
47 *Tājgozāri-ye A'lāhazrat Homāyun Mohammad Rezā Pahlavi Āryāmehr Shāhanshāh-e Irān va 'Olyāhazrat Farah Pahlavi Shahbānu-ye Irān* [The Coronation of His Imperial Majesty Mohammad Reza Pahlavi Āryāmehr Shāhanshāh of Iran and Her Majesty Farah Pahlavi Shahbanou of Iran], 4 Ābān 1346, 46–52.
48 Javād Bushehri report, 27 Dey 1339/ 17 January 1961, *Bazm-e Ahriman*, vol. 1, 101.
49 Shakibi, 'Pahlavism', 118.
50 Gholam Reza Afkhami, *The Life and Times of the Shah* (Monterey: University of California Press, 2008), 248–9.
51 *Jashn-e Tājgozāri*, 313.
52 See Afkhami, *The Life and Times of the Shah*, 247–9.
53 Gregory Lima, *The Revolutionizing of Iran* (Tehran: International Communications, 1973), 103.
54 Ibid.
55 *Jashn-e Tājgozāri*, 46–52.
56 Denis Wright Report, 30 November 1967, 4, FO 248/1637.
57 *Jashn-e Tājgozāri*, 55.
58 Ibid., 141–3.
59 *Programme of the Coronation Ceremony: Summary* (Tehran: Ministry of Information, 1967), 9.
60 Javād Bushehri to Mehdi Sami'i, 9 Mehr 1346/ 1 October 1967, 'Asnād-e Mahramāneh-ye Jashnhā', 131; *Programme of the Coronation Ceremony*, 9.
61 *Jashn-e Tājgozāri*, 55.
62 J. R. Rich to D. Allen, 28 August 1968, FCO 57/69.
63 '2,500th Year of Monarchy', *Kayhan International*, 8 May 1969.
64 Abdolreza Ansari, *The Shah's Iran – Rise and Fall: Conversations with an Insider* (London: I.B. Tauris, 2017), 249.
65 Ibid., 250.
66 Ibid., 250–1.
67 According to Deputy Minister of Court Mohammad Bāheri, 'Alam was against the idea of the Celebrations, but followed the orders of the Shah. See his interview with Habib Ladjevardi, Cannes, France, 7, 8, 10, 11, 13, 14 August 1982, Iranian Oral History Collection, Harvard University, tape 20, 2. Interestingly, according to British records, although they note that 'Alam's loyalty to the Shah is unquestionable', he was also opposed to the coronation: 'Both the Minister of Court and his wife made it clear to the Ambassador during a dinner party conversation on 30 January that they are unhappy about the forthcoming coronation, and the consequential expense involved,

on public relations grounds.' See C. D. Wiggin to W. Morris, 4 February 1967, FO 248/1637.
68 Diary entry 5 Ordibehesht 1352/ 25 April 1973, *Yāddāshthā-ye 'Alam*, vol. 3, 27.
69 Conversation with 'Abdolrezā Ansāri, Paris, 2016.
70 Shafā to Hendrik Jonker, 28 January 1971, NA 2.05.191/554.
71 Ibid. In his memoir 'Abdolrezā Ansāri gives a slightly different account of the members of the committee. For instance, Rezā Qotbi is listed on Ansāri's list, whereas Cyrus Farzāneh is absent. See Ansari, *The Shah's Iran*, 252. Shafā's account has been used here because Farzāneh was listed elsewhere as having attended meetings of the Executive Committee. See, for example, SAVAK report, 5 Mordād 1350/ 27 July 1971, *Bazm-e Ahriman*, vol. 4, 210–11. In the weeks prior to the Celebrations, a list of twenty-six people was published, who would oversee the implementation of events during the Celebrations. See, *Ruznāmeh-ye Jashn-e Shāhanshāhi-ye Irān*, 30 Shahrivar 1350/ 21 September 1971, 8.
72 Shafā to Hendrik Jonker, 28 January 1971, NA 2.05.191/554.
73 Shafā to 'Alam, 8 Khordād 1349/ 29 May 1970, 'Asnād-e Mahramāneh-ye Jashnhā', 156–9.
74 Cyrus Kadivar, 'We Are Awake: 2500-Year Celebrations Revisited', *Iranian*, 25 January 2002. Available online: http://iranian.com/CyrusKadivar/2002/January/2500/index.html (accessed 19 December 2016).
75 Ansari, *The Shah's Iran*, 257.
76 It was due to be completed by 1 Shahrivar 1350/ 23 August 1971. See Javād Bushehri to 'Alam, 1 Āzar 1348/ 22 November 1969, *Bazm-e Ahriman*, vol. 3, 108–10.
77 Jonker to Minister of Foreign Affairs, 14 September 1971; and Jonker to Foreign Ministry, 22 September 1971, NA 2.05.191/554.
78 *Iran '71: An Independent Survey of the Iranian Economy on the Occasion of the 2500th Anniversary of the Founding of the Persian Empire* (Tehran: Iran Trade and Industry, 1971), 10.
79 Dutch Embassy Tehran to Ministry of Foreign Affairs, 11 March 1970, NA 2.05.191/554.
80 The eagle was an almost exact copy of one depicted on Egyptian Blue, discovered at Persepolis in 1948. See Ali Mousavi, *Persepolis: Discovery and Afterlife of a World Wonder* (Boston: Walter de Gruyter, 2012), 250. Thanks to Dr Mousavi for bringing this to my attention.
81 Ansari, *The Shah's Iran*, 255.
82 Ibid., 256.
83 Ibid., 253.
84 Ibid., 254.
85 Cyrus Kadivar, '2500-Year Revisited', *The Iranian*, 25 January 2002. Available online: http://iranian.com/CyrusKadivar/2002/January/2500/index.html (accessed 19 December 2016).
86 Ansari, *The Shah's Iran*, 264–5.
87 Arthur Upham Pope to Amir Ebrahimi, 4 December 1960, in Gluck and Siver, *Surveyors of Persian Art*, 427.
88 Memo from Asadollah Behroozan, ibid., 427.
89 Pope to Ebrahimi, 4 December 1960, ibid., 429.
90 G. W. Harrison to Roger Stevens, 2 September 1959, FO 371/140887.
91 Though curiously guests were not placed in their continent-wing. For example, the Afghan Princess Bilqis Begum and her husband Abdul Wali Khan were placed in

America Avenue, flanked by Korea's Jung Pil Kim on one side and Mauritania's Ould Daddah on the other. See 'Where the Guests Slept', *Tehran Journal*, 20 October 1971.
92 Antony Mann, 'Paris Wins Order of the Bath', *Daily Telegraph*, 11 October 1971; and *Tehran Journal*, 3 July 1971.
93 'Qālichehhā-ye Yādbud Barāye Sarān-e Keshvarhā' [Commemorative Carpets for Heads of State], *Haftehnāmeh-ye Komiteh-ye Ettelā'āt va Enteshārāt-e Jashn-e Dohezār o Pānsadomin Sāl-e Bonyāngozāri-ye Shāhanshāhi*, no. 12, 7 Shahrivar 1350/ 29 August 1971, 12–13. *Paris Match* reported that the value of each woven portrait was 350,000 francs ($65,000, the equivalent of $500,000 today), an exorbitant and unrealistic amount. See 'Persépolis: La fête d'un empereur et de son peuple', *Paris Match*, 23 October 1971, 33. For five guests who accepted their invitations at the last minute, leaving no time for the tapestries to be made, they were sent in August 1975. Diary entry 2 August 1975, Asadollah Alam, *The Shah and I: Confidential Diary of Iran's Royal Court, 1969–1977*, ed. Alinaghi Alikhani (London: I.B. Tauris, 1991), 432.
94 *Tehran Journal*, 3 July 1971.
95 Gregory Lima, 'Inside Agnew's Tent', *Kayhan International*, 13 October 1971, 1.
96 Jonker report, 3 November 1971, NA 2.05.191/554.
97 Charlotte Curtis, 'Tent City Awaits Celebration: Shah's "Greatest Show"', *New York Times*, 12 October 1971, 39.
98 Danish ambassador to Jonker, 3 July 1971, NA 2.05.191/554.
99 'Necessary Information and Questions', undated, NA 2.05.191/554.
100 'Abdolrezā Ansāri to Gholāmrezā Nikpey, 2 Shahrivar 1350/ 24 August 1971, 'Asnād-e Mahramāneh-ye Jashnhā', 179.
101 Quoted in Loren Jenkins, 'Iran's Birthday Party', *Newsweek*, 25 October 1971, 33. Funds were allocated to modernize areas in Fars close to where foreigners might pass by, such as Marvdasht and Sa'ādatābād and other areas on the way from Shiraz to Pasargadae. See Governor of Fars to Minister of Interior, 30 Farvardin 1350/ 19 April 1971, *Bazm-e Ahriman*, vol. 4, 32–3.
102 'Alam to Bushehri, 12 Khordād 1349/ 2 June 1970, *Bazm-e Ahriman*, vol. 3, 183; and Bushehri to 'Alam, 18 Khordād 1349/ 8 June 1970, ibid., 191.
103 Ansari, *The Shah's Iran*, 263–4.
104 See Amir Mottaqi to Ministry of Foreign Affairs, 1 Esfand 1350/ 20 February 1972, 'Asnād-e Mahramāneh-ye Jashnhā', 181.
105 Abbas Milani, *The Shah* (New York: Palgrave Macmillan, 2011), 326.
106 Farah Pahlavi, *An Enduring Love: My Life with the Shah* (New York: Turnaround Distributor, 2004), 216–17.
107 Curtis, 'Tent City Awaits Celebration', 39.
108 Vincent Mulchrone, 'The Biggest Beano Since Babylon...', *Daily Mail*, 11 October 1971.
109 For example, a statue of Empress Farah was constructed in a public park in Shiraz. Anonymous report, *Bazm-e Ahriman*, vol. 4, 108. Displays of the twelve points of the White Revolution were set up in towns and villages across the country.
110 Some of these events were funded by local governments and some by private individuals and organizations. In Khorasan, for instance, there was a suggestion that new taxes could be introduced for a limited period to fund local festivities, Amir Mottaqi to Javād Bushehri, 29 Ābān 1348/ 20 November 1969, 'Asnād-e Mahramāneh-ye Jashnhā', 154.

111 'Surat-e majles komisiyon-e barnāmeh va tashrifāt' [Parliamentary report of commission for programme and protocol], 12 Ābān 1347/ 3 November 1968, 'Asnād-e Mahramāneh-ye Jashnhā', 151.
112 Fariborz Mokhtari, *In the Lion's Shadow: The Iranian Schindler and His Homeland in the Second World War* (Stroud: History Press, 2011), 127.
113 Jewish Council for the Celebrations to Javād Bushehri, 23 Khordād 1349/ 13 June 1970, *Bazm-e Ahriman*, vol. 3, 192–4.
114 Khān-bābā Bayāni to Javād Bushehri, 2 Khordād 1348/ 23 May 1969, *Bazm-e Ahriman*, vol. 3, 67–70.
115 Hamid Naficy, *A Social History of Iranian Cinema, Volume 2: The Industrializing Years, 1941–1978* (Durham, NC: Duke University Press, 2012), 139; 'Film about Celebrations Ready Soon', *Kayhan International*, 2 September 1972, 3; SAVAK report, 12 Āzar 1351/ 3 December 1972, *Bazm-e Ahriman*, vol. 4, 393–4. The film cost around 50 million rials to produce ($670,000).
116 Hamid Naficy, 'Nonfiction Fiction: Documentaries on Iran', *Iranian Studies*, 12: 3/4 (1979): 229.
117 Javād Bushehri to Amir 'Abbās Hoveydā, 27 Mordād 1348/ 18 August 1969, *Bazm-e Ahriman*, vol. 3, 85–6.
118 Pope to H. Amir-Ebrahimi, 12 December 1960, in *Surveyors of Persian Art*, ed. Gluck and Siver, 430–2.
119 The daily *Ruznāmeh-ye Jashn-e Shāhanshāhi-ye Irān* ran in 100 issues from 3 Mordād until 30 Ābān 1350.
120 *Gāhnāmeh-ye Panjāh Sāl-e Shāhanshāhi-ye Pahlavi* [Chronology of Fifty Years of the Pahlavi Monarchy] (Paris: Soheil Publishers, 1985), 2042.
121 'Irān Āmādeh Bargozāri-ye Bozorgtarin Jashn-e Tārikh-e Khod Shod', *Keyhān*, 12 Mehr 1350/ 4 October 1971, 1.
122 Walter Schwarz, 'A Kingdom Remembered – 2,500 Years on', *The Guardian*, 13 October 1971, 1.
123 David Stronach, *Pasargadae: A Report on the Excavations Conducted by the British Institute of Persian Studies* (Oxford: Clarendon Press, 1978), 173.
124 David Stronach, 'Cyrus and Pasargadae', in *Cyrus the Great: An Ancient Iranian King*, ed. Touraj Daryaee (Santa Monica, CA: Afshar Publishing, 2013), 63. When he heard of imminent plans to remove these features, Stronach rushed to Pasargadae so that he could record the precise measurements before the removal. Conversation with David Stronach, Berkeley, 2014.
125 This sort of state-sponsored vandalism of historical monuments is not uncommon and reflects the problems inherent in using history and archaeology for political propaganda. During Mussolini's Augustus celebration in 1936–7, layers of history were removed from the site of Augustus's tomb. Similarly, in the 19th century in Europe, medieval churches were purged of later additions in the hope that this would reveal the true nature of the monuments and bring the restorers closer to the pure spirit of the Christian faith. See David Lowenthal, *The Past Is a Foreign Country* (Cambridge: Cambridge University Press, 1985), 278.
126 *The Glorification of Cyrus the Great Achaemenian King of Kings*, Pasargad, 12 October 1971 [programme].
127 Ibid.
128 'Misāq-e Shāhanshāh bā Bonyāngozār-e Shāhanshāhi-ye Irān' [The Shah's Covenant with the Founder of Imperial Iran], *Keyhān*, 20 Mehr 1350/ 12 October 1971, 1.
129 Quoted in Margaret Laing, *The Shah* (London: Sigwick and Jackson, 1977), 22.

130 'Isā Sadiq, *Yādgār-e ʿOmr: Khāterāti az Sargozasht-e Doktor ʿIsā Sadiq*, vol. 4 (Tehran: Ketābforushi-ye Dekhodā, 2536), 35.
131 See, for example, Peter Chelkowski interviewed in *Decadence and Downfall*.
132 Schwarz, 'A Kingdom Remembered'.
133 'Sjah belooft aan Cyrus een nog groter Iran' [Shah Promises Cyrus an Even Greater Iran], *Leidsch Dagblad*, 13 October 1971, 9.
134 Roy Mottahedeh, *The Mantle of the Prophet: Religion and Politics in Iran* (Oxford: Oneworld, 2009), 327.
135 Bani Sadr interviewed in *Decadence and Downfall*.
136 Houchang Nahavandi, *The Last Shah of Iran: Fatal Countdown of a Great Patriot Betrayed by the Free World, a Great Country Whose Fault Was Success*, trans. Steeve Reed (Slough: Aquillon, 2005), 21–2.
137 Ibid., 22.
138 R. K. Karanjia, *The Mind of a Monarch* (London: George Allen & Unwin, 1977), 29.
139 Roger Savory, 'Iran: A 2500-year Historical and Cultural Tradition', in *Iranian Civilization and Culture*, ed. Adams, 77.
140 Ibid.
141 *World Congress of Iranology: On the Occasion of the Celebration of the 2500th Anniversary of the Founding of the Persian Empire by Cyrus the Great*, Shiraz, 13–15 October 1971 [programme]; 'Bozorgtarin Kongreh-ye Irānshenāsān-e Jahān Diruz bā Sherkat-e 250 Irānshenās dar Shirāz Āghāz beh Kār Kard' [The Largest Conference of Iranologists in the World Got to Work Yesterday in Shiraz with the Participation of 250 Iranologists], *Keyhān*, 22 Mehr 1350/ 14 October 1971, 12.
142 Sadiq, *Yādgār-e ʿOmr*, 31.
143 Walter Schwarz, 'Finale Saves the Cyrus Show', *The Guardian*, 16 October 1971, 1.
144 'Hāyleh Selāsi Emperātur-e 81 Sāleh-ye Etiyupi dar Tehrān' [Haile Selassie 81-year-old Emperor of Ethiopia in Tehran], *Keyhān*, 21 Mehr 1350/ 13 October 1971, 28.
145 'Necessary Information and Questions', undated, NA 2.05.191/554.
146 Ramsbotham report, 22 October 1971, FCO 17/1529.
147 *Dāneshgāh-e Pahlavi beh Revāyat-e Asnād* [The Pahlavi University According to Documents] (Tehran: Markaz-e Asnād-e Enqelāb-e Eslāmi, 1397), 327–8.
148 Milani, *The Shah*, 199.
149 General Nasiri to Central Commander of the Gendarmerie, 26 Mehr 1350/ 18 October 1971, *Bazm-e Ahriman*, vol. 4, 340.
150 'The Shahanshah's Speech at the Banquet on 14 October 1971', NA 2.05.191/554.
151 Ibid.
152 'Reply of His Imperial Majesty Haile Selassie I at Iran Banquet', ibid.
153 According to one of the catering staff, the food for the guests was flown in on special aircraft and included 2,700 kilograms of meat and 1,280 kilograms of fowl and game. See Beglinger, 'The Most Expensive Party Ever'.
154 *Chicago Tribune*, 10 October 1971. One Dutch newspaper made the extraordinary claim that 50 tonnes (50,000 kg) of caviar was supplied, one-eighth of the global yearly production. See 'Uitbundig feest in Persepolis' [Exuberant Party at Persepolis], *Gelderlander Pers*, 4 August 1971. This again highlights the fallibility of the press coverage of the Celebrations.
155 'Diner Persepolis op 14 Oktober 1971', NA 2.05.191/554.
156 Quoted in Martin Clark, 'The Party', in *Celebration at Persepolis*, ed. Michael Stevenson (Bristol: Arnolfini, 2008), 23.
157 Ansari, *The Shah's Iran*, 267.

158 Maria Anna Harley, 'Music of Sound and Light: Xenakis's Polytopes', *Leonardo*, 31:1 (1998): 59.
159 Ansari, *The Shah's Iran*, 258.
160 In April 1971, the light and sound machine suffered a technical fault and the organizers were concerned that this might occur again during the Celebrations. To avoid such embarrassment, the company that installed the equipment arranged for a specialist to be sent to Iran in the months leading up to the Celebrations and for a number of individuals in Iran to be given specialist training. See Mehrdād Pahlbod to 'Abdolrezā Ansāri, 25 Farvardin 1350/ 14 April 1971, *Bazm-e Ahriman*, vol. 4, 31.
161 Talinn Grigor, 'Preserving the Antique Modern: Persepolis '71', *Future Anterior*, 2:1 (2005): 26.
162 'Surat jalaseh-ye komisiyon-e arteshi-ye jashn-e shāhanshāhi-ye Irān' [Proceedings of the military commission of the imperial celebrations], *Bazm-e Ahriman*, vol. 3, 154–6. When the commission was founded, Amānollāh Jahānbāni was in charge. See *Bazm-e Ahriman*, vol. 1, 104; vol. 2, 22.
163 Ibid., 40–1; and 154–6.
164 Shafa, *Facts about the Celebration*, 28.
165 *Rāhnamā-ye Rezheh* [Guide to the Parade] (Tehran: Ministry of Information, 1971).
166 Yahyā Zokā', *Artesh-e Shāhanshāhi-ye Irān az Kurosh tā Pahlavi* (Tehran: Shurā-ye Arteshi-ye Jashn-e Dohezār o Pānsadomin Sāl-e Bonyāngozāri-ye Shāhanshāhi-ye Irān, 1350); and Yahyā Zokā', *Pishineh-ye Sān va Rezheh dar Irān* (Tehran: Komiteh-ye Farhang-e Jashn-e Shāhanshāhi-ye Irān, 1350[?]).
167 V. Romanowski de Boncza, *Les Costumes Militaires de L'Empire Perse depuis sa Fondation* (Athens: imprimé par Aspioti-Elka, 1965).
168 Jalil Ziyā'pur, *Pushāk-e Hakhāmaneshihā va Mādihā dar Takht-e Jamshid* (Tehran: Komiteh-ye Farhang-e Jashn-e Shāhanshāhi-ye Irān, 1350[?]).
169 E. R. Chamberlin, *Preserving the Past* (London: J.M. Dent and Sons, 1979), 25.
170 For example, Kaveh Farrokh, *Shadows in the Desert: Ancient Persia at War* (Oxford: Osprey, 2007).
171 'Shahanshah's Message at the Grand Parade 15 October 1971', NA 2.05.191/554.
172 *Parade of the Celebration of the 2500th Anniversary of the Founding of the Persian Empire by Cyrus the Great*, Persepolis, 15 October 1971 [programme]. The Revolutionary Corps, established as part of the White Revolution in 1963, was an educational programme that sought to improve literacy levels in Iran. For a comprehensive study of the Literacy Corps, see Farian Sabahi, *The Literacy Corps in Pahlavi Iran (1963–1979): Political Social and Literary Implications* (Lugano: Sapiens Lugano cop., 2002).
173 Grigor, 'Preserving the Antique Modern', 26–27. Although some of the facial hair in the published pictures appears to be artificial.
174 Ansari, *The Shah's Iran*, 267.
175 Jonker to Head of Protocol, 8 September 1971, NA 2.05.191/554.
176 Pahlavi, *An Enduring Love*, 225.
177 On this festival, see H. E. Chehabi, 'The Shiraz Festival and Its Place in Iran's Revolutionary Mythology', in *The Age of Aryamehr: Late Pahlavi Iran and Its Global Entanglements*, ed. Roham Alvandi (London: Gingko Library, 2018), 168–201.
178 'Invitations', *Kayhan International*, 26 July 1971.
179 Farajollāh Āq Oli to Bushehri, 15 Ordibehesht 1343/ 5 May 1964, *Bazm-e Ahriman*, vol. 2, 11.
180 Court Minister to Bushehri, 10 Khordād 1343/ 31 May 1964, ibid., 18.

181 See Faryār Javāheriyān, 'Shahyād: Nomādi do Pahlu' [Shahyād: A Two-Faceted Symbol], *Irān Nāmeh*, 24:4 (1387/2009): 482.
182 Ibid. Javāheriyān provides a direct quote for this (*beh andāzeh-ye kāfi 'azemat nadārad*), but from the text it is unclear to whom this quote should be attributed.
183 Ibid.
184 Ibid., 486.
185 Ibid.
186 Talinn Grigor, 'Of Metamorphosis Meaning on Iranian Terms', *Third Text*, 17:3 (2003): 211.
187 Hoseyn Amānat to Javād Bushehri, 30 Esfand 1346/ 20 March 1968, 'Asnād-e Mahramāneh-ye Jashnhā', 131–2; Peter Ayres, 'The Geometry of Shahyad Ariamehr', *Arup Journal*, 5:1 (1970): 34. Footage of building at different stages of its construction can be observed in the documentary *Hargez Nakhab Kurush* (2012), [film] Manoto, London.
188 'The Official Ceremonies' by the Committee of the International Affairs of the Festivities, July 1971, NA 2.05.191/554.
189 See letter Javād Bushehri to Mayor of Tehran Fathollāh Forud, 24 Bahman 1339/ 13 February 1961, 'Asnād-e Mahramāneh-ye Jashnhā', 129.
190 Talinn Grigor, 'Orientalism and Mimicry of Selfness', in *L'Orientalisme architectural entre imaginaires et savoirs*, ed. Nabila Oulebsir and Mercedes Volait (Paris: Picard, 2009), 6. Available online: http://journals.openedition.org/inha/4911 (accessed 29 April 2019).
191 This loan will be discussed at length in Chapter 3.
192 Ansāri to 'Alam, 23 Mordād 1350/ 14 August 1971, *Bazm-e Ahriman*, vol. 4, 204. It was to be on permanent display at the entrance to the monument.
193 'Tehran's Ctesiphon', *Kayhan International*, 23 October 1971.
194 Public Relations Office of the Military Council of the Imperial Celebrations to Head of the Central Council of the Imperial Celebrations, 21 Mehr 1350/ 13 October 1971, *Bazm-e Ahriman*, vol. 4, 334–5. The same bands also performed the following day at the inauguration of the Āryāmehr Stadium.
195 'Marāsem-e Eftetāh-e Banā-ye Bāshokuh-e Shahyād-e Āryāmehr' [Inauguration Ceremony of the Magnificent Shahyād Āryāmehr], *Ettelā'āt*, 20 Mehr 1350/ 17 October 1971. 12. It was planned to last two and a half hours and cost 1.9 million rials ($25,300), but was evidently scaled down. See Gholāmrezā Nikpey to Ansāri, 20 Bahman 1349/ 9 February 1971, *Bazm-e Ahriman*, vol. 3, 287–90.
196 *Echo of Iran*, 5 July 1971.
197 'Cyrus Cup Stays at Home', *Kayhan International*, 10 July 1971, 3.
198 *Gāhnāmeh-ye Panjāh Sāl-e Shāhanshāhi-ye Pahlavi*, vol. 5, 2008.
199 The final was played between Iran and America on 9 May, with Empress Farah in attendance. Ibid., 2006.
200 Abbas Milani, *Eminent Persians: The Men and Women Who Made Modern Iran, 1941–1979*, vol. 1 (Syracuse, NY: Syracuse University Press, 2008), 151; and Nahavandi, *The Last Shah of Iran*, 37–8. Iran withdrew its bid shortly after the revolution, leaving Los Angeles as the only remaining candidate.
201 'Aryamehr Sports Centre', *Iran Tribune*, October 1971, 43.
202 Ibid., 42.
203 For footage of the event, see *Forugh-e Jāvidān*.
204 *Iran Tribune*, November 1971, 10.
205 Ibid., 11.

206 'Injā, Diruz Markaz-e Shādi-ye Jahān Bud', *Keyhān*, 26 Mehr 1350/ 18 October 1971, 1.
207 After the revolution, it was renamed Borj-e Āzādi (Freedom Tower).
208 'Grand Finale', *Kayhan International*, 23 October 1971, 6.
209 *Ettelā'āt*, 26 Mehr 1350/ 18 October 1971, 5. For full details, see *Celebration of the 2500th Anniversary of the Founding of the Persian Empire* [programme], 14–22.
210 'Necessary Information and Questions', undated, NA 2.05.191/554.
211 Chamberlin, *Preserving the Past*, 26.
212 See Chapter 6.

3 International diplomacy at Persepolis

1 For the Russian and British imperial competition in Persia, see Firuz Kazemzadeh, *Russia and Britain in Persia: Imperial Ambitions in Qajar Iran* (London: I.B. Tauris, 2013).
2 Michael Axworthy, *Iran: Empire of the Mind* (London: Penguin, 2008), 192.
3 For a fascinating study of the constitutional crisis in the context of British imperial policy, see Mansour Bonakdarian, *Britain and the Iranian Constitutional Revolution of 1906–1911: Foreign Policy, Imperialism, and Dissent* (Syracuse: Syracuse University Press, 2006).
4 Stephanie Cronin, *The Army and the Pahlavi State in Iran, 1910–1926* (London: I.B. Tauris, 1997), 86.
5 Michael P. Zirinsky, 'Imperial Power and Dictatorship: Britain and the Rise of Reza Shah, 1921–1926', *International Journal of Middle East Studies* 24 (1992): 658.
6 Ibid., 647.
7 See Annabelle Sreberny and Massoumeh Torfeh, *Persian Service: The BBC and British Interests in Persia* (London: I.B. Tauris, 2014), 39–43.
8 Fariborz Mokhtari, *In the Lion's Shadow: The Iranian Schindler and His Homeland in the Second World War* (Stroud: History Press, 2011), 69.
9 Ibid.
10 Fereydoun Hoveyda, *The Fall of the Shah* (New York: Wyndham Books, 1980), 70; and Peter Frankopan, *Silk Roads: A New History of the World* (London: Bloomsbury, 2015), 400.
11 Abbas Milani, *The Shah* (New York: Palgrave Macmillan, 2011), 101.
12 R. K. Karanjia, *The Mind of a Monarch* (London: George Allen & Unwin, 1977), 69.
13 Ramsbotham, Diplomatic Report, 'The Dynasty Blessed by the Gods', 11 October 1971, 2, FCO 57/323.
14 Though as more evidence comes to light, the central roles of the CIA and MI6 have become increasingly clear. For a flavour of the debate, see Mark Gasiorowski and Malcolm Byrne (eds), *Mohammad Mosaddeq and the 1953 Coup in Iran* (New York: Syracuse University Press, 2004); Ervand Abrahamian, *The Coup* (New York: New Press, 2013); and Darioush Bayandor, *Iran and the CIA: The Fall of Mosaddeq Revisited* (New York: Palgrave Macmillan, 2010).
15 *Jashn-e Tājgozāri: Beh Revāyat-e Asnād-e Sāvāk* (Tehran: Markaz-e Barresi-ye Asnād-e Tārikhi-ye Vezārat-e Ettelā'āt, 1385/2006), 53.
16 Diary entry 2–14 Shahrivar 1353/ 24 August–5 September 1974, *Yāddāshthā-ye 'Alam*, vol. 4, 18.

17 Zhand Shakibi, 'The Rastakhiz Party and Pahlavism: The Beginnings of State Anti-Westernism in Iran', *British Journal of Middle Eastern Studies*, 45:2 (2018): 255.
18 'Special Mementoes for Special Guests', *Kayhan International*, 23 October 1971, 6.
19 Mohammad Reza Pahlavi, *Iran, Philosophy Behind the Revolution* (London: Orient Commerce Establishment, 1971), 131.
20 Ibid., 229.
21 'The Shahanshah's speech at the banquet on 14 October 1971', 17–19, NA 2.05.191/554.
22 'Shahanshah's message at the Grand Parade, 15 October 1971', 21, ibid.
23 Michael Axworthy, *Revolutionary Iran: A History of the Islamic Republic* (London: Penguin Books, 2013), 77.
24 Quoted in William A. McWhirter, 'The Shah's Princely Party', *Life Magazine*, 29 October 1971, 26.
25 'Dānmārk: Qadimitarin Keshvar-e Pādeshāhi-ye Orupā', *Etteláʿāt*, 21 Mehr 1350/ 13 October 1971, 25.
26 R. Tarverdi and Ali Massoudi (eds), *The Land of Kings* (Tehran: Ettelaʿat Publications, 1971), 1.
27 The only other option open to the organizers would have been to follow the protocol of the day as they saw it, in which countries were ordered according to their success in the Second World War. Following these rules, Britain, the Soviet Union, France and America would be accorded the highest status. See Abdolreza Ansari, *The Shah's Iran – Rise and Fall: Conversations with an Insider* (London: I.B. Tauris, 2017), 266.
28 Cyrus Kadivar, '2500-Year Revisited', *The Iranian*, 25 January 2002. Available online: http://iranian.com/CyrusKadivar/2002/January/2500/index.html (accessed 19 December 2016).
29 Ramsbotham to Hormoz Qarib, 28 August 1971, 'Asnād-e Mahramāneh-ye Jashnhā', 141.
30 See Anthony Mann, 'Shah Attacks Pompidou for Missing Party', *Daily Telegraph*, 8 October 1971.
31 Peter Ramsbotham in an interview with Habib Ladjevardi, London, UK, 18 October 1985, Iranian Oral History Collection, Harvard University, tape 1, 26–7.
32 Peter Ramsbotham in an interview with Shusha Assar, 20 January 1986, Hampshire, UK, in the Oral History of Iran Collection of the Foundation of Iranian Studies, 65–6.
33 A carillon is a set of bells typically housed in the bell tower of a church. Jonker to Ministry of Foreign Affairs, 28 January 1970, NA 2.05.191/554.
34 Ministry of Foreign Affairs to Embassy Tehran, 1 March 1970, ibid.
35 Jonker to Ministry of Foreign Affairs, 6 April 1970, ibid.
36 Jonker to Ministry of Foreign Affairs, 20 March 1970, ibid. To the ambassador's disappointment, the Ministry of Foreign Affairs decided to send the Shah a concert organ instead, before changing their minds and taking to Persepolis a silver model of the famous Dutch flagship of Admiral De Ruyter, *De Zeven Provinciën*, weighing 13 kilograms.
37 George Middleton in an interview with Habib Ladjevardi, London, England, 16 October 1985, Iranian Oral History Collection, Harvard University, tape 3.
38 Diary entry 8 Khordād 1348/ 29 May 1969, *Yāddāshthā-ye ʿAlam*, vol. 1, 207.,.
39 Amelie Kuhrt, *The Persian Empire: A Corpus of Sources from the Achaemenid Period* (Oxon: Routledge, 2009), 72.
40 Josef Wiesehöfer, *Ancient Persia* (London: I.B. Tauris, 2001), 49.

41 A. T. Olmstead, *History of the Persian Empire* (Chicago: University of Chicago Press, 1948), 52.
42 Richard Frye, *The Heritage of Persia*, 2nd edn (London: Cardinal, 1976), 89.
43 C. B. F. Walker, 'A Recently Identified Fragment of the Cyrus Cylinder', *Iran* 10 (1972): 158–9.
44 Pierre Nora, 'Between Memory and History', in *Realms of Memory: Rethinking the French Past*, vol. 1, ed. Pierre Nora, trans. Arthur Goldhammer (New York: Columbia University Press, 1996), 7.
45 David Lowenthal, *The Past Is a Foreign Country* (Cambridge: Cambridge University Press, 1985), 64.
46 *Echo of Iran*, 26 August 1968.
47 Ramsbotham to Sir Denis Greenhill, 20 August 1971, FCO 17/1528.
48 Ibid.
49 Greenhill to Ramsbotham, 15 September 1971, FCO 17/1529.
50 S. L. Egerton to Parsons, 13 September 1971, FCO 17/1529.
51 FCO Correspondence, 26 October 1971, FCO 17/1529.
52 Ibid.
53 Conversation with David Stronach, Berkeley, 2014.
54 "Cyrus' Cylinder Flown to Tehran', *Kayhan International*, 23 October 1971, 4.
55 Conversation with David Stronach, Berkeley, 2014.
56 Ramsbotham to Greenhill, 21 October 1971, FCO 17/1529.
57 Barnett to Ramsbotham, 5 November 1971, FCO 17/1529. Barnett even took the Cylinder to Israel where he stopped off to see his son on his way back to London.
58 Hartley Shawcross to Barnett, 18 November 1971, FCO 17/1529.
59 Clive Bossom to Edward Heath, 18 October 1971, FCO 17/1529. The problem to which the letter referred was Britain's military withdrawal from the Persian Gulf.
60 Shawcross to Heath, 20 October 1971, FCO 17/1529.
61 Shawcross to Greenhill, 21 October 1971, FCO 17/1529.
62 Quoted in Martin Bailey, 'How Britain Tried to Use a Persian Antiquity for Political Gain', *The Art Newspaper*, 150, September 2004, 19.
63 Jakob Jónsson to Shafā, undated, Shafā Archives.
64 'Cyrus the Great Clay Cylinder (Defensive)', October 1971, FCO 17/1529.
65 Heath to Shawcross, 4 November 1971, FCO 17/1529. Shawcross had apparently planned to use a speech to the Iran Society in London on 4 November to argue this.
66 'Cyrus the Great Clay Cylinder (Defensive)', October 1971, FCO 17/1529.
67 Shojaeddin Shafa, *Facts about the Celebration of the 2500th Anniversary of the Founding of the Persian Empire by Cyrus the Great* (Tehran: Committee of International Affairs of the Festivities, 1971), 60.
68 Press Release, 'Iran Presents Replica of Ancient Edict to United Nations', 14 October 1971, UN HQ/264, S-0882-0002.
69 Farah Pahlavi, *An Enduring Love* (New York: Turnaround Distributor, 2004), 219.
70 'The Cyrus Cylinder', The British Museum. Available online: http://www.britishmuseum.org/research/collection_online/collection_object_details.aspx?objectId=327188&partId=1 (accessed 18 February 2016).
71 St John Simpson, 'The Cyrus Cylinder: Display and Replica', in *The Cyrus Cylinder: The Great Persian Edict from Babylon*, ed. Irving Finkel (London: I.B. Tauris, 2012), 82.

72 Shirin Ebadi, *Nobel Lecture*, 10 December 2003. Available online: http://www.nobelprize.org/nobel_prizes/peace/laureates/2003/ebadi-lecture-e.html (accessed 13 September 2016).
73 William Shawcross, *The Shah's Last Ride* (London: Chatto and Windus, 1989), 47.
74 Charles Issawi, 'The Iranian Economy 1925–1975: Fifty Years of Economic Development', in George Lenczowski (ed.), *Iran Under the Pahlavis* (Stanford: Hoover Institution Press, 1978), 141.
75 See, for example, *Iran 71: An independent survey on the Iranian economy*.
76 'Necessary Information and Questions', 2, NA 2.05.191/554.
77 'Decorations', *Kayhan International*, 5 June 1971.
78 'Alam to Ansāri, 11 Khordād 1350/ 01 June 1971, *Bazm-e Ahriman*, vol. 4, 91.
79 Letter dated 26 Khordād 1350/ 16 June 1971, ibid., 100.
80 Minister of Water and Electricity to Ansāri and Nikpey, 22 Tir 1350/ 13 July 1971, ibid., 149.
81 'Barnāmeh-ye otomobilrāni-ye sitro'en dar Irān' [Programme of Citroën's car show in Iran], 5 Mordād 1350/27 July 1971, ibid., 173–4.
82 Ramsbotham report, 23 October 1971, 4, FCO 57/323.
83 Denis Wright, in an interview with Habib Ladjevardi, Aylesbury, UK, 10 and 11 October 1984, Iranian Oral History Collection, Harvard University, tape 6, 44. Some two years later, 'Alam recorded in his diary that the Shah refused to arrange a formal greeting for Pompidou upon a brief stopover in Iran: 'the Shah really wants to get back at Pompidou for not attending the Imperial Celebrations.' Diary entry 31 Mordād 1352/ 22 August 1973, *Yāddāshthā-ye 'Alam*, vol. 3, 122.
84 Ramsbotham report, 23 October 1971, 4, FCO 57/323.
85 'Heinemann rechtfertigt seine Persien-Reise' [Heinemann Justifies His Trip to Persia], *Frankfurter Allgemeine Zeitung*, 18 August 1971.
86 Ibid.
87 'Zwitserland: Feestje in Perzië is niet leuk' [Switzerland: Party in Persia Is No Fun], *Nieuwe Leidsche Courant*, 13 October 1971, 9.
88 SAVAK report, 7 Mordād 1350/ 29 July 1971, *Bazm-e Ahriman*, vol. 4, 179.
89 SAVAK report, 15 Shahrivar 1350/ 6 September 1971, ibid., 248–50.
90 Ramsbotham to A. D. Parsons, 21 October 1971, FCO 17/1529.
91 'Intimidatie van 'Nederlandse' Pers: Opponent van Sjah krijgt geen pas' [Intimidation of 'Dutch' Persian: Opponent of the Shah refused passport], *Trouw*, 12 October 1971.
92 'Kamerleden laken gedrag Perzische ambassadeur' [MPs Reproach Behaviour of Persian Ambassador], *Volkskrant*, 13 October 1971.
93 Norbert Schmelzer, 'Reply', 27 October 1971, *Aanhangsel tot het verslag van de handelingen der Tweede Kamer*, Zitting 1971–1972, 479, NA 2.02.28.3882.
94 'We Stand on Our Own Feet Monarch Tells World Press', *Kayhan International*, 23 October 1971, 7.
95 *Anglo-Iranian Trade*, 4:4 (1971).
96 John O'Regan, *From Empire to Commonwealth* (London: Radcliffe Press, 1994), 169.
97 Wright, Iranian Oral History Collection, Harvard University, tape 4, 6–7.
98 J. R. Rich to Sir Denis Allen, 10 September 1968, FCO 57/69.
99 Ramsbotham, Iranian Oral History Collection, Harvard University, tape 1, 23.
100 Denis Wright telegram, 9 January 1971, FCO 57/323.
101 Queen Elizabeth II to the Shah, January 1971, FCO 57/323. In the handwritten version that was delivered to the Shah, the queen merely addresses the note to 'Your

Imperial Majesty' but signs the letter 'Your good friend Elizabeth'. See *Yāddāshthā-ye 'Alam*, vol. 2, 203–4.
102 In his diary, 'Alam writes that after reading the letter 'I became very angry', but that the Shah accepted the queen's suggestion that Prince Philip and Princess Anne should be invited instead of Prince Charles. Diary entry 10–23 Bahman 1349/ 30 January–12 February 1971, *Yāddāshthā-ye 'Alam*, vol. 2, 192.
103 Loren Jenkins, 'Iran's Birthday Party', *Newsweek*, 25 October 1971, 33.
104 Jonker report, 3 November 1971, NA 2.05.191/554.
105 Memorandum Henry Kissinger to President Nixon, 6 April 1971, FRUS, 1969–1976, Volume E-4, Iran and Iraq, 1969–1972, doc. 121.
106 'List of Heads of States and the Imperial Missions to whom instructions for invitation have been issued', FCO 248/1708.
107 SAVAK report, 23 Farvardin 1350/ 12 April 1971, *Bazm-e Ahriman*, vol. 4, 25. He sent his eldest daughter, Princess Bilqis Begum, and her husband Abdul Wali Khan.
108 For the letter signed by Jean-Paul Sartre, Simone de Beauvoir and fourteen British Members of Parliament, see 'A Hungry Nation Does Not Need a 2500 Year Celebration: Appeal', in *Corruption and Struggle in Iran: A Defense Publication of the Iranian Student Association in the United States* (June 1972), 8–10. The issue of internal opposition will be explored in greater detail in Chapter 6.
109 Then, according to 'Alam, she came to Iran to apologize personally to the Shah. See diary entry 9 Shahrivar 1355/ 31 August 1976, *Yāddāshthā-ye 'Alam*, vol. 6, 222.
110 Jonker report, 3 November 1971, NA 2.05.191/554.
111 Andrew Scott Cooper, *The Fall of Heaven: The Pahlavis and the Final Days of Imperial Iran* (New York: Henry Holt, 2016), 170.
112 J. M. Pontaut, 'La Fête des fêtes', *Paris Match*, 30 October 1971, 63.
113 For a reproduction of the letter see *Iran Free Press*, 1:2, October 1971, 8.
114 R. T. Eland to Drace-Francis, 1 October 1970, FCO 248/1708.
115 C. D. S. Drace-Francis report, 5 October 1970, FCO 248/1708.
116 Letter from Lieutenant General Riyāhi, undated. Available online: http://iichs.org/index_en.asp?img_cat=126&img_type=1 (accessed 26 April 2019).
117 Intelligence Report 2035–72, Washington, May 1972, FRUS, Volume E-4, doc. 180.
118 As was the official title, see Shafā press conference, 6 July 1971, NA 2.05.191/554. The activities of these committees will be explored in Chapter 5.
119 Pope to Jay Gluck, 12 December 1960, in Gluck and Siver, *Surveyors of Persian Art*, 426.
120 For a list of these honorary chairs, see Shafa, *Facts about the Celebration*, 22–4.
121 Cyrus Committees Forge Friendship, *Kayhan International*, 28 October 1971.
122 Ramsbotham report, 11 October 1971, 4, FCO 57/323.
123 E. M. Westwood to A. L. Mayall, 4 May 1971, FCO 57/323.
124 Ramsbotham to A. L. Mayall, 20 February 1971, FCO 57/322.
125 *Jashn-e Tājgozāri*, 56–7.
126 This statue can be seen in the Fine Art Museum at the Sa'dābād Palace in Tehran.
127 Report: 'Coronation Gifts for the Shah', 30 October 1967, FO 248/1637.
128 H. A. Hoogendoorn to Dutch Minister of Foreign Affairs, 21 October 1971, NA 2.05.191/554.
129 Memorandum Kissinger to Agnew, 9 October 1971, 1, FRUS, Volume E-4, doc. 121.
130 Ibid.
131 Ibid., 2.
132 Ramsbotham report, 23 October 1971, 7, FCO 57/323.

133 Richard Sisson and Leo Rose, *War and Secession: Pakistan, India, and the Creation of Bangladesh* (Oxford: University of California Press, 1990), fn. 4, 307.
134 Roham Alvandi, *Nixon, Kissinger, and the Shah* (Oxford: Oxford University Press, 2014), 61.
135 'Shahanshah's interview', NA 2.05.191/554. In his memoir published in exile, the Shah blamed Yahya Khan's 'intransigence' for his failure to bring the peace talks to a successful conclusion. Mohammad Reza Pahlavi, *The Shah's Story*, trans. Teresa Waugh (London: Michael Joseph, 1980), 134.
136 Karanjia, *The Mind of a Monarch*, 27.
137 'The Master Builder of Iran', *Newsweek*, 14 October 1974, 27.
138 Houchang Chehabi, 'South Africa and Iran in the Apartheid Era', *Journal of Southern African Studies*, 42:4 (2016): 694.
139 'Visit to Senegal of Shahbanou of Iran', March 1976, FCO 8/2766.
140 Diana Murphy (ed.), *Moshe Safdie 1* (Victoria: The Images Publishing Group, 2009), 243.
141 'Visit to Senegal of Shahbanou of Iran', FCO 8/2766.
142 Murphy, *Moshe Safdie 1*, 243.
143 Richard Frye in an interview with Shahla Haeri, Cambridge, MA, 3, 10 and 24 October 1984, Iranian Oral History Collection, Harvard University, tape 3, 35.
144 David Ben-Gurion, 'Cyrus, King of Persia', in *Acta Iranica*, vol. 1, ed. Jacques Duchesne-Guillemin (Tehran: Bibliothèque Pahlavi; Leiden: Brill, 1974), 127–34.
145 Maier Asher, 'Israel Resent Cold Shoulder', *Sunday Telegraph*, 17 October 1971.
146 *Gāhnāmeh-ye Panjāh Sāl-e Shāhanshāhi-ye Pahlavi*, vol. 5, 2058.
147 'Princess Ashraf Pahlavi of Iran Visits China', *Peking Review*, 14:17 (23 April 1971): 4. For her account of the trip, see Ashraf Pahlavi, *Faces in a Mirror: Memoirs from Exile* (Englewood Cliffs: Prentice-Hall, 1980), 178–80.
148 'Princess Fatemeh Pahlavi in Peking', *Peking Review*, 14:19 (7 May 1971): 30.
149 Parviz Mohajer, 'Chinese-Iranian Relations v. Diplomatic and Commercial Relations, 1949–90', *Encyclopaedia Iranica*, 5:4 (1991): 438–41; Fred Halliday, *Dictatorship and Development* (Harmondsworth: Penguin, 1979), 263. For text of the agreement, see 'Joint Communique on Establishment of Diplomatic Relations Between China and Iran', *Peking Review*, 14:34 (20 August 1971): 4.
150 'Iran's 2,500th Anniversary of Persian Empire Greeted', *Peking Review*, 14:43 (22 October 1971): 3–4.
151 *Gāhnāmeh-ye Panjāh Sāl-e Shāhanshāhi-ye Pahlavi*, vol. 5, 2058.
152 Amir Taheri, 'Ties as Old as the Silk Road: Empress, Chou pledge expanded co-operation', *Kayhan International*, 23 September 1972, 1.
153 Denis Wright, Iranian Oral History Collection, Harvard University, tape 3, 10–11.
154 Ramsbotham report, 11 October 1971, 4, FCO 57/323.
155 Diary entry 5 Khordād 1352/ 26 May 1973, *Yāddāshthā-ye 'Alam*, vol. 3, 63.
156 Quoted in Ehsan Naraghi, *From Palace to Prison*, trans. Nilou Mobasser (London: I.B. Tauris, 1994), 19.

4 The Celebrations and cultural policy

1 Yahyā Dustdār and Hoseyn Tayyebāti, *Ketābshenāsi-ye Jashn-e Shāhanshāhi-ye Irān* [Bibliography of the Imperial Celebrations] (Tehran: Shurā-ye Markazi-ye Jashnhā-ye Shāhanshāhi-ye Irān, 1351).

2 Quoted in Zaven N. Davidian, *Iran in the Service of World Peace: On the Occasion of the 2500th Anniversary of the Celebration of the Founding of the Iranian Empire* (Tehran: Davidian, 1971), 28.
3 Talinn Grigor, 'Recultivating "Good Taste": The Early Pahlavi Modernists and Their Society for National Heritage', *Iranian Studies*, 37:1 (2004): 43.
4 Afshin Marashi, *Nationalizing Iran* (Seattle: University of Washington Press, 2008).
5 'Shah's Speech to the Campaign to End Illiteracy', September 1965, Shafā Archives.
6 'World Conference of Ministers of Education on the Eradication of Illiteracy', Tehran, 8–19 September 1965, Final Report, UNESCO/ED/217.
7 Farian Sabahi, *The Literacy Corps in Pahlavi Iran* (Lugano: Sapiens Lugano, 2002), 157.
8 J. A. Warder to Shafā, 18 September 1965, Shafā Archives.
9 Shafā report to the Imperial Court, 18 Ābān 1344/ 9 November 1965, Shah Archives.
10 'Shah's Donation to UNESCO to Fight Illiteracy', *Karachi Morning News*, 4 May 1966, Newspaper cutout in the Shafā Archives.
11 'A Good Documentary on the Literacy Corps', *Kayhan International*, 19 February 1972, 4.
12 'Commemorative Schools', *Kayhan International*, 20 March 1971, 2.
13 Abdolreza Ansari, *The Shah's Iran* (London: I.B. Tauris, 2017), 279–80.
14 'Surat-e Kāmel-e Nām va Mahal-e Madāres-e Yādbud-e Jashn-e Shāhanshāhi-ye Irān keh Sākhtemān-e Ānhā dar Rustāhā-ye Sarāsar-e Keshvar beh Pāyān Resideh ast' [Complete List of Names and Places of Commemorative Schools of the Imperial Celebrations of Iran Whose Construction Has Been Completed in Villages Across the Country], *Keyhān*, 18 Mehr 1350/ 10 October 1971, 11. Complete list on pages 8–20.
15 'Empress Buys Shares Towards 50 Schools', *Kayhan International*, 17 April 1971.
16 Minister of Information to Central Council for the Celebrations, 21 Farvardin 1350/ 10 April 1971, *Bazm-e Ahriman*, vol. 4, 16–19.
17 See 'Surat-e Kāmel-e Nām va Mahal-e Madāres-e Yādbud-e Jashn-e Shāhanshāhi-ye Irān keh Sākhtemān-e Ānhā dar Rustāhā-ye Sarāsar-e Keshvar beh Pāyān Resideh ast', *Keyhān*, 18 Mehr 1350/ 10 October 1971, 8–20.
18 The extent to which this participation was voluntary is questionable. There were certainly some instances of forced contributions. In one reported incident, students at a school in Isfahan were asked to contribute 20 rials each, and in another bazaaris were forced to pay towards the purchase of a school. Some civil servants apparently even had money taken from their salaries. See SAVAK internal reports, 27 Ordibehesht 1350/ 17 May 1971, *Bazm-e Ahriman*, vol. 4, 74; and 28 Ordibehesht 1350/ 18 May 1971, 75.
19 'Empress Buys Shares Towards 50 Schools' *Kayhan International*, 17 April 1971.
20 It is possible that more schools were built after this date. Ansari suggests that up to 3,200 schools were constructed. See Ansari, *The Shah's Iran*, 281.
21 *Gāhnāmeh-ye Panjāh Sāl-e Shāhanshāhi-ye Pahlavi*, vol. 5 (Paris: Soheil Publishers, 1985), 2022.
22 Ibid., 1289.
23 'Conseil Culturel Royal De L'Iran, sous le Haut Patronage de Sa Majesté Impériale Mohammad-Reza Chah Pahlavi', undated document, 1–8, Shafā Archives; and 'Shafā az Zabān-e Khodash', 73.
24 'Conseil Culturel Royal de L'Iran', 12–13.
25 'Conseil Culturel Impérial', *Journal de Teheran*, 26 September 1963.
26 Ibid.

Notes

27 For more on this, see Robert Steele, 'The Pahlavi National Library Project: Education and Modernization in Late Pahlavi Iran', *Iranian Studies*, 52:1–2 (2019): 85–110.
28 Ketābkhāneh-ye Pahlavi, report, c. 1346, Shafā Archives; 'Kārnāmeh-ye Dah Sāleh-ye Ketābkhāneh-ye Pahlavi' [Record of Ten Year's Work of the Pahlavi Library], *Keyhān*, 27 Mehr 1354/ 19 October 1975, 10.
29 'Iranian Study Center Now Being Established', *Tehran Journal*, 12 November 1964.
30 Shafā document on creation of Pahlavi library, undated, Shafā Archives.
31 'Isā Sadiq to Central Council of the Imperial Celebrations of Iran, 27 Bahman 1339/ 16 February 1961, *Bazm-e Ahriman*, vol. 1, 129–30.
32 'Asāsnāmeh-ye ketābkhāneh-ye Pahlavi' [Statute of the Pahlavi Library], 2, Shafā Archives.
33 Ibid., 3.
34 Letter from Shafā to international cultural institutions, 24 August 1965, 3, Shafā Archives.
35 Felix Tauer to Shafā, 29 September 1965, Shafā Archives.
36 Shafā document on creation of Pahlavi Library, undated, 2, Shafā Archives.
37 Fazllollāh Safā to Komiteh-ye Ta'lif-e Tārikh-e Irān, 5 Bahman 1344/ 25 January 1966, Shafā Archives.
38 Fazllollāh Safā to Komiteh-ye Ta'lif-e Tārikh-e Irān, 23 Dey 1344/ 13 January 1966, Shafā Archives.
39 Including, for example, Abulhasan Dehghān, Hasan Khub Nazar and 'Ali Sāmi from the Pahlavi University in Shiraz. See president of the Pahlavi University Asadollāh 'Alam to Minister of Education Mr Hedāyati, 15 Esfand 1344/ 6 March 1966, Shafā Archives.
40 Marashi, *Nationalizing Iran*, 99.
41 Mohammad Reza Pahlavi, 'Speech to the International Congress of Iranologists, Tehran, 31 August 1966', in *Iran, Philosophy behind the Revolution*, 205.
42 Shojāʿ al-Din Shafā, *Jahān-e Irānshenāsi* [World of Iranology], vol. 1 (Tehran: Ketābkhāneh-ye Pahlavi, 1348/1969).
43 'Conseil Culturel Impérial', *Journal de Teheran*, 26 September 1963.
44 The original documents on which the publication was based are contained in the Shafā archives at the Bibliothèque universitaire des langues et civilisations in Paris. The US section alone consists of three huge boxes, packed with files full of research and correspondence. To give an impression of the scale of the project, see the photograph of the *Jahān-e Irānshenāsi* archives in *Yādnāmeh-ye Shojāʿ al-Din Shafā*.
45 Rouhollah Ramazani to Shafā, 18 February 1970, Shafā Archives.
46 Ferydoon Firoozi, based at a university in the United States, for example, wrote a personal letter to Shafā requesting that he send him a copy of the volume containing the Shah's collection of speeches in 5,000 pages that he had been unable to attain. See Ferydoon Firoozi to Shafā, 2 February 1970, Shafā Archives.
47 Ketābkhāneh-ye Pahlavi, report, c. 1346, 7, Shafā Archives.
48 Ibid., 3; 'Gozāresh-e kārhā-ye jāri-ye daftar-e farhangi va ketābkhāneh-ye Pahlavi' [report on the current work of the cultural office and the Pahlavi Library], 31 Ordibehesht 1345/ 21 May 1966, Shafā Archives.
49 Shurā-ye farhangi-ye saltanati, report of year 1342 (1963–1964), 11, Shafā Archives.
50 Passage from *Tehran Journal*, 11 April 1968, cited in Jay Gluck and Noël Siver (eds), *Surveyors of Persian Art: A Documentary Biography of Arthur Upham Pope and Phillis Ackerman* (Costa Mesa, CA: Mazda Publishers, 1996), 509.
51 Gluck and Siver, *Surveyors of Persian Art*, 516.

52　Ibid., 530.
53　Ibid. It appears that although lectures were delivered in different languages, the collected papers were translated and printed in Persian. In a letter from Richard Frye to the Iranian ambassador in Washington, DC, Frye submitted his paper 'in accordance with his [Shafa's] wishes ... so it might be translated into Persian'. Frye to Khosro Khosrovani, 2 August 1966, Shafā Archives.
54　'Permanent Body to Be Set Up for Future Congresses', *Tehran Journal*, 7 September 1966.
55　Ketābkhāneh-ye Pahlavi, report, c. 1346, 8–9, Shafā Archives.
56　Letter from C. M. Le Quesne, 27 August 1959, FCO 371/140887.
57　Ansari, *The Shah's Iran*, 250.
58　Ibid., 250–1.
59　Richard Frye, Iranian Oral History Collection, Harvard University, tape 3, 35.
60　For a complete list of invited scholars, see *World Congress of Iranology* [programme].
61　See Elwell-Sutton, '2500th Anniversary Celebrations', *Bulletin of the British Association of Orientalists*, 6 (1973): 20–5.
62　Bernard Lewis, *Notes on a Century: Reflections of a Middle East Historian* (London: Orion Books, 2013), 184.
63　See Chapter 3.
64　'The Reverend Norman Sharp: A Tribute by Paul Gotch and Ronald Ferrier', Iran Society, 18 December 1996, Gotch Papers, BM.
65　Norman Sharp to Zabih Ghorban, 17 January 1984, Gotch Papers, BM.
66　Ibid. According to Sharp, the design of the emblem was supposed to resemble the 'Door of Knowledge', with Old Persian cuneiform characters inscribed beneath. The words in cuneiform were *Kharathu*, meaning 'wisdom', and *Arawasta*, meaning 'activity', two qualities ascribed to Darius the Great.
67　Ralph Norman Sharp, *The Inscriptions in Old Persian Cuneiform of the Achaemenian Emperors* (Tehran: Central Council of the Celebration of the 2500th Anniversary of the Founding of the Persian Empire by Cyrus the Great, 1966); *Nazariāti Darbāreh-ye Neveshtehhā-ye (Katibehhā-ye) Pārsi-ye Bāstān* (Tehran: Shurā-ye Markazi-ye Jashn-e Shāhanshāhi-ye Irān, undated).
68　Sayyed Mohammad Taqi Mostafavi, *The Land of Pars: The Historical Monuments and the Archaeological Sites of the Province of Fars*, trans. R. N. Sharp (Chippenham: Picton Publishing, 1978).
69　Ibid.
70　Inscription translation in Paul Gotch Papers, BM.
71　Norman Sharp to Paul Gotch, 13 November 1970, Gotch Papers, BM.
72　Sharp to Gotch, 7 September 1971, Gotch Papers, BM.
73　Sharp to Gotch, 9 October, Gotch Papers, BM.
74　Elwell-Sutton, '2500th Anniversary Celebrations', 22.
75　This was according to her other sister, Hebe Kohlbrugge. Sadly, Hebe Kohlbrugge died in 2016 before we had chance to meet, but she recorded the story to Piet van Veldhuizen, who passed it on to me.
76　For an overview of her career, see David Morgan, 'Ann K.S. Lambton (1912–2008) and Persian Studies', *Journal of the Royal Asiatic Society*, 21 (2011): 99–109.
77　K. S. McLachlan, 'Professor AKS Lambton', *The Telegraph*, 8 August 2008. Available online: http://www.telegraph.co.uk/news/obituaries/2524891/Professor-AKS-Lambton.html (accessed 18 September 2016).

78 Peter Avery in an interview with Shusha Assar Guppy, Cambridge, UK, 9 and 10 October 1985, Oral History of Iran Collection of the Foundation of Iranian Studies, 79–81.
79 Peter Avery 'Iran: Cultural Crossroads for 2,500 Years', *The UNESCO Courier*, October 1971, 9.
80 Curiously, just four years earlier, Avery had written, in a review of *The Revolution of the Shah and the People*, published in 1967 on the occasion of the Shah's coronation, that 'Certainly, the Shah, Mohammad Reza Shah Pahlavi, and his people have become one to a degree not known since Shah Abbas.' Cited in Ramesh Sanghvi, *Aryamehr: A Political Biography* (London: Macmillan, 1969), 320.
81 Italian ambassador to Ministry of Foreign Affairs, 9 Mehr 1350/ 1 October 1971, *Bazm-e Ahriman*, vol. 4, 319.
82 Javād Bushehri to head of the Iran and Italy Cultural Association, 22 Ordibehesht 1347/ 12 May 1968, *Bazm-e Ahriman*, vol. 3, 4–5.
83 Richard Frye, 'Asia Institute', *Encyclopaedia Iranica*, online edition, 2011. Available online: http://www.iranicaonline.org/articles/asia-institute-the-1 (accessed 13 September 2016).
84 Richard Frye letter to Noël Siver, 7 July 1971, in *Surveyors of Persian Art*, ed. Gluck and Siver, 564.
85 Such as US journalist Barbara Walters. Richard Frye in an interview with Shahla Haeri, Cambridge, MA, 10 October 1984, Iranian Oral History Collection, Harvard University, tape 3, 10.
86 Donald N. Wilber, *Adventures in the Middle East: Excursions and Incursions* (Princeton: Darwin, 1986), 233. As well as attending the Congress of Iranology, Wilber contributed to the Celebrations with his publication *Four Hundred Forty-Six Kings of Iran* (Shiraz: Pahlavi University, 1972).
87 Elwell-Sutton, '2500th Anniversary Celebrations', 21.
88 Ibid.
89 *World Congress of Iranology* [programme].
90 Mohammad Reza Pahlavi, 'An Excerpt from the Message of His Imperial Majesty Shahanshah Aryamehr at the Inauguration of the World Congress of Iranology', *Journal of the Regional Cultural Institute (Iran, Pakistan, Turkey)*, 4 (1971): 8.
91 Ibid., 7.
92 Muhammad A. Dandamaev, 'Préliminaire', in *Acta Iranica*, vol. 1 (Tehran: Bibliothèque Pahlavi, 1974), 1.
93 *World Congress of Iranology* [programme].
94 'Cultural Contributions', *Iran Tribune*, November 1971, 14.
95 For an overview of papers see Dandamaev, 'Préliminaire', 3–12.
96 Elwell-Sutton, '2500th Anniversary Celebrations', 21. The international shipping of the books from Iran was covered by the event organizers.
97 See John Hansman, 'Elamites, Achaemenians and Anshan', *Iran*, 10 (1972): 101–25.
98 Conversation with David Stronach, Berkeley 2014.
99 Charlotte Curtis, 'First Party of Iran's 2,500-Year Celebration', *New York Times*, 13 October 1971, 3.
100 *Celebration of the 2500th Anniversary of the Founding of the Persian Empire by Cyrus the Great*, 15.
101 Elwell-Sutton, '2500th Anniversary Celebrations', 22.
102 Ibid.
103 Ibid., 23.

104 According to official figures there were 400 Iranologists and religious representatives present at this audience. *Gāhnāmeh-ye Panjāh Sāl-e Shāhanshāhi-ye Pahlavi*, vol. 5, 2059.
105 Elwell-Sutton, '2500th Anniversary Celebrations', 23–4.
106 'Cultural Contributions', *Iran Tribune*, November 1971, 14. Over 1,000 research papers were said to have been collected from scholars participating in the conference and others from around the world, with the intention that they would be published by the Imperial Court. According to Shafā, these were intended to be sent to research centres around the world and placed at the disposal of students and scholars. This does not appear to have happened, and the collected works are thought to have been destroyed following the revolution, lost along with some of the other important collections of the Pahlavi Library. Houchang Nahavandi, *The Last Shah of Iran*: trans. Steeve Reed (Slough: Aquillon, 2005), 46; 'Cultural Contributions', 14; Farah Pahlavi, *An Enduring Love: My Life with the Shah* (New York: Turnaround Distributor, 2004), 221.
107 Jacques Duchesne-Guillemin, 'Avertissement', *Acta Iranica*, vol. 1 (Tehran: Bibliothèque Pahlavi, 1974), v.
108 Although Hinnells was not invited to the Congress itself, he organized the International Congress of Mithraic Studies that was held at the University of Manchester and which was dedicated to the Celebrations.
109 'Kārnāmeh-ye Dah Sāleh-ye Ketābkhāneh-ye Pahlavi', *Keyhān*, 27 Mehr 1354/ 19 October 1975, 10. There were plans to publish a Persian translation, but this does not appear to have happened.
110 Court Minister to Javād Bushehri, 9 Shahrivar 1345/ 31 August 1966, 'Asnād-e Mahramāneh-ye Jashnhā', 143.
111 Minutes of the 309th session of the Historical Council, 1 Mordād 1345/ 23 July 1966, 'Asnād-e Mahramāneh-ye Jashnhā', 140–3.
112 Minutes of the 886th session of the Historical Council, 21 Shahrivar 1349/ 12 September 1970, 'Asnād-e Mahramāneh-ye Jashnhā', 143–5.
113 Minutes of the 309th session of the Historical Council.
114 Vice president of the Central Council for the Celebrations to Minister of Education Dr Hedāyat, 26 Dey 1344/ 16 January 1966, Shafā Archives.
115 Nāser al-Din Shāh Hoseyni, *Peyvastegi-ye Shāhanshāhi va Mellat-e Irān* (Tehran: Komiteh-ye Farhang-e Jashn-e Shāhanshāhi-ye Irān); Eqbāl Yaghmā'i, *Cherā mā Shāh va Shāhanshāhi rā Dust Dārim* (Tehran: Komiteh-ye Farhang-e Jashn-e Shāhanshāhi-ye Irān); and 'Abbās Parviz, *Qiyām-e Irāniān dar rāh-e Tajdid va 'Azemat-e Irān* (Tehran: Shurā-ye Markazi-ye Jashn-e Shāhanshāhi-ye Irān, 1348).
116 To give an idea of the cost to produce these works, Shirin Bayāni was paid 8,000 rials ($107) for writing her eighty-page booklet on Cyrus the Great. For list of booklets and costs, see 'List-e pādāsh-e nevisandegān-e maghālāt dar shurā-ye markazi-ye jashn-e shāhanshāhi' [list of fees for writers of articles], undated, *Bazm-e Ahriman*, vol. 3, 263–5.
117 *12 Maqāleh: Beh Monāsebat-e Bozorgdāsht-e Jashn-e Dohezār o Pānsadomin Sāl-e Bonyāngozāri-ye Shāhanshāhi-ye Irān* (Tehran: Madreseh-ye 'Āli-ye Adabiyāt va Zabānhā-ye Khāreji, 1350).
118 *Sahm-e Rejāl-e Khorāsān dar Baqā-ye Shāhanshāhi-ye Irān* (Mashhad: Shurā-ye Jashn-e Shāhanshāhi-ye Khorāsān, 1349); Birām Qalij Āqcheh-li, *Chehreh-ye Shahrestān-e Gonbad-e Qābus dar 'asr-e Poreftekhār-e Dudmān-e Pahlavi* (Gonbad-e

Qābus: Komiteh-ye Āmuzesh va Parvaresh-e Shurā-ye Jashn-e Dohezār o Pānsadomin Sāl-e Bonyāngozāri-ye Shāhanshāhi-ye Irān, 1350); and Mohammad 'Ali Tāheriyā, *Dāmghān-e Sheshhezār Sāleh* (Dāmghān: Shurā-ye Jashn-e Shāhanshāhi-ye Dāmghān, 1347).
119 Hoseyn Ahmadipur, *Tārikh-e Kohan va Gozashtehhā-ye por Eftekhār-e Shāhanshāhi-ye Irān, az Didgāh-e Shāhanshāh Āryāmehr* (Tabriz: Shurā-ye Markazi-ye Jashn-e Shāhanshāhi-ye Āzarbāyejān, 1347); *Āzarbāyejān dar Doreh-ye Sāzandegi va Enqelāb* (Tabriz: Shurā-ye Markazi-ye Jashn-e Shāhanshāhi-ye Āzarbāyejān, 1345); and *Naqsh-e Āzarbāyejān dar Tārikh-e Dohezār o Pānsad Sāleh-ye Shāhanshāhi-ye Irān* (Tabriz: Shurā-ye Markazi-ye Jashn-e Shāhanshāhi-ye Āzarbāyejān, 1345).
120 Hoseyn Ahmadipur, *Qalbi keh beh Khāter-e Vatan va Mellat Mitapad* (Tabriz: Shurā-ye Markazi-ye Jashn-e Shāhanshāhi-ye Āzarbāyejān-e Sharqi, 1341).
121 Another contributor to this volume was Mohammad Esmāʿil Rezvāni, who served on the Committee for Authoring the History of Iran.
122 Sayyed Hoseyn Nasr, 'Foreword', in *Atlas-e Tārikhi-ye Irān* [Historical Atlas of Iran], ed. Sayyed Hoseyn Nasr, Ahmad Mostowfi and 'Abbās Zaryāb (Tehran: University of Tehran Press, 1971).
123 Manoutchehr Mortazavi, *Le Rôle de l'Azarbaïdjan au cours de XXV siècles d'histoire de l'empire d'Iran*, trans. Mohammad Gharavi (Tabriz: University of Tabriz, 1971).
124 *Namāyeshgāh-e Noskhehhā va Asnād-e Khatti* [Exhibition of Manuscripts and Documents] (Tehran: Dāneshgāh-e Tehrān, 1350).
125 Shojaeddin Shafa, *Facts about the Celebration of the 2500th Anniversary of the Founding of the Persian Empire by Cyrus the Great* (Tehran: Committee of International Affairs of the Festivities, 1971), 16.
126 For instance, Louis Vanden Berghe, *Bāstānshenāsi-ye Irān-e Bāstān* [Archéologie de l'Iran ancien] (Tehran: Dāneshgāh-e Tehrān, 1345); Henri Massé, *Ferdowsi va Hamāseh-ye Melli* [Ferdowsi and the National Epic] (Tabriz: Dāneshgāh-e Tabriz, 1350).
127 Sylvia Matheson to Javād Bushehri, 23 April 1970, FO 248/1708.
128 Report of the British embassy in Tehran, 27 May 1970, FO 248/1708.
129 'Gozāresh-e 'amaliyāt-e hesābdāri-ye shurā-ye markazi-ye jashn-e shāhanshāhi-ye Irān az aval-e Mehr māh-e 1339 leghāyat Shahrivar māh-e 1351' [Report of accounts of the Central Council for the Celebrations from Mehr 1339 until Shahrivar 1351] 13 Mehr 1351/ 5 October 1972, *Bazm-e Ahriman*, vol. 4, 389–91. By contrast, the total sum of the production of all other books paid for by the Central Council (not including the *Shāhnāmeh-ye Bāysonghori*), was 9,331,222 rials ($124,400).
130 Roman Ghirshman, 'The Classical Age', in, *Persia: The Immortal Kingdom*, ed. Roman Ghirshman, Vladimir Minorsky and Ramesh Sanghvi (London: Orient Commerce Establishment, 1971), 34. Ghirshman was perhaps chosen as a contributor as much for his eminence as for his previous writings on Cyrus's reign. In his book on Iranian history published in the early 1950s, for instance, Ghirshman writes of the 'generous character of Cyrus, who sought to bring peace to mankind'. See Roman Ghirshman, *Iran* (Harmondsworth: Penguin Books, 1954), 132–3.
131 Vladimir Minorsky, 'The Medieval Age', *Persia*, ed. Ghirshman, Minorsky and Sanghvi, 152.
132 Michael Axworthy, *The Sword of Persia: Nader Shah, from Tribal Warrior to Conquering Tyrant* (London: I.B. Tauris, 2006), 8.

133 For an analysis of Nāder Shāh in the historiography, see Rudolph Matthee, 'Nader Shah in Iranian Historiography: Warlord or National Hero', *Institute for Advanced Study* (2018). Available online: http://www.ias.edu/ideas/2018/matthee-nader-shah (accessed 19 January 2019).
134 *Gāhnāmeh-ye Panjāh Sāl-e Shāhanshāhi-ye Pahlavi*, vol. 2, 1025.
135 D. K. Timms to G. L. Merrells, 5 December 1967, FO 248/1637.
136 Ramesh Sanghvi, 'Iran Today and Tomorrow', in *Persia*, ed. Ghirshman, Minorsky and Sanghvi, 208–9.
137 Ibid.
138 Ibid.
139 Ibid.
140 Sanghvi also wanted to organize a touring exhibition, for which he would charge $1.5 million. This was dismissed by Amir Mottaqi, who felt that it would be too expensive and would not produce the desired effect. See Amir Mottaqi to 'Alam, 21 Farvardin 1349/ 10 April 1970, 'Asnād-e Mahramāneh-ye Jashnhā', 145–6.
141 'Kholāseh-ye dariyāfti' [summary of receipts], 21 August 1972, *Bazm-e Ahriman*, vol. 4, 386–8.
142 *Gāhnāmeh-ye Panjāh Sāl-e Shāhanshāhi-ye Pahlavi*, vol. 2, 1017. Instead of taking high-quality photographs of the original work, the publishers had watercolour copies made on the basis of photographs. The British Museum's Basil Gray, who composed the introduction and commentary, was apparently unaware of the procedure, or else he was misled by his patrons, for he wrote that they were 'reproduced in facsimile from the original'. See Robert Hillenbrand, 'Exploring a Neglected Masterpiece: The Gulistan Shahnama of Baysunghur', *Iranian Studies* 43:1 (2010): 107.
143 'Aliqoli E'temād Moqaddam, *Shāh va Sepāh Bar Bonyād-e Shāhnāmeh-ye Ferdowsi* (Tehran: Vezārat-e Farhang va Honar, 1350); Hoseyn Ahmadipur, *Hamāsehhā-ye Bozorg-e Melli, Shāhnāmeh Bozorgtarin Shāhkār-e Hamāsi-ye - Jahān* (Tabriz: Shurā-ye Jashn-e Shāhanshāhi-ye Āzarbāyejān-e Sharqi, 1345); and Tal'at Basāri, *Zanān-e Shāhnāmeh* (Tehran: Dāneshsarā-ye 'Āli, 1350).
144 Ali M. Ansari, *The Politics of Nationalism in Modern Iran* (Cambridge: Cambridge University Press, 2012), 176.
145 Text of address to the Congress of Iranology, 1967, Shafā Archives.
146 Richard Frye, Iranian Oral History Collection, Harvard University, tape 5, 17.
147 Rezā Pahlavi, *Safarnāmeh-ye Māzandarān* (Tehran: Markaz-e Pazhuhesh va Nashr-e Farhang-e Siyāsi-ye Dowrān-e Pahlavi, 1355); and Diary entry 27 Mordād 1355/ 18 August 1976, *Yāddāshthā-ye 'Alam*, vol. 6, 207–8.

5 International cultural activity

1 'Payām-e Shāhanshāh Āryāmehr, dar Tārikh Sabt Shod', *Rastākhiz*, 19 Mehr 2535 (1355)/ 11 October 1976, 12.
2 'Yekhezār Mohaqeq' [One Thousand Scholars], *Keyhān*, 19 Mehr 1350/ 11 October 1971, 5.
3 Letter from C. M. Le Quesne, 27 August 1959, FCO 371/140887.
4 Quoted in 'A Royal Visit to the United States', *Persian Panorama: Publication of the Imperial Embassy of Iran*, London, 1:3 (1965), 62.
5 Quoted in Sabahi, *The Literacy Corps in Pahlavi Iran*, 22.

6 *Sept mille ans d'art en Iran* (Paris: Musée du Petit Palais, 1961).
7 Dutch ambassador in Tehran, H. J. Levelt, to Minister of Foreign Affairs, 13 September 1962, NA 2.05.118/14175.
8 Peter Andrews, *The Turcoman of Iran* (Kendal: Titus Wilson & Son, 1971).
9 Report of dinner in Rome, 19 June 1964, Shafā Archives.
10 '2,500ème Anniversaire de la Fondation de l'État Perse par Cyrus-le-Grand: Comité Français', Shafā Archives.
11 André Malraux in the introduction to *Comité Français Cyrus-le-Grand pour la Commémoration du 2.500ᵉ Anniversaire de la Fondation de l'Empire Perse* (Tehran: Kayhan Press, 1960).
12 L. G. M. Jaquet to Minister of Education, Arts and Sciences, 10 February 1961, NA 2.05.191/42.
13 Amir Khosrow Afshar to Denis Greenhill, 'The United Kingdom Committee of Cyrus the Great', 28 September 1971, FCO 17/1528.
14 Listed in Wilhelm Eilers (ed.), *Festgabe Deutscher Iranisten zur 2500 Jahrfeier Irans* (Stuttgart: Hochwacht Druck, 1971).
15 'Comité Italien pour la Célébration de Cyrus', undated, Shafā Archives.
16 'Komiteh-ye Jashnhā-ye Shāhanshāhi dar Pākestān' [Committee of the Imperial Celebrations in Pakistan], *Haftehnāmeh-ye Komiteh-ye Ettelāʿāt va Enteshārāt-e Jashn-e Dohezār o Pānsadomin Sāl-e Bonyāngozāri-ye Shāhanshāhi*, 12, 7 Shahrivar 1350/ 29 August 1971, 6–7.
17 *Gāhnāmeh-ye Panjāh Sāl-e Shāhanshāhi-ye Pahlavi*, 2005–60.
18 Shafā to ʿAlam, 8 Khordād 1349/ 29 May 1970, 'Asnād-e Mahramāneh-ye Jashnhā', 156–9.
19 Richard Escritt to Richard Fell, 2 November 1971, FCO 17/1529.
20 Ahmad Nabi Khan, *Iran and Pakistan: The Story of a Cultural Relationship through the Ages* (Karachi: National Publishing House, 1971).
21 See introduction to Charles J. Adams (ed.), *Iranian Civilization and Culture* (Montreal: McGill University, Institute of Islamic Studies, 1973).
22 Quoted in Shojaeddin Shafa, *Facts about the Celebration of the 2500th Anniversary of the Founding of the Persian Empire by Cyrus the Great* (Tehran: Committee of International Affairs of the Festivities, 1971), 21.
23 Adams (ed.), *Iranian Civilization and Culture*.
24 Muhammad A. Dandamaev, 'Préliminaire' in *Acta Iranica*, vol. 1, ed. Jacques Duchesne-Guillemin (Tehran: Bibliothèque Pahlavi, 1974), 1–2.
25 'Yekhezār Mohaqeq', *Keyhān*, 19 Mehr 1350/ 11 October 1971, 5.
26 Malik Ram and S. Balu Rao (eds), *Indo-Iran: Papers Presented at the Congress of Iranologists and Indologists, New Delhi, on the Occasion of the 2500th Anniversary of the Founding of Monarchy in Iran, 4–6 October, 1971* (New Delhi: Indo-Iran Society, 1974).
27 *Kurus: Memorial Volume: Essays on Indology and Indo-Iran Relations in Memory of Cyrus Celebration Held in the City of Bombay on 2500th Anniversary of the Foundation of the Persian Empire* (Bombay: The House, 1974).
28 *Gāhnāmeh-ye Panjāh Sāl-e Shāhanshāhi-ye Pahlavi*, 2057.
29 Ibid., 2056.
30 Wilhelm Eilers (ed.), *Festgabe Deutscher Iranisten zur 2500 Jahrfeier Irans* (Stuttgart: Hochwacht Druck, 1971), viii.
31 Ibid., vii.

32 Eröffnung der Sonderausstellung "2500 Jahre Kaiserreich Iran" im Museum für Völkerkunde am Montag, 4 Oktober 1971, 15 Uhr – Rede des Herrn Bundespräsidenten, Österreichisches Staatsarchiv, AT-OeSA/AdR PK 2Rep AR Reden Jonas 1613.
33 'Yekhezār Mohaqeq', *Keyhān*, 19 Mehr 1350/ 11 October 1971, 5.
34 See foreword to *Indo-Iran*, ed. Ram and Rao.
35 Mumtaz Hasan, in the foreword to Mohammad Ashraf, *Persian Manuscripts in the National Museum of Pakistan at Karachi* (Karachi, 1971).
36 'Report on the activities of the Working Committee of the Cyrus the Great Committee in the Netherlands: June–December 1971', 1–3, NA 2.05.191/554.
37 Subsequently published by the British Institute of Persian Studies and as a chapter of the *Cambridge History of Iran*. See Max Mallowan, 'Cyrus the Great', *Iran*, 10 (1972): 1–17; and Max Mallowan, 'Cyrus the Great' in *Cambridge History of Iran*, vol. 2, ed. Ilya Gershevitch (Cambridge: Cambridge University Press, 1985), 392–419.
38 'List of events in the United Kingdom and Ireland in celebration of the 2500th Anniversary of the Founding of the Persian Empire by Cyrus the Great', 28 September 1971, FCO 17/1528.
39 'Anniversary Meeting', *Journal of the Royal Asiatic Society of Great Britain and Ireland*, 2 (1972): 183.
40 'List of Events in the United Kingdom and Ireland', 28 September 1971, FCO 17/1528.
41 Sir John Wolfenden in Ralph Pinder-Wilson, *Royal Persia: A Commemoration of Cyrus the Great and His Successors* (London: British Museum, 1971), iii.
42 Robert Shackleton to Robin Campbell, 24 May 1971, FCO 17/1528.
43 BBC Persian Programme Organiser John Dunn to British Embassy, Tehran, 27 September 1971, FCO 17/1528.
44 Arthur Upham Pope to Amir Ebrahimi, 4 December 1960, in *Surveyors of Persian Art*, ed. Gluck and Siver, 427.
45 Pope to Jay Gluck, 12 December 1960, in *Surveyors of Persian Art*, ed. Gluck and Siver, 426.
46 'Mosāhebeh-ye Chāp Nashodeh az Shojāʻ al-Din Shafā', 191.
47 Ibid.
48 Ibid., 192–3.
49 Corning Museum of Glass, *A Tribute to Persia: Persian Glass* (Corning: Corning Museum of Glass, 1972).
50 *From Persia's Ancient Looms: An Exhibition in Honor of the 2500th Anniversary of the Founding of the Persian Empire by Cyrus the Great*, 23 January–30 September 1972, under the patronage of His Excellency, the ambassador of Iran and Mrs Aslan Afshar (Washington, DC: Textile Museum, 1972).
51 'Mosāhebeh-ye Chāp Nashodeh az Shojāʻ al-Din Shafā Darbāreh-ye: Jashnhā-ye Dohezār o Pānsad Sāleh', *Rahāvard*, 95 (2011), 191.
52 'Centenary Fires World Interest', *Kayhan International*, 3 April 1971, 3.
53 Letter Aslān Afshār to Froelich G. Rainey, 27 July 1971, in *Expedition*, 13:3–4 (August 1971): 3.
54 'Mosāhebeh-ye Chāp Nashodeh az Shojāʻ al-Din Shafā', 191.
55 Ibid.
56 'The Shahyad Monument', *Iran Tribune*, November 1971, 42.
57 *Persische Teppiche* (Hamburg: Museum für Kunst und Gewerbe, 1971).
58 Nobusuke Kishi, *Persian Art Exhibition Celebrating the 2,500th Anniversary of the Founding of the Persian Empire of Iran* (Tokyo: Japanese Committee for the 2,500th Anniversary of the Founding of the Persian Empire, 1971).

59 Jarmila Stěpková, *2500 let Íránského Mincovnictví* (V Praze: Narodni Galerie, 1971).
60 *De Iraanse kunst in de Belgische verzamelingen* (Bruxelles: Musées Royaux d'Art et d'Histoire, 1971).
61 *Iran: Hommes du vent, gens de terre* (Paris: Musée de l'Homme, 1971).
62 *Conmemoración del xxv centenario de la fundación del imperio persa: Catalogo de la exposición de antigüedades persas* (Madrid: Ministerio de Asuntos Exteriores Dirección General de Relaciones Culturales, 1971).
63 Mahmud Kashfiyān to Minister of Economy, 1 Ordibehesht 1350/ 20 April 1971, *Bazm-e Ahriman*, vol. 4, 38; Mehdi Bushehri to Mehrdād Pahlbod, 2 Ordibehesht 1350/ 21 April 1971, *Bazm-e Ahriman*, vol. 4, 40-1.
64 'Abdolrezā Ansāri to Ardeshir Zāhedi, 6 Ordibehesht 1350/ 25 April 1971, *Bazm-e Ahriman*, vol. 4, 47.
65 SAVAK report, 21 Ordibehesht 1350/ 11 May 1971, *Bazm-e Ahriman*, vol. 4, 59-60.
66 'Abdolrezā Ansāri to Hushang Ansāri, 1 Tir 1350/ 22 June 1971, *Bazm-e Ahriman*, vol. 4, 117.
67 Mehrdād Pahlbod to Ministry of Information, 7 Shahrivar 1350/ 29 August 1971, *Bazm-e Ahriman*, vol. 4, 227.
68 Pahlbod to Zāhedi, 27 Mordād 1350/ 18 August 1971, *Bazm-e Ahriman*, vol. 4, 213-14.
69 'Mosāhebeh-ye Chāp Nashodeh az Shojāʿ al-Din Shafāʾ, 191-3.
70 Personal correspondence with John Hinnells, December 2013.
71 Ibid.
72 John Hinnells in the introduction to *Mithraic Studies: Proceedings of the First International Congress of Mithraic Studies*, ed. John Hinnells (Manchester: University of Manchester Press, 1975), xiii-xiv.
73 Ibid.
74 Ugo Bianchi, 'The Second International Congress of Mithraic Studies, Tehran, September 1975', *Journal of Mithraic Studies*, 1:1 (1976): 77.
75 Head of Bureau of General Information and Events, Ms. S. Dörr to Dutch ambassador in Tehran, 1 April 1970, NA 2.05.191/554; and C. D. S. Drace-Francis, British Embassy, Tehran, to M. L. Dooley, Cultural Relations Department, Foreign Office, 15 October 1970, FCO 248/1708.
76 Protocol Department of the Imperial Ministry of Foreign Affairs to the Dutch Embassy Tehran, 30 April 1969, NA 2.05.191/554.
77 See Chapter 2.
78 'Report on the activities of the Working Committee', 3, NA 2.05.191/554.
79 Houchang Nahavandi, *The Last Shah of Iran* (Slough: Aquillon, 2005), 45.
80 'Centenary', *Kayhan International*, 5 June 1971. The street in Rome is in the EUR district and is called Via Ciro Il Grande. Brazil also pledged to name a major street after Iran and an 'important school' after Cyrus the Great. See *The Echo of Iran*, 27 July 1971, 1.
81 *Gāhnāmeh-ye Panjāh Sāl-e Shāhanshāhi-ye Pahlavi*, vol. 5, (Paris: Soheil Publishers, 1985). 2054-5.
82 Ibid., 2046.
83 Ibid., 2047.
84 Ibid., 2044. There were two prizes of 75,000 Indonesian rupees (around $190).
85 Ibid., 2032.
86 Maryam Borjian, 'The Rise and Fall of a Partnership: The British Council and the Islamic Republic of Iran (2001-2009)', *Iranian Studies*, 44:4 (2011): 545.

87 Annual Report 1940–1941, quoted in Robert Phillipson, *Linguistic Imperialism* (Oxford: Oxford University Press, 1992), 138–9.
88 Ibid., 142.
89 Ibid., 143.
90 Quoted in Annabelle Sreberny and Massoumeh Torfeh, *Persian Service: The BBC and British Interests in Persia* (London: I.B. Tauris, 2014), 45.
91 Report from C. D. S. Drace-Francis, 22 October 1970, FCO 248/1708.
92 Denis Wright to Mehrdād Pahlbod, 7 August 1970, FCO 248/1708.
93 Pahlbod to Wright, 19 August 1970, FCO 248/1708.
94 FAAC (72) 1, 1971, 8, BW 49/31.
95 Ibid.
96 Ibid., 9.
97 Ibid. After Iran, it moved to Istanbul where attendance figures were much higher, though still rather low by Istanbul standards. Ibid., 10. The Australian government also proposed to hold an exhibition in Iran on the 200th anniversary of Captain Cook as part of the Imperial Celebrations. See Report from J. G. Bruton, 1971, BW 49/31.
98 David Stronach, 'Director's Report November 1st 1970 to October 31st 1971', *Iran*, 10 (1972): xi. For text of the speech, see Sadiq, *Yādgār-e 'Omr*, vol. 4, 57–72.
99 Roy Mottahedeh, *The Mantle of the Prophet* (Oxford: Oneworld, 2009), 64.
100 Ibid., 55.
101 'Īsā Sadiq, *Yādgār-e 'Omr*, vol. 4 (Tehran: Ketābforushi-ye Dekhodā, 2536/1356/1977), 56–8.
102 Stronach, 'Director's Report', xi.
103 Max Mallowan, David Stronach, David Blow, Basil Gray and Gavin Hambly, *British Contributions to Persian Studies* (Tehran: Ramin Printers, 1971). In 1942, during the British Council's formative years in Iran, Arthur Arberry had also written a book titled *British Contributions to Persian Studies*, published by the Council. See Arthur J. Arberry, *British Contributions to Persian Studies* (London: The British Council, 1942).
104 Report on visit to Ahwaz by Deputy Representative, 10–12 March 1972, BW 49/31.
105 Ibid.
106 FAAC (72) 1, 9, BW 49/31. The piece is called the 'Working Model for Oval with Points' and is currently held at the Museum for Contemporary Art in Tehran.
107 'IsMEO Activities', *East and West* 22:3/4 (1972): 390.
108 Peter Ramsbotham letter to Rt Hon Sir Alec Douglas-Home, 25 July 1972, BW 49/31.
109 Banri Namikawa, *The Legacy of Cyrus the Great: On the Occasion of the 2500th Anniversary of the Founding of the Persian Empire* (Tokyo: Tokyo International Publishers, 1971); Jayad Haidari, *Iran: In Celebration of the 2500th Anniversary of the Founding of the Persian Empire by Cyrus the Great* (New York: St. John's University, 1971); and *Türkiye'de Basılmış Farsça Eserler, çeviriler ve İran'la Ilgili Yayınlar Bibliyografyası* [Bibliography of Persian Works, Translations and Publications About Iran, Published in Turkey] (Ankara, 1971). Portuguese books include the following five works published by the Calouste Gulbenkian Foundation on behalf of the Portuguese committee for the Celebrations: Luís de Matos, *Das Relações entre Portugal e a Pérsia, 1500–1758: Catálogo Bibliográfico da Exposição Comemorativa do XXV Centenário de Accommodatie Monarquia no Irão* (Lisbon: Fundação Calouste Gulbenkian, 1972); *Portugal e a Pérsia: Exposição Integrada no Âmbito*

das Comemorações do 2.500.o Aniversário da Fundação da Monarquia no Irão (Lisbon: Fundação Calouste Gulbenkian, 1972) [Exhibition programme]; Roberto Gulbenkian, ed. and trans., *L'ambassade en Perse de Luís Pereira de Lacerda et des Pères Portugais de L'ordre de Saint-Augustin, Belchior dos Anjos et Huilherme de Santo Agostinho 1604–1605* (Lisbon: Fundação Calouste Gulbenkian, 1972); Jean Aubin, *L'ambassade de Gregório Pereira Fidalgo à la Cour de Châh Soltân-Hosseyn, 1696–1697* (Lisbon: Fundação Calouste Gulbenkian, 1971); and Joaquim Veríssimo Serrão, *Un Voyageur Portugais en Perse au Début du XVIIe Siècle: Nicolau de Orta Rebelo*, trans. into French by Simone Biberfeld (Lisbon: Fundação Calouste Gulbenkian, 1972).

110 *Divān-e Hāfez-e Shirāzi* (Karachi-Dhaka: Komiteh-ye Markazi-ye Jashn-e Shāhanshāhi, 1971); *Mobārak Nāmeh* [Book of Congratulations] (Rawalpindi: Majles-e Taqribāt-e Jashn-e Shāhanshāhi-ye Irān, 1971); Hozur Ahmad Salim, *Āmuzgāh-e Fārsi* [Persian Coursebook] (Hyderabad, 1350); Ja'far Qāsemi, *Ta'sir-e Ma'navi-ye Irān dar Pākestān* [Spiritual Influence of Iran on Pakistan] (Lahore: Edāreh-ye Oqāf-e Panjāb, 1350); Khan, *Iran and Pakistan*; and Ashraf, *Persian Manuscripts*.

111 Mumtaz Hasan in the foreword to Ashraf, *Persian Manuscripts*.

112 Franz Jonas in the introduction to *Imperium Persicum: 2500jähriges Bestehen des Persischen Kaiserreiches* (Wien: Kaiserlich Iranische Botschaft, 1971), 2.

113 Ibid., 84.

114 In addition to those already mentioned, see Jean-Paul Deschatelets's introduction in *Iranian Civilization and Culture*, ed. Adams.

115 *Terre D'Europe*, 'Iran', 12:40–1, October–December, 1971; and 'Cultural Crossroads for 2,500 Years', *The UNESCO Courier*, October 1971.

116 Giuseppe Tucci, 'Celebration of the 25th Centenary of Cyrus the Great: International Competition', Rome, November 1964 [poster], Shafā Archives.

117 Alessandro Bausani, *L'Iran e la sua tradizione millenaria* (Rome: Istituto Italiano per il Medio ed Estremo Oriente, 1971); and Giuseppe Tucci, *Ciro Il Grande* (Rome: Istituto Italiano per il Medio ed Estremo Oriente, 1971).

118 Carlo Paoloni, *I fuochi sacri dell'antica Persia* (Milan: Carlo Paoloni, 1971), viii. The work is only tangentially related to Iranian culture and civilization. It is more a geological survey of natural gas resources in Iran throughout history.

119 *Kurus: Memorial Volume*.

120 Ibid., 140.

121 B. M. Gai, 'Concept of Monarchy in Ancient and Medieval Iran as Gleaned from Classical Persian Poetry', in *Indo-Iran*, ed. Ram and Rao, 19–20.

122 B. H. Zaidi, in the introduction to *Indo-Iran*, ed. Ram and Rao, xiii.

123 John Manuel Cook, *Ancient Persia* (London: Dent, 1983), iii.

124 Ilya Gershevitch, quote in his preface to Richard Hallock, 'The Evidence of the Persepolis Tablets', *The Cambridge History of Iran*, vol. 2, preprinted chapter (Cambridge: Middle East Centre, 1971).

125 For example, Roger Stevens, *The Land of the Great Sophy* (London: Methuen, 1971); Alessandro Bausani, *The Persians*, trans. J. B. Donne (London: Elek Books, 1971); Ali Dashti, *In Search of Omar Khayyam*, trans. Laurence Elwell-Sutton (London: George Allen & Unwin, 1971).

126 Jean Perrot, *The Palace of Darius at Susa* (London: I.B. Tauris, 2013), xii.

127 Shafā to 'Alam, 5 Tir 1350/ 26 June 1971, Shafā Archives.

6 Criticizing the Celebrations

1 Jalal Al-e Ahmad, *Plagued by the West (Gharbzadegi)*, trans. Paul Sprachman (New York: Caravan Books, 1981), 51.
2 Roy Mottahedeh, *The Mantle of the Prophet* (Oxford: Oneworld, 2009), 312.
3 For analysis, see Ali Mirsepassi, *Intellectual Discourse and the Politics of Modernization: Negotiating Modernity in Iran* (Cambridge: Cambridge University Press, 2000), 97–114.
4 Mehrzad Boroujerdi, *Iranian Intellectuals and the West: The Tormented Triumph of Nativism* (Syracuse: Syracuse University Press, 1996), 72.
5 SAVAK report, 10 Shahrivar 1350/ 1 September 1971, *Bazm-e Ahriman*, vol. 4, 237–8.
6 Milani quotes Shafā as saying that one of the goals of the Celebrations was to 'accentuate the pre-Islamic imperial grandeur of Persia to the detriment of its Islamic component'. Abbas Milani, *The Shah* (New York: Palgrave Macmillan, 2011), 324.
7 For the *ulema* in the Constitutional Revolution, see Matteo Farzaneh, *The Iranian Constitutional Revolution and the Clerical Leadership of Khurasani* (New York: Syracuse University Press, 2015).
8 Michael Axworthy, *Empire of the Mind* (London: Penguin, 2008), 227.
9 Ali Gheissari and Vali Nasr, *Democracy in Iran: History and the Quest for Liberty* (Oxford: Oxford University Press, 2006), 42.
10 Homa Katouzian, *Sadeq Hedayat: The Life and Legend of an Iranian Writer* (London: I.B. Tauris, 2002), 191–2.
11 Nikki Keddie, *Modern Iran* (New Haven: Yale University Press, 2003), 191.
12 Ruhollah Ramazani, *Independence Without Freedom: Iran's Foreign Policy* (Charlottesville: University of Virginia Press, 2013), 9.
13 Michael Axworthy, *Revolutionary Iran* (London: Penguin Books, 2013), 62; Milani, *The Shah*, 297–99.
14 Diary entry 22 January 1973, *The Shah and I*, 279.
15 Diary entry 11 November 1972, *The Shah and I*, 155.
16 Ruhollah Khomeini, *Islam and Revolution 1: Writings and Declarations of Imam Khomeini (1941–1980)*, translated and annotated by Hamid Algar (Berkeley: Mizan Press, 1981), 181–2.
17 Amin Saikal, *The Rise and Fall of the Shah: From Autocracy to Religious Rule* (Princeton, NJ: Princeton University Press, 1980), 193.
18 Ali Ansari, *Modern Iran Since 1921* (Harlow: Longman, 2003), 162–3.
19 SAVAK report, 28 Shahrivar 1346/ 19 September 1967, *Jashn-e Tājgozāri*, 247; and 30 Shahrivar 1346/ 21 September, 255.
20 SAVAK report, undated, *Jashn-e Tājgozāri*, 266.
21 Ibid., 266–7.
22 David Menashri, 'Shi'ite Leadership: In the Shadow of Conflicting Ideologies', *Iranian Studies*, 13:1/4 (1980): 129.
23 Said Arjomand, 'Traditionalism in Twentieth-century Iran', in *From Nationalism to Revolutionary Islam*, ed. Said Arjomand (Albany: State University of New York Press, 1984), 223. For the complete text of the speech, see Khomeini, *Islam and Revolution 1*, 200–8.
24 SAVAK special bulletin, 29 Tir 1350/ 20 July 1971, *Bazm-e Ahriman*, vol. 4, 156–7.
25 SAVAK internal report, 20 Mordād 1350/ 11 August 1971, *Bazm-e Ahriman*, vol. 4, 193–4.

26 SAVAK report, 26 Mordād 1350/ 17 August 1971, *Bazm-e Ahriman*, vol. 4, 212.
27 SAVAK report, 16 Mordād 1350/ 7 August 1971, *Bazm-e Ahriman*, vol. 4, 142–3.
28 This was a reference to the faith of the architect Hoseyn Amānat, who designed the monument.
29 SAVAK report, 11 Ābān 1350/ 2 November 1971, *Bazm-e Ahriman*, vol. 4, 350–2.
30 Ibid.
31 See, for example, Ervand Abrahamian, "Ali Shari'ati: Ideologue of the Iranian Revolution", *MERIP Reports*, 102 (1982): 24–8.
32 Mirsepassi, *Intellectual Discourse*, 116.
33 Ali Shariati, *Man and Islam: Extraction and Refinement of Cultural Resources*. Available online: http://www.shariati.com/english/culture.html (accessed 13 May 2019).
34 Quoted in Mottahedeh, *The Mantle of the Prophet*, 331.
35 Najibullah Lafraie, *Revolutionary Ideology and Islamic Militancy: The Iranian Revolution and Interpretations of the Quran* (London: Tauris Academic Studies, 2009), 138.
36 Ali Shariati, *On the Plight of the Oppressed People*. Available online: http://www.al-islam.org/articles/plight-oppressed-people-ali-shariati (accessed 17 March 2017).
37 Ali Rahnema, 'Ali Shariati: Teacher, Preacher, Rebel', in *Pioneers of Islamic Revival*, ed. Ali Rahnema (London: Zed Books, 1994), 235.
38 Mozaffar Firouz, *L'Iran face à l'imposture de l'histoire* (Paris: L'Herne, 1971), 15.
39 Ibid., 34.
40 Ibid., 78.
41 Ibid., 10.
42 Cyrus Ghani, *Iran and the West: A Critical Bibliography* (London: Kegan Paul International, 1987), 131–2.
43 'Iran: Annual Review for 1961', Sir Geoffrey Harrison to Lord Home, 3 January 1962, FO 371/164179, 9–10.
44 Gregory Lima, *The Revolutionizing of Iran* (Tehran: International Communications, 1973), 126.
45 Matthew K. Shannon, *Losing Hearts and Minds: American-Iranian Relations and International Education During the Cold War* (Ithaca: Cornell University Press, 2017), 10–11.
46 Ibid., 53.
47 Axworthy, *Revolutionary Iran*, 70.
48 James Buchan, *Days of God* (London: John Murray, 2012), 182.
49 Axworthy, *Revolutionary Iran*, 70.
50 SAVAK report, 18 Ābān 1346/ 9 November, *Jashn-e Tājgozāri*, 407.
51 Ibid., 408.
52 Ibid., 410.
53 Christopher Hewitt, *Political Violence and Terrorism in Modern America: A Chronology* (Westport: Praeger Security International, 2005), 85.
54 Telegram 189359 from the Department of State to the US Delegation to the 25th Centenary Celebration in Shiraz, Iran, 15 October 1971, FRUS, Volume E-4, doc. 150.
55 'Iranian Émigrés in Masked Protests Against Shah's Regime', *San Francisco Examiner*, 16 October 1971.
56 'Shah Celebrates Monarchy While Iranians Suffer', *The Stanford Daily*, 160:16, 18 October 1971.

57 'A Hungry Nation Does Not Need a 2500 Year Celebration: Appeal', in *Corruption and Struggle in Iran*, 8–10.
58 Press release from the Executive Committee for the Dhofar Liberation Front, in *Corruption and Struggle in Iran*, 10–11.
59 'A Time for Peaceful Revolution', *Iran Free Press*, 1:2, October 1971, 4.
60 SAVAK special bulletin, 29 Tir 1350/ 20 July 1971, *Bazm-e Ahriman*, vol. 4, 158–9.
61 SAVAK internal report, 16 Farvardin 1350/ 5 April 1971, *Bazm-e Ahriman*, vol. 4, 9–10. Other SAVAK reports express similar frustrations, see reports from 9 Khordād 1350/ 30 May 1971, 85; and 7 Tir 1350/ 28 June 1971, 125–6.
62 SAVAK internal report, 9 Mordād 1350/ 31 July 1971, *Bazm-e Ahriman*, vol. 4, 181–2.
63 Ramsbotham report, 22 October 1971, 3, FCO 17/1529.
64 Airgram 136 from the Embassy in Iran to the Department of State, 'Student Disturbances at Universities in Tehran', 10 May 1971, FRUS, Volume E-4, doc. 126.
65 SAVAK report, 5 Mehr 1350/ 27 September 1971, *Bazm-e Ahriman*, vol. 4, 301–3.
66 SAVAK report, 2 Mordād 1350/ 24 July 1971, *Bazm-e Ahriman*, vol. 4, 165.
67 SAVAK report, 8 Mehr 1350/ 30 September 1971, *Bazm-e Ahriman*, vol. 4, 315.
68 'Jashn-e Zed-e Mardomi-ye Shāh', *Bazm-e Ahriman*, vol. 4, fn., 315–16.
69 Reza Baraheni, *Crowned Cannibals* (New York: Vintage Books, 1977), 100.
70 *Time*, 25 October 1971, cut out in *Corruption and Struggle in Iran*, 28.
71 Press Statement from Amnesty International, 2 November 1971, cut out in *Corruption and Struggle in Iran*, 13.
72 See Andrew Scott Cooper, *The Fall of Heaven* (New York: Henry Holt, 2016), 237.
73 Abdolreza Ansari, *The Shah's Iran* (London: I.B. Tauris, 2017), 279.
74 Letter Parren James Mitchell to Amir Aslan Afshar, 24 February 1972, in *Corruption and Struggle in Iran*, 22.
75 Ibid., 17–26.
76 Abbas Milani, *Eminent Persians*, vol. 1 (Syracuse, NY: Syracuse University Press, 2008), 100.
77 Peter Ramsbotham, Iranian Oral History Collection, Harvard University, tape 1, 28.
78 Jonker report, 5 October 1971, NA 2.05.191/554.
79 Telegram 331 from the embassy in Iran to the Department of State, January 17, 1972, footnote 1, FRUS, Volume E-4, doc. 16.
80 Baqer Moin, *Khomeini: The Life of the Ayatollah* (London: I.B. Tauris, 2009), 164.
81 Ramsbotham dispatch to London, 5 October 1971, FCO 17/1528.
82 Memorandum Henry Kissinger to President Nixon, 6 April 1971, FRUS, Volume E-4, doc. 121.
83 Telegram no. 591 from Douglas-Home to Tehran, 12 October, FCO 57/323.
84 Telegram 2495 from the embassy in Iran to the Department of State, 12 May 1971, FRUS, Volume E-4, doc. 127.
85 SAVAK report, 29 Shahrivar 1350/ 20 September 1971, *Bazm-e Ahriman*, vol. 4, 287–9.
86 Arthur Upham Pope to Amir Ebrahimi, 4 December 1960, in *Surveyors of Persian Art*, ed. Jay Gluck and Noël Siver (Costa Mesa, CA: Mazda Publishers, 1996), 429.
87 Jonker to Ministry of Foreign Affairs, 5 October 1971, NA 2.05.191/554.
88 Ramsbotham to Foreign Office, 26 September 1971, FCO 17/1528.
89 Jonker to Ministry of Foreign Affairs, 5 October 1971, NA 2.05.191/554.
90 Ansari, *The Shah's Iran*, 275–6.
91 Ramsbotham to Foreign Office, 26 September 1971, FCO 17/1528. Emphasis was added by Ramsbotham.

92 Quoted in E. R. Chamberlin, *Preserving the Past* (London: J.M. Dent and Sons, 1979), 25.
93 'Economic Review: Iran', *The Economist Intelligence Unit*, London, 4 (1971): 7.
94 Milani, *Eminent Persians*, vol. 1, 55.
95 Ansari, *The Shah's Iran*, 268.
96 Ramsbotham report, 22 October 1971, 3, FCO 17/1529.
97 See *Jashn-e Tājgozāri*, fn. 1, 338–9.
98 Milani, *The Shah*, 3.
99 *Jashn-e Tājgozāri*, fn. 1, 339.
100 Often the documents published by the Islamic Republic on the Pahlavi elite read like character assassinations, inviting the reader to be repulsed by the decadence and immorality of the subjects. The author of one such article on Shojāʿ al-Din Shafā, Qāsem Tabrizi, characterizes Shafā as a womanizer and heavy drinker, who 'had a vulgar face and was immersed in moral corruption'. See Tabrizi, 'Shojāʿ al-Din Shafā beh Revāyat-e Asnād-e Sāvāk', 124–6.
101 'Decorations', *Kayhan International*, 5 June 1971.
102 SAVAK report, 28 Tir 1350/ 19 July 1971, *Bazm-e Ahriman*, vol. 4, 151.
103 SAVAK special bulletin, 29 Tir 1350/ 20 July 1971, *Bazm-e Ahriman*, vol. 4, 156.
104 Ramsbotham report, 22 October 1971, 5–6, FCO 17/1529.
105 Diary entry 18 Mehr 1351/ 10 October 1972, *Yāddāshthā-ye ʿAlam*, vol. 2, 363.
106 ʿAlam to Hoveydā, 1352(?), 'Asnād-e Mahramāneh-ye Jashnhā', 188.
107 Dustdār and Tayyebāti, *Ketābshenāsi-ye Jashn-e Shāhanshāhi-ye Irān*.
108 SAVAK to Head of State Police, 20 Mehr 1351/ 12 October 1972, *Bazm-e Ahriman*, vol. 4, 392.
109 'Country Marks Anniversary of Celebrations', *Kayhan International*, 21 October 1972, 3.
110 Ramsbotham report, 22 October 1971, 3, FCO 17/1529.
111 Jahangir Amuzegar, *The Dynamics of the Iranian Revolution: The Pahlavis' Triumph and Tragedy* (Albany: State University of New York Press, 1991), 226.
112 Milani, *The Shah*, 372.
113 Ali M. Ansari, *The Politics of Nationalism in Modern Iran* (Cambridge: Cambridge University Press, 2012), 175.

7 The cost of the Celebrations

1 '1350 Named Cyrus the Great Year', *Kayhan International*, 27 March 1971, 1.
2 Houchang Nahavandi, *The Last Shah of Iran*, trans. Steeve Reed (Slough: Aquillon, 2005), 44.
3 'Fun in the Sand: 2500 Year Celebration', *Washington Daily News*, 16 October 1971.
4 Jenkins, 'Iran's Birthday Party', *Newsweek*, 25 October 1971, 33.
5 SAVAK special bulletin, 29 Tir 1350/ 20 July 1971, *Bazm-e Ahriman*, vol. 3, 161.
6 Andrew Scott Cooper, *The Fall of Heaven: The Pahlavis and the Final Days of Imperial Iran* (New York: Henry Holt, 2016), 197.
7 *Decadence and Downfall*, Dir. Hassan Amini, London: BBC (2016).
8 Equivalent to around $1.9 billion in 2019, based on a cumulative rate of inflation of 532.5 per cent.

9 'Het zeer rijke, zeer arme Perzië' [Very Rich, Very Poor Persia], *NRC Handelsblad*, 1 October 1971, 6.
10 'Opponent van Sjah Krijgt geen Pas', *Trouw*, 12 October 1971, 3.
11 *5th Development Plan: A Summary* (Tehran: Plan and Budget Organisation, 1973), 131.
12 Khodādād Farmānfarmā'iyān quoted in Frances Bostock and Geoffrey Jones, *Planning and Power in Iran: Ebtehaj and Economic Development Under the Shah* (London: Routledge, 2013), 97.
13 Farhad Daftary, 'Barnāma-Rizi', *Encyclopaedia Iranica* (1988). Available online: http://www.iranicaonline.org/articles/barnama-rizi-planning (accessed 2 February 2017).
14 Speaking at a conference in San Francisco in 1961. Quoted in Bostock and Jones, *Planning and Power in Iran*, 93.
15 Farhad Daftary, 'Development and Planning in Iran: A Historical Survey', *Iranian Studies*, 6:4 (1973): 196.
16 Ibid.
17 Ibid., 206.
18 Farhad Daftary, 'Barnāma-Rizi'.
19 'Gozāresh va barnāmeh-ye jashnhā-ye 2500 sāleh', 24 Esfand 1337/ 15 March 1959, *Bazm-e Ahriman*, vol. 1, 1–5.
20 '1350 Named Cyrus the Great Year', *Kayhan International*, 27 March 1971, 1.
21 *Iran '71: A Survey of the Iranian Economy* (Tehran: Iran Trade and Industry, 1971), 123.
22 Ibid., 114.
23 R. K. Karanjia, *The Mind of a Monarch* (London: George Allen & Unwin, 1977), 21.
24 'Ministry to establish 2500 co-ops during 1350', *Kayhan International*, 22 May 1971.
25 For an evaluation of the land reform programme and the establishment of cooperatives, see Jahangir Amuzegar, *The Dynamics of the Iranian Revolution* (Albany: State University of New York Press, 1991), 183–8.
26 Jonker to Ministry of Foreign Affairs, 2 June 1971, NA 2.05.191/554.
27 *Oil and the Economy of Iran* (Tehran: Ministry of Information, 1972), 3.
28 Karanjia, *The Mind of a Monarch*, 21.
29 'Mammoth Airlift by HOMA', *Iran Tribune*, November 1971, 36.
30 'Dar Hāshiyeh-ye Jashnhā: Khadamāt-e Homā dar Hameh jā Cheshmgir Bud' [On the Side of the Celebrations: The Services of Iran Air Were Noticeable Everywhere], *Keyhān*, 26 Mehr 1350/ 18 October 1971, 28.
31 *Iran '71: A Survey of the Iranian Economy*, 92.
32 As early as 1959, the Central Council was urged to have regular contact with the governor of Fars. See report of meeting at Sa'dābād, 9 Tir 1338/ 1 July 1959, *Bazm-e Ahriman*, vol. 1, 6–7.
33 See Cynthia Helms, *An Ambassador's Wife in Iran* (New York: Dodd, Mead, and Co., 1981), 67–8.
34 *Economic Review of the Year 1346: 21 March 1967–20 March 1968* (Tehran: Bank of Iran and the Middle East, 1968), 125–6.
35 'L'Organisation nationale du tourisme iranien veille au développement de l'équipement hôtelier', *Le Monde Diplomatique*, December 1965, 33.
36 *Economic Review of the Year 1346: 21 March 1967–20 March 1968* (Tehran: Bank of Iran and the Middle East, 1968), 125–6.
37 *Economic Review of the Year 1348: 21 March 1969 to 20 March 1970* (Tehran: Bank of Iran and the Middle East, 1970), 81.

38 *Economic Review of the Year 1349: 21 March 1970 to 20 March 1971* (Tehran: Bank of Iran and the Middle East, 1971), 82.
39 *Iranian Tourist Industry Strongly Benefits from Anniversary Celebrations* (Tehran: Foreign Relations Department, Ministry of Information, 1972), 2.
40 Ibid., 2–6.
41 *Iran '71: A Survey of the Iranian Economy*, 105.
42 Record of a Meeting of the Celebrations Committee, 24 Mehr 1340/ 16 October 1961, *Bazm-e Ahriman*, vol. 1, 232–3.
43 *Iran '71: A Survey of the Iranian Economy*, 103.
44 Ibid., 111.
45 'Turkey-Iran Railway Opened: European and Iranian systems linked by 159-mile line through rugged terrain', *The Railway Magazine*, 117:848, December 1971, 646–7.
46 For example, *Isfahan* (Tehran: Iran National Tourist Organization, 1971); Aziz Hatami, *Persepolis, Pasargadae and Nagsh-e Rustam: Presentation on the Occasion of the 2500th Anniversary of the Founding of the Achaemenian Dynasty* (Tehran: Ministry of Information, 1966); and *The 2500th Anniversary of the Founding of the Persian Empire* (Tehran: Iran Air, 1971) [tourism pamphlet]. There are a number of references to other tourism pamphlets and books, published in English, French and Persian. See, for example, Amir Moʿezz to ʿAbdolrezā Ansāri, 11 Khordād 1350/ 31 May 1971, *Bazm-e Ahriman*, vol. 4, 88.
47 *Türkiye/Iran Transit Route: For the "Celebration of the 2500th Anniversary of the Founding of the Persian Empire by Cyrus the Great"* (Istanbul: Touring and Automobile Club of Turkey, 1971).
48 Henri Stierlin, *Iran of the Master Builders: 2500 Years of Architecture* (Geneva: Editions Sigma, 1971). Published in a number of languages including French, English and German.
49 Banri Namikawa, *Iran* (Tokyo: Kodansha International, 1975).
50 *Economic Review of the Year 1348*, 82; and *Economic Review of the Year 1346*, 126.
51 Qāsem Rezāi report to the prime minister, 10 Tir 1349/ 1 July 1970, *Asnādi az Sanʿat-e Jahāngardi dar Irān* [Documents on the Tourism Industry in Iran], vol. 3 (Tehran: Tahyeh va Tanzim: Moʿāvenat-e khadamāt-e modiriyat va ettelāʿresāni-ye daftar-e raʾis jomhur, 1380), 891.
52 Ibid., 892–3.
53 'New Hotels', *Iran Tribune*, November 1971, 46.
54 Ramsbotham report, 22 October 1971, 4, FCO 17/1529.
55 Ibid., 5.
56 Cyrus Farzāneh to prime minister, 26 Bahman 1350/ 15 February 1972, *Asnādi az Sanʿat-e Jahāngardi dar Irān*, vol. 3, 961.
57 Jean Bechara to Cyrus Farzāneh, 18 Bahman 1350/ 7 February 1972, *Asnādi az Sanʿat-e Jahāngardi dar Irān*, vol. 3, 962–3.
58 *Tourism: Investment Opportunities in Iran* (Tehran: Iranian National Tourist Organization Research and Planning Department, February 1972), 11.
59 See Cyrus Farzāneh to ʿAlam, 26 Ordibehesht 1351/ 16 May 1972, 'Asnād-e Mahramāneh-ye Jashnhā', 183–5.
60 Naomi Barry, 'Feest in Persepolis, reclame zonder te betalen' [Party in Persepolis: Advertisement Without Paying], *Haagsche Courant*, 25 September 1971, 7.
61 Shafā to Jonker, 28 January 1971, NA 2.05.191/554.
62 *Iranian Tourist Industry Strongly Benefits from Anniversary Celebrations*, 2.

63 Eckart Ehlers, 'Some Geographic and Socio-Economic Aspects of Tourism in Iran', *Sonderdruck aus ORIENT*, 15:3 (1974): 103.
64 Ramsbotham report, 22 October 1971, FCO 17/1529.
65 *Summary of the Fifth National Development Plan: 1973–1978* (Tehran: Plan and Budget Organization, 1973), 444.
66 *INTO Weekly News Bulletin*, 8 July 1973.
67 *Tourist Statistics of Iran: 1977* (Tehran: Ministry of Information and Tourism, 1977).
68 *Summary of the Fifth National Development Plan*, 446.
69 Approximately $307 million. 'Iran: Approaching the Crossroads', *Euro Finance Report*, 24 November 1976, 219.
70 *INTO Weekly News Bulletin*, 30 December 1973.
71 On 1 October 1973, for instance, visa-free travel was introduced between Iran and Britain. *INTO Weekly News Bulletin*, 13 August 1973.
72 See William A. Dorman and Mansour Farhang, *The U.S. Press and Iran: Foreign Policy and the Journalism Deference* (Berkeley: University of California Press, 1987), 117–20.
73 'Het zeer rijke, zeer arme Perzië', *NRC Handelsblad*, 1 October 1971, 6.
74 'The Shah: Poor Imitation of a Real Ruler of Iran', *Iran Free Press*, 1:2, October 1971, 6.
75 'Opponent van Sjah Krijgt geen pas', *Trouw*, 12 October 1971, 3.
76 James Bill, *The Eagle and the Lion* (New Haven: Yale University Press, 1988), fn. 2, 482.
77 Publicity for the 2500th Anniversary Celebrations, 25 October 1971, FCO 17/1529.
78 Ibid.
79 Ibid.
80 For example, the aforementioned hairdressers. See 'The 2500th Anniversary of the Crown', *Kayhan International*, 12 July 1971.
81 Abdolreza Ansari, *The Shah's Iran – Rise and Fall: Conversations with an Insider* (London: I.B. Tauris, 2017), 295.
82 'The 2500th Anniversary of the Crown'.
83 Jonker to Minister of Foreign Affairs, 2 June 1971, NA 2.05.191/554.
84 It was originally planned to be funded from the Tehran municipal budget, see Javād Bushehri to Fathollāh Farud, mayor of Tehran, 24 Bahman 1339/ 13 February 1961, 'Asnād-e Mahramāneh-ye Jashnhā', 129.
85 Jonker to Minister of Foreign Affairs, 2 June 1971, NA 2.05.191/554. It must be pointed out that the final accounts of the Central Council of the Celebrations show that the complete funds for the Shahyād Tower were actually taken out of its budget, so it could be that the money contributed went to other Celebrations-related projects instead.
86 'Alam to Manuchehr Eqbāl, 2 Mordād 1350/ 24 July 1971, 'Asnād-e Mahramāneh-ye Jashnhā', 162–3. This, incidentally, is almost exactly the amount that the Shahyād Tower cost.
87 Amuzegar, *The Dynamics of the Iranian Revolution*, 181.
88 Abbas Milani, *Eminent Persians: The Men and Women Who Made Modern Iran, 1941– 1979*, vol. 2 (Syracuse, NY: Syracuse University Press, 2008), 671.
89 SAVAK report, 7 Ābān 1346/ 29 October 1971, *Jashn-e Tājgozāri*, 393.
90 Ramsbotham report, 22 October 1971, 4, FCO 17/1529.
91 Imperial Court to Mr Jahānshāhi, president of the Central Bank, Khordād 1350/ May/ June 1971, 'Asnād-e Mahramāneh-ye Jashnhā', 171.
92 Wife of the half-brother of the Shah, 'Abdolrezā Pahlavi.
93 'Alam to Ansāri, 14 Tir 1350/ 5 July 1971, 'Asnād-e Mahramāneh-ye Jashnhā', 172.

94 Hormoz Gharib to Amir Mottaqi, 6 November 1350/ 2 September 1971, 'Asnād-e Mahramāneh-ye Jashnhā', fn., 180.
95 Mehdi Bushehri to Central Bank, 5 Ordibehesht 1350/ 24 April 1971, *Bazm-e Ahriman*, vol. 4, 46.
96 'Alam to Hoveydā, 24 Farvardin 1350/ 13 April 1971, 'Asnād-e Mahramāneh-ye Jashnhā', 171.
97 'Kholāseh-ye dariyāfti', 30 Mordād 1351/ 21 August 1972, *Bazm-e Ahriman*, vol. 4, 386–8.
98 'Alam to Hoveydā, undated, 1973/1974, 'Asnād-e Mahramāneh-ye Jashnhā', 188.
99 'Alam to Bushehri, 30 Āzar 1348/ 21 December 1969, 'Asnād-e Mahramāneh-ye Jashnhā', 155.
100 'Alam to Eqbāl, Āzar 1349/ December 1970, 'Asnād-e Mahramāneh-ye Jashnhā', 161.
101 Hoseyn Amānat to Javād Bushehri, 15 Mordād 1347/ 6 August 1968, *Bazm-e Ahriman*, vol. 3, 15–17.
102 'Gozāresh-e 'amaliyāt-e hesābdāri-ye shurā-ye markazi-ye jashn-e shāhanshāhi-ye Irān az aval-e Mehr māh-e 1339 leghāyat Shahrivar māh-e 1351' [Report of accounts of the Central Council for the Celebrations from Mehr 1339 until Shahrivar 1351, 13 Mehr 1351/ 5 October 1972], *Bazm-e Ahriman*, vol. 4, 389–91.
103 James Buchan, *Days of God* (London: John Murray, 2012), fn. 205, 406.
104 'Kholāseh-ye dariyāfti', 30 Mordād 1351/ 21 August 1972, *Bazm-e Ahriman*, vol. 4, 386–8.
105 'Gozāresh-e 'amaliyāt-e hesābdāri', 13 Mehr 1351/ 5 October 1972, *Bazm-e Ahriman*, vol. 4, 389–91.
106 'Kholāseh-ye dariyāfti',386–8.
107 Ansari, *The Shah's Iran*, 251. The rest of the money, as stated above, came from donations.
108 'Kholāseh-ye dariyāfti', *Bazm-e Ahriman*, vol. 4, 386–8.
109 Ansari, *The Shah's Iran*, 296.
110 The others being the Colosseum in Rome, Baalbek in Lebanon and the Palais de Versailles. See *Outline of the Celebration of the 2500th Anniversary of the Founding of the Persian Empire by Cyrus the Great* (Tehran: Central Council of the Celebration of the 2500th Anniversary of the Founding of the Persian Empire by Cyrus the Great, 1971), 8.
111 Peter Ramsbotham, Foundation for Iranian Studies, tape 3, 67.
112 *Economic review of the year 1349*, 83.

Conclusion

1 Christopher de Bellaigue, *The Islamic Enlightenment: The Modern Struggle Between Faith and Reason* (London: Bodley Head, 2017), 342.
2 C. B. F. Walker, 'A Recently Identified Fragment of the Cyrus Cylinder', *Iran*, 10 (1972):158–9.
3 Heleen Sancisi-Weerdenburg, *Sources, Structures and Synthesis: Proceedings of the Groningen 1983 Achaemenid History Workshop* (Leiden: Nederlands Instituut voor het Nabije Oosten, 1987), xiii.
4 St John Simpson and John Curtis (eds), *The World of Achaemenid Persia: History and Society in Iran and the Ancient Near East* (London: I.B. Tauris, 2010), xiii.

5. Sayyed Nimā Hoseyni, 'Kurosh beh Revāyat-e Khalkhāli: Dorughin va jenāyatkār, jāhtalab va 'ayyāsh' [Cyrus according to Khalkhāli: False and criminal, opportunist and pleasure seeker], *Tārikh-e Irāni*, 28 Farvardin 1390/ 17 April 2011. Available online: http://tarikhirani.ir/fa/files/26/bodyView/151 (accessed 11 June 2019).
6. 'Mosāhebeh-ye Chāp Nashodeh az Shojā' al-Din Shafā', 182.
7. Hoseyni, 'Kurosh beh Revāyat-e Khalkhāli'.
8. Ali M. Ansari, *The Politics of Nationalism in Modern Iran* (Cambridge: Cambridge University Press, 2012), 223.
9. Houchang Nahavandi, *The Last Shah of Iran*, trans. Steeve Reed (Slough: Aquillon, 2005), 47.
10. Ruhollah Khomeini, *Islam and Revolution*, translated and annotated by Hamid Algar (Berkeley: Mizan Press, 1981), 201.
11. Ansāri to 'Alam, 12 Tir 1350/ 3 June 1971, *Bazm-e Ahriman*, vol. 4, 134–5.
12. Abdolreza Ansari, *The Shah's Iran* (London: I.B. Tauris, 2017), 284.
13. Ansāri to 'Alam, 12 Tir 1350/ 3 June 1971, Bazm-e Ahriman, vol. 4, 134–5.
14. 'Sāl-e 2500 Shāhanshāhi Bejāye Sāl-e 1350 Shamsi' [Year 2500 Imperial Instead of 1350 Shamsi], *Khāndanihā*, 14 Farvardin 1350/ 3 April 1971, 7.
15. SAVAK report, 30 Farvardin 1350/ 19 April 1971, *Bazm-e Ahriman*, vol. 4, 34–5.
16. Ibid.
17. 'Āghāz-e Sāl-e 2535 Shāhanshāhi' [The Beginning of Year 2535 Imperial], *Rastākhiz*, 28 Esfand 1354/ 18 March 1976, 1.
18. Laurence Elwell-Sutton, 'The Pahlavi Era', in *Persia: History and Heritage*, ed. J. A. Boyle (London: Melland for the British Institute of Persian Studies, 1978), 64.
19. Marvin Zonis, *Majestic Failure: The Fall of the Shah* (Chicago: University of Chicago Press, 1991), 81–2.
20. Michael Axworthy, *Revolutionary Iran* (London: Penguin Books, 2013), 92.
21. Ervand Abrahamian, *Iran between Two Revolutions* (Princeton, NJ: Princeton University Press, 1983), 505.
22. John Simpson, *A Mad World, My Masters: Tales from a Traveller's Life* (London: Pan Books, 2008), 223–5.
23. Elaine Sciolino, *Persian Mirrors: The Elusive Face of Iran* (London: Free Press, 2000), 165.
24. Saeid Jafari, "'Cyrus the Great' Enters Iranian Politics', *Al-Monitor*, 2 November 2016. Available online: http://www.al-monitor.com/pulse/originals/2016/11/iran-cyrus-day-commeoration-nouri-hamedani-protest.html (accessed 13 June 2017).
25. Ian Black and Saeed Kamali Dehghan, 'Iran Lays Claim to British Museum's Cyrus Cylinder', *The Guardian*, 15 September 2010. Available online: https://www.theguardian.com/world/2010/sep/15/iran-cyrus-cylinderbritish-museum (accessed 14 June 2019).
26. Ansari, *The Politics of Nationalism in Modern Iran*, 279.
27. Pejman Abdolmohammadi, 'The Revival of Nationalism and Secularism in Modern Iran', *LSE Middle East Centre Paper Series*, 11 (2015): 18.
28. 'Cherā Ra'is-e Majles-e Korowāsi Nām-e Keshvarash rā beh Kurosh-e Hakhāmaneshi Rabt Midahad?' [Why does the Speaker of Croatian Parliament Relate the Name of his Country to Cyrus the Achaemenid?], BBC Persian, 4 September 2015. Available online: http://www.bbc.com/persian/iran/2015/09/150904_l45_coratia_cyrus (accessed 21 October 2018).

29 'The Cyrus Cylinder Travels to the US', British Museum Press Release, 28 November 2012. Available online: http://www.britishmuseum.org/about_us/news_and_press/press_releases/2012/cyrus_cylinder_travels_to_us.aspx (accessed 18 September 2017).
30 '"Los Angeles Embodies Diversity." The City's New Sculpture Celebrating Freedom Is Unveiled', *Los Angeles Times*, 4 July 2017. Available online: http://www.latimes.com/local/lanow/la-me-freedom-sculpture-20170704-story.html (accessed 2 October 2017).
31 'United States Stands with People of Iran', House of Representatives Foreign Affairs Committee Press Release, 9 January 2018. Available online: http://foreignaffairs.house.gov/press-release/united-states-stands-people-iran/ (accessed 22 January 2018).
32 'Aryamehr Sports Stadium', *Iran Tribune*, October 1971, 44.
33 'Out of the Blue Iran Told "No Deal"', *Kayhan International*, 23 March 1974, 8. As the title of the article indicates, Clough turned down the offer.
34 Jason Burke, 'Shah's Opulent Tent City Awaits Rebirth in Desert', *The Observer*, 9 September 2001.
35 Diary entry 17 Farvardin 1349/ 6 April 1970, *Yāddāshthā-ye ʿAlam*, vol. 2, 22.
36 'Mosāhebeh-ye Chāp Nashodeh az Shojāʿ al-Din Shafā', 188.

Bibliography

Archives

British Museum, London.
British National Archives, Kew.
Bibliothèque universitaire des langues et civilisations, Paris.
Iranian Institute for Contemporary Historical Studies, Tehran. Documents available online: http://iichs.org/index_en.asp?img_cat=126&img_type=1 (accessed 28 October 2016).
Nationaal Archief (Dutch National Archives), The Hague.
Österreichisches Staatsarchiv (Austrian State Archives), Vienna.
UNESCO Archives, Paris.
United Nations Archives, New York.

Newspaper and magazines

Chicago Tribune
Daily Mail
The Daily Telegraph
Echo of Iran
Ettelāʿāt
Euro Finance Report
Frankfurter Allgemeine Zeitung
Gelderlander Pers
The Guardian
Haagsche Courant
Haftehnāmeh-ye Komiteh-ye Ettelāʿāt va Enteshārāt-e Jashn-e Dohezār o Pānsadomin Sāl-e Bonyāngozāri-ye Shāhanshāhi
Iran Tribune
Journal de Teheran
Kayhan International
Keyhān
Khāndanihā
Leidsch Dagblad
Le Monde
Le Monde Diplomatique
Life Magazine
Los Angeles Times

Newsweek
New York Times
NRC Handelsblad
The Observer
Paris Match
Peking Review
The Railway Magazine
Rastākhiz
Ruznāmeh-ye Jashn-e Shāhanshāhi-ye Irān
Tages-Anzeiger
Tehran Journal
Trouw
Volkskrant
Washington Daily News
The Washington Post

Films

Decadence and Downfall: The Shah of Iran's Ultimate Party (2016), Dir. Hassan Amini, London: BBC.
Forugh-e Jāvidān (1972), Dir. Farrokh Golestan.
Hargez Nakhab Kurush (2012), Prod. Raha Etemadi, London: Manoto.

Oral histories

Denis Wright, in an interview with Habib Ladjevardi, Aylesbury, UK, 10 and 11 October 1984, Iranian Oral History Collection, Harvard University.
George Middleton in an interview with Habib Ladjevardi, London, England, 16 October 1985, Iranian Oral History Collection, Harvard University.
Mohammad Baheri in an interview with Habib Ladjevardi, Cannes, France, 7, 8, 10, 11, 13, 14 August 1982, Iranian Oral History Collection, Harvard University.
Peter Avery in an interview with Shusha Assar Guppy, Cambridge, UK, 9 and 10 October 1985, Oral History of Iran Collection of the Foundation of Iranian Studies.
Peter Ramsbotham in an interview with Habib Ladjevardi, London, UK, 18 October 1985, Iranian Oral History Collection, Harvard University.
Peter Ramsbotham in an interview with Shusha Assar Guppy, 20 January 1986, Hampshire, UK, Oral History of Iran Collection of the Foundation of Iranian Studies.
Richard Frye in an interview with Shahla Haeri, Cambridge, MA, 3, 10 and 24 October 1984, Iranian Oral History Collection, Harvard University.

Classical sources

Arrian, *The Campaigns of Alexander*, trans. Aubrey de Sélincourt (London: Penguin Books, 1971).

Herodotus, *The Histories*, trans. George Rawlinson (London: Everyman's Library, 1997).
Plato, *Laws*, trans. Benjamin Jowett. Available online: http://classics.mit.edu/ (accessed on 18 September 2016).
Xenophon, *Cyropaedia: The Education of Cyrus*, trans. Henry G. Dakyns (Breinigsville: Dodo Press, 2010).

Persian sources

12 Maqāleh: Beh Monāsebat-e Bozorgdāsht-e Jashn-e Dohezār o Pānsadomin Sāl-e Bonyāngozāri-ye Shāhanshāhi-ye Irān [12 Articles: On the Occasion of the Celebrations of the 2500th Anniversary of the Founding of Imperial Iran] (Tehran: Madreseh-ye ʿĀli-ye Adabiyāt va Zabānhā-ye Khāreji, 1350/1971).
2500 Sāl Shāhanshāhi-ye Irān: az Kurosh tā Pahlavi [2500 Years of Imperial Iran: From Cyrus to Pahlavi] (Tehran: Vezārat-e Behdāri, 1350/1971).
Ahmadipur, Hoseyn, *Āzarbāyejān dar Doreh-ye Sāzandegi va Enqelāb* [Azerbaijan During the Period of Construction and Revolution] (Shurā-ye Markazi-ye Jashn-e Shāhanshāhi-ye Āzarbāyejān, 1345/1966).
Ahmadipur, Hoseyn, *Hamāsehhā-ye Bozorg-e Melli, Shāhnāmeh Bozorgtarin Shāhkār-e Hamāsi-ye Jahān* [The Great National Epics: Shahnameh, the World's Greatest Epic Masterpiece] (Tabriz: Shurā-ye Jashn-e Shāhanshāhi-ye Āzarbāyejān-e Sharqi, 1345/1966).
Ahmadipur, Hoseyn, *Naqsh-e Āzarbāyejān dar Tārikh-e Dohezār o Pānsad Sāleh-ye Shāhanshāhi-ye Irān* [The Role of Azerbaijan in the 2500-Year History of Imperial Iran] (Tabriz: Shurā-ye Markazi-ye Jashn-e Shāhanshāhi-ye Āzarbāyejān, 1345/1966).
Ahmadipur, Hoseyn, *Qalbi keh beh Khāter-e Vatan va Mellat Mitapad* [The Heart That Beats for the People and the Nation] (Tabriz: Shurā-ye Markazi-ye Jashn-e Shāhanshāhi-ye Āzarbāyejān-e Sharqi, 1341/1962).
Ahmadipur, Hoseyn, *Tārikh-e Kohan va Gozashtehhā-ye por Eftekhār-e Shāhanshāhi-ye Irān, az Didgāh-e Shāhanshāh Āryāmehr* [The Ancient History and the Glorious Past of Imperial Iran, from the Perspective of Shāhanshāh Āryāmehr] (Tabriz: Shurā-ye Markazi-ye Jashn-e Shāhanshāhi-ye Āzarbāyejān, 1347/1968).
ʿAlam, Asadollāh, *Yāddāshthā-ye ʿAlam* [The Diaries of ʿAlam], ed. ʿAli-Naqi ʿĀlikhāni, 7 vols (Tehran: Ketābsarā, 1393/2014).
Āqcheh-li, Birām Qalij, *Chehreh-ye Shahrestān-e Gonbad-e Qābus dar ʿAsr-e Poreftekhār-e Dudmān-e Pahlavi* [The Face of Gonbad Qābus in the Period of the Glorious Pahlavi Dynasty] (Gonbad-e Qābus: Komiteh-ye Āmuzesh va Parvaresh-e Shurā-ye Jashn-e Dohezār o Pānsadomin Sāl-e Bonyāngozāri-ye Shāhanshāhi-ye Irān, 1350/1971).
Asnādi az Sanʿat-e Jahāngardi dar Irān [Documents on the Tourism Industry in Iran], 3 vols (Tehran: Tahyeh va Tanzim: Moʿāvenat-e Khadamāt-e Modiriyat va Ettelāʿresāni-ye Daftar-e Raʾis Jomhur, 1380/2001).
Basāri, Talʿat, *Zanān-e Shāhnāmeh* [Women of the Shāhnāmeh] (Tehran: Dāneshsarā-ye ʿĀli, 1350/1971).
Bazm-e Ahriman: Jashnhā-ye 2500 Sāleh-ye Shāhanshāhi beh Revāyat-e Asnād-e Sāvāk va Darbār [The Devil's Feast: The 2500th Anniversary Celebrations According to SAVAK and Court Documents], 4 vols (Tehran: Markaz-e Barresi-ye Asnād-e Tārikhi-ye Vezārat-e Ettelāʿāt, 1377–8/1998–9).

Berghe, Louis Vanden, *Bāstānshenāsi-ye Irān-e Bāstān* [Archéologie de l'Iran ancien] (Tehran: Dāneshgāh-e Tehrān, 1345/1966).

'Cherā Ra'is-e Majles-e Korowāsi Nām-e Keshvarash rā beh Kurosh-e Hakhāmaneshi Rabt Midahad?' [Why Does the Speaker of Croatian Parliament Relate the Name of His Country to Cyrus the Achaemenid?], *BBC Persian*, 4 September 2015. Available online: http://www.bbc.com/persian/iran/2015/09/150904_l45_coratia_cyrus (accessed 21 October 2018).

Dāneshgāh-e Pahlavi beh Revāyat-e Asnād [Pahlavi University According to Documents] (Tehran: Markaz-e Asnād-e Enqelāb-e Eslāmi, 1397/2018).

Dustdār, Yahyā and Hoseyn Tayyebāti, *Ketābshenāsi-ye Jashn-e Shāhanshāhi-ye Irān* [Bibliography of the Imperial Celebrations] (Tehran: Shurā-ye Markazi-ye Jashnhā-ye Shāhanshāhi-ye Irān, 1351/1972).

Gāhnāmeh-ye Panjāh Sāl-e Shāhanshāhi-ye Pahlavi [Chronology of Fifty Years of the Pahlavi Monarchy] (Paris: Soheil Publishers, 1985).

Hadidi, Mokhtār, 'Pahlavi-ye Dovvom va Nemuneh-ye Andishehhā-ye Bāstāngarāyāneh: Negāhi beh Asnād-e Mahramāneh-ye Jashnhā-ye 2500 Sāleh-ye Shāhanshāhi' [The Second Pahlavi and some Elements of Archaistic Thoughts: A Look to the Secret Documents Relating to the 2500th Anniversary Celebrations], *Tārikh-e Moʿāser-e Irān*, 2:5 (1377/1998): 103–88.

Hāfez, *Divān-e Hāfez-e Shirāzi* (Karachi-Dhaka: Komiteh-ye Markazi-ye Jashn-e Shāhanshāhi, 1971).

Hoseyni, Nāser al-Din Shāh, *Peyvastegi-ye Shāhanshāhi va Mellat-e Irān* [The Connection between the Shah and the Nation of Iran] (Tehran: Komiteh-ye Farhang-e Jashn-e Shāhanshāhi-ye Irān, undated).

Hoseyni, Sayyed Nimā, 'Kurosh beh Revāyat-e Khalkhāli: Dorughin va Jenāyatkār, Jāhtalab va ʿAyyāsh' [Cyrus According to Khalkhāli: False and Criminal, Opportunist and Pleasure Seeker], *Tārikh-e Irāni*, 28 Farvardin 1390/ 17 April 2011. Available online: http://tarikhirani.ir/fa/files/26/bodyView/151 (accessed 11 June 2019).

Jashn-e Tājgozāri: Beh Revāyat-e Asnād-e Sāvāk [The Coronation Celebration: According to SAVAK Documents] (Tehran: Markaz-e Barresi-ye Asnād-e Tārikhi-ye Vezārat-e Etteláʿāt, 1385/2006).

Javāheriyān, Faryār, 'Shahyād: Nomādi do Pahlu' [Shahyād: A Two-Faceted Symbol], *Irān Nāmeh*, 24:4 (1387/2009): 481–96.

Kiyā, Sādeq, *Āryāmehr* (Tehran: Vezārat-e Farhang va Honar, 1346/1967).

Massé, Henri, *Ferdowsi va Hamāseh-ye Melli* [Ferdowsi and the National Epic] (Tabriz: Dāneshgāh-e Tabriz, 1350/1971).

Mirghafāri, Marjān, 'Mardom Jashnhā-ye 2500 Sāleh rā Farmāyeshi Midānestand: Goftogu bā Shojāʿ al-Din Shafā, Mobtaker-e Bargozāri-ye Jashnhā-ye Shāhanshāhi' [The People Knew the 2500th Anniversary Celebrations Were Ordered: Conversation with Shojāʿ al-Din Shafā, Initiator of the Imperial Celebrations], *Tārikh-e Irāni*, 11 Ābān 1395/ 1 November 2016. Available online: http://tarikhirani.ir/fa/news/53/bodyView/5631 (accessed 21 May 2019).

Moqaddam, ʿAliqoli Eʿtemād, *Shāh va Sepāh bar Bonyād-e Shāhnāmeh-ye Ferdowsi* [The Shah and the Army According to Ferdowsi's Shāhnāmeh] (Tehran: Vezārat-e Farhang va Honar, 1350/1971).

'Mosāhebeh-ye Chāp Nashodeh az Shojāʿ al-Din Shafā Darbāreh-ye: Jashnhā-ye Dohezār o Pānsad Sāleh' [Unpublished Interview with Shojāʿ al-Din Shafā About: The 2500th Anniversary Celebrations], *Rahāvard*, 95 (2011): 180–193.

Mobārak Nāmeh [Book of Congratulations] (Rawalpindi: Majles-e Taqribāt-e Jashn-e Shāhanshāhi-ye Irān, 1971).
Namāyeshgāh-e Noskhehhā va Asnād-e Khatti [Exhibition of Manuscripts and Documents] (Tehran: Dāneshgāh-e Tehrān, 1350/1971).
Nāmeh-ye Tāj (Tabriz: Dāneshgāh-e Adabiyat va 'Olum-e Ensāni-ye Tabriz, 1346/1967).
Nasr, Sayyed Hoseyn, Ahmad Mostowfi and 'Abbās Zaryāb (eds), *Atlas-e Tārikhi-ye Irān* [Historical Atlas of Iran] (Tehran: University of Tehran Press, 1350/1971).
Pahlavi, Mohammad Rezā, *Enqelāb-e Sefid* [White Revolution] (Tehran: Ketābkhāneh-ye Pahlavi, 1967).
Pahlavi, Rezā, *Safarnāmeh-ye Māzandarān* [Mazandaran Travelogue] (Tehran: Markaz-e Pazhuhesh va Nashr-e Farhang-e Siyāsi-ye Dowrān-e Pahlavi, 1355/1976).
Parviz, 'Abbās, *Qiyām-e Irāniān dar rāh-e Tajdid va 'Azemat-e Irān* [Iranian Uprising on the Way to the Revival and Glory of Iran] (Tehran: Shurā-ye Markazi-ye Jashn-e Shāhanshāhi-ye Irān, 1348/1969).
Pirniyā, Hasan, 'Abbās Eqbāl Āshtiyāni and Bāqer 'Āqeli, *Tārikh-e Irān* [History of Iran] (Tehran: Nashr Nāmak, 1393/2014).
Qāsemi, Ja'far, *Ta'sir-e Ma'navi-ye Irān dar Pākestān* [Spiritual Influence of Iran on Pakistan] (Lahore: Edāreh-ye Oqāf-e Panjāb, 1350/1971).
Rāhnamā-ye Rezheh [Guide to the Parade] (Tehran: Ministry of Information, 1350/1971).
Sadiq, 'Isā, *Yādgār-e 'Omr: Khāterāti az Sargozasht-e Doktor 'Isā Sadiq* [Memoirs], vol. 4 (Tehran: Ketābforushi-ye Dekhodā, 2536/1356/1977).
Safā, Zabihollāh, *Āyin-e Shāhanshāhi-ye Irān* [Imperial Traditions of Iran] (Tehran: University of Tehran, 1346/1967).
Sahm-e Rejāl-e Khorāsān dar Baqā-ye Shāhanshāhi-ye Irān [The Contribution of the People of Khorasan to the Survival of Imperial Iran] (Mashhad: Shurā-ye Jashn-e Shāhanshāhi-ye Khorāsān, 1349/1970).
Salim, Hozur Ahmad, *Āmuzgāh-e Fārsi* [Persian Coursebook] (Hyderabad, 1350/1971).
Shafā, Shojā' al-Din, *Jahān-e Irānshenāsi* [World of Iranology], vol. 1 (Tehran: Ketābkhāneh-ye Pahlavi, 1348/1969).
Shafā, Shojā' al-Din, 'Shojā' al-Din Shafā az Zabān-e Khodash', in *Yādnāmeh-ye Shojā' al-Din Shafā*, ed. Claudine Shafa (Paris, 2013), 37–113.
Sharp, Ralph Norman, *Nazariāti Darbāreh-ye Neveshtehhā-ye (Katibehhā-ye) Pārsi-ye Bāstān* [Theories about Ancient Persian Inscriptions] (Tehran: Shurā-ye Markazi-ye Jashn-e Shāhanshāhi-ye Irān, undated).
Tabrizi, Qāsem, 'Shojā' al-Din Shafā beh Revāyat-e Asnād-e Sāvāk' [Shojā' al-Din Shafā According to SAVAK Documents], *Faslnāmeh-ye Motāle'āt-e Tārikhi*, 60 (1397/2018): 123–39.
Tāheriyā, Mohammad 'Ali, *Dāmghān-e Sheshhezār Sāleh* [6,000-Year-Old Damghan] (Dāmghān: Shurā-ye Jashn-e Shāhanshāhi-ye Dāmghān, 1347/1968).
Tājgozāri-ye A'lāhazrat Homāyun Mohammad Rezā Pahlavi Āryāmehr Shāhanshāh-e Irān va 'Olyāhazrat Farah Pahlavi Shahbānu-ye Irān [The Coronation of His Imperial Majesty Mohammad Reza Pahlavi Āryāmehr Shāhanshāh of Iran and Her Majesty Farah Pahlavi Shahbanou of Iran], 4 Ābān 1346/ 26 October 1967 [programme].
Tājgozāri-ye Shāhanshāhān-e Irān [The Coronation of the Kings of Iran] (Tehran: Shurā-ye Markazi-ye Jashn-e Shāhanshāhi-ye Irān, 1346/1967).
Yaghmā'i, Eqbāl, *Cherā mā Shāh va Shāhanshāhi rā Dust Dārim* [Why We Love the King and the Monarchy] (Tehran: Komiteh-ye Farhang-e Jashn-e Shāhanshāhi-ye Irān, undated).

Zanān-e Darbār beh Revāyat-e Asnād-e Sāvāk: Farah Pahlavi [Women of the Court According to SAVAK Documents: Farah Pahlavi], vol. 2 (Tehran: Markaz-e Barresi-ye Asnād-e Tārikhi-ye Vezārat-e Ettelāʿāt, 1388/2009).

Zokā', Yahyā, *Artesh-e Shāhanshāhi-ye Irān az Kurosh tā Pahlavi* [The Army of Imperial Iran from Cyrus to Pahlavi] (Tehran: Shurā-ye Arteshi-ye Jashn-e Dohezār o Pānsadomin Sal-e Bonyāngozāri-ye Shāhanshāhi-ye Irān, 1350/1971).

Zokā', Yahyā, *Pishineh-ye Sān va Rezheh dar Irān* [Background to Pageants and Parades in Iran] (Tehran: Komiteh-ye Farhang-e Jashn-e Shāhanshāhi-ye Irān, 1350/1971).

Ziyā'pur, Jalil, *Pushāk-e Hakhāmaneshihā va Mādihā dar Takht-e Jamshid* [Garments of the Achaemenids and Medes at Takht-e Jamshid] (Tehran: Komiteh-ye Farhang-e Jashn-e Shāhanshāhi-ye Irān, 1350/1971).

Non-Persian sources

The 2500th Anniversary of the Founding of the Persian Empire (Tehran: Iran Air, 1971) [tourism pamphlet].

5th Development Plan: A Summary (Tehran: Plan and Budget Organization, 1973).

Abdolmohammadi, Pejman, 'History, National Identity and Myths in Iranian Contemporary Political Thought: Mirza Fathali Akhundzadeh (1812–78), Mirza Aqa Khan Kermani (1853–96) and Hassan Taqizadeh (1878–1970)', in *Perceptions of Iran: History, Myths and Nationalism from Medieval Persia to the Islamic Republic*, ed. Ali M. Ansari (London: I.B. Tauris, 2014), 27–38.

Abdolmohammadi, Pejman, 'The Political Thought of Mirzā Aqā Khān Kermani, the Father of Persian National Liberalism', *Oriente Moderno*, 94:1 (2014): 148–61.

Abdolmohammadi, Pejman, 'The Revival of Nationalism and Secularism in Modern Iran', *LSE Middle East Centre Paper Series*, 11 (2015).

Abrahamian, Ervand, "Ali Shariʿati: Ideologue of the Iranian Revolution', *MERIP Reports*, 102 (1982): 24–8.

Abrahamian, Ervand, *The Coup* (New York: New Press, 2013).

Abrahamian, Ervand, *Iran between Two Revolutions* (Princeton, NJ: Princeton University Press, 1983).

Abrahamian, Ervand, 'Revolutionary Iran: A History of the Islamic Republic by Michael Axworthy', *Times Higher Education*, 4 April 2013. Available online: https://www.timeshighereducation.com/books/revolutionary-iran-a-history-of-the-islamic-republic-by-michael-axworthy/2002873.article (accessed 23 October 2016).

Adams, Charles J. (ed.), *Iranian Civilization and Culture: Essays in Honour of the 2,500th Anniversary of the Founding of the Persian Empire* (Montreal: McGill University, Institute of Islamic Studies, 1973).

Afkhami, Gholam Reza, *Life and Times of the Shah* (Monterey: University of California Press, 2008).

Aghaie, Kamran Scot, 'Islamist Historiography in Post-Revolutionary Iran', in *Iran in the 20th Century: Historiography and Political Culture*, ed. Touraj Atabaki (London: I.B. Tauris, 2009), 233–63.

Aghaie, Kamran Scot, 'Religious Rituals, Social Identities and Political Relationships in Tehran under Qajar Rule, 1850s-1920s', in *Religion and Society in Qajar Iran*, ed. Robert Gleave (Oxon: Routledge, 2005), 373–92.

Alam, Asadollah, *The Shah and I: Confidential Diary of Iran's Royal Court, 1969–1977*, ed. Alinaghi Alikhani (London: I.B. Tauris, 1991).
Al-e Ahmad, Jalal, *Plagued by the West (Gharbzadegi)*, trans. Paul Sprachman (New York: Caravan Books, 1981).
Allen, Lindsey, *The Persian Empire: A History* (London: British Museum Press, 2005).
Alvandi, Roham, *Nixon, Kissinger and the Shah* (Oxford: Oxford University Press, 2014).
Amanat, Abbas, *Iran: A Modern History* (New Haven: Yale University Press, 2017).
Amanat, Abbas and Farzin Vajdani, 'Jalal-al-din-Mirza', *Encyclopaedia Iranica*, online edition, 2008. Available online: http://www.iranicaonline.org/articles/jalal-al-din-mirza (accessed 4 September 2018).
Amuzegar, Jahangir, *The Dynamics of the Iranian Revolution: The Pahlavis' Triumph and Tragedy* (Albany: State University of New York Press, 1991).
Amuzegar, Jahangir, *Managing Oil Wealth: OPEC's Windfalls and Pitfalls* (London: I.B. Tauris, 2001).
Andrews, Peter, *The Turcoman of Iran* (Kendal: Titus Wilson and Son, 1971).
Anglo-Iranian Trade, 4:4 (1971).
'Anniversary Meeting', *Journal of the Royal Asiatic Society of Great Britain and Ireland* 2 (1972): 182–91.
Ansari, Abdolreza, *The Shah's Iran – Rise and Fall: Conversations with an Insider* (London: I.B. Tauris, 2017).
Ansari, Ali M., 'Iranian Nationalism and the Question of Race', in *Constructing Nationalism in Iran: From the Qajars to the Islamic Republic*, ed. Meir Litvak (Oxon: Routledge, 2017), 101–17.
Ansari, Ali M. (ed.), *Iran's Constitutional Revolution of 1906: Narratives of the Enlightenment* (London: Gingko Library, 2016).
Ansari, Ali M., *Modern Iran Since 1921* (Harlow: Longman, 2003).
Ansari, Ali M., 'Mohammad Ali Foroughi and the Construction of Civic Nationalism in Early Twentieth-Century Iran', in *Iran in the Middle East: Transnational Encounters and Social History*, ed. H. E. Chehabi, Peyman Jafari and Maral Jefroudi (London: I.B. Tauris, 2015), 11–26.
Ansari, Ali M., 'Persia in the Western Imagination', in *Anglo-Iranian Relations Since 1800*, ed. Vanessa Martin (London: Routledge, 2005), 8–20.
Ansari, Ali M., *The Politics of Nationalism in Modern Iran* (Cambridge: Cambridge University Press, 2012).
Arberry, Arthur J., *British Contributions to Persian Studies* (London: British Council, 1942).
Arjomand, Said, 'Traditionalism in Twentieth-century Iran', in *From Nationalism to Revolutionary Islam*, ed. Said Arjomand (Albany: State University of New York Press, 1984), 195–232.
Ashraf, Mohammad, *Persian Manuscripts in the National Museum of Pakistan at Karachi* (Karachi: National Museum of Pakistan, 1971).
Aubin, Jean, *L'ambassade de Gregório Pereira Fidalgo à la cour de Châh Soltân-Hosseyn, 1696–1697* (Lisbon: Fundação Calouste Gulbenkian, 1971).
Axworthy, Michael, *Iran: Empire of the Mind* (London: Penguin, 2008).
Axworthy, Michael, *Revolutionary Iran: A History of the Islamic Republic* (London: Penguin Books, 2013).
Axworthy, Michael, *The Sword of Persia: Nader Shah, from Tribal Warrior to Conquering Tyrant* (London: I.B. Tauris, 2006).
Ayres, Peter, 'The Geometry of Shahyad Ariamehr', *The Arup Journal*, 5:1 (1970): 29–35.

Azimi, Fakhreddin, *Quest for Democracy in Iran: A Century of Struggle against Authoritarian Rule* (Cambridge, MA: Harvard University Press, 2008).
Bailey, Martin, 'How Britain Tried to Use a Persian Antiquity for Political Gain', *The Art Newspaper*, 150 (September 2004): 18–19.
Ball, George, *The Past Has Another Pattern* (New York: Norton, 1982).
Baraheni, Reza, *Crowned Cannibals: Writings on Repression in Iran* (New York: Vintage Books, 1977).
Bausani, Alessandro, *L'Iran e la sua tradizione millenaria* (Rome: Istituto Italiano per il Medio ed Estremo Oriente, 1971).
Bausani, Alessandro, *The Persians*, trans. J. B. Donne (London: Elek Books, 1971).
Bayandor, Darioush, *Iran and the CIA: The Fall of Mosaddeq Revisited* (New York: Palgrave Macmillan, 2010).
Beckman, Daniel, 'The Many Deaths of Cyrus the Great', *Iranian Studies*, 51:1 (2018): 1–21.
de Bellaigue, Christopher, *The Islamic Enlightenment: The Modern Struggle between Faith and Reason* (London: Bodley Head, 2017).
Ben-Gurion, David, 'Cyrus, King of Persia', in *Acta Iranica*, vol. 1, ed. Jacques Duchesne-Guillemin (Tehran: Bibliothèque Pahlavi, 1974), 127–34.
Bernhardsson, Magnus T., *Reclaiming a Plundered Past: Archaeology and Nation Building in Modern Iraq* (Austin: University of Texas Press, 2005).
Bianchi, Ugo, 'The Second International Congress of Mithraic Studies, Tehran, September 1975', *Journal of Mithraic Studies*, 1:1 (1976): 77.
Bill, James, *The Eagle and the Lion: The Tragedy of American-Iranian Relations* (New Haven: Yale University Press, 1988).
Bonakdarian, Mansour, *Britain and the Iranian Constitutional Revolution of 1906–1911: Foreign Policy, Imperialism, and Dissent* (Syracuse: Syracuse University Press, 2006).
Borjian, Maryam, 'The Rise and Fall of a Partnership: The British Council and the Islamic Republic of Iran (2001–2009)', *Iranian Studies*, 44:4 (2011): 541–62.
Boroujerdi, Mehrzad, *Iranian Intellectuals and the West: The Tormented Triumph of Nativism* (Syracuse: Syracuse University Press, 1996).
Bostock, Frances and Geoffrey Jones, *Planning and Power in Iran: Ebtehaj and Economic Development under the Shah* (London: Routledge, 2013).
Bowring, Joanna, *Chronology of Temporary Exhibitions at the British Museum* (London: British Museum, 2012).
Breuilly, John, *Nationalism and the State* (Manchester: Manchester University Press, 2001).
Brotton, Jerry, *This Orient Isle: Elizabethan England and the Islamic World* (London: Allen Lane, 2016).
Buchan, James, *Days of God* (London: John Murray, 2012).
Calmard, Jean, 'Shi'i Rituals and Power II. The Consolidation of Safavid Shi'ism: Folklore and Popular Religion', in *Safavid Persia: The History and Politics of an Islamic Society*, ed. Charles Melville (London: I.B. Tauris, 2009), 139–90.
Celebration of the 2500th Anniversary of the Founding of the Persian Empire by Cyrus the Great (Tehran: Ministry of Information, 1971) [programme].
Chamberlin, E. R., *Preserving the Past* (London: J.M. Dent and Sons, 1979).
Chehabi, H. E., 'The Shiraz Festival and Its Place in Iran's Revolutionary Mythology', in *The Age of Aryamehr: Late Pahlavi Iran and Its Global Entanglements*, ed. Roham Alvandi (London: Gingko Library, 2018), 168–201.

Chehabi, H. E., 'South Africa and Iran in the Apartheid Era', *Journal of Southern African Studies*, 42:4 (2016): 687–709.
Clark, Martin, 'The Party', in *Celebration at Persepolis*, ed. Michael Stevenson (Bristol: Arnolfini, 2008), 16–29.
Conmemoración del xxv Centenario de la Fundación del Imperio Persa: Catalogo de la Exposición de Antigüedades Persas (Madrid: Ministerio de Asuntos Exteriores Dirección general de Relaciones Culturales, 1971).
Cook, John Manuel, *Ancient Persia* (London: Dent, 1983).
Cooper, Andrew Scott, *The Fall of Heaven: The Pahlavis and the Final Days of Imperial Iran* (New York: Henry Holt, 2016).
Corning Museum of Glass, *A Tribute to Persia: Persian Glass* (Corning: Corning Museum of Glass, 1972).
Cronin, Stephanie, *The Army and the Pahlavi State in Iran, 1910–1926* (London: I.B. Tauris, 1997).
'Cultural Crossroads for 2,500 Years', *The UNESCO Courier*, October 1971.
Curzon, George, *Persia and the Persian Question*, vol. 2 (London: Longmans Green, 1892).
'The Cyrus Cylinder', The British Museum. Available online: http://www.britishmuseum.org/research/collection_online/collection_object_details.aspx?objectId=327188&partId=1 (accessed 18 February 2016).
'Cyrus Cylinder: How a Persian Monarch Inspired Jefferson', *BBC*, 11 March 2013. Available online: http://www.bbc.co.uk/news/world-us-canada-21747567 (accessed 7 September 2016).
'The Cyrus Cylinder Travels to the US', British Museum Press Release, 28 November 2012. Available online: http://www.britishmuseum.org/about_us/news_and_press/press_releases/2012/cyrus_cylinder_travels_to_us.aspx (accessed 18 September 2017).
Daftary, Farhad, 'Barnāma-Rizi', *Encyclopaedia Iranica* (1988). Available online: http://www.iranicaonline.org/articles/barnama-rizi-planning (accessed 2 February 2017).
Daftary, Farhad, 'Development and Planning in Iran: A Historical Survey', *Iranian Studies*, 6:4 (1973): 176–228.
Dandamaev, Muhammad A., 'Préliminaire', in *Acta Iranica*, vol. 1, ed. Jacques Duchesne-Guillemin (Tehran: Bibliothèque Pahlavi, 1974), 1–12.
Dashti, Ali, *In Search of Omar Khayyam*, trans. Laurence Elwell-Sutton (London: George Allen & Unwin, 1971).
Davidian, Zaven N., *Iran in the Service of World Peace: On the Occasion of the 2500th Anniversary of the Celebration of the Founding of the Iranian Empire* (Tehran: Davidian, 1971).
De Iraanse kunst in de Belgische verzamelingen (Bruxelles: Musées Royaux d'Art et d'Histoire, 1971).
Dorman, William A. and Mansour Farhang, *The U.S. Press and Iran: Foreign Policy and the Journalism Deference* (Berkeley: University of California Press, 1987).
Ebadi, Shirin, *Nobel Lecture*, 10 December 2003. Available online: http://www.nobelprize.org/nobel_prizes/peace/laureates/2003/ebadi-lecture-e.html (accessed 13 September 2016).
The Economist Intelligence Unit, London, 4 (1971).
Economic Review of the Year 1346: 21 March 1967–20 March 1968 (Tehran: Bank of Iran and the Middle East, 1968).
Economic Review of the Year 1348: 21 March 1969 to 20 March 1970 (Tehran: Bank of Iran and the Middle East, 1970).

Economic Review of the Year 1349: 21 March 1970 to 20 March 1971 (Tehran: Bank of Iran and the Middle East, 1971).

Edelman, Murray, *Constructing the Political Spectacle* (Chicago: University of Chicago Press, 1987).

Ehlers, Eckart, 'Some Geographic and Socio-Economic Aspects of Tourism in Iran', *Sonderdruk aus ORIENT*, 15:3 (1974): 97–105.

Eilers, Wilhelm (ed.), *Festgabe Deutscher Iranisten zur 2500 Jahrfeier Irans* (Stuttgart: Hochwacht Druck, 1971).

Eley, Geoff and Ronald Grigor Suny, 'Introduction: From the Moment of Social History to the Work of Cultural Representation', in *Becoming National: A Reader*, ed. Geoff Eley and Ronald Grigor Suny (Oxford: Oxford University Press, 1996), 3–37.

Elwell-Sutton, Laurence, '2500th Anniversary Celebrations', *Bulletin of the British Association of Orientalists*, 6 (1973): 20–25.

Elwell-Sutton, Laurence, 'The Iranian Press, 1941–1947', *Iran*, 6 (1968): 65–104.

Elwell-Sutton, Laurence, 'The Pahlavi Era', in *Persia: History and Heritage*, ed. J. A. Boyle (London: Melland for the British Institute of Persian Studies, 1978), 49–64.

Elwell-Sutton, Laurence, 'Reza Shah the Great', in *Iran under the Pahlavis*, ed. George Lenczowski (Stanford, CA: Hoover Institute Press, 1978), 1–50.

Emami, Farshid, 'Urbanism of Grandiosity: Planning a New Urban Centre for Tehran (1973–76)', *International Journal of Islamic Architecture*, 3:1 (2014): 69–102.

Expedition, 13:3–4 (August 1971), published by Penn Museum.

Farrokh, Kaveh, *Shadows in the Desert: Ancient Persia at War* (Oxford: Osprey, 2007).

Farzaneh, Matteo, *The Iranian Constitutional Revolution and the Clerical Leadership of Khurasani* (New York: Syracuse University Press, 2015).

Fazeli, Nematollah, *Politics of Culture in Iran: Anthropology, Politics and Society in the Twentieth Century* (Oxon: Routledge, 2006).

Figes, Orlando, *A People's Tragedy: The Russian Revolution 1891–1924* (London: Pimlico, 1997).

Firouz, Mozaffar, *L'Iran face à l'imposture de l'histoire* (Paris: L'Herne, 1971).

Foreign Relations of the United States, 1969–1976, Volume E-4, Documents on Iran and Iraq, 1969–1972 (Washington, DC, 2006). Available online: http://history.state.gov/historicaldocuments/frus1969-76ve04 (accessed 27 April 2017).

Frankopan, Peter, *Silk Roads: A New History of the World* (London: Bloomsbury, 2015).

From Persia's Ancient Looms: An Exhibition in Honor of the 2500th Anniversary of the Founding of the Persian Empire by Cyrus the Great, 23 January–30 September 1972, under the patronage of His Excellency, the ambassador of Iran and Mrs Aslan Afshar (Washington, DC: Textile Museum, 1972).

Frye, Richard, 'Asia Institute', *Encyclopaedia Iranica*, online edition, 2011. Available online: http://www.iranicaonline.org/articles/asia-institute-the-1 (accessed 13 September 2016).

Frye, Richard, *The Heritage of Persia*, 2 edn (London: Cardinal, 1976).

Frye, Richard, 'Persia in the Mind of the West', *Islam and Christian-Muslim Relations*, 14:4 (2003): 403–6.

Gasiorowski, Mark and Malcolm Byrne (eds), *Mohammad Mosaddeq and the 1953 Coup in Iran* (New York: Syracuse University Press, 2004).

Ghani, Cyrus, *Iran and the West: A Critical Bibliography* (London: Kegan Paul International, 1987).

Gheissari, Ali, *Iranian Intellectuals in the 20th Century* (Austin: University of Texas Press, 1998).

Gheissari, Ali and Vali Nasr, *Democracy in Iran: History and the Quest for Liberty* (Oxford: Oxford University Press, 2006).
Ghirshman, Roman, *Iran* (Harmondsworth: Penguin Books, 1954).
Ghirshman, Roman, Vladimir Minorsky and Ramesh Sanghvi, *Persia: The Immortal Kingdom* (London: Orient Commerce Establishment, 1971).
The Glorification of Cyrus the Great Achaemenian King of Kings, Pasargad, 12 October 1971 [programme].
Gluck, Jay and Noël Siver (eds), *Surveyors of Persian Art: A Documentary Biography of Arthur Upham Pope and Phillis Ackerman* (Costa Mesa, CA: Mazda Publishers, 1996).
Grigor, Talinn, *Building Iran* (New York: Periscope Publishing, 2009).
Grigor, Talinn, 'Of Metamorphosis Meaning on Iranian Terms', *Third Text*, 17:3 (2003): 207–25.
Grigor, Talinn, 'Orientalism and Mimicry of Selfness: Archaeology of the Neo-Achaemenid Style', in *L'Orientalisme architectural entre imaginaires et savoirs*, ed. Nabila Oulebsir and Mercedes Volait (Paris: Picard, 2009). Available online: http://journals.openedition.org/inha/4911 (accessed 29 April 2019).
Grigor, Talinn, 'Preserving the Antique Modern: Persepolis '71', *Future Anterior*, 2:1 (2005): 22–9.
Grigor, Talinn, 'Recultivating "Good Taste": The Early Pahlavi Modernists and Their Society for National Heritage', *Iranian Studies*, 37:1 (2004): 17–45.
Grigor, Talinn, '"They Have Not Changed in 2,500 Years": Art, Archaeology, and Modernity in Iran', in *Unmasking Ideology in Imperial and Colonial Archaeology: Vocabulary, Symbols, and Legacy*, ed. Bonnie Effros and Guolong Lai (Los Angeles: Cotsen Institute of Archaeology Press at UCLA, 2018), 121–46.
Gulbenkian, Roberto ed. and trans., *L'ambassade en Perse de Luís Pereira de Lacerda et des Pères Portugais de l'ordre de Saint-Augustin, Belchior dos Anjos et Huilherme de Santo Agostinho 1604–1605* (Lisbon: Fundação Calouste Gulbenkian, 1972).
Gurney, John, 'Ann Katharine Swynford Lambton', in *Bibliographical Memoirs of Fellows of the British Academy*, 12 (Oxford: Published for the British Academy by Oxford University Press, 2013), 235–73.
Haidari, Jayad, *Iran: In Celebration of the 2500th Anniversary of the Founding of the Persian Empire by Cyrus the Great* (New York: St. John's University, 1971).
Halliday, Fred, *Iran: Dictatorship and Development* (Harmondsworth: Penguin, 1979).
Hallock, Richard, 'The Evidence of the Persepolis Tablets', *Cambridge History of Iran*, vol. 2, preprinted chapter (Cambridge: Middle East Centre, 1971).
Handley-Taylor, Geoffrey, *Bibliography of Iran* (London: Bibliography of Iran, 1967).
Hansman, John, 'Elamites, Achaemenians and Anshan', *Iran*, 10 (1972): 101–25.
Harley, Maria Anna, 'Music of Sound and Light: Xenakis's Polytopes', *Leonardo*, 31:1 (1998): 55–65.
Harrison, Thomas, 'Reinventing Achaemenid Persia', in *The World of Achaemenid Persia: History and Society in Iran and the Ancient Near East*, ed. St John Simpson and John Curtis (London: I.B. Tauris, 2010), 21–31.
Hatami, Aziz, *Persepolis, Pasargadae and Nagsh-e Rustam: Presentation on the Occasion of the 2500th Anniversary of the Founding of the Achaemenian Dynasty* (Tehran: Ministry of Information, 1966).
Helms, Cynthia, *An Ambassador's Wife in Iran* (New York: Dodd, Mead, and Co., 1981).
Hewitt, Christopher, *Political Violence and Terrorism in Modern America: A Chronology* (Westport: Praeger Security International, 2005).

Hillenbrand, Robert, 'Exploring a Neglected Masterpiece: The Gulistan Shahnama of Baysunghur', *Iranian Studies* 43:1 (2010): 97–126.
Hinnells, John (ed.), *Mithraic Studies: Proceedings of the First International Congress of Mithraic Studies* (Manchester: University of Manchester Press, 1975).
Hoveyda, Fereydoun, *The Fall of the Shah* (New York: Wyndham Books, 1980).
Imperium Persicum: 2500jähriges Bestehen des Persischen Kaiserreiches (Wien: Kaiserlich Iranische Botschaft, 1971).
INTO Weekly News Bulletin, 8 July 1973.
INTO Weekly News Bulletin, 13 August 1973.
INTO Weekly News Bulletin, 30 December 1973.
Iran '71: An Independent Survey of the Iranian Economy on the Occasion of the 2500th Anniversary of the Founding of the Persian Empire (Tehran: Iran Trade and Industry, 1971).
Iran Free Press, 1:2, October 1971.
Iran: Hommes du vent, gens de terre (Paris: Musée de l'Homme, 1971).
Iranian Student Association in the United States, *Corruption and Struggle in Iran: A Defense Publication of the Iranian Student Association in the United States* (United States: Iranian Student Association in the United States, 1972).
Iranian Tourist Industry Strongly Benefits from Anniversary Celebrations (Tehran: Foreign Relations Department, Ministry of Information, 1972).
Isfahan (Tehran: Iran National Tourist Organization, 1971).
'IsMEO Activities', *East and West*, 22:3/4 (1972): 375–95.
Issawi, Charles, 'The Iranian Economy 1925–1975: Fifty Years of Economic Development', in *Iran under the Pahlavis*, ed. George Lenczowski (Stanford: Hoover Institution Press, 1978), 129–66.
Jafari, Saeid, '"Cyrus the Great" Enters Iranian Politics', *Al-Monitor*, 2 November 2016. Available online: http://www.al-monitor.com/pulse/originals/2016/11/iran-cyrus-day-commeoration-nouri-hamedani-protest.html (accessed 13 June 2017).
Kadivar, Cyrus, 'We Are Awake: 2500-Year Celebrations Revisited', *The Iranian*, 25 January 2002. Available online: http://iranian.com/CyrusKadivar/2002/January/2500/index.html (accessed 19 December 2016).
Kallis, Aristotle, 'Framing Romanità: The Celebrations for the Bimillenario Augusteo and the Augusteo-Ara Pacis Project', *Journal of Contemporary History*, 46:4 (2011): 809–31.
Karanjia, R. K., *The Mind of a Monarch* (London: George Allen & Unwin, 1977).
Katouzian, Homa, *State and Society in Iran: The Eclipse of the Qajars and the Emergence of the Pahlavis* (London: I.B. Tauris, 2006).
Kaye, John William, *The Life and Correspondence of Major-General Sir John Malcolm*, vol. 1 (London: Smith and Elder, 1856).
Kazemzadeh, Firuz, *Russia and Britain in Persia: Imperial Ambitions in Qajar Iran* (London: I.B. Tauris, 2013).
Keddie, Nikki, *Modern Iran* (New Haven: Yale University Press, 2003).
Kertzer, David, *Ritual, Politics, and Power* (New Haven: Yale University Press, 1988).
Khan, Ahmad Nabi, *Iran and Pakistan: The Story of a Cultural Relationship through the Ages* (Karachi: National Publishing House, 1971).
Khomeini, Ruhollah, *Islam and Revolution 1: Writings and Declarations of Imam Khomeini (1941–1980)*, translated and annotated by Hamid Algar (Berkeley: Mizan Press, 1981).
Kia, Mehrdad, 'Persian Nationalism and the Campaign for Language Purification', *Middle Eastern Studies*, 34:2 (1998): 9–36.

Kishi, Nobusuke, *Persian Art Exhibition Celebrating the 2,500th Anniversary of the Founding of the Persian Empire of Iran* (Tokyo: Japanese Committee for the 2,500th Anniversary of the Founding of the Persian Empire, 1971).

Kuhrt, Amelie, *The Persian Empire: A Corpus of Sources from the Achaemenid Period* (Oxon: Routledge, 2009).

Kurus: Memorial Volume: Essays on Indology and Indo-Iran Relations in Memory of Cyrus Celebration Held in the City of Bombay on 2500th Anniversary of the Foundation of the Persian Empire (Bombay: The House, 1974).

Lafraie, Najibullah, *Revolutionary Ideology and Islamic Militancy: The Iranian Revolution and Interpretations of the Quran* (London: Tauris Academic Studies, 2009).

Laing, Margaret, *The Shah* (London: Sigwick and Jackson, 1977).

Lewis, Bernard, *Notes on a Century: Reflections of a Middle East Historian* (London: Orion Books, 2013).

Lima, Gregory, *The Revolutionizing of Iran* (Tehran: International Communications, 1973).

Loloi, Parvin, 'Portraits of the Achaemenid Kings in English Drama: Sixteenth-Eighteenth Centuries', in *The World of Achaemenid Persia: History and Society in Iran and the Ancient Near East*, ed. St John Simpson and John Curtis (London: I.B. Tauris, 2010), 34–40.

Louis, W. R., 'The British Withdrawal from the Gulf, 1967–71', *Journal of Imperial and Commonwealth History*, 33:1 (2003): 83–108.

Lowenthal, David, *The Heritage Crusade and the Spoils of History* (Cambridge: Cambridge University Press, 1998).

Lowenthal, David, *The Past Is a Foreign Country* (Cambridge: Cambridge University Press, 1985).

Malcolm, John, *The History of Persia from the Most Early Period to the Present Time*, vol. 1 (London: John Murray, 1815).

Mallowan, Max, 'Cyrus the Great', *Iran*, 10 (1972): 1–17.

Mallowan, Max, 'Cyrus the Great' in *Cambridge History of Iran*, vol. 2, ed. Ilya Gershevitch (Cambridge: Cambridge University Press, 1985), 392–419.

Mallowan, Max, David Stronach, David Blow, Basil Gray and Gavin Hambly, *British Contributions to Persian Studies* (Tehran: Ramin Printers, 1971).

Malraux, André, *Comité Français Cyrus-le-Grand pour la Commémoration du 2.500ᵉ Anniversaire de la Fondation de l'Empire Perse* (Tehran: Kayhan Press, 1960).

Manning, Frank E., 'Cosmos and Chaos: Celebration in the Modern World', in *The Celebration of Society: Perspectives on Contemporary Cultural Performance* ed. Frank E. Manning (Bowling Green, Ontario: Bowling Green University Popular Press, 1983), 3–30.

Marashi, Afshin, *Nationalizing Iran: Culture, Power, and the State, 1870–1940* (Seattle: University of Washington Press, 2008).

Marashi, Afshin, 'The Nation's Poet: Ferdowsi and the Iranian National Imagination', in *Iran in the 20th Century*, ed. Touraj Atabaki (London: I.B. Tauris, 2009), 93–111.

Matin-Asgari, Afshin, *Both Eastern and Western: An Intellectual History of Modern Iran* (Cambridge: Cambridge University Press, 2018).

Matos, Luís de, *Das Relações entre Portugal e a Pérsia, 1500–1758: Catálogo Bibliográfico da Exposição Comemorativa do XXV Centenário de Accommodatie Monarquia no Irão* (Lisbon: Fundação Calouste Gulbenkian, 1972).

Matthee, Rudolph, 'Nader Shah in Iranian Historiography: Warlord or National Hero', *Institute for Advanced Study* (2018). Available online: http://www.ias.edu/ideas/2018/matthee-nader-shah (accessed 19 January 2019).

McDaniel, Tim, *Autocracy, Modernization, and Revolution in Russia and Iran* (Princeton, NJ: Princeton University Press, 1991).
Menashri, David, 'Shi'ite Leadership: In the Shadow of Conflicting Ideologies', *Iranian Studies*, 13:1/4 (1980): 119–45.
Milani, Abbas, *Eminent Persians: The Men and Women Who Made Modern Iran, 1941-1979*, vol. 1 (Syracuse, NY: Syracuse University Press, 2008).
Milani, Abbas, *The Shah* (New York: Palgrave Macmillan, 2011).
Mirsepassi, Ali, *Intellectual Discourse and the Politics of Modernization: Negotiating Modernity in Iran* (Cambridge: Cambridge University Press, 2000).
Mohajer, Parviz, 'Chinese-Iranian Relations v. Diplomatic and Commercial Relations, 1949–90', *Encyclopaedia Iranica*, 5:4 (1991), 438–41.
Moin, Baqer, *Khomeini: The Life of the Ayatollah* (London: I.B. Tauris, 2009).
Mokhtari, Fariborz, *In the Lion's Shadow: The Iranian Schindler and His Homeland in the Second World War* (Stroud: History Press, 2011).
Morgan, David, 'Ann K.S. Lambton (1912–2008) and Persian Studies', *Journal of the Royal Asiatic Society*, 21 (2011): 99–109.
Mortazavi, Manoutchehr, *Le rôle de l'Azarbaïdjan au cours de XXV siècles d'histoire de l'empire d'Iran*, trans. Mohammad Gharavi (Tabriz: University of Tabriz, 1971).
Mostafavi, Sayyed Mohammad Taqi, *The Land of Pars: The Historical Monuments and the Archaeological Sites of the Province of Fars*, trans. R. N. Sharp (Chippenham: Picton Publishing, 1978).
Motadel, David, 'Iran and the Aryan Myth', in *Perceptions of Iran: History, Myths and Nationalism from Medieval Persia to the Islamic Republic*, ed. Ali M. Ansari (London: I.B. Tauris, 2014), 119–45.
Mottahedeh, Roy, *The Mantle of the Prophet: Religion and Politics in Iran* (Oxford: Oneworld, 2009).
Mousavi, Ali, *Persepolis: Discovery and Afterlife of a World Wonder* (Boston: Walter de Gruyter, 2012).
Mousavi, Ali, 'Pilgrimage to Pasargadae: A Brief History of the Site from the Fall of the Achaemenids to the Early Twentieth Century', in *Cyrus the Great: An Ancient Iranian King*, ed. Touraj Daryaee (Santa Monica, CA: Afshar Publishing, 2013), 28–39.
Murphy, Diana (ed.), *Moshe Safdie 1* (Victoria: Images Publishing Group, 2009).
Naficy, Hamid, 'Nonfiction Fiction: Documentaries on Iran', *Iranian Studies*, 12:3/4 (1979): 217–38.
Naficy, Hamid, *A Social History of Iranian Cinema, Volume 2: The Industrializing Years, 1941–1978* (Durham, NC: Duke University Press, 2012).
Nahavandi, Houchang, *The Last Shah of Iran: Fatal Countdown of a Great Patriot Betrayed by the Free World, a Great Country Whose Fault Was Success*, trans. Steeve Reed (Slough: Aquillon, 2005).
Namikawa, Banri, *Iran* (Tokyo: Kodansha International, 1975).
Namikawa, Banri, *The Legacy of Cyrus the Great: On the Occasion of the 2500th Anniversary of the Founding of the Persian Empire* (Tokyo: Tokyo International Publishers, 1971).
Naraghi, Ehsan, *From Palace to Prison: Inside the Iranian Revolution*, trans. Nilou Mobasser (London: I.B. Tauris, 1994).
Nasiri-Moghaddam, Nader, 'Archaeology and the Iranian National Museum', in *Culture and Cultural Politics under Reza Shah: The Pahlavi State, New Bourgeoisie and the Creation of a Modern Society in Iran*, ed. Bianca Devos and Christoph Werner (London: Routledge, 2014), 121–48.

Nelis, Jan, 'Constructing Fascist Identity: Benito Mussolini and the Myth of "Romanità"', *The Classical World*, 100:4 (2007): 391–415.
Nemet-Nejat, Karen Rhea, *Daily Life in Ancient Mesopotamia* (London: Greenwood Press, 1998).
Nora, Pierre, 'General Introduction: Between Memory and History', in *Realms of Memory: Rethinking the French Past*, vol. 1, ed. Pierre Nora, trans. Arthur Goldhammer (New York: Columbia University Press, 1996), 1–20.
Oil and the Economy of Iran (Tehran: Ministry of Information, 1972).
Olmstead, A. T., *History of the Persian Empire* (Chicago: University of Chicago Press, 1948).
Outline of the Celebration of the 2500th Anniversary of the Founding of the Persian Empire by Cyrus the Great (Tehran: Central Council of the Celebration of the 2500th Anniversary of the Founding of the Persian Empire by Cyrus the Great, 1971).
O'Regan, John, *From Empire to Commonwealth* (London: Radcliffe Press, 1994).
Pahlavi, Ashraf, *Faces in a Mirror: Memoirs from Exile* (Englewood Cliffs: Prentice-Hall, 1980).
Pahlavi, Farah, *An Enduring Love: My Life with the Shah* (New York: Turnaround Distributor, 2004).
Pahlavi, Mohammad Reza, 'An Excerpt from the Message of His Imperial Majesty Shahanshah Aryamehr at the Inauguration of the World Congress of Iranology', *Journal of the Regional Cultural Institute (Iran, Pakistan, Turkey)*, 4 (1971): 7–9.
Pahlavi, Mohammad Reza, *Iran, Philosophy Behind the Revolution* (London: Orient Commerce Establishment, 1971).
Pahlavi, Mohammad Reza, *Mission for My Country* (London: Hutchinson, 1961).
Pahlavi, Mohammad Reza, *The Shah's Story*, trans. Teresa Waugh (London: Michael Joseph, 1980).
Paoloni, Carlo, *I fuochi sacri dell'antica Persia: studio redatto in occasione della celebrazione del 2500⁰ anniversario della fondazione dell' impero persiano da parte di Ciro il Grande* (Milan: Carlo Paoloni, 1971).
Parade of the Celebration of the 2500th Anniversary of the Founding of the Persian Empire by Cyrus the Great, Persepolis, 15 October 1971 [programme].
Perrot, Jean, *The Palace of Darius at Susa: The Great Royal Residence of Achaemenid Persia* (London: I.B. Tauris, 2013).
Persian Panorama: Publication of the Imperial Embassy of Iran, London, 1:3 (1965).
Persische Teppiche (Hamburg: Museum für Kunst und Gewerbe, 1971).
Phillipson, Robert, *Linguistic Imperialism* (Oxford: Oxford University Press, 1992).
Pinder-Wilson, Ralph, *Royal Persia: A Commemoration of Cyrus the Great and His Successors* (London: British Museum, 1971).
Podeh, Elie, *The Politics of National Celebration in the Arab Middle East* (Cambridge: Cambridge University Press, 2011).
Pope, Arthur Upham, 'The Celebrations of the Thousandth Anniversary of the Birth of Firdawsi, Epic Poet of Persia', *Bulletin of the American Institute for Persian Art and Archaeology*, 7 (1934): 39–42.
Portugal e a Pérsia: Exposição Integrada no âmbito das Comemorações do 2.500.o Aniversário da Fundação da Monarquia no Irão (Lisbon: Fundação Calouste Gulbenkian, 1972) [exhibition programme].
Programme of the Coronation Ceremony: Summary (Tehran: Ministry of Information, 1967).

Quiles, Ismael, 'La Philosophie sous-jacente au message de Cyrus', in *Acta Iranica*, vol. 1, ed. Jacques Duchesne-Guillemin (Tehran: Bibliothèque Pahlavi, 1974), 19–23.

Rahimi, Babak, *Theater State and the Formation of Early Modern Public Sphere in Iran: Studies on Safavid Muharram Rituals, 1590–1641 CE* (Leiden: Brill, 2012).

Rahnema, Ali, 'Ali Shariati: Teacher, Preacher, Rebel', in *Pioneers of Islamic Revival*, ed. Ali Rahnema (London: Zed Books, 1994), 208–50.

Ram, Malik and S. Balu Rao (eds), *Indo-Iran: Papers Presented at the Congress of Iranologists and Indologists, New Delhi, On the Occasion of the 2500th Anniversary of the Founding of Monarchy in Iran, 4–6 October, 1971* (New Delhi: Indo-Iran Society, 1974).

Ramazani, Ruhollah, *Independence Without Freedom: Iran's Foreign Policy* (Charlottesville: University of Virginia Press, 2013).

Renan, Ernest, 'What Is a Nation?', paper delivered at the Sorbonne 11 March 1882. Available online: http://www.ucparis.fr/files/9313/6549/9943/what_is_a_nation.pdf (accessed 6 March 2017).

Romanowski de Boncza, V., *Les Costumes Militaires de L'Empire Perse depuis sa Fondation* (Athens: : imprimé par Aspioti-Elka, 1965).

Rose, Hugh James (ed.), *A New General Biographical Dictionary*, vol. 3 (London: Fellowes, 1841).

Rousseau, Jean-Jacques, *Constitutional Project for Corsica* (1765). Available online: http://www.constitution.org/jjr/corsica.htm (accessed 6 March 2017).

Ruoff, Kenneth James, *Imperial Japan at Its Zenith: The Wartime Celebration of the Empire's 2,600th Anniversary* (Ithaca: Cornell University Press, 2010).

Sabahi, Farian, *The Literacy Corps in Pahlavi Iran (1963–1979): Political Social and Literary Implications* (Lugano: Sapiens Lugano, 2002).

Saikal, Amin, *The Rise and Fall of the Shah: From Autocracy to Religious Rule* (Princeton, NJ: Princeton University Press, 1980).

Sancisi-Weerdenburg, Heleen, *Sources, Structures and Synthesis: Proceedings of the Groningen 1983 Achaemenid History Workshop* (Leiden: Nederlands Instituut voor het Nabije Oosten, 1987).

Sanghvi, Ramesh, *Aryamehr: A Political Biography* (London: Macmillan, 1969).

Savory, Roger, 'Iran: A 2500-Year Historical and Cultural Tradition' in *Iranian Civilization and Culture: Essays in Honour of the 2,500th Anniversary of the Founding of the Persian Empire*, ed. Charles Adams (Montreal: McGill University, Institute of Islamic Studies, 1973), 77–89.

Sciolino, Elaine, *Persian Mirrors: The Elusive Face of Iran* (London: Free Press, 2000).

Serrão, Joaquim Veríssimo, *Un Voyageur Portugais en Perse au Début du XVIIe siècle: Nicolau de Orta Rebelo*, translated into French by Simone Biberfeld (Lisbon: Fundação Calouste Gulbenkian, Comité National Portugais Pour la Célébration du 2,500e Anniversaire de la Fondation de la Monarchie en Iran, 1972).

Sept Mille Ans d'Art en Iran (Paris: Musée du Petit Palais, 1961).

Shafa, Shojaeddin, *Facts about the Celebration of the 2500th Anniversary of the Founding of the Persian Empire by Cyrus the Great* (Tehran: Committee of International Affairs of the Festivities, 1971).

Shahbazi, A. Shahpur, 'Ferdowsi, Abu'l-Qāsem iv. Millenary Celebration', *Encyclopaedia Iranica*, 9:5 (1999), 527–30.

Shakibi, Zhand, 'Pahlavism: The Ideologization of Monarchy in Iran', *Politics, Religion and Ideology*, 14:1 (2013): 114–35.

Shakibi, Zhand, 'The Rastakhiz Party and Pahlavism: The Beginnings of State Anti-Westernism in Iran', *British Journal of Middle Eastern Studies*, 45:2 (2018): 251–68.

Shannon, Matthew K., *Losing Hearts and Minds: American-Iranian Relations and International Education During the Cold War* (Ithaca: Cornell University Press, 2017).
Shariati, Ali, *Man and Islam: Extraction and Refinement of Cultural Resources*. Available online: http://www.shariati.com/english/culture.html (accessed 13 May 2019).
Shariati, Ali, *On the Plight of the Oppressed People*. Available online: http://www.al-islam.org/articles/plight-oppressed-people-ali-shariati (accessed 17 March 2017).
Sharp, Ralph Norman, *The Inscriptions in Old Persian Cuneiform of the Achaemenian Emperors* (Tehran: Central Council of the Celebration of the 2500th Anniversary of the Founding of the Persian Empire by Cyrus the Great, 1966).
Shawcross, William, *The Shah's Last Ride* (London: Chatto and Windus, 1989).
Shojaeddin Shafa and His Literary and Research Works (Tehran: Kayhan Press, 1972).
Siebertz, Roman 'Depicting Power: The Commemorative Stamp Set of 1935', in *Culture and Cultural Politics under Reza Shah: The Pahlavi State, New Bourgeoisie and the Creation of a Modern Society in Iran*, ed. Bianca Devos and Christoph Werner (London: Routledge, 2014), 149-80.
Simpson, John, *A Mad World, My Masters: Tales from a Traveller's Life* (London: Pan Books, 2008).
Simpson, St John, 'The Cyrus Cylinder: Display and Replica', in *The Cyrus Cylinder: The Great Persian Edict from Babylon*, ed. Irving Finkel (London: I.B. Tauris, 2012), 69-84.
Simpson, St John, 'Making Their Mark: Foreign Travellers at Persepolis', *Arta*, 1 (2005): 1-77.
Simpson, St John, 'Pottering Around Persepolis: Observations on Early European Visitors to the Site', in *Persian Responses: Political and Cultural Interaction with(in) the Achaemenid Empire*, ed. Christopher Tuplin (Swansea: Classical Press of Wales, 2007), 343-56.
Simpson, St John and John Curtis (eds), *The World of Achaemenid Persia: History and Society in Iran and the Ancient Near East* (London: I.B. Tauris, 2010).
Sisson, Richard and Leo Rose, *War and Secession: Pakistan, India, and the Creation of Bangladesh* (Oxford: University of California Press, 1990).
Sreberny, Annabelle and Massoumeh Torfeh, *Persian Service: The BBC and British Interests in Persia* (London: I.B. Tauris, 2014).
Steele, Robert, 'Pahlavi Iran on the Global Stage: The Shah's 1971 Persepolis Celebrations', in *The Age of Aryamehr: Late Pahlavi Iran and Its Global Entanglements*, ed. Roham Alvandi (London: Gingko Library, 2018), 110-46.
Steele, Robert, 'The Pahlavi National Library Project: Education and Modernization in Late Pahlavi Iran', *Iranian Studies*, 52:1-2 (2019): 85-110.
Štěpková, Jarmila, *2500 let íránského mincovnictví* (V Praze: Narodni galerie, 1971).
Stevens, Roger, *The Land of the Great Sophy* (London: Methuen, 1971).
Stierlin, Henri, *Iran of the Master Builders: 2500 Years of Architecture* (Geneva: Editions Sigma, 1971).
Stronach, David, 'Cyrus and Pasargadae', in *Cyrus the Great: An Ancient Iranian King*, ed. Touraj Daryaee (Santa Monica, CA: Afshar Publishing, 2013), 53-77.
Stronach, David, 'Director's Report November 1st 1970 to October 31st 1971', *Iran*, 10 (1972): xi.
Stronach, David, *Pasargadae: A Report on the Excavations Conducted by the British Institute of Persian Studies* (Oxford: Clarendon Press, 1978).
Summary of the Fifth National Development Plan: 1973-1978 (Tehran: Plan and Budget Organization, 1973).

Tarverdi, R. and Ali Massoudi (eds), *The Land of Kings* (Tehran: Ettelaʿat Publications, 1971).
Tavakoli-Targhi, Mohamad, 'From Patriotism to Matriotism: A Tropological Study of Iranian Nationalism, 1870–1909', *International Journal of Middle East Studies*, 34:2 (2002): 217–38.
Tavakoli-Targhi, Mohamad, *Refashioning Iran: Orientalism, Occidentalism and Historiography* (Houndmill: Palgrave, 2001).
Terre D'Europe, 'Iran', 12:40–41 (1971).
Ting, Helen, 'Social Construction of Nation – A Theoretical Exploration', *Nationalism and Ethnic Politics*, 14:3 (2008): 453–82.
Tourism: Investment Opportunities in Iran (Tehran: Iranian National Tourist Organization Research and Planning Department, February 1972).
Tourist Statistics of Iran: 1977 (Tehran: Ministry of Information and Tourism, 1977).
Tucci, Giuseppe, *Ciro Il Grande* (Rome: Istituto Italiano per il Medio ed Estremo Oriente, 1971).
Türkiye'de Basılmış Farsça Eserler, çeviriler ve İran'la Ilgili Yayınlar Bibliyografyası [Bibliography of Persian Works, Translations and Publications about Iran, Published in Turkey] (Ankara: Millî Kütüphane, 1971).
Türkiye/Iran Transit Route: For the "Celebration of the 2500th Anniversary of the Founding of the Persian Empire by Cyrus the Great" (Istanbul: Touring and Automobile Club of Turkey, 1971).
'United States Stands with People of Iran', House of Representatives Foreign Affairs Committee Press Release, 9 January 2018. Available online: http://foreignaffairs.house.gov/press-release/united-states-stands-people-iran/ (accessed 22 January 2018).
Vaziri, Mostafa, *Iran as Imagined Nation: The Construction of National Identity* (New York: Paragon House, 1993).
Walker, C. B. F., 'A Recently Identified Fragment of the Cyrus Cylinder', *Iran*, 10 (1972): 158–9.
Wilber, Donald N., *Adventures in the Middle East: Excursions and Incursions* (Princeton: Darwin, 1986).
Wilber, Donald N., *Four Hundred Forty-Six Kings of Iran* (Shiraz: Pahlavi University, 1972).
Wilber, Donald N., *Reza Shah Pahlavi: The Resurrection and Reconstruction of Iran* (Hicksville: Exposition Press, 1975).
Wiesehöfer, Josef, *Ancient Persia* (London: I.B. Tauris, 2001).
World Congress of Iranology: On the Occasion of the Celebration of the 2500th Anniversary of the Founding of the Persian Empire by Cyrus the Great, Shiraz, 13–15 October 1971 [programme].
Wortman, Richard S., *Scenarios of Power: Myth and Ceremony in Russian Monarchy*, vol. 2 (Princeton, NJ: Princeton University Press, 1995).
Zarghamee, Reza, *Discovering Cyrus: The Persian Conqueror Astride the Ancient World* (Washington: Mage Publishers, 2013).
Zia-Ebrahimi, Reza, 'Better a Warm Hug than a Cold Bath: Nationalist Memory and the Failures of Iranian Historiography', *Iranian Studies*, 49:5 (2016): 837–54.
Zia-Ebrahimi, Reza, *The Emergence of Iranian Nationalism: Race and the Politics of Dislocation* (New York: Columbia University Press, 2016).
Zia-Ebrahimi, Reza, 'Self-Orientalization and Dislocation: The Uses and Abuses of the "Aryan" Discourse in Iran', *Iranian Studies*, 44:4 (2011): 445–72.

Zirinsky, Michael P., 'Imperial Power and Dictatorship: Britain and the Rise of Reza Shah, 1921–1926', *International Journal of Middle East Studies*, 24 (1992): 639–63.

Zonis, Marvin, *Majestic Failure: The Fall of the Shah* (Chicago: University of Chicago Press, 1991).

Zonis, Marvin, *The Political Elite of Iran* (Princeton, NJ: Princeton University Press, 1971).

Index

Abrahamian, Ervand 8
Acta Iranica 70, 84, 91
Achaemenid Persia 11, 16, 20–1, 48–9, 53, 83, 88, 140
Addis Ababa University 96
Afghanistan 66
Afkhami, Gholam Reza 6
Afshār, Amir Aslān 99, 118
Afshār, Amir Khosrow 100
Afshār, Iraj 79
Agnew, Spiro 3, 9, 46, 68–9
Ahmadinejad, Mahmoud 142
Ākhundzādeh, Mirzā Fath ʿAli 14, 15–16, 31
ʿAlā, Hoseyn 11, 22, 31–4, 76, 79, 110
ʿAlam, Asadollāh 9, 37–8, 44, 46, 57, 59, 65, 71, 82–3, 90, 111, 114, 120, 122, 126, 128–9, 131, 133–6, 144
Āl-e Ahmad, Jalāl 109–10
Alvandi, Roham 8
Amānat, Hoseyn 51
Amnesty International 118
Āmuzegār, Jahāngir 123
Āmuzegār, Jamshid 36
Anjoman-e Āsār-e Melli-ye Irān. See Society for the National Heritage of Iran
Ansāri, ʿAbdolrezā 36–41, 75, 79, 88, 118, 136, 141
Ansari, Ali 16, 18, 90, 112, 124, 140
Āryāmehr (title) 16, 30, 35
Āryāmehr Cup (tennis tournament) 52
Āryāmehr Stadium 2, 50, 52, 101, 128, 144
Āryāmehr University 117
Aryan race 16–17, 29–30
Asia Institute 82
Asian Games (1974) 52
Ātābāy, ʿAbolfath 38, 41
Avery, Peter 81, 104
Axworthy, Michael 8, 55, 58, 115, 141

Baader-Meinhof Group 115
Bahādori, Karim Pāshā 121
Bahaʾism 10, 46, 113
Bahremand, Mehdi 120
Bailey, Sir Harold 100
Ball, George 3
Banisadr, Abulhasan 126
Baraheni, Reza 9
Barnett, Richard 61–3, 79
Bāstān Museum 18, 21, 78, 99, 143
Bausani, Alessandro 105
Bayāni, Khān-bābā 85
Bazm-e Ahriman 10
Beatrix, Princess of the Netherlands 67, 97
Ben-Gurion, David 70, 84
Bill, James 133
Bliss, Sir Arthur 102
Borj-e Shahyād-e Āryāmehr. See Shahyād Tower
Boyle, John 79, 95, 97, 102
Brandt, Willy 95–7
Britain
    16–19th century travellers to Iran 18–20
    Ferdowsi celebration 22
    imperialism 55–6
    loan of Cyrus Cylinder 51, 61–3, 80
British Contributions to Persian Studies, exhibition 102–3
British Council 101–3, 106
British Institute of Persian Studies 43, 46, 80, 83, 103
British Museum 51, 60–3, 79–80, 98
Browne, Edward Granville 102
Buchan, James 4, 135
Bullard, Sir Reader 101
Bushehri, Javād 33–4, 36–7, 134
Bushehri, Mehdi 33, 36–7

Cambridge History of Iran 88, 90, 106
Cameron, George 83

Index

Ceauşescu, Nicolae 67
Cerulli, Enrico 82
Chamberlin, Eric 19, 49, 53
China 70–1
Christensen, Arthur 22, 25, 87
Churchill, Winston 56, 68
Cold War 8, 57, 68, 94
Commission on Education (*Anjoman-e Maʿāref*) 77
Committee for Authoring the History of Iran (*Komiteh-ye Taʾlif-e Tārikh-e Irān*) 74, 77–8, 85, 139
Committee for Free Iran 67, 116–17
Committee for the International Fight Against Illiteracy (*Komiteh-ye Peykār-e Jahāni bā Bisavādi*) 74–6
Confederation of Iranian Students National Union 67, 115–16, 123
Congress of Mithraic Studies 100
Constantine II of Greece 58
Constitutional Revolution (1905–11) 17, 110
Cook, John Manuel 106
Cooper, Andrew Scott 8, 126
Corbin, Henri 79, 83–4
Corruption, allegations of 120
Curzon, George Nathaniel 18–19
Cyrus Cylinder 1, 7, 27, 39, 51, 53, 57, 60–3, 80, 88, 139, 142–3
Cyrus Hotel 38–9, 130
Cyrus the Great
  comparison with Mohammad Reza Pahlavi 1, 4, 26–8, 59–60, 63
  film about 42–3
  in Greek and Biblical sources 23–4
  in Pahlavi era texts 25–6, 31
  in Pahlavi foreign policy 57, 62
  in publications 88
Cyrus the Great Committees
  Britain 68, 95–6, 97
  Canada 96
  France 68, 95
  Germany 95
  international 12, 64, 67–8, 93, 95–7
  Italy 95, 101, 105
  the Netherlands 95
  Pakistan 95–6, 104
  Spain 68
  United States 67, 98–9

Cyrus the Great Cup (football tournament) 51–2
Cyrus the Great Polo Tournament 52
Cyrus the Great Year 125–8

Dār al-Fonun 15, 18
Darius Hotel 38–9, 43, 84, 130
Darke, Hubert 79
de Boncza, V. Romanowski 48–9
Decadence and Downfall, documentary 5, 12, 50
de Gaulle, Charles 68, 71, 94
Deschatelets, Jean-Paul 96
Duchesne-Guillemin, Jacques 84
Durham University 102

Ebadi, Shirin 63
Ebtehāj, Abulhasan 126–7
Edelman, Murray 7
Eilers, Wilhelm 95
Elizabeth II, Queen of England 11, 34, 46, 55, 66
Elwell-Sutton, Laurence 5, 21, 45, 80–1, 84, 102, 139, 141, 145
Emāmi, Taqi 41
En-lai, Chou 70–1
Enqelāb-e Sefid. *See* White Revolution
Ettelāʿāt newspaper 58, 141

Fadāiyān-e Eslām 111
Fadāiyān-e Khalq 118
Farahmand, Mohammad 141
Farhād, Ahmad 32
Farhangestān 17
Farmānfarmāʾiyān, ʿAbdolʿaziz 52
Farmānfarmāʾiyān, Khodādād 126
Farzāneh, Cyrus 37, 120–1, 130–1
Fath ʿAli Shāh 15
Ferdowsi
  1000th anniversary celebration 13, 22
  Shāhnāmeh 22, 42, 73, 85, 89–90, 98, 105, 140
Firouz, Mozaffar 113–12
Flames of Persia, film. *See Forugh-e Jāvidān*
Forugh-e Jāvidān (Eternal Flame), film 42, 50
Foroughi, Mohammad ʿAli 16–17, 22
Foroughi, Mohsen 51
Foruzānfar, Badiʿal-Zamān 76

Fouché, Jacobus 68
Frederick IX of Denmark 58
Frye, Richard 18, 82–3, 90, 100

Gāhnāmeh-ye Panjāh Sāl-e
  Shāhanshāhi-ye Pahlavi 95–6
Gandhi, Indira 97
Ganjeʿi, Farhad 76
Gershevitch, Ilya 80, 83
Gharbzadegi 109
Ghirshman, Roman 83–4, 88, 95, 175 n.130
Giri, V. V. 46, 69, 97
Gnägi, Rudolf 64
Gohariyān, Rāmin 75
Golestan, Farrokh 42
Golestān Palace 35–6, 53
Goruh-e Māziyār 115–16
Gray, Basil 80, 98, 102–3
Great Civilization 30–1
Grigor, Talinn 22, 48, 51
Grousset, Rene 87
The Guardian newspaper 3, 4

Hadidi, Mokhtār 31
Haile Selassie 46–7
Hallock, Richard 106
Hansman, John 80, 83
Harmatta, János 79
Harmsworth, Vere 62, 95
Hasan, Mumtaz 104
Heath, Edward 62
Heinemann, Gustav 64, 66, 95–6
Hejāzi, Mohammad 32, 76, 110
Hekmat, ʿAli Asghar 21, 76, 110
Helms, Cynthia 128
Helms, Richard 128
Herodotus 23
Hinnells, John 84, 100
Hirohito, Emperor of Japan 66
Hoveydā, Amir ʿAbbās 35, 64, 71, 118, 127–8

Imperial calendar 141
Imperial Celebrations
  anniversary (1972) 122
  Central Council of the Imperial
    Celebrations of Iran 32, 34, 50, 87–8, 93, 122, 134–6, 141
  commemorative schools 74, 134
  conception 31–2
  cost 3, 117, 121, 126–7, 132–4, 144
  Cultural Committee of the 2500th
    Anniversary Celebrations of Imperial
    Iran (*Komiteh-ye Farhangi-ye
    Jashn-e Dohezār o Pānsadomin Sāl-e
    Shāhanshāhi-ye Irān*) 85
  delays 33–4
  gala dinner 2, 41, 46–8, 59, 84
  glorification ceremony at Pasargadae 1, 13–14, 43–5, 82–3, 119
  High Executive Committee 37–9, 50, 75, 120
  Historical Committee of the Imperial
    Celebrations (*Komisiyon-e Motāleʿāt-e
    Tārikhi-ye Jashn-e Shāhanshāhi-ye
    Irān*) 85
  logo, 27, 39, 61, 143
  parade at Persepolis 48–50, 119
  reception at Bāgh-e Eram 83–4
  regional and religious minority
    participation 42, 86
  son et lumière 2, 39, 45, 48, 82, 84, 144, 162 n.160
  tent city 2, 39–40, 45, 68, 84, 121, 130–1, 133, 135, 140, 144
Imperial Court 11, 30–2, 37–8, 76, 79, 96, 107, 110, 122, 134–6, 139, 145
Imperial Cultural Council (*Shurā-ye
  Farhangi-ye Saltanati*) 74, 76, 77, 91
Indo-Iran Society 105–6
Institut für Orientalistik, Vienna 97
Inter-Continental Hotel, Tehran 130
International Congress of Iranology
  (First, 1966) 78–9, 90
International Congress of Iranology
  (Second, 1971) 6, 11–12, 45, 61, 70, 78–85, 102
International Day of Cyrus the Great 143
International Union of Iranologists
  (*Etehādi-ye Jahāni-ye
  Irānshenāsān*) 79
Iran Air 76, 80, 128, 130
Iran Bāstān Museum 18, 21, 78, 102
Iran Culture House, Bombay 105
Iran Free Press 133
Iranian Liberation Front 125–6
Iranian National Tourist Organization
  (INTO) 120, 129–31

Irānshahr newspaper 17, 21
Israel 31, 70, 79, 140
Istituto Italiano per il Medio ed Estremo Oriente (IsMEO) 82, 104–5

Jahānbāni, Amānollāh 32, 48, 51
Jahān-e Irānshenāsi (World of Iranology) 78
Jansen 39–40, 120
Jashn-e Zed-e Mardomi-ye Shāh 117
Jewish Council for the Celebrations 42
Jonas, Franz 97, 104
Jonker, Hendrik, Dutch ambassador 2–3, 38–9, 40, 59, 67, 118
Juliana, Queen of the Netherlands 46, 67, 97

Kampman, Arie 97
Kāveh newspaper 17, 21
Kermāni, Mirzā Āqā Khān 14, 16, 24–5, 31
Ketābshenāsi-ye Jashn-e Shāhanshāhi-ye Irān 73, 122
Keyhān newspaper 26, 52, 76, 85, 93
Khalkhāli, Sādeq 140–2
Khān, Mirzā Malkam 14
Khan, Yahya 69
Khāndanihā magazine 141
Khānlari, Parviz Nātel, 76
Khayyam, Omar 73, 22
Khomeini, Ruhollah 12, 53, 109–12, 114, 123, 140–2
Kissinger, Henry 68
Kiyā, Sādeq 30, 79
Kiyānpur, Gholāmrezā 121
Kohlbrugge, Hanna 59, 81
Kollek, Teddy 128
König, Franz 79

Lambton, Ann 81
Lewis, Bernard 80, 95
Literacy Corps (*Sepāh-e Dānesh*) 74–5, 77
Lockhart, Laurence 80, 102
London Symphony Orchestra 102, 145
Lowenthal, David 15, 27, 60

MacArthur, Douglas 118
Maison de l'Iran 36, 97, 99
Malcolm, Sir John 15, 19–20
Malraux, André 95

Manning, Frank 6
Maqsudi, Hoseyn 41
Marashi, Afshin 15–16, 21–2, 74, 77
Massé, Henri 22, 95
Matheson, Sylvia 88
Maxim's 41, 120, 133, 140
Metropolitan Museum of Art 98, 143
Milani, Abbas 6, 123
Ministry of Culture and Art (Iran) 38–9, 50, 99, 102, 122, 135, 145
Minorsky, Vladimir 88–9
Mirzā, Jalāl al-Din 15, 21
Moʿiniyān, Nosratollāh 33
Mojāhedin-e Khalq 118
Moore, Henry 102–3
Mosaddeq, Mohammad 31, 56, 89
Mostafavi, Mohammad Taqi 48, 51
Mottaqi, Amir 37
Museum für Kunst und Gewerbe, Hamburg 99
Museum für Völkerkunde, Vienna 97

Nāder Shāh 30, 88–9
Nafisi, Saʿid 32, 76, 87
Nahāvandi, Hushang 80, 125, 140
Namikawa, Banri 103, 130
Naraghi, Ehsan 31
Nāser al-Din Shāh 18
Nasiri, Neʿmatollāh 38, 118–19
Nasr, Sayyed Hoseyn 83, 104
National Front 114
The Netherlands 65, 67–8, 95
Newsweek magazine 2, 125
Nikpey, Gholāmrezā 51, 99
Nikpey, Manuchehr 38
Nixon, Richard 11, 55, 67–70, 119
Niyāvarān Palace 38
Nora, Pierre 13, 28, 60

Ohnesorg, Benno 115

Pahlavi, Ashraf 36, 63, 70, 74–6
Pahlavi, Farah 2, 7–9, 35, 38, 41, 50, 69–70, 75, 79, 83, 96, 100, 120–2, 131
Pahlavi Library (*Ketābkhāneh-ye Pahlavi*) 74, 76–9, 84–5, 91, 139
Pahlavi, Mohammad Reza:
  coronation 3, 34–6, 56, 68, 112, 123, 134–6

early reign 56
global vision 57, 68–72
Mission for My Country 26
negotiations between India and
    Pakistan 69
Persepolis 45–6
speech at gala dinner 46–7
speech at parade at Persepolis, 49
speech at Pasargadae 4, 44–5, 63
Pahlavi, Reza 18, 21–2, 28, 30, 35, 50, 55,
    89–90, 111
Pahlavi University, Shiraz 6, 78, 80, 82–3,
    87, 102, 125
Pahlavism 29, 57, 90–1, 109, 123, 142
Pahlbod, Mehrdād 36–7, 42, 61, 78, 97,
    100, 102
Pasargadae 43, 46, 80, 128
Perrot, Jean 1, 106
Persepolis 1, 3, 18–19, 43, 48, 57, 59, 64,
    65–6, 82, 106, 119, 124, 128, 130–1,
    135, 142–3
Persia: Immortal Kingdom 88–9, 134
Philip, Prince of England 45–6, 58, 68, 71
Pirniyā, Hasan 21–2, 25
Plan Organization (*Sāzemān-e Barnāmeh*)
    9, 12, 36, 52, 75–6, 125–8, 136, 144
Podgorny, Nikolai 46, 69
Pompidou, Georges 59, 64, 67, 69
Pope, Arthur Upham 21, 25–6, 39–40, 67,
    79, 84, 98, 119
Purdāvud, Ebrāhim 76

Qarib, Hormoz 37–8, 42, 58–9, 67
Qatar 70
Qotbi, Rezā 42, 158 n.71

Rafsanjani, Hashemi, 142
Rāhnamā-ye Rezheh 48–9
Ramsbotham, Peter 59, 61–2, 68, 71, 103,
    118–21, 123, 132, 137
Renan, Ernest 14–15
Romanov celebration 8, 13
Roosevelt, Franklin D. 56
Rouhani, Hassan 142
Rousseau, Jean-Jacques 14
Rudaki Hall 36, 102, 122

Saʿādatmand, Abulhasan 48
Sābeti, Parviz 121

Saʿdābād Palace 49, 51, 84
Sadiq, ʿIsā 21–2, 76–7, 79, 102
Sāmi, ʿAli 63, 80
Samiʿi, Mehdi 36
Samiʿi, Mohammad ʿAli 58
Sanghvi, Ramesh 89
Sartre, Jean-Paul 67, 116
SAVAK (*Sāzemān-e Ettelāʿāt va
    Amniyat-e Keshvar*) 10, 110, 112, 116,
    118–21, 141–2
Savory, Roger 45, 96
Scarcia, Gianroberto 82
Scheel, Walter 95
School of Oriental and African Studies
    (SOAS), London 22, 80, 102
Senegal 69–70
Senghor, Léopold Sédar 69
Shādmān, Fakhr al-Din 76
Shafā, Shojāʿ al-Din 3–4, 11, 25, 28, 30–3,
    37–8, 45, 62, 73–5, 76, 77, 82–3, 87,
    91, 93–4, 96, 98, 100, 106–7, 110, 120,
    139, 145, 185 n.100
Shafaq, Sādeq Rezāzādeh 32, 76, 110
Shāh ʿAbbās 13, 19, 35
Shāh ʿAbbās Hotel 84
Shāh Ismāʿil 30, 35
Shāh Tahmāsp 19, 98
Shahyād Tower 2, 36, 50–1, 52, 61–2, 64,
    101, 113, 122, 124, 133, 135, 137
Shariʿati, ʿAli 113, 123, 142
Sharif-Emāmi, Jaʿfar 35, 141
Sharp, Norman 80
Shawcross, Lord Hartley 62, 95
Shawcross, William 4, 63
Shazar, Zalman 70
Shiraz Arts Festival 50
*Shurā-ye Markazi-ye Jashn-e
    Shāhanshāhi-ye Irān*. See Central
    Council of the Imperial Celebrations
    of Iran
Society for the National Heritage of Iran
    13, 17, 21–2
South Africa 68
Stalin, Joseph 56
Stewart, Michael 60
Stronach, David 43, 46, 80, 83,
    102–3
Student protests 114–15, 121
Suratgar, Lotfʿali 35

Tāleqāni, Mahmud 113
Taqizādeh, Sayyed Hasan 16–17, 32, 76, 110
Tavakoli-Targhi, Mohamad 15, 16
Tehran Congress (UNESCO, 1965) 74–5
Tito, Josip Broz 68
Tobacco Concession (1891–92) 110
Tourism 7–8, 126, 128–32, 136–7
Toynbee, Arnold 84
Treaty of Turkmenchay 55
Tucci, Giuseppe 82, 84, 94–5, 105
Turkomen of Iran exhibition 94

ulema 16, 53, 111
UN. *See* United Nations
UNESCO. *See* United Nations Educational, Scientific and Cultural Organization
United Nations 1, 34, 63, 143
United Nations Educational, Scientific and Cultural Organization 25, 32, 74, 81, 93–4
United States 67–70
University of Cambridge 80, 102
University of Chicago 98
University of Edinburgh 5, 102
University of Manchester 98–100, 102
University of Oxford 80–1, 102
University of Pennsylvania 99
University of Tabriz 86–7, 102
University of Tehran 85, 87, 102, 114–15, 117, 141
University of Toronto 96

University of Tunis 96

Vanden Berghe, Louis 104
Velāyat-e Faqih 112
von Fürstenberg, Maximilian 46
von Grunebaum, Gustave 81

Washington Daily News newspaper 2, 125
White Revolution 24–6, 28, 43, 53, 74, 111, 127, 133, 145
Wilber, Donald 21, 82
Wright, Sir Denis 66, 71, 95, 102

Xenakis, Iannis 48
Xenophon 23–5, 87

Yādnāmeh-ye Jashn-e Shāhanshāhi-ye Irān 122, 134
Yaghmā'i, Eqbāl 85
Yārshāter, Ehsān 79
Yazdānpanāh, Morteẓā 34, 51

Zaehner, Robert 81
Zāhedi, Ardeshir 36, 41, 67
Zahir Shah, Mohammad 66
Zarghām, 'Ali Akbar 38
Zarrinkub, 'Abdolhoseyn 79
Zia-Ebrahimi, Reza 14, 20, 27
Ziyā'pur, Jalil 49
Zokā', Yahyā 48
Zonis, Marvin 2, 4

Figure 1 Shojāʿ al-Din Shafā (picture taken 1971), the Shah's cultural counsellor at the Imperial Court, who first proposed a celebration commemorating Cyrus the Great in 1958. Courtesy of Claudine Shafa.

Figure 2 A headline from *Keyhān* (19 Mehr 1350/ 11 October 1971) that reads 'The Immortality of Imperial Iran'. On the left side is an image of Cyrus the Great, on the right the Shah. Below Cyrus is text of the Cyrus Cylinder, below the Shah text from his White Revolution. From the British Library's collection.

Figure 3 Shojāʿ al-Din Shafā beside a map marking the international committees established for the Imperial Celebrations. Courtesy of Claudine Shafa.

Figure 4 Advertisement from Iran Air (Homā), in the newspaper *Keyhān*, which reads, 'Greetings and welcome to the two thousand five hundredth Anniversary Celebrations of Imperial Iran'. Images inside the number 2,500 illustrate Iran's continuity from ancient times to the present. Above is written 'Ancient Iran' and 'Modern Iran'. At the top of the page is the official logo of the Celebrations. From the British Library's collection.

Figure 5 Set of stamps from Tunisia commemorating the 2500th Anniversary Celebrations. Author's collection.

Figure 6 Set of stamps from Fujairah commemorating the 2500th Anniversary Celebrations. Author's collection.

Figure 7 Three stamps from Iran. On the top left corner of each is the original logo of the Celebrations, depicting an image of an eagle found at Persepolis. Author's collection.

Figure 8 Stamp from Belgium depicting the tomb at Buzpar, discovered by Belgian archaeologist Louis Vanden Berghe during his sixth Fars expedition (18 November 1960–17 January 1961). Author's collection.

Figure 9 Stamp from Oman depicting Iranian footballer Parviz Ghelichkhani, issued as part of a set of six stamps commemorating the 2500th Anniversary Celebrations. Author's collection.

Figure 10 Illustration published on the front page of *Iran Free Press*, October 1971. The caption below the illustration reads: 'Shah: "Here's to us, forget about those beggars outside, they're just Iranians." Cyrus: "Have your cruel joke, Shah, your thieving, murdering days are numbered."' From the collection of the International Institute of Social History, Amsterdam.

Figure 11 The Shahyād Tower, shortly before its inauguration in 1971 (Photo by Bettmann via Getty Images).

Figure 12 Inauguration of the Āryāmehr Stadium (Photo by Rolls Press/Popperfoto via Getty Images).

Figure 13 Soldiers marching during the parade at Persepolis (Photo by Georges Galmiche/INA via Getty Images).

Figure 14 View of the tent city from Persepolis (Photo by Georges Galmiche/INA via Getty Images).

Figure 15 Frontal view of one of the tent structures (Photo by the author, 2017).

Figure 16 The grand banquet in the dining hall of the tent city (Photo by Georges Galmiche/INA via Getty Images).